ID0463893

Webster's
International
Atlas

Created in Cooperation with the Editors of
MERRIAM-WEBSTER

BARNES & NOBLE

NEW YORK

Contents

Preface

This atlas provides basic information about each of the nearly 200 countries in the world and about the 50 states of the United States. A full page is provided for each country and two for each state with information including a color map showing both populated places and major natural features, a locator map, a fact box containing important information about the country or state, and a representation of the country or state flag with interesting information about it.

Additional information is provided in tables showing country capitals and membership in international organizations, communications, longest rivers, tallest mountains, and largest lakes. There is also a country by country listing showing many of the largest cities with their geographical coordinates.

This colorful, portable book was created by the Cartography Department of Encyclopædia Britannica in association with the editors of Merriam-Webster, and is designed to help readers visualize the changing world in which we live in a handy, affordable format.

Abbreviations

Ala.	Alabama	Mt.	Mount
Ark.	Arkansas	Mtn.	Mountain
Arm.	Armenia	Mts.	Mountains
ASEAN	Association of Southeast Asian Nations	N	north(ern)
		Nat'l	National
Azer.	Azerbaijan	N.C.	North Carolina
Belg.	Belgium	NE	northeast(ern)
Calif.	California	N.H.	New Hampshire
C.A.R	Central African Republic	N.J.	New Jersey
		N.P.	National Park
Caricom	Caribbean Community	NW	northwest(ern)
CFA	Communauté Financière Africaine (African Financial Community)	N.Y.	New York
		N.Z.	New Zealand
		Okla.	Oklahoma
		Penin.	Peninsula
Conn.	Connecticut	Penn.	Pennsylvania
D.C.	District of Columbia	Pk.	Peak
Del.	Delaware	Port.	Portugal
Dem.	Democratic	Pt.	Point
Den.	Denmark	Rep.	Republic
E	east(ern)	R.I.	Rhode Island
Fla.	Florida	S	south(ern)
Fr.	France	S.C.	South Carolina
ft.	foot (feet)	SE	southeast(ern)
GNP	gross national product	sq.	square
		St.	Saint
I.	Island	SW	southwest(ern)
Ill.	Illinois	Switz.	Switzerland
Ind.	Indiana	Tenn.	Tennessee
Indon.	Indonesia	Turkmen.	Turkmenistan
Is.	Islands	U.A.E.	United Arab Emirates
km.	kilometer(s)	U.K.	United Kingdom
La.	Louisiana	U.S.	United States
Mass.	Massachusetts	Va.	Virginia
Md.	Maryland	Vt.	Vermont
mi.	mile(s)	W	west(ern)
Mich.	Michigan	Wash.	Washington
Minn.	Minnesota	Wis.	Wisconsin
Miss.	Mississippi	W.Va.	West Virginia

Guide to Map Projections

Technically, the earth is not round but is flattened at the poles and takes a shape most accurately described as an ellipsoid. The deviation from a perfect sphere is relatively minor, and although the distinction is of critical importance in surveying and geodesy, for most purposes it can be assumed that the earth is spherical.

A globe is the only true means of representing the surface of the earth and maintaining accurate relationships of location, direction, and distance, but it is often more desirable to have a flat map for reference. However, in order for a round globe to be portrayed as a flat map, various parts of the globe's surface must stretch or shrink, thereby altering the geometric qualities associated with it. To control this distortion, a systematic transformation of the sphere's surface must be made. The transformation and resultant new surface is usually derived mathematically and is referred to as the map projection.

An infinite number of map projections can be conceived, but the only ones which are effective are those projections which ensure that the spatial relationships between true (known) locations on the three-dimensional sphere are preserved on the two-dimensional flat map.

The four basic spatial properties of location are area, angle, distance, and direction. No map projection can preserve all four of these basic properties simultaneously. In fact, every map will possess some level of distortion in one or more of these dimensions. The map surface can be developed such that individual properties are preserved to a certain extent, or that certain combinations of properties are preserved to some extent, but every projection is, in some way, a compromise and must distort some properties in order to portray others accurately.

Choosing a Map Projection

The question of which map projection is best might be better stated as which map projection is most appropriate for the intended purpose of the map. For example, navigation demands correct direction, while road atlases will be concerned with preserving distance. Another important consideration is the extent and area of the region to be mapped. Some common guidelines include the use of cylindrical projections for low latitudes, conic projections for middle latitudes, and azimuthal projections for polar views. World maps are rather special cases and are commonly shown on a class of projection that may be neither equal-area nor conformal, referred to as compromise projections, typically on an oval grid.

Common Map Projections

Name	Class	Attribute	Common Uses
Mercator	Cylindrical	Conformal	Best suited for navigation uses, but often used inappropriately for world maps.
Sinusoidal	(Pseudo-cylindrical)	Equal-area	Used occasionally for world maps and in combination with Mollweide to derive other projections.
Mollweide	(Pseudo-cylindrical)	Equal-area	Used for world maps, especially for showing thematic content.
Lambert Conformal Conic	Conic	Conformal	Used extensively for mapping areas of extensive east-west extent in the mid-latitudes (such as the U.S.).
Albers Equal-area	Conic	Equal-area	Similar to Lambert Conformal Conic in use.
Polyconic	Polyconic	Neither Equal-area nor Conformal	Used by U.S. Geological Survey in mapping topographic quadrangles and was used for early coastal charts and some military mapping.
Bonne	(Pseudo-conic)	Equal-Area	Frequently used in atlases for showing continents.
Gnomonic	Azimuthal	Equal-Area	Used most frequently in navigation.
Stereographic	Azimuthal	Conformal	Most often used for topographic maps of polar regions and for navigation.
Orthographic	Azimuthal	Neither Equal-area nor Conformal	Most popular use is for pictorial views of earth, especially as seen from space.

Map Legend

Cities and Towns

Ottawa ⊛   National Capital

Edinburgh ◉   Second level
political capital

São Paulo ●   City symbol

Boundaries

▬▬   International

▬ ▬   Disputed

---   Defacto

·······   Line of control

———   Political subdivisions

Other Features

SERENGETI
NATIONAL PARK ■   National park

Mount Everest
29,028 ft. ▲   Mountain Peak

⌒⌒   Dam

⌒⌒   Falls

⌒⌒   Rapids

········   River

- - -   Intermittent river

———   Canal

•—•—•   Aqueduct

∧∧∧   Reef

Countries
of the
World

@2000, Encyclopædia Britannica, Inc.

Official name: Islamic State of Afghanistan
Head of government: President
Official languages: Dari (Persian); Pashto
Monetary unit: afghani
Area: 251,825 sq. mi. (652,225 sq. km.)
Population (2001): 26,813,000
GNP per capita (1998): U.S.$280
Principal exports (1995): carpets and
  rugs 54.3%; dried fruits and nuts 15.6%
  to: Pakistan 20.1%; Belgium-
  Luxembourg 8.7%; France 7.4%; U.S.
  6.7%; Japan 6.0%

Scale 1: 19,568,000

| 0 | 80 | 160 mi |
| 0 | 120 | 240 km |

Ethnic Composition

Ḥazāra 19%
Other 18%
Tadzhik 25%
Pashtun 38%

After the fall of the Taliban in 2001, the newly established
Afghan Interim Authority restored, in a modified form,
the national flag first introduced in 1928. Black represents
the dark ages of the past; red, the blood shed in the
struggle for independence; and green, hope and prosperity
for the future.

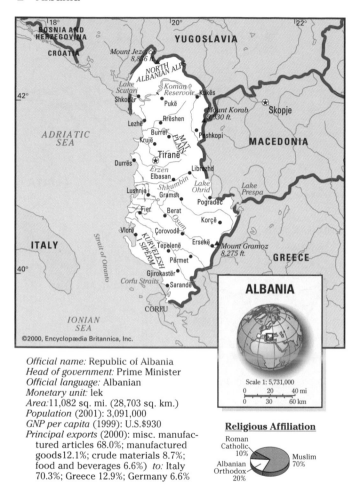

Official name: Republic of Albania
Head of government: Prime Minister
Official language: Albanian
Monetary unit: lek
Area: 11,082 sq. mi. (28,703 sq. km.)
Population (2001): 3,091,000
GNP per capita (1999): U.S.$930
Principal exports (2000): misc. manufactured articles 68.0%; manufactured goods 12.1%; crude materials 8.7%; food and beverages 6.6%) *to:* Italy 70.3%; Greece 12.9%; Germany 6.6%

Scale 1: 5,731,000

| 0 | 20 | 40 mi |
| 0 | 30 | 60 km |

Religious Affiliation

Roman Catholic 10%
Muslim 70%
Albanian Orthodox 20%

On Nov. 28, 1443, the flag was first raised by Skanderbeg, the national hero. After independence from Turkish rule was proclaimed on Nov. 28, 1912, the flag was flown by various regimes, each of which identified itself by adding a symbol above the double-headed eagle. The current flag, which features only the eagle, was adopted on May 22, 1993.

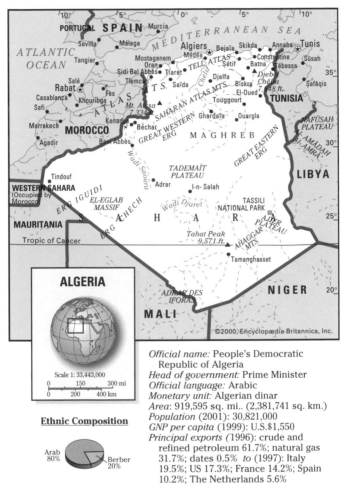

ALGERIA

Scale 1: 33,443,000

| 0 | 150 | 300 mi |
| 0 | 200 | 400 km |

Ethnic Composition

Arab 80%

Berber 20%

Official name: People's Democratic Republic of Algeria
Head of government: Prime Minister
Official language: Arabic
Monetary unit: Algerian dinar
Area: 919,595 sq. mi.. (2,381,741 sq. km.)
Population (2001): 30,821,000
GNP per capita (1999): U.S.$1,550
*Principal exports (*1996): crude and refined petroleum 61.7%; natural gas 31.7%; dates 0.5% *to* (1997): Italy 19.5%; US 17.3%; France 14.2%; Spain 10.2%; The Netherlands 5.6%

In the early 19th century, during the French conquest of North Africa, Algerian resistance fighters led by Emir Abdelkader supposedly raised the current flag. Its colors and symbols are associated with Islam and the Arab dynasties of the region. The flag was raised over an independent Algeria on July 2, 1962.

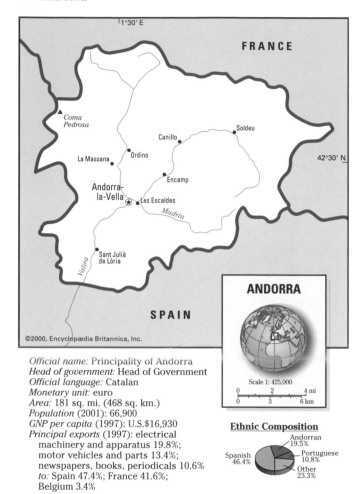

©2000, Encyclopædia Britannica, Inc.

ANDORRA

Scale 1: 425,000

0 — 2 — 4 mi
0 — 3 — 6 km

Official name: Principality of Andorra
Head of government: Head of Government
Official language: Catalan
Monetary unit: euro
Area: 181 sq. mi. (468 sq. km.)
Population (2001): 66,900
GNP per capita (1997): U.S.$16,930
Principal exports (1997): electrical
   machinery and apparatus 19.8%;
   motor vehicles and parts 13.4%;
   newspapers, books, periodicals 10.6%
   to: Spain 47.4%; France 41.6%;
   Belgium 3.4%

Ethnic Composition

Andorran 19.5%
Spanish 46.4%
Portuguese 10.8%
Other 23.3%

The flag may date to 1866, but the first legal authority for it is
unknown. The design was standardized in July 1993. Possible
sources for its colors are the flags of neighboring Spain (red-
yellow-red) and France (blue-white-red). The coat of arms
incorporates both French and Spanish elements dating to the
13th century or earlier.

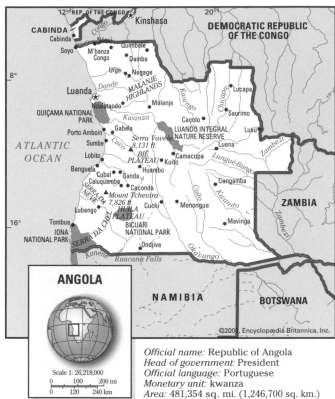

Scale 1: 26,218,000

0   100   200 mi

0   120   240 km

Ethnic Composition

Other 28%

Kongo 13.2%

Ovimbundu 37.2%

Mbundu 21.6%

Official name: Republic of Angola
Head of government: President
Official language: Portuguese
Monetary unit: kwanza
Area: 481,354 sq. mi. (1,246,700 sq. km.)
Population (2001): 10,366,000
GNP per capita (1999): U.S.$270
Principal exports (1999) mineral fuels
87.8%; diamonds 11.8% *to* (1999): U.S.
59.5% China 8.2%; Taiwan 7.7%;
Germany 2.4%; France 2.1%

After Portugal withdrew from Angola on Nov. 11, 1975, the flag of the leading rebel group gained recognition. Inspired by designs of the Viet Cong and the former Soviet Union, it includes a star for internationalism and progress, a cogwheel for industrial workers, and a machete for agricultural workers. The black stripe is for the African people.

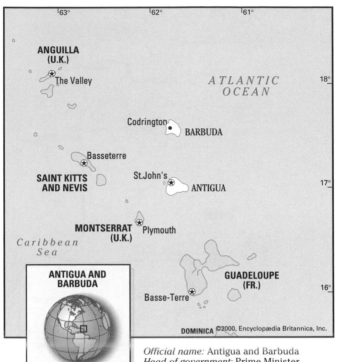

Scale 1: 4,945,000

| 0 | 20 | 40 mi |
| 0 | 30 | 60 km |

Religious Affiliation

Other 15.5%
Roman Catholic 10.8%
Protestant 73.7%

Official name: Antigua and Barbuda
Head of government: Prime Minister
Official language: English
Monetary unit: Eastern Caribbean dollar
Area: 170.5 sq. mi. (441.6 sq. km.)
Population (2001): 71,500
GNP per capita (1999): U.S.$8,990
Principal exports (1998): reexports
(significantly, petroleum products
reexported to neighboring islands)
59.1%; domestic exports 40.9%
to (1994): U.S. 40.0%; also United
Kingdom; Canada; and Caricom

When "associated statehood" was granted by Britain on Feb.
27, 1967, the flag was introduced, and it remained after independence (Nov. 1, 1981). Red is for the dynamism of the people, the V-shape is for victory, and the sun is for the climate.
Black is for the majority population and the soil, blue is for
the sea, and white is for the beaches.

©2000, Encyclopædia Britannica, Inc.

ARGENTINA

Scale 1: 57,746,000

| 0 | 250 | 500 mi |
| 0 | 400 | 800 km |

Official name: Argentine Republic
Head of government: President
Official language: Spanish
Monetary unit: peso
Area: 1,073,400 sq. mi. (2,780,092 sq. km.)
Population (2001): 37,487,000
GNP per capita (1999): U.S.$7,550
Principal exports (1999): food products
and live animals 35.1%; petroleum and
petroleum products 12.1%; machinery
and transport equipment 12.0%;
manufactured products 10.8%;
to: Brazil 24.4%; U.S. 11.4%; Chile 8.0%

Ethnic Composition

European 85%

Mestizo and Amerindian 15%

The uniforms worn by Argentines when the British attacked
Buenos Aires (1806) and the blue ribbons worn by patriots in
1810 may have been the origin of the celeste-white-celeste
flag hoisted on Feb. 12,1812. The flag's golden "sun of May"
was added on Feb. 25,1818, to commemorate the yielding of
the Spanish viceroy in 1810.

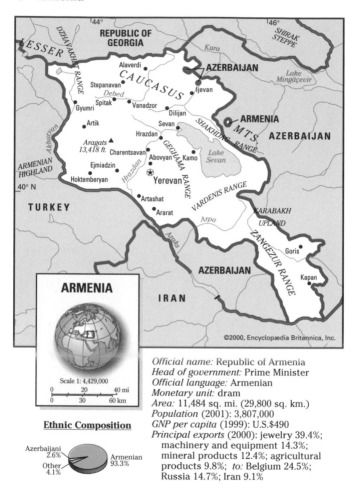

©2000, Encyclopædia Britannica, Inc.

ARMENIA

Scale 1: 4,429,000

| 0 | 20 | 40 mi |
| 0 | 30 | 60 km |

Ethnic Composition

Azerbaijani 2.6%
Other 4.1%
Armenian 93.3%

Official name: Republic of Armenia
Head of government: Prime Minister
Official language: Armenian
Monetary unit: dram
Area: 11,484 sq. mi. (29,800 sq. km.)
Population (2001): 3,807,000
GNP per capita (1999): U.S.$490
Principal exports (2000): jewelry 39.4%;
    machinery and equipment 14.3%;
    mineral products 12.4%; agricultural
    products 9.8%; *to:* Belgium 24.5%;
    Russia 14.7%; Iran 9.1%

In 1885 an Armenian priest proposed adopting the "rainbow flag given to the Armenians when Noah's Ark came to rest on Mt. Ararat." On Aug. 1, 1918, a flag was sanctioned with stripes of red (possibly symbolizing blood), blue (for homeland), and orange (for courage and work). Replaced during Soviet rule, it was readopted on Aug. 24, 1990.

AUSTRALIA

Scale 1: 70,500,000

| 0 | 300 | 600 mi |
| 0 | 400 | 800 km |

©2000, Encyclopædia Britannica, Inc.

Official name: Commonwealth of
   Australia
Head of government: Prime Minister
Official language: English
Monetary unit: Australian dollar
Area: 2,969,910 sq. mi. (7,692,030 sq. km.)
Population (2001): 19,358,000
GNP per capita (1999): U.S.$20,950
Principal exports (1999–2000): crude
   materials excluding fuels 18.9%;
   mineral fuels and lubricants 18.6%;
   food and live animals 17.3% *to:* Japan
   19.3%; U.S. 9.8%

Age Breakdown

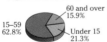

60 and over
15.9%

15–59
62.8%

Under 15
21.3%

After Australian confederation was achieved on Jan. 1, 1901,
the flag was chosen in a competition. Like the blue flags of
British colonies, it displays the Union Jack in the canton. Also
shown are the Southern Cross and a "Commonwealth Star."
The design became official on May 22, 1909, and it was recognized as the national flag on Feb. 14, 1954.

©2000, Encyclopædia Britannica, Inc.

Official name: Republic of Austria
Head of government: Chancellor
Official language: German
Monetary unit: euro
Area: 32,378 sq. mi. (83,858 sq. km.)
Population (2001): 8,069,000
GNP per capita (1999): U.S.$25,430
Principal exports (1999): machinery and
  transport equipment 43.1%; chemical
  products 9.4%; fabricated metals 4.9%;
  paper and paper products 4.7%
  to: Germany 34.9%; Italy 8.4%

AUSTRIA

Scale 1: 8,842,000

| 0 | 40 | 80 mi |
| 0 | 40 | 80 | 120 km |

Religious Affiliation

Nonreligious and atheist 8.6%
Other 8.6%
Lutheran 4.8%
Roman Catholic 78%

The colors of the Austrian coat of arms date from the seal of
Duke Frederick II in 1230. With the fall of the Austro-
Hungarian Empire in 1918, the new Austrian republic adopted
the red-white-red flag. The white is sometimes said to represent the Danube River. The imperial eagle, with one or two
heads, has been an Austrian symbol for centuries.

Map of Azerbaijan showing cities, mountains, rivers, and surrounding countries (Georgia, Russia, Armenia, Turkey, Iran) and the Caspian Sea.

Labels on the map include:

46° 48° 50°

RUSSIA 44°

GEORGIA
GREATER CAUCASUS MOUNTAINS
Tbilisi
Balakän
Kura
Khrami
Zaqatala
Qax
SHIRAK STEPPE
Xudat
Xaçmaz
CASPIAN SEA
Mount Shakhdag 13,917 ft.
Qazax
Ağstafa
Toyuz
Kura
Şäki
Qäbälä
Däväçi
Siyäzän
LESSER
Lake Mingäçevir
Şämkir
Gäncä
Mingäçevir
İsmayıllı
Samaxi
ABŞERON PENINSULA
ARMENIA
CAUCASUS MTS.
Daʻkäsän
Yevlax
Ağdaş
Göyçay
Ağsu
Sumqayıt
Baku
Yerevan
Mount Däliläc 11,550 ft.
NAGORNO-KARABAKH
Bärdä
Ucar
Kürdämir
Qazımämmäd
40°
Araz
Ağcabädi
KURA-ARAS LOWLAND
Ağdam
İmişli
Ali-Bayramlı
TURKEY
KARABAKH UPLAND
Xankändi
ZANGEZUR RANGE
Füzuli
Araks
Selyan
SHIRVANSKY NATURE RESERVE
Nakhichevan
Kapydzhik 12,815 ft.
Jalal-Abad
Neftçala
KYZYLAGACH NATURE RESERVE
Masallı
Ordubad
LÄNKÄRAN LOWLAND
Mount Kyumyurkyoy 8,174 ft.
Länkäran
Astara
IRAN 36°

©2000, Encyclopædia Britannica, Inc.

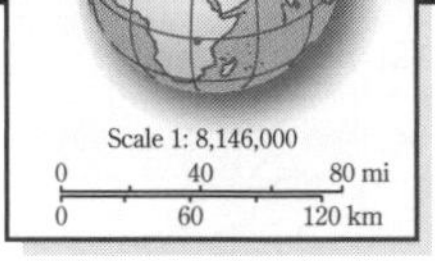

AZERBAIJAN

Scale 1: 8,146,000

0 40 80 mi
0 60 120 km

Ethnic Composition

Azerbaijani 82.7%
Other 6%
Armenian 5.6%
Russian 5.7%

Official name: Azerbaijani Republic
Head of government: President
Official language: Azerbaijani
Monetary unit: manat
Area: 33,400 sq. mi. (86,600 sq. km.)
Population (2001): 8,105,000
GNP per capita (1999): U.S.$460
Principal exports (1998): petroleum products 69.1%; textiles 9.2%; food 7.7%; machinery and equipment 6.0% *to:* Turkey 22.4%; Russia 17.4%; Georgia 12.7%

In the early 20th century anti-Russian nationalists exhorted the Azerbaijanis to "Turkify, Islamicize, and Europeanize," and the 1917 flag was associated with Turkey and Islam. In 1918 the crescent and star (also symbols of Turkic peoples) were introduced. Suppressed under Soviet rule, the flag was re-adopted on Feb. 5, 1991.

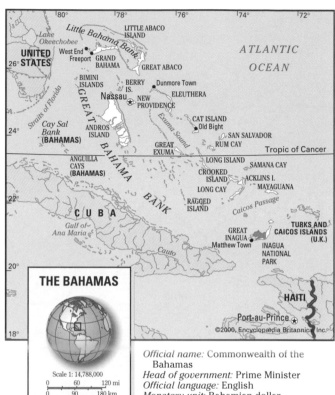

Official name: Commonwealth of the
Bahamas
Head of government: Prime Minister
Official language: English
Monetary unit: Bahamian dollar
Area: 5,382 sq. mi. (13,939 sq. km.)
Population (2001): 298,000
GNP per capita (1998): U.S.$11,890
Principal exports (1999): domestic
exports 48.3%, of which crayfish 14.9%
rum, reexports 44.2%, petroleum
exports 7.5% *to* (1998): U.S. 56.5%;
EC 31.4%; Canada 2.1%

Ethnic Composition

Asian or
Hispanic
3%

White
12%

Black 85%

The flag of The Bahamas was adopted on July 10, 1973, the
date of independence from Britain. Several entries from a
competition were combined to create the design. The two
aquamarine stripes are for the surrounding waters, the gold
stripe is for the sand and other rich land resources, and the
black triangle is for the people and their strength.

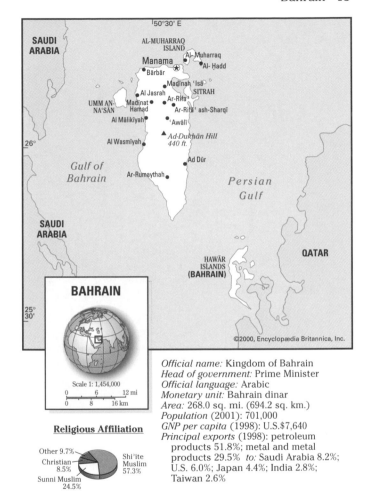

©2000, Encyclopædia Britannica, Inc.

Scale 1: 1,454,000

0   6   12 mi
0   8   16 km

Religious Affiliation

Other 9.7%
Christian 8.5%
Sunni Muslim 24.5%
Shi'ite Muslim 57.3%

Official name: Kingdom of Bahrain
Head of government: Prime Minister
Official language: Arabic
Monetary unit: Bahrain dinar
Area: 268.0 sq. mi. (694.2 sq. km.)
Population (2001): 701,000
GNP per capita (1998): U.S.$7,640
Principal exports (1998): petroleum
  products 51.8%; metal and metal
  products 29.5% *to:* Saudi Arabia 8.2%;
  U.S. 6.0%; Japan 4.4%; India 2.8%;
  Taiwan 2.6%

Red was the color of the Kharijite Muslims of Bahrain about 1820, and white was chosen to show amity with the British. The flag was recognized in 1933 but was used long before. The current flag law was adopted on Aug. 19, 1972. Between the white and red there may be a straight or serrated line, but the latter is most common.

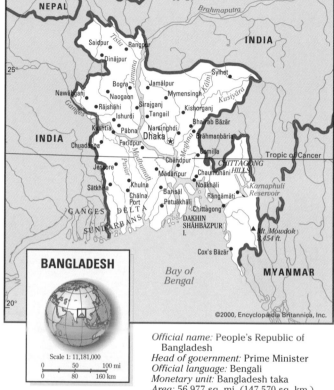

BANGLADESH

Scale 1: 11,181,000

0   50   100 mi
0   80   160 km

Religious Affiliation

Muslim 88.3%

Hindu 10.5%

Other 1.2%

Official name: People's Republic of Bangladesh
Head of government: Prime Minister
Official language: Bengali
Monetary unit: Bangladesh taka
Area: 56,977 sq. mi. (147,570 sq. km.)
Population (2001): 131,270,000
GNP per capita (1998): U.S.$350
Principal exports (1997–98): ready-made garments 61.9%; fish and prawns 7.3%
to: Western Europe 49.0%; U.S. 32.0%; Hong Kong 3.0%

The flag is dark green to symbolize Islam, plant life, and the hope placed in Bengali youth. Its original design included a red disk and a silhouette of the country. On Jan. 13, 1972, the silhouette was removed and the disk shifted off-center. The disk is the "rising sun of a new country" colored by the blood of those who fought for independence.

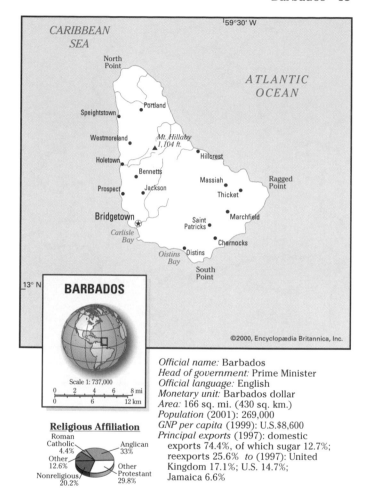

CARIBBEAN
SEA

North
Point

Portland

Speightstown

ATLANTIC
OCEAN

Westmoreland

Mt. Hillaby
1,104 ft.

Hillcrest

Holetown

Bennetts

Massiah

Ragged
Point

Prospect

Jackson

Thicket

Bridgetown

Saint
Patricks

Marchfield

Carlisle
Bay

Charnocks

Oistins
Bay

Oistins

South
Point

13° N

BARBADOS

©2000, Encyclopædia Britannica, Inc.

Scale 1: 737,000

0 2 4 6 8 mi
0   6   12 km

Religious Affiliation

Roman
Catholic
4.4%

Anglican
33%

Other
12.6%

Nonreligious
20.2%

Other
Protestant
29.8%

Official name: Barbados
Head of government: Prime Minister
Official language: English
Monetary unit: Barbados dollar
Area: 166 sq. mi. (430 sq. km.)
Population (2001): 269,000
GNP per capita (1999): U.S.$8,600
Principal exports (1997): domestic
  exports 74.4%, of which sugar 12.7%;
  reexports 25.6% *to* (1997): United
  Kingdom 17.1%; U.S. 14.7%;
  Jamaica 6.6%

The flag was designed by Grantley Prescod, a Barbadian art teacher. Its stripes of blue-yellow-blue are for sea, sand, and sky. The black trident head was inspired by the colonial flag of Barbados, which featured a trident-wielding Poseidon, or Neptune, figure. The flag was first hoisted on Nov. 30, 1966, the date of independence from Britain.

Scale 1: 9,358,000

| 0 | | 40 | | 80 mi |
| 0 | 60 | | 120 km |

Ethnic Composition

Other 5.6%
Ukrainian 3%
Russian 13.5%
Belarusian 77.9%

Official name: Republic of Belarus
Head of government: President
Official languages: Belarusian; Russian
Monetary unit: rubel
Area: 80,153 sq. mi. (207,595 sq. km.)
Population (2001): 9,986,000
GNP per capita (1998): U.S.$2,620
Principal exports (1997): industrial products 98.3%, of which machinery and metalworking 32.9%, chemical and petroleum products 20.9% *to:* Russia 64.8%; Ukraine 5.8%

In 1951 the former Soviet republic created a striped flag in red (for communism) and green (for fields and forests), with the hammer, sickle, and star of communism. In 1991–95 an older design was used, but the Soviet-era flag was then altered and readopted without communist symbols. The vertical stripe is typical of embroidery on peasant clothing.

NORTH SEA
THE NETHERLANDS
Brugge-Zeebrugge Canal
Blankenberge
Ostend
Nieuwpoort
Breda
Tilburg
Brecht
Turnhout
Eindhoven
East Schelde
Westerschelde
Kalmthout
Zandvliet
Antwerp
KEMPENLAND
Neerpelt
Maas
Brugge
Eeklo
Torhout
Aalter
Ghent
Sint-Niklaas
Geel
Peer
Bree
IJzer
Steden
Roeselare
Mechelen
Rupel
Tessenderlo
Demer
Poperinge
Ypres
Kortrijk
Schelde
Aalst
Schaerbeek
Louvain
Hasselt
Genk
GERMANY
Moeskron
Lille
Tournai
Péruwelz
Enghien
Brussels
Uccle
Ixelles
Tienen
Riemst
Maastricht
Ruhr
Ath
Braine-l'Alleud
Waremme
Liège
Eupen
Aachen
Mons
Boussu
Le Louvière
Spy
Wanze
Meuse
Seraing
Verviers
Sambre
Charleroi
Namur
CONDROZ
Spa
Botrange
Thuin
Dinant
Ciney
HAUTES FAGNES-EIFEL NATIONAL PARK
Lake Plate Taille
Philippeville
Lesse
Marche-en-Famenne
FRANCE
Couvin
Saint-Hubert
ARDENNES
Bastogne
Bouillon
Florenville
Arlon
LUXEMBOURG
Luxembourg
Athus
Our
Moselle

©2000, Encyclopædia Britannica, Inc.

BELGIUM

Scale 1: 4,176,000

0 — 20 — 40 mi
0 — 30 — 60 km

Language Composition

Other 8%
Dutch 59%
French 33%

Official name: Kingdom of Belgium
Head of government: Prime Minister
Official languages: Dutch; French; German
Monetary unit: euro
Area: 11,787 sq. mi. (30,528 sq. km.)
Population (2001): 10,268,000
GNP per capita (1999): U.S.$24,650
Principal exports (1999): machinery and transport equipment 30.0%; chemicals 20.3%; food 8.7% *to:* Germany 17.9%; France 17.7%; The Netherlands 12.8%; United Kingdom 10.0%

A gold shield and a black lion appeared in the seal of Count Philip of Flanders as early as 1162, and in 1787 cockades of black-yellow-red were used in a Brussels revolt against Austria. After a war for independence, the flag was recognized on Jan. 23, 1831. By 1838 the design, which was influenced by the French tricolor, became standard.

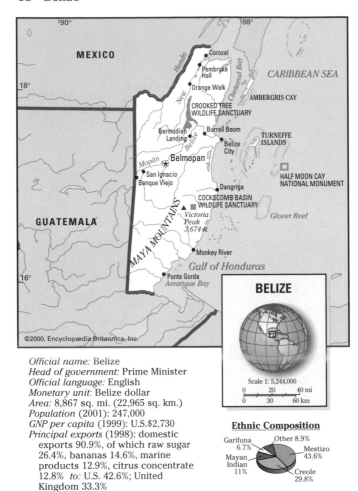

©2000, Encyclopædia Britannica, Inc.

BELIZE

Scale 1: 5,244,000

| 0 | 20 | 40 mi |
| 0 | 30 | 60 km |

Official name: Belize
Head of government: Prime Minister
Official language: English
Monetary unit: Belize dollar
Area: 8,867 sq. mi. (22,965 sq. km.)
Population (2001): 247,000
GNP per capita (1999): U.S.$2,730
Principal exports (1998): domestic
    exports 90.9%, of which raw sugar
    26.4%, bananas 14.6%, marine
    products 12.9%, citrus concentrate
    12.8% *to:* U.S. 42.6%; United
    Kingdom 33.3%

Ethnic Composition

Garifuna 6.7%
Other 8.9%
Mayan Indian 11%
Mestizo 43.6%
Creole 29.8%

The flag of Belize (former British Honduras) was based on the
flag of the nationalist People's United Party. Its coat of arms
shows a mahogany tree, a shield, and a Creole and a Mestizo.
The red stripes, symbolic of the United Democratic Party,
were added on independence day (Sept. 21, 1981), when the
flag was first officially hoisted.

BURKINA FASO
⊛ Ouagadougou
NIGER
PENDJARI NATIONAL PARK
"W" NATIONAL PARK
NIGERIA
• Kandi
ATAKORA MOUNTAINS
Mékrou
Alibori
Sota
• Natitingou
• Djougou
TOGO
• Parakou
Ouémé
Niger
8° N
• Savé
GHANA
• Savalou
Lake Volta
Lake Togo
• Abomey
Ogou
Mono
Porto-Novo ⊛
BENIN
Cotonou
S L A V E   C O A S T
Bight of Benin
©2000, Encyclopædia Britannica, Inc.

Scale 1: 13,517,000

0 — 60 — 120 mi
0 — 80 — 160 km

Ethnic Composition

Other 19.9%
Fon 39.7%
Adjara 11.1%
Aizo 8.6%
Yoruba 12.1%
Bariba 8.6%

Official name: Republic of Benin
Head of government: President
Official language: French
Monetary unit: CFA franc
Area: 43,500 sq. mi. (114,760 sq. km.)
Population (2001): 6,591,000
GNP per capita (1999): U.S.$380
Principal exports (1997): cotton yarn 51.6%; reexport 38.5% *to* (1997): Brazil 18.0%; Portugal 11.0%; Morocco 10.0%; India 6.5%; Libya 6.0%

Adopted on Nov. 16, 1959, the flag of the former French colony used the Pan-African colors. Yellow was for the savannas in the north and green was for the palm groves in the south. Red stood for the blood of patriots. In 1975 a Marxist-oriented government replaced the flag, but after the demise of Communism it was restored on Aug. 1, 1990.

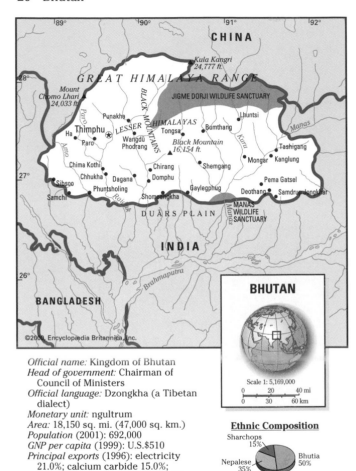

Official name: Kingdom of Bhutan
Head of government: Chairman of
  Council of Ministers
Official language: Dzongkha (a Tibetan
  dialect)
Monetary unit: ngultrum
Area: 18,150 sq. mi. (47,000 sq. km.)
Population (2001): 692,000
GNP per capita (1999): U.S.$510
Principal exports (1996): electricity
  21.0%; calcium carbide 15.0%;
  particle board 8.0%; cement 7.1%;
  to (1997-98): India 94.5%

Ethnic Composition

Sharchops 15%

Nepalese 35%

Bhutia 50%

The flag of Bhutan ("Land of the Dragon") features a dragon
grasping jewels; this represents natural wealth and perfec-
tion. The white color is for purity and loyalty, the gold is for
regal power, and the orange-red is for Buddhist sects and religious commitment. The flag may have been introduced as
recently as 1971.

©2000, Encyclopædia Britannica, Inc.

Official name: Republic of Bolivia
Head of government: President
Official languages: Spanish, Aymara,
  Quechua
Monetary unit: boliviano
Area: 424,164 sq. mi. (1,098,581 sq. km.)
Population (2001): 8,516,000
GNP per capita (1999): U.S.$990
Principal exports (1998): zinc 14.1%;
  soybeans 13.6%; gold 10.1%; silver
  6.6% *to:* U.S. 18.4%; United Kingdom
  17.8%; Peru 11.9%

Scale 1: 23,517,000

Ethnic Composition

White 14.5%
Aymara 16.9%
Other 12%
Quechua 25.4%
Mestizo 31.2%

A version of the flag was first adopted on July 25, 1826, but on Nov. 5, 1851, the order of the stripes was changed to red-yellow-green. The colors were often used by the Aymara and Quechua peoples; in addition, red is for the valor of the army, yellow for mineral resources, and green for the land. The current flag law dates from July 14, 1888.

Scale 1: 6,252,000

| 0 | 30 | 60 mi |
| 0 | 40 | 80 km |

Ethnic Composition

Serb 31.3%
Muslim 49.2%
Croat 17.3%
Other 2.2%

Official name: Bosnia and Herzegovina
Head of government: Prime Minister
Official languages: Bosnian (Serbo-Croatian)
Monetary unit: marka
Area: 19,741 sq. mi. (51,129 sq. km.)
Population (2001): 3,922,000. (excludes nearly 300,000 refugees in adjacent countries and Western Europe)
GNP per capita (1999): U.S.$1,210
Principal exports (2000): *to:* Italy 23.4%; Yugoslavia 21.6%; Switzerland 11.9%; Germany 9.2%; Croatia 7.9%

Upon independence from Yugoslavia on March 3, 1992, the Bosnian-led government chose a neutral flag in order to appease the Serb and Croat populations. The flag was adopted on May 4, 1992, and although civil war caused the administrative division of the country in 1995, the white flag is recognized internationally.

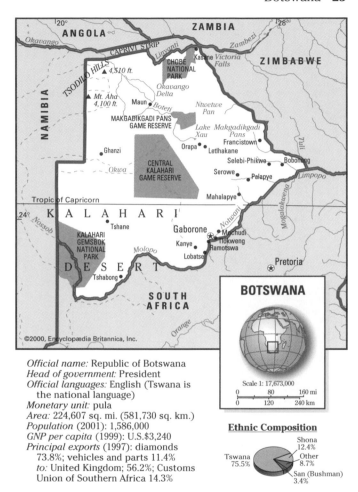

Official name: Republic of Botswana
Head of government: President
Official languages: English (Tswana is the national language)
Monetary unit: pula
Area: 224,607 sq. mi. (581,730 sq. km.)
Population (2001): 1,586,000
GNP per capita (1999): U.S.$3,240
Principal exports (1997): diamonds 73.8%; vehicles and parts 11.4% *to:* United Kingdom; 56.2%; Customs Union of Southern Africa 14.3%

Scale 1: 17,673,000

| 0 | 80 | 160 mi |
| 0 | 120 | 240 km |

Ethnic Composition

Shona 12.4%
Other 8.7%
San (Bushman) 3.4%
Tswana 75.5%

Adopted in 1966, the flag was designed to contrast symbolically with that of neighboring South Africa, where apartheid was then in effect. The black and white stripes in Botswana's flag are for racial cooperation and equality. The background symbolizes water, a scarce resource in the expansive Kalahari Desert.

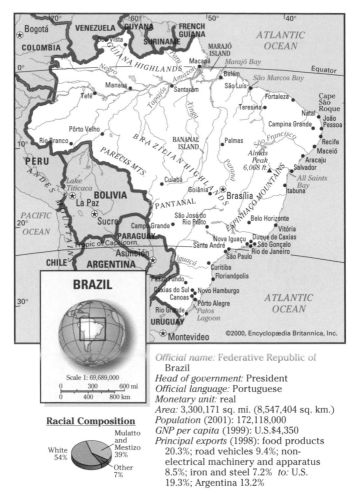

Official name: Federative Republic of
  Brazil
Head of government: President
Official language: Portuguese
Monetary unit: real
Area: 3,300,171 sq. mi. (8,547,404 sq. km.)
Population (2001): 172,118,000
GNP per capita (1999): U.S.$4,350
Principal exports (1998): food products
  20.3%; road vehicles 9.4%; non-
  electrical machinery and apparatus
  8.5%; iron and steel 7.2% *to:* U.S.
  19.3%; Argentina 13.2%

Racial Composition

White 54%
Mulatto and Mestizo 39%
Other 7%

Scale 1: 69,689,000

The original flag was introduced on Sept. 7, 1822, when Dom
Pedro declared independence from Portugal. In 1889 the blue
disk and the motto Ordem e Progresso ("Order and
Progress") were added. The Brazilian states and territories
are symbolized by the constellations of stars. Green is for the
land, while yellow is for gold and other mineral wealth.

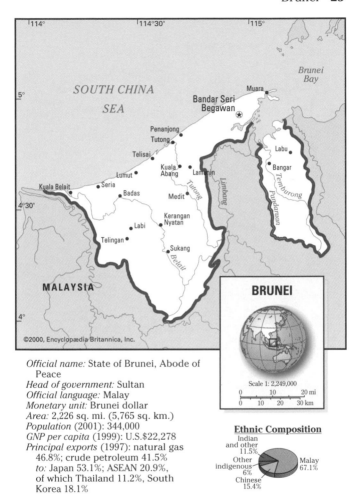

114° 114°30' 115°

SOUTH CHINA
SEA

Brunei
Bay

Muara

Bandar Seri
Begawan

Penanjong
Tutong

Telisai

Kuala
Abang Lamunin

Lumut

Kuala Belait

Seria

Badas

Medit

Labu

Bangar

5°

4°30'

4°

Kerangan
Nyatan

Labi

Telingan

Sukang

Belait

Tutong

Limbang

Temburong

Pandaruan

MALAYSIA

©2000, Encyclopædia Britannica, Inc.

BRUNEI

Scale 1: 2,249,000

| 0 | 10 | 20 mi |
| 0 | 10 | 20 | 30 km |

Official name: State of Brunei, Abode of
Peace
Head of government: Sultan
Official language: Malay
Monetary unit: Brunei dollar
Area: 2,226 sq. mi. (5,765 sq. km.)
Population (2001): 344,000
GNP per capita (1999): U.S.$22,278
Principal exports (1997): natural gas
46.8%; crude petroleum 41.5%
to: Japan 53.1%; ASEAN 20.9%,
of which Thailand 11.2%, South
Korea 18.1%

Ethnic Composition

Indian
and other
11.5%

Other
indigenous
6%

Chinese
15.4%

Malay
67.1%

When Brunei became a British protectorate in 1906, diagonal
stripes were added to its yellow flag. The yellow stood for the
sultan, while white and black were for his two chief ministers.
Introduced in September 1959, the coat of arms has a parasol
as a symbol of royalty and a crescent and inscription for the
state religion, Islam.

Official name: Republic of Bulgaria
Head of government: Prime Minister
Official language: Bulgarian
Monetary unit: lev
Area: 110,971.4 sq. mi. (8,190,876 sq. km.)
Population (2001): 7,953,000
GNP per capita (1999): U.S.$1,410
Principal exports (1997): chemicals and
  plastics 22.3%; food, beverages and
  tobacco 13.5%; machinery and
  metalworking equipment 9.6%
  to: Italy 11.7%; Germany 9.5%;
  Turkey 9.0%

Scale 1: 8,710,000
0   40   80 mi
0   60   120 km

Ethnic Composition

Bulgarian 85.7%
Turkish 9.4%
Other 4.9%

The flag was based on the Russian flag of 1699, but with green
substituted for blue. Under communist rule, a red star and
other symbols were added, but the old tricolor was reestablished on Nov. 27, 1990. The white is for peace, love, and freedom; green is for agriculture; and red is for the independence
struggle and military courage.

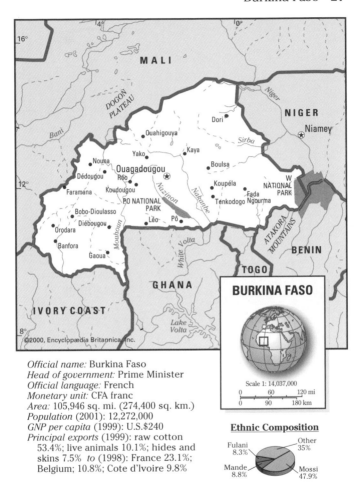

Official name: Burkina Faso
Head of government: Prime Minister
Official language: French
Monetary unit: CFA franc
Area: 105,946 sq. mi. (274,400 sq. km.)
Population (2001): 12,272,000
GNP per capita (1999): U.S.$240
Principal exports (1999): raw cotton
  53.4%; live animals 10.1%; hides and
  skins 7.5% to (1998): France 23.1%;
  Belgium; 10.8%; Cote d'Ivoire 9.8%

Scale 1: 14,037,000
0   60   120 mi
0   90   180 km

Ethnic Composition

Fulani 8.3%
Other 35%
Mande 8.8%
Mossi 47.9%

On Aug. 4, 1984, Upper Volta was renamed Burkina Faso by
the revolutionary government of Thomas Sankara, and the
current flag was adopted with Pan-African colors. The yellow
star symbolizes leadership and revolutionary principles. The
red stripe is said to stand for the revolutionary struggle,
while the green stripe represents hope and abundance.

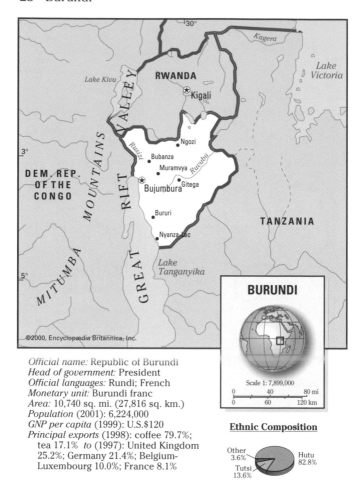

Official name: Republic of Burundi
Head of government: President
Official languages: Rundi; French
Monetary unit: Burundi franc
Area: 10,740 sq. mi. (27,816 sq. km.)
Population (2001): 6,224,000
GNP per capita (1999): U.S.$120
Principal exports (1998): coffee 79.7%;
   tea 17.1% *to* (1997): United Kingdom
   25.2%; Germany 21.4%; Belgium-
   Luxembourg 10.0%; France 8.1%

Ethnic Composition

Other 3.6%
Tutsi 13.6%
Hutu 82.8%

The flag became official on June 28, 1967. Its white saltire (diagonal cross) and central disk symbolize peace. The red color is for the independence struggle, and green is for hope. The stars correspond to the national motto, "Unity, Work, Progress." They also recall the Tutsi, Hutu, and Twa peoples and the pledge to God, king, and country.

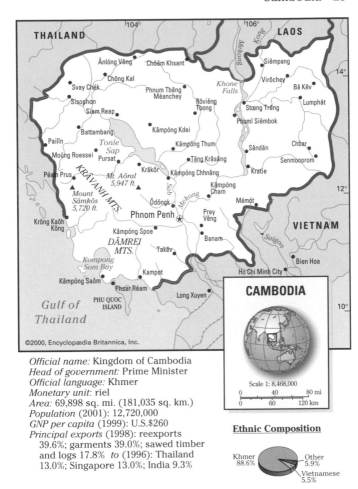

THAILAND

LAOS

Ânlóng Vêng   Chôăm Khsant

Chŏng Kal

Svay Chék

Sisophon

Siĕm Reap

Phnum Tbêng
Méanchey

Rôviĕng
Tbong

*Khone
Falls*

Siĕmpang

Virôchey

Bâ Kêv

Lumphăt

Stœng Trêng

Phumĭ Siĕmbok

Battambang

Pailĭn

*Tonle
Sap*

Kâmpóng Kdei

Kâmpóng Thum

Tăng Krâsăng

Sândăn

Chbar

Senmonorom

Moŭng Roessei   Pursat

Péam Prus

Krâkôr

Kâmpóng Chhnăng

Mt. Aôral
5,947 ft.

Kâmpóng
Cham

Kratie

Mount
Sāmkôs
5,720 ft.

Ŏdôngk

Phnom Penh

Prey
Vêng

Mémót

VIETNAM

Krŏng Kaôh
Kŏng

Kâmpóng Spoe

*DÂMREI
MTS.*

Takêv

Banam

Saigon

*Kompong
Som Bay*

Kâmpóng Saôm

Phsar Réam

Kampot

Long Xuyen

Ho Chi Minh City

Bien Hoa

*Gulf of
Thailand*

PHU QUOC
ISLAND

Mekong

Kong

Mekong

KRAVANH MTS.

©2000, Encyclopædia Britannica, Inc.

CAMBODIA

Scale 1: 8,468,000

| 0 | 40 | 80 mi |
| 0 | 60 | 120 km |

Official name: Kingdom of Cambodia
Head of government: Prime Minister
Official language: Khmer
Monetary unit: riel
Area: 69,898 sq. mi. (181,035 sq. km.)
Population (2001): 12,720,000
GNP per capita (1999): U.S.$260
Principal exports (1998): reexports
   39.6%; garments 39.0%; sawed timber
   and logs 17.8% *to* (1996): Thailand
   13.0%; Singapore 13.0%; India 9.3%

Ethnic Composition

Khmer
88.6%

Other
5.9%

Vietnamese
5.5%

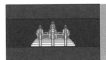

Artistic representations of the central ruined temple of
Angkor Wat, a 12th-century temple complex, have appeared
on Khmer flags since the 19th century. The current flag
design dates to 1948. It was replaced in 1970 under the
Khmer Republic and in 1976 under communist leadership,
but it was again hoisted on June 29, 1993.

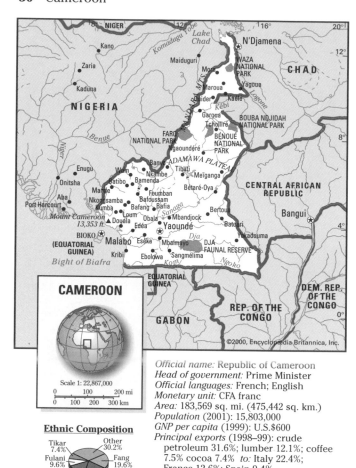

Official name: Republic of Cameroon
Head of government: Prime Minister
Official languages: French; English
Monetary unit: CFA franc
Area: 183,569 sq. mi. (475,442 sq. km.)
Population (2001): 15,803,000
GNP per capita (1999): U.S.$600
Principal exports (1998–99): crude
   petroleum 31.6%; lumber 12.1%; coffee
   7.5% cocoa 7.4% to: Italy 22.4%;
   France 12.6%; Spain 9.4%

Ethnic Composition

Tikar 7.4%
Fulani 9.6%
Duala, Luanda, and Basa 14.7%
Bamileke and Bamum 18.5%
Fang 19.6%
Other 30.2%

The flag was officially hoisted on Oct. 29, 1957, prior to independence (Jan. 1, 1960). Green is for the vegetation of the south, yellow for the savannas of the north, and red for union and sovereignty. Two yellow stars were added (for the British Cameroons) in 1961, but these were replaced in 1975 by a single star symbolizing national unity.

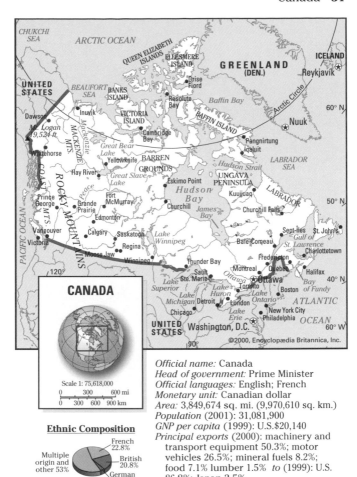

Official name: Canada
Head of government: Prime Minister
Official languages: English; French
Monetary unit: Canadian dollar
Area: 3,849,674 sq. mi. (9,970,610 sq. km.)
Population (2001): 31,081,900
GNP per capita (1999): U.S.$20,140
Principal exports (2000): machinery and
transport equipment 50.3%; motor
vehicles 26.5%; mineral fuels 8.2%;
food 7.1% lumber 1.5% *to* (1999): U.S.
86.8%; Japan 2.5%

CANADA

Scale 1: 75,618,000

0   300   600 mi
0   300   600   900 km

Ethnic Composition

Multiple
origin and
other 53%

French
22.8%

British
20.8%

German
3.4%

During Canada's first century of independence the Union Jack
was still flown, but with a Canadian coat of arms. The maple
leaf design, with the national colors, became official on Feb.
15, 1965. Since 1868 the maple leaf has been a national symbol, and in 1921 a red leaf in the coat of arms stood for
Canadian sacrifice during World War I.

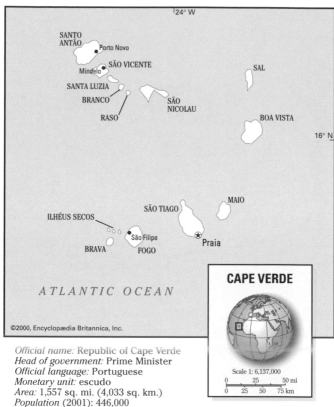

24° W

SANTO
ANTÃO
• Porto Novo
SÃO VICENTE
Mindelo
SANTA LUZIA
BRANCO
RASO
SÃO
NICOLAU
SAL
BOA VISTA

16° N

ILHÉUS SECOS
SÃO TIAGO
MAIO
São Filipe
BRAVA   FOGO
⊛ Praia

ATLANTIC OCEAN

©2000, Encyclopædia Britannica, Inc.

Official name: Republic of Cape Verde
Head of government: Prime Minister
Official language: Portuguese
Monetary unit: escudo
Area: 1,557 sq. mi. (4,033 sq. km.)
Population (2001): 446,000
GNP per capita (1999): U.S.$1,330
Principal exports (1998): shoes 22.5%;
   clothing 7.1%; fish and fish
   preparations 6.7%; reexports 62.1%
   to: Portugal 89.3%; Spain 7.9%

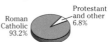

CAPE VERDE

Scale 1: 6,137,000
0   25   50 mi
0   25   50   75 km

Religious Affiliation

Roman
Catholic
93.2%

Protestant
and other
6.8%

After the elections of 1991, the flag was established with a
blue field bearing a ring of 10 yellow stars to symbolize the
10 main islands of Cape Verde. The stripes of white-red-white
suggest peace and national resolve. Red, white, and blue also
are a symbolic link to Portugal and the United States. The
new flag became official on Sept. 25, 1992.

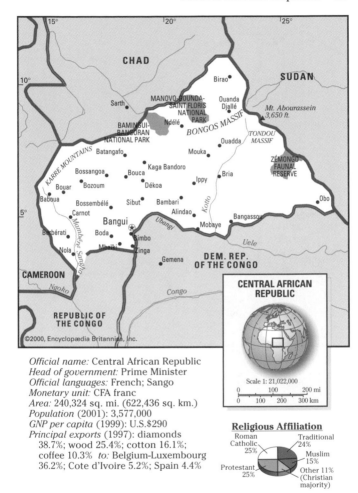

Official name: Central African Republic
Head of government: Prime Minister
Official languages: French; Sango
Monetary unit: CFA franc
Area: 240,324 sq. mi. (622,436 sq. km.)
Population (2001): 3,577,000
GNP per capita (1999): U.S.$290
Principal exports (1997): diamonds
   38.7%; wood 25.4%; cotton 16.1%;
   coffee 10.3% *to:* Belgium-Luxembourg
   36.2%; Cote d'Ivoire 5.2%; Spain 4.4%

Scale 1: 21,022,000
0   100   200 mi
0   100   200   300 km

Religious Affiliation
Roman   Traditional
Catholic   24%
25%   Muslim
                                15%
Protestant   Other 11%
25%   (Christian
                              majority)

Barthélemy Boganda designed the flag in 1958. It combines
French and Pan-African colors. The star is a guide for
progress and an emblem of unity. The blue stripe is for liberty, grandeur, and the sky; the white is for purity, equality, and
candor; the green and yellow are for forests and savannas;
and the red is for the blood of humankind.

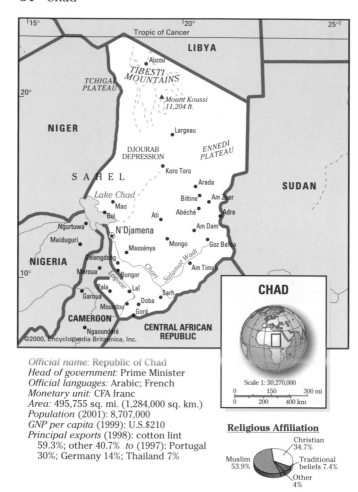

Tropic of Cancer

LIBYA

Aozou

TCHIGAI
PLATEAU

TIBESTI
MOUNTAINS

▲ Mount Koussi
11,204 ft.

NIGER

Largeau

ENNEDI
PLATEAU

DJOURAB
DEPRESSION

SAHEL

Koro Toro

SUDAN

Arada

Lake Chad

Biltine   Am Zoer

Mao

Ati   Abéché   Adre

Bol

Ngurtuwa

N'Djamena   Am Dam

Maiduguri

Massénya   Mongo   Goz Beïda

NIGERIA

Gelengdeng   Salamat Wadi   Am Timan

Maroua   Bongor

Pala   Laï

Garoua   Sarh

Moundou   Doba   Goré

CAMEROON   CENTRAL AFRICAN
REPUBLIC

Ngaoundéré

©2000, Encyclopædia Britannica, Inc.

CHAD

Scale 1: 30,270,000

0   150   300 mi

0   200   400 km

Official name: Republic of Chad
Head of government: Prime Minister
Official languages: Arabic; French
Monetary unit: CFA franc
Area: 495,755 sq. mi. (1,284,000 sq. km.)
Population (2001): 8,707,000
GNP per capita (1999): U.S.$210
Principal exports (1998): cotton lint
   59.3%; other 40.7% *to* (1997): Portugal
   30%; Germany 14%; Thailand 7%

Religious Affiliation

Christian
34.7%

Muslim
53.9%

Traditional
beliefs 7.4%

Other
4%

In 1958 a tricolor of green-yellow-red (the Pan-African colors)
was proposed, but that design was already used by the Mali-
Senegal federation, another former French colony. Approved
on Nov. 6, 1959, the current flag substitutes blue for the original green stripe. Blue is for hope and sky, yellow for the sun,
and red for the unity of the nation.

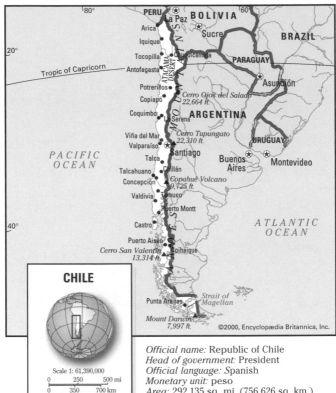

©2000, Encyclopædia Britannica, Inc.

CHILE

Scale 1: 61,390,000

| 0 | 250 | 500 mi |
| 0 | 350 | 700 km |

Religious Affiliation

Protestant 13.2%
Atheist and nonreligious 5.8%
Other 4.3%
Roman Catholic 76.7%

Official name: Republic of Chile
Head of government: President
Official language: Spanish
Monetary unit: peso
Area: 292,135 sq. mi. (756,626 sq. km.)
Population (2001): 15,402,000
GNP per capita (1999): U.S.$4,630
Principal exports (1999): mining 44.4%; industrial products 38.5%; foodstuffs 17.1%. *to:* U.S. 19.4%; Japan 14.3%; United Kingdom 6.8% Argentina 4.6%; Brazil 4.3%

On Oct. 18, 1817, the flag was established for the new republic. The blue is for the sky, and the star is "a guide on the path of progress and honor." The white is for the snow of the Andes Mountains while the red recalls the blood of patriots. In the 15th century the Araucanian Indians gave red-white-blue sashes to their warriors.

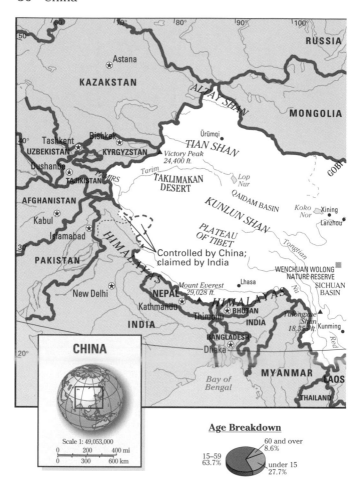

Age Breakdown

60 and over
8.6%

15–59
63.7%

under 15
27.7%

CHINA

Scale 1: 49,053,000

0   200   400 mi

0   300   600 km

Controlled by China;
claimed by India

The flag was hoisted on Oct. 1, 1949. The red is for communism and the Han Chinese. The large star was originally for the Communist Party, and the smaller stars were for the proletariat, the peasants, the petty bourgeoisie, and the "patriotic capitalists." The large star was later said to stand for China, the smaller stars for minorities.

Official name: People's Republic of China
Head of government: Premier
Official language: Mandarin Chinese
Monetary unit: Renminbi (yuan)
Area: 3,696,100 sq. mi. (9,572,900 sq. km.)
Population (2001): 1,274,915,000
GNP per capita (1999): U.S.$750
Principal exports (1998): machinery and transport equipment 27.3%;
   products of the textile industries, rubber and metal products 17.6%
   to: Hong Kong 21.1%; U.S. 20.7%; Japan 16.2%

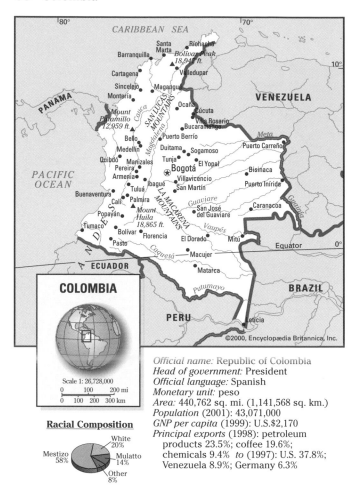

Official name: Republic of Colombia
Head of government: President
Official language: Spanish
Monetary unit: peso
Area: 440,762 sq. mi. (1,141,568 sq. km.)
Population (2001): 43,071,000
GNP per capita (1999): U.S.$2,170
Principal exports (1998): petroleum
    products 23.5%; coffee 19.6%;
    chemicals 9.4% to (1997): U.S. 37.8%;
    Venezuela 8.9%; Germany 6.3%

COLOMBIA

Scale 1: 26,728,000

0   100   200 mi
0   100 200 300 km

Racial Composition

White 20%
Mestizo 58%
Mulatto 14%
Other 8%

In the early 19th century "the Liberator" Simon Bolivar created a yellow-blue-red flag for New Granada (which included
Colombia, Venezuela, Panama, and Ecuador). The flag symbolized the yellow gold of the New World separated by the
blue ocean from the red of "bloody Spain." The present
Colombian flag was established on Nov. 26, 1861.

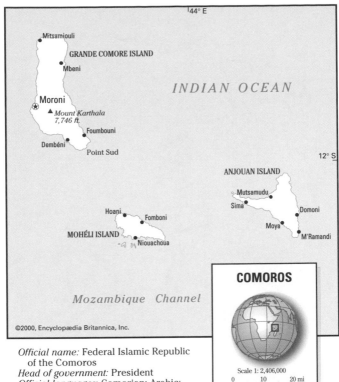

©2000, Encyclopædia Britannica, Inc.

Official name: Federal Islamic Republic of the Comoros
Head of government: President
Official languages: Comorian; Arabic; French
Monetary unit: Comorian franc
Area: 719 sq. mi. (1,862 sq. km.)
Population (2001): 566,000
GNP per capita (1999): U.S.$350
Principal exports (1999): vanilla 43.2%; cloves 27.7%; ylang-ylang 13.3%
to: U.S. 26.8%; France 25.4%; Germany 12.2%

COMOROS

Scale 1: 2,406,000
0   10   20 mi
0   15   30 km

Age Breakdown

15–59
47.5%
Under 15
48.5%
60 and over
4%

The flag was adopted on Oct. 3, 1996. Its green background and white crescent are symbols of Islam, and the Arabic words for Allah and Muhammad are inscribed in the corners. The four stars are for the islands of Njazidja (formerly Grande-Comore), Mwali (Mohéli), Nzwani (Anjouan), and Mayotte (a French territory that is claimed by Comoros).

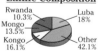

Official name: Democratic Republic of the Congo
Head of government: President
Official languages: French; English
Monetary unit: Congolese franc
Area: 905,354 sq. mi. (2,344,858 sq. km.)
Population (2001): 53,625,000
GNP per capita (2000): U.S.$85
Principal exports (1999): diamonds 61.3%; crude petroleum 12.4%; coffee 9.8%; cobalt 8.6%; copper 5.1%
to (1999): Belgium-Luxembourg; U.S.; Finland; Italy

Ethnic Composition

Rwanda 10.3%
Mongo 13.5%
Kongo 16.1%
Luba 18%
Other 42.1%

In 1877 the flag of the Congo Free State was blue with a gold star, for a shining light in the "Dark Continent." At independence (June 30, 1962) six stars were added for the existing six provinces, but in 1971 the flag was replaced with a green flag depicting an arm and a torch. The regime led by Laurent Kabila restored the old flag on May 17, 1997.

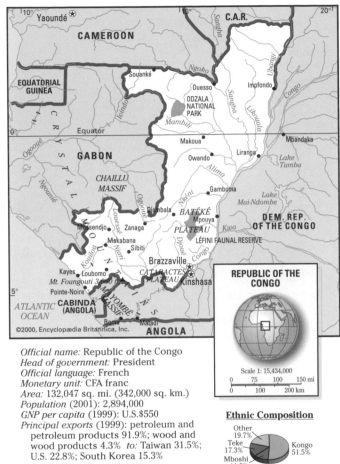

Official name: Republic of the Congo
Head of government: President
Official language: French
Monetary unit: CFA franc
Area: 132,047 sq. mi. (342,000 sq. km.)
Population (2001): 2,894,000
GNP per capita (1999): U.S.$550
Principal exports (1999): petroleum and
   petroleum products 91.9%; wood and
   wood products 4.3% *to:* Taiwan 31.5%;
   U.S. 22.8%; South Korea 15.3%

Scale 1: 15,434,000

| 0 | 75 | 100 | 150 mi |
| 0 | 100 | 200 km |

Ethnic Composition

Other 19.7%
Teke 17.3%
Mboshi 11.5%
Kongo 51.5%

First adopted on Sept. 15, 1959, the flag uses the Pan-African colors. Green was originally said to stand for Congo's agriculture and forests, and yellow for friendship and the nobility of the people, but the red was unexplained. Altered in 1969 by a Marxist government, the flag was restored to its initial form on June 10, 1991.

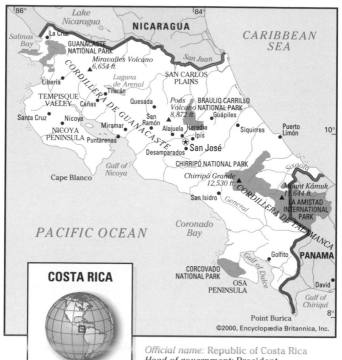

©2000, Encyclopædia Britannica, Inc.

COSTA RICA

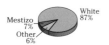

Scale 1: 5,424,000

| 0 | 25 | 50 mi |
| 0 | 40 | 80 km |

Ethnic Composition

White 87%
Mestizo 7%
Other 6%

Official name: Republic of Costa Rica
Head of government: President
Official language: Spanish
Monetary unit: Costa Rican colon
Area: 19,730 sq. mi. (51,100 sq. km.)
Population (2001): 3,936,000
GNP per capita (1999): U.S.$3,570
Principal exports (1998): bananas 21.8%; coffee 13.3%; processed food and tobacco products 9.3%; fish and shrimp 7.6% *to:* U.S. 42%; United Kingdom 7%; Germany 7%

The blue and white stripes originated in the flag colors of the United Provinces of Central America (1823–40). On Sept. 29, 1848, the red stripe was added to symbolize sunlight, civilization, and "true independence." The current design of the coat of arms, which is included on government flags, was established in 1964.

©2000, Encyclopædia Britannica, Inc.

CROATIA

Scale 1: 7,071,000

0   30   60 mi
0   30   60   90 km

Ethnic Composition

Croat 78.1%
Serb 12.1%
Other 9.8%

Official name: Republic of Croatia
Head of government: Prime MInister
Official language: Croatian (Serbo-
   Croatian)
Monetary unit: kuna
Area: 21,359 sq. mi. (56,542 sq. km.)
Population (2001): 4,393,000
GNP per capita (1999): U.S.$4,530
Principal exports (1998): machinery and
   transport equipment 30.4%; clothing
   12.2% *to:* Italy 17.7%; Germany 16.9%;
   Bosnia and Herzegovina 14.4%

During the European uprisings of 1848, Croatians designed a flag based on that of Russia. In April 1941 the fascistic Ustasa used this flag, adding the checkered shield of Croatia. A communist star soon replaced the shield, but the current flag was adopted on Dec. 22, 1990. Atop the shield is a "crown" inlaid with historic coats of arms.

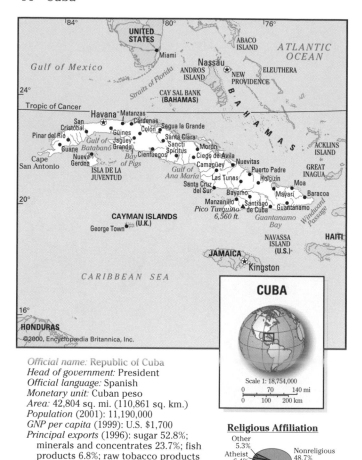

©2000, Encyclopædia Britannica, Inc.

Official name: Republic of Cuba
Head of government: President
Official language: Spanish
Monetary unit: Cuban peso
Area: 42,804 sq. mi. (110,861 sq. km.)
Population (2001): 11,190,000
GNP per capita (1999): U.S. $1,700
Principal exports (1996): sugar 52.8%;
minerals and concentrates 23.7%; fish
products 6.8%; raw tobacco products
5.9% *to* (1999): Russia 23.3%; Canada
14.5%; The Netherlands 12.9%

CUBA

Scale 1: 18,754,000

0   70   140 mi
0   100   200 km

Religious Affiliation

Other
5.3%

Atheist
6.4%

Roman
Catholic
39.6%

Nonreligious
48.7%

In the mid-19th century Cuban exiles designed the flag, which
was later carried into battle against Spanish forces. It was
adopted on May 20, 1902. The stripes were for the three military districts of Cuba and the purity of the patriotic cause.
The red triangle was for strength, constancy, and equality,
and the white star symbolized independence.

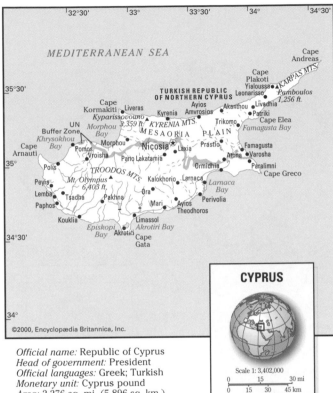

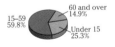

Official name: Republic of Cyprus
Head of government: President
Official languages: Greek; Turkish
Monetary unit: Cyprus pound
Area: 2,276 sq. mi. (5,896 sq. km.)
Population (2001): 675,000
GNP per capita (1999): U.S.$11,950
Principal exports (1998): reexports
55.6%; domestic exports 38.7%, of
which clothing 5.3%, chemicals 5.2%
to: United Kingdom 14.6%; Russia
10.3%; Greece 9.8%

Age Breakdown

60 and over
14.9%

15–59
59.8%

Under 15
25.3%

On Aug. 7, 1960, the Republic of Cyprus was proclaimed with
a national flag of a neutral design. It bears the island in silhouette and a green olive wreath, for peace. In 1974 there was
a Turkish invasion of the island. A puppet government, which
adopted a flag based on the Turkish model, was set up on the
northern third of Cyprus.

©2000, Encyclopædia Britannica, Inc.

CZECH REPUBLIC

Scale 1: 6,810,000

0   20   40 mi
0   40   60 km

Official name: Česka Republika
Head of government: Prime Minister
Official language: Czech
Monetary unit: koruna
Area: 30,450 sq. mi. (78,864 sq. km.)
Population (2001): 10,269,000
GNP per capita (1999): U.S.$5,020
Principal exports (1998): machinery and apparatus 32.7%; transport equipment 9.8%; chemicals and chemical products 6.9% *to* (1999): Germany 42.1%; Slovakia 8.2%; Austria 6.4%

Ethnic Composition

Czech 81.2%
Moravian 13.2%
Other 5.6%

When Czechs, Slovaks, and Ruthenians united to form Czechoslovakia in 1918, a simple white-red bicolor flag was chosen; in 1920 it incorporated a blue triangle at the hoist. Czechoslovakia divided into Slovakia and the Czech Republic in 1993, but the latter country readopted the Czechoslovak flag as its own.

Official name: Kingdom of Denmark
Head of government: Prime Minister
Official language: Danish
Monetary unit: Danish krone
Area: 16,639 sq. mi. (43,096 sq. km.)
Population (2001): 5,358,000
GNP per capita (1999): U.S.$32,050
Principal exports (2000): machinery and
    apparatus 23.5%; food and live
    animals 18.4%; pharmaceuticals 5.1%
    to: Germany 18.9%; Sweden 13.0%;
    United Kingdom 9.8%

Scale 1: 6,930,000

| 0 | 20 | 40 mi |
| 0 | 30 | 60 km |

Age Breakdown

Under 15
17.3%

15–59
62.9%

60 and over
19.8%

A traditional story claims that the Danish flag fell from
heaven on June 15, 1219, but the previously existing war flag
of the Holy Roman Empire was of a similar design, with its
red field symbolizing battle and its white cross suggesting
divine favor. In 1849 the state and military flag was altered
and adopted as a symbol of the Danish people.

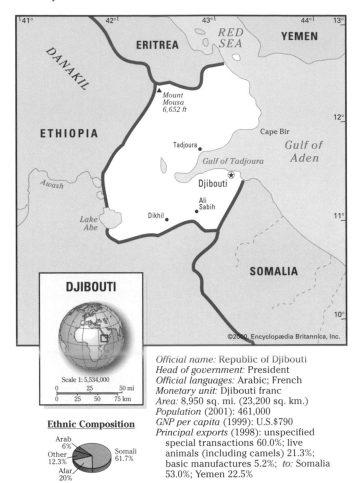

©2000, Encyclopædia Britannica, Inc.

DJIBOUTI

Scale 1: 5,534,000

0   25   50 mi
0   25   50   75 km

Ethnic Composition

Arab 6%
Other 12.3%
Afar 20%
Somali 61.7%

Official name: Republic of Djibouti
Head of government: President
Official languages: Arabic; French
Monetary unit: Djibouti franc
Area: 8,950 sq. mi. (23,200 sq. km.)
Population (2001): 461,000
GNP per capita (1999): U.S.$790
Principal exports (1998): unspecified
   special transactions 60.0%; live
   animals (including camels) 21.3%;
   basic manufactures 5.2%; *to:* Somalia
   53.0%; Yemen 22.5%

First raised by anti-French separatists, the flag was officially hoisted on June 27, 1977. The color of the Afar people, green, stands for prosperity. The color of the Issa people, light blue, symbolizes sea and sky, and recalls the flag of Somalia. The white triangle is for equality and peace; the red star is for unity and independence.

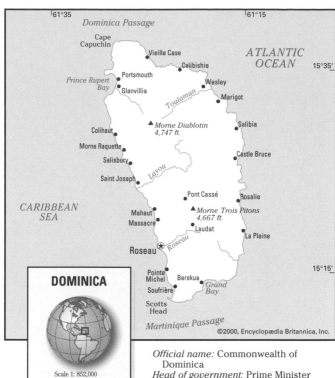

61°35   Dominica Passage

Cape
Capuchin
Vieille Case
Calibishie

ATLANTIC
OCEAN   15°35'

Portsmouth
Wesley
Prince Rupert
Bay
Glanvillia
Marigot

Toulaman

▲ Morne Diablotin
4,747 ft.
Salibia

Colihaut
Morne Raquette
Castle Bruce
Salisbury

Layou

Saint Joseph

Pont Cassé
Rosalie
▲ Morne Trois Pitons
4,667 ft.

CARIBBEAN
SEA
Mahaut
Massacre
Laudat
La Plaine

Roseau ✪

Roseau

15°15'

Pointe
Michel   Berekua
Grand
Soufrière   Bay

Scotts
Head

Martinique Passage

61°15

©2000, Encyclopædia Britannica, Inc.

DOMINICA

Scale 1: 852,000
0   3   6 mi
0   5   10 km

Religious Affiliation

Other
12.7%

Protestant
17.2%

Roman
Catholic
70.1%

Official name: Commonwealth of
   Dominica
Head of government: Prime Minister
Official language: English
Monetary unit: East Caribbean dollar
Area: 285.3 sq. mi. (739.0 sq. km.)
Population (2001): 71,700
GNP per capita (1999): U.S.$3,260
Principal exports (1999): manufactured
   exports 61.7%; coconut-based soaps
   26.7%; agricultural exports 38.3%
   to: Caricom 55.3%; United
   Kingdom 27.5%

The flag was hoisted on Nov. 3, 1978, at independence from
Britain. Its background symbolizes forests; its central disk is
red for socialism and bears a sisserou (a rare local bird). The
stars are for the parishes of the island. The cross of yellow,
white, and black is for the Carib, Caucasian, and African peoples and for fruit, water, and soil.

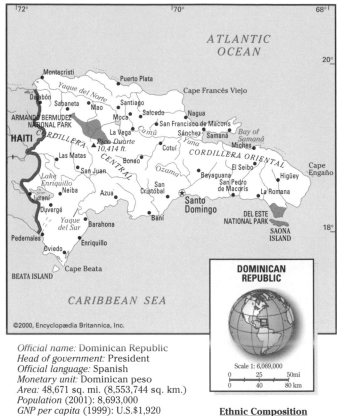

72° 70° 68°

ATLANTIC OCEAN

20°

Montecristi
Puerto Plata
Cape Francés Viejo
Yaque del Norte
Dababón
Sabaneta Mao Santiago Salcedo Nagua
Moca San Francisco de Macorís
ARMANDO BERMUDEZ
NATIONAL PARK La Vega *Camú*
HAITI *CORDILLERA* Sánchez Samaná Miches
Pico Duarte *Bay of Samaná*
CENTRAL 10,414 ft. Cotuí *Yuna*
Bonao *CORDILLERA ORIENTAL*
Las Matas *Ozama* El Seibo Cape Engaño
San Juan Bayaguana Higüey
Lake Enriquillo San Pedro
Neiba Azua San de Macorís La Romana
Jimaní Cristóbal
Duvergé Santo DEL ESTE
Yaque del Sur Baní Domingo NATIONAL PARK
Barahona SAONA
Pedernales Enriquillo ISLAND
Oviedo 18°
BEATA ISLAND Cape Beata

CARIBBEAN SEA

©2000, Encyclopædia Britannica, Inc.

Official name: Dominican Republic
Head of government: President
Official language: Spanish
Monetary unit: Dominican peso
Area: 48,671 sq. mi. (8,553,744 sq. km.)
Population (2001): 8,693,000
GNP per capita (1999): U.S.$1,920
Principal exports (1998): ships' stores
15.8%; ferronickel 15.0%; cacao
and cocoa 13.6%; raw sugar 13.2%;
to: U.S. 53.9%; Belgium 11.9%;
Puerto Rico 7.0%

DOMINICAN REPUBLIC

Scale 1: 6,069,000
0 25 50mi
0 40 80 km

Ethnic Composition

Mixed 73%
White 16%
Black 11%

On Feb. 28, 1844, Spanish-speaking Dominican revolutionaries added a white cross to the simple blue-red flag of eastern Hispaniola, in order to emphasize their Christian heritage. On November 6 of that same year the new constitution established the flag, but with the colors at the fly end reversed so that the blue and red would alternate.

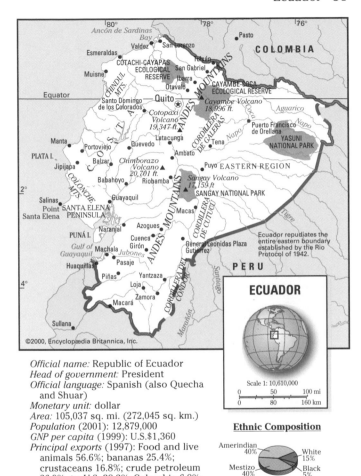

©2000, Encyclopædia Britannica, Inc.

Official name: Republic of Ecuador
Head of government: President
Official language: Spanish (also Quecha and Shuar)
Monetary unit: dollar
Area: 105,037 sq. mi. (272,045 sq. km.)
Population (2001): 12,879,000
GNP per capita (1999): U.S.$1,360
Principal exports (1997): Food and live animals 56.6%; bananas 25.4%; crustaceans 16.8%; crude petroleum 26.9% *to:* U.S. 38.2%; Colombia 6.8%; Italy 5.2%; Chile 4.6%

Scale 1: 10,610,000

| 0 | 50 | 100 mi |
| 0 | 80 | 160 km |

Ethnic Composition

Amerindian 40%
White 15%
Mestizo 40%
Black 5%

Victorious against the Spanish on May 24, 1822, Antonio José de Sucre hoisted a yellow-blue-red flag. Other flags were later used, but on Sept. 26, 1860, the current flag design was adopted. The coat of arms is displayed on the flag when it is used abroad or for official purposes, to distinguish it from the flag of Colombia.

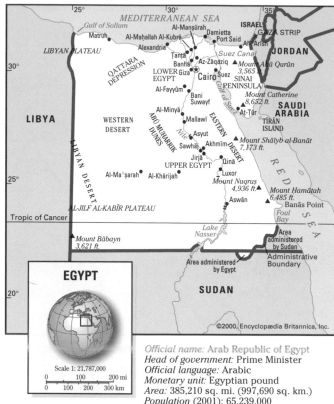

MEDITERRANEAN SEA

Gulf of Sollum
Matrûh
LIBYAN PLATEAU
Al-Maḥallah Al-Kubrá
Alexandria
Tanta
Banha
Az-Zaqaziq
LOWER EGYPT
Giza
Cairo
Al-Mansûrah
Damietta
Port Said
Suez Canal
ISRAEL
GAZA STRIP
Al-'Arîsh
JORDAN

QATTARA DEPRESSION

Al-Fayyûm
Bani Suwayf

Suez
SINAI PENINSULA
▲ Mount Abû Qurûn 3,565 ft.

Al-Minyā
Mallawī

LIBYA

WESTERN DESERT

Asyut
Sawhāj
Akhmîm
Jirjā
UPPER EGYPT
Qinā
Luxor

ABÛ MUHARRIK DUNES

LIBYAN DESERT

EASTERN DESERT

Mount Catherine 8,652 ft.
At-Tûr
SAUDI ARABIA
TÎRÂN ISLAND
▲ Mount Shāyb al-Banāt 7,173 ft.

Al-Ma'ṣarah
Al-Khārijah
Mount Nuqrus 4,936 ft.▲
Aswân
▲ Mount Hamâtah 6,485 ft.
RED SEA

AL-JILF AL-KABÎR PLATEAU

Tropic of Cancer

Banâs Point
Foul Bay

Lake Nasser
▲ Mount Bābayn 3,621 ft.
Area administered by Sudan
Administrative Boundary

Area administered by Egypt
SUDAN

©2000, Encyclopædia Britannica, Inc.

EGYPT

Scale 1: 21,787,000

0   100   200 mi
0   100   200   300 km

Religious Affiliation

Christian 10%
Sunni Muslim 90%

Official name: Arab Republic of Egypt
Head of government: Prime Minister
Official language: Arabic
Monetary unit: Egyptian pound
Area: 385,210 sq. mi. (997,690 sq. km.)
Population (2001): 65,239,000
GNP per capita (1999): U.S.$1,380
Principal exports (1999): petroleum and
    petroleum products 22.9%; cotton,
    yarn, textiles, and clothing 9.7%;
    bunkers and ships'stores 10.3%
    to: U.S. 12.4%; Italy 10.1%; The
    Netherlands 7.1%

The 1952 revolt against British rule established the red-white-black flag with a central gold eagle. Two stars replaced the eagle in 1958, and in 1972 a federation with Syria and Libya was formed, adding instead the hawk of Quraysh (the tribe of Muhammad). On Oct. 9, 1984, the eagle of Saladin (a major 12th-century ruler) was substituted.

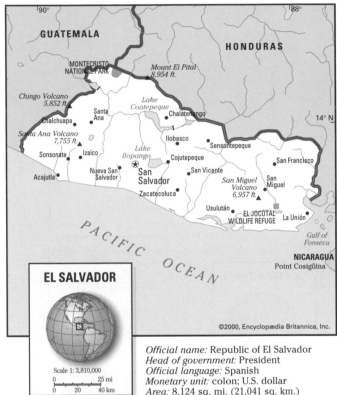

©2000, Encyclopædia Britannica, Inc.

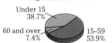

Scale 1: 3,810,000

0   25 mi

0   20   40 km

Age Breakdown

Under 15
38.7%

60 and over
7.4%

15–59
53.9%

Official name: Republic of El Salvador
Head of government: President
Official language: Spanish
Monetary unit: colon; U.S. dollar
Area: 8,124 sq. mi. (21,041 sq. km.)
Population (2001): 6,238,000
GNP per capita (1999): U.S.$1,920
Principal exports (1997): coffee 38.1%;
   paper and paper products 4.8%;
   pharmaceuticals 3.9%; raw sugar
   products 3.9% *to:* Guatemala 19.5%;
   U.S. 19.2%; Germany 17.5%

In the early 19th century a blue-white-blue flag was designed for the short-lived United Provinces of Central America, in which El Salvador was a member. On Sept. 15, 1912, the flag was reintroduced in El Salvador. The coat of arms in the center resembles that used by the former federation and includes the national motto, "God, Union, Liberty."

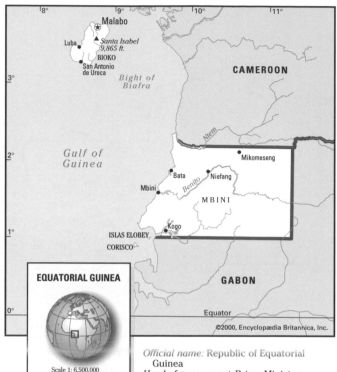

Scale 1: 6,500,000

0   20   40 mi
0   30   60 km

Ethnic Composition

Fang 82.9%

Bubi 9.6%

Other 7.5%

Official name: Republic of Equatorial Guinea
Head of government: Prime Minister
Official language: Spanish; French
Monetary unit: CFA franc
Area: 10,831 sq. mi. (28,051 sq. km.)
Population (2001): 486,000
GNP per capita (1999): U.S.$1,170
Principal exports (1998): petroleum 87.6%; wood 9.2%; cocoa 1.5%
  to: U.S. 62.0%; Spain 17.3%

The flag was first hoisted at independence (Oct. 12, 1968). Its coat of arms shows the silk-cotton tree, or god tree, which recalls early Spanish influence in the area. The sea, which links parts of the country, is reflected in the blue triangle. The green is for vegetation, white is for peace, and red is for the blood of martyrs in the liberation struggle.

Scale 1: 11,150,000

0   50   100 mi

0   50   100   150 km

Language Composition

Semitic languages 81%

Cushitic languages 14%

Nilotic languages 5%

Official name: State of Eritrea
Head of government: President
Official language: (none)
Monetary unit: nakfa
Area: 46,770 sq. mi. (121,100 sq. km.)
Population (2001): 4,298,000
GNP per capita (1999): U.S.$200
Principal exports (1998): raw materials 45.5%; food products 29.6%; manufactured goods 13.2%
to: The Sudan 27.2%; Ethiopia 26.5%; Japan 13.2%

Officially hoisted at the proclamation of independence on May 24, 1993, the national flag was based on that of the Eritrean People's Liberation Front. The red triangle is for the blood of patriots, the green is for agriculture, and the blue is for maritime resources. Around a central branch is a circle of olive branches with 30 leaves.

©2000, Encyclopædia Britannica, Inc.

ESTONIA

Scale 1: 4,840,000

| 0 | 20 | 40 mi |
| 0 | 30 | 60 km |

Ethnic Composition

Estonian 63.9%

Russian 29%

Other 7.1%

Official name: Republic of Estonia
Head of government: Prime Minister
Official language: Estonian
Monetary unit: kroon
Area: 16,769 sq. mi. (43,431 sq. km.)
Population (2001): 1,363,000
GNP per capita (1999): U.S.$3,400
Principal exports (2000): electrical and
  non-electrical machinery 37.5%; wood
  and wood products 13.4%; textiles and
  clothing 11.3% *to:* Finland 32.3%;
  Sweden 20.5%; Germany 8.5%

In the late 19th century an Estonian students' association
adopted the blue-black-white flag. Blue was said to stand for
the sky, black for the soil, and white for aspirations to freedom and homeland. The flag was officially recognized on July
4, 1920. It was replaced under Soviet rule, and readopted on
Oct. 20, 1988.

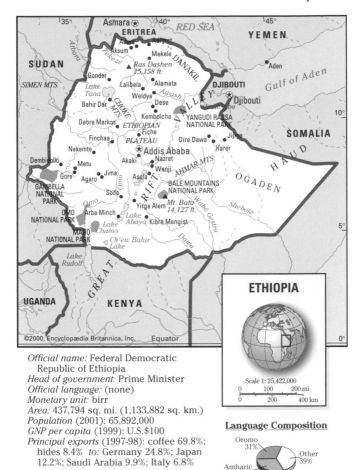

Official name: Federal Democratic
  Republic of Ethiopia
Head of government: Prime Minister
Official language: (none)
Monetary unit: birr
Area: 437,794 sq. mi. (1,133,882 sq. km.)
Population (2001): 65,892,000
GNP per capita (1999): U.S.$100
Principal exports (1997-98): coffee 69.8%;
  hides 8.4% *to:* Germany 24.8%; Japan
  12.2%; Saudi Arabia 9.9%; Italy 6.8%

ETHIOPIA

Scale 1: 25,422,000

0   100   200 mi
0   200   400 km

Language Composition

Oromo
31%

Other
39%

Amharic
30%

The flag is red (for sacrifice), green (for labor, development,
and fertility), and yellow (for hope, justice, and equality).
Tricolor pennants were used prior to the official flag of Oct. 6,
1897, and a tricolor was flown by antigovernment forces in
1991. On Feb. 6, 1996, the disk (for peace) and star (for unity
and the future) were added.

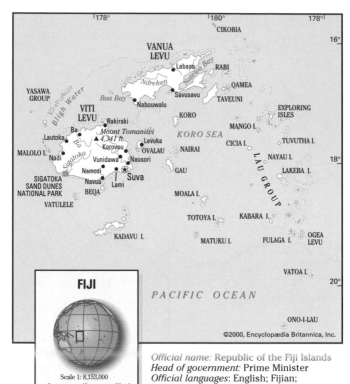

©2000, Encyclopædia Britannica, Inc.

FIJI

Scale 1: 8,153,000

| 0 | 40 | 80 mi |
| 0 | 60 | 120 km |

Ethnic Composition

Indian 43.5%
Fijian 50.7%
Other 5.8%

Official name: Republic of the Fiji Islands
Head of government: Prime Minister
Official languages: English; Fijian; Hindustani
Monetary unit: Fiji dollar
Area: 7,055 sq. mi. (18,272 sq. km.)
Population (2001): 827,000
GNP per capita (1999): U.S.$2,310
Principal exports (1997): sugar 24.4%; clothing 23.5%; gold 8.7%; fish 5.3%; timber 3.5% *to:* Australia 40.5%; United Kingdom 21.4%; Japan 13.4%; U.S. 10.2%

The national flag, introduced on Oct. 10, 1970, is a modified version of Fiji's colonial flag. It includes the Union Jack on a light blue field. The shield has the red cross of St. George on a white background, below a yellow lion, which holds a cocoa pod. Local symbols (sugar cane, coconuts, bananas, and the Fiji dove) are also shown.

Official name: Republic of Finland
Head of government: Prime Minister
Official language: (none)
Monetary unit: euro
Area: 130,559 sq. mi. (338,145 sq. km.)
Population (2001): 5,185,000
GNP per capita (1999): U.S.$24,730
Principal exports (1999): electrical
   machinery and apparatus 23.7%;
   paper and paper products 20.5%
   to: Germany 13.1%; Sweden 9.9%;
   United Kingdom 9.1%; U.S. 7.9%;
   France 5.3%

Scale 1: 18,656,000

| 0 | 25 | 50 | 150 mi |
| 0 | 120 | 240 km |

Religious Affiliation

Nonreligious 12%
Other 2.1%
Evangelical Lutheran 85.9%

In 1862, while Finland was under Russian control, a flag was
proposed that would have a white background for the snows
of Finland and blue for its lakes. The blue was in the form of a
"Nordic cross" similar to those used by other Scandinavian
countries. The flag was officially adopted by the newly independent country on May 29, 1918.

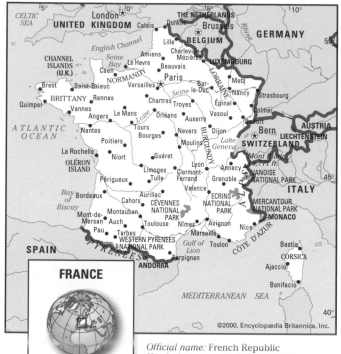

FRANCE

Scale 1 : 18,620,000

| 0 | 80 | 160 mi |
| 0 | 80 | 160 | 240 km |

Religious Affiliation

Roman Catholic 76.4%   Other 23.6%

Official name: French Republic
Head of government: Prime Minister
Official language: French
Monetary unit: euro
Area: 210,026 sq. mi. (543,965 sq. km.)
Population (2001): 59,090,000
GNP per capita (1999): U.S.$24,170
Principal exports (1998): machinery and
   apparatus 26.1%; transport equipment
   17.7%; chemicals and chemical
   products 12.7%; agricultural products
   12.0% *to:* Germany 16.1%; United
   Kingdom 10.0%; Italy 9.2%; Spain 8.7%

From 1789 blue and red, the traditional colors of Paris, were
included in flags with Bourbon royal white. In 1794 the tricol-
or was made official. It embodied liberty, equality, fraternity,
democracy, secularism, and modernization, but there is no
symbolism attached to the individual colors. It has been the
sole national flag since March 5, 1848.

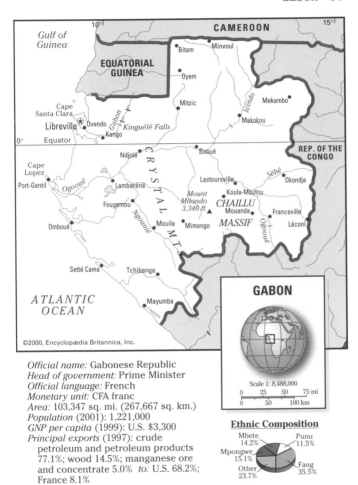

©2000, Encyclopædia Britannica, Inc.

Official name: Gabonese Republic
Head of government: Prime Minister
Official language: French
Monetary unit: CFA franc
Area: 103,347 sq. mi. (267,667 sq. km.)
Population (2001): 1,221,000
GNP per capita (1999): U.S. $3,300
Principal exports (1997): crude
  petroleum and petroleum products
  77.1%; wood 14.5%; manganese ore
  and concentrate 5.0% *to:* U.S. 68.2%;
  France 8.1%

Scale 1: 8,488,000

0   25   50   75 mi
0   50   100 km

Ethnic Composition

Mbete 14.2%
Punu 11.5%
Mpongwe 15.1%
Other 23.7%
Fang 35.5%

After proclaiming independence from France, Gabon adopted
its national flag on Aug. 9, 1960. The central yellow stripe is
for the Equator, which runs through the country. Green
stands for the tropical forests that are one of Gabon's most
important resources. Blue represents its extensive coast
along the South Atlantic Ocean.

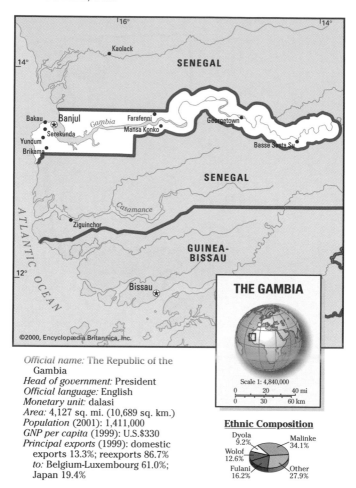

©2000, Encyclopædia Britannica, Inc.

Official name: The Republic of the Gambia
Head of government: President
Official language: English
Monetary unit: dalasi
Area: 4,127 sq. mi. (10,689 sq. km.)
Population (2001): 1,411,000
GNP per capita (1999): U.S.$330
Principal exports (1999): domestic exports 13.3%; reexports 86.7% *to:* Belgium-Luxembourg 61.0%; Japan 19.4%

THE GAMBIA

Scale 1: 4,840,000

0   20   40 mi
0   30   60 km

Ethnic Composition

Dyola 9.2%
Malinke 34.1%
Wolof 12.6%
Fulani 16.2%
Other 27.9%

The Gambia achieved independence from Britain on Feb. 18, 1965, under the current flag. The center stripe is blue to symbolize the Gambia River. The red stripe is for the sun and the equator. The green stripe is for agricultural produce (peanuts, grains, and citrus fruits), while the white stripes are said to stand for peace and unity.

Official name: Georgia
Head of government: President
Official language: Georgian
Monetary unit: lari
Area: 26,911 sq. mi. (69,700 sq. km.)
Population (2001): 4,989,000
GNP per capita (1999): U.S.$620
Principal exports (2000): scrap metals
    11.5%; wine 8.6%; nuts 6.8%; fertilizers
    4.7% *to:* Turkey 22.3%; Russia 20.6%;
    Germany 9.4%; Azerbaijan 6.4%

Ethnic Composition

Georgian 70.1%
Armenian 8.1%
Russian 6.3%
Other 15.5%

According to tradition, Queen Tamara (1184–1213) and other
rulers used white, black, and cherry red for their flags. The
current flag was first hoisted on March 25, 1917. It was
replaced under Soviet rule, but readopted on Nov. 14, 1990.
Cherry red is the national color, black stands for past
tragedies, and white is for hope.

Official name: Federal Republic of Germany
Head of government: Chancellor
Official language: German
Monetary unit: euro
Area: 137,846 sq. mi. (357,021 sq. km.)
Population (2001): 82,386,000
GNP per capita (1999): U.S.$25,620
Principal exports (2000): machinery and transport equipment 51.2%; chemicals and chemical products 12.7%
to: France 11.4%; U.S. 10.2%

GERMANY

Scale 1: 15,019,000

| 0 | 40 | 80 | 120 mi |
| 0 | 60 | 120 | 180 km |

Age Breakdown

60 and over
20.7%
15–59
63%
Under 15
16.3%

In the early 19th century German nationalists displayed black, gold, and red on their uniforms and tricolor flags. The current flag was used officially from 1848 to 1852 and re-adopted by West Germany on May 9, 1949. East Germany flew a similar flag but only the flag of West Germany was maintained upon reunification in 1990.

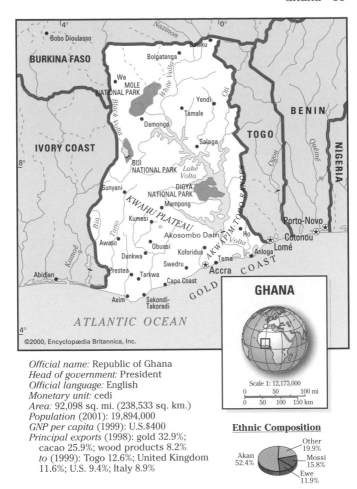

GHANA

Scale 1: 12,173,000

| 0 | 50 | 100 mi |

| 0 | 50 | 100 | 150 km |

Official name: Republic of Ghana
Head of government: President
Official language: English
Monetary unit: cedi
Area: 92,098 sq. mi. (238,533 sq. km.)
Population (2001): 19,894,000
GNP per capita (1999): U.S.$400
Principal exports (1998): gold 32.9%;
  cacao 25.9%; wood products 8.2%
  to (1999): Togo 12.6%; United Kingdom
  11.6%; U.S. 9.4%; Italy 8.9%

Ethnic Composition

Akan
52.4%

Other
19.9%

Mossi
15.8%

Ewe
11.9%

On March 6, 1957, independence from Britain was granted
and a flag, based on the red-white-green tricolor of a nationalist organization, was hoisted. A black "lodestar of African
freedom" was added and the white stripe was changed to yellow, symbolizing wealth. Green is for forests and farms, red
for the independence struggle.

©2000, Encyclopædia Britannica, Inc.

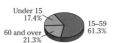

GREECE

Scale 1: 11,646,000

| 0 | 50 | 100 mi |
| 0 | 80 | 160 km |

Age Breakdown

Under 15 17.4%
60 and over 21.3%
15–59 61.3%

Official name: Hellenic Republic
Head of government: Prime Minister
Official language: Greek
Monetary unit: euro
Area: 50,949 sq. mi. (131,957 sq. km.)
Population (2001): 10,975,000
GNP per capita (1999): U.S.$12,110
Principal exports (1998): food 18.4%;
   clothing and apparel 16.8%; petroleum
   6.4%; aluminum 4.2%; tobacco
   products 4.1% *to:* Germany 18.3%;
   Italy 11.9%; United Kingdom 7.9%;
   U.S. 4.7%

In March 1822, during the revolt against Ottoman rule, the first Greek national flags were adopted; the most recent revision to the flag was made on Dec. 22, 1978. The colors symbolize Greek Orthodoxy while the cross stands for "the wisdom of God, freedom and country." The stripes are for the battle cry for independence: "Freedom or Death."

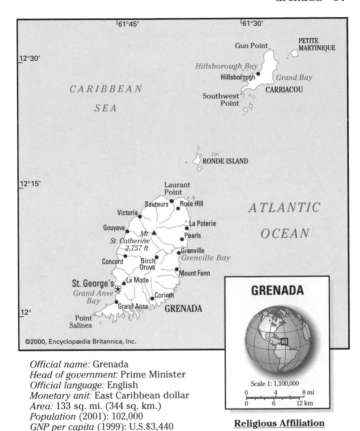

©2000, Encyclopædia Britannica, Inc.

Official name: Grenada
Head of government: Prime Minister
Official language: English
Monetary unit: East Caribbean dollar
Area: 133 sq. mi. (344 sq. km.)
Population (2001): 102,000
GNP per capita (1999): U.S.$3,440
Principal exports (1997): domestic
  exports 91.5%, of which nutmeg 26.3%,
  fish 14.3%, cocoa beans 7.3%;
  reexports 8.5% *to:* Germany 46.9%;
  U.S. 12.2%; St. Lucia 6.1%

Scale 1: 1,100,000

| 0 | 4 | 8 mi |
| 0 | 6 | 12 km |

Religious Affiliation

Roman Catholic 53.1%

Protestant 38.1%

Other 8.8%

Grenada's flag was officially hoisted on Feb. 3, 1974. Its background is green for vegetation and yellow for the sun, and its red border is symbolic of harmony and unity. The seven stars are for the original administrative subdivisions of Grenada. Nutmeg, a crop for which the "Isle of Spice" is internationally known, is represented as well.

©2000, Encyclopædia Britannica, Inc.

Official name: Republic of Guatemala
Head of government: President
Official language: Spanish
Monetary unit: quetzal
Area: 42,042 sq. mi. (108,889 sq. km.)
Population (2001): 11,687,000
GNP per capita (1999): U.S.$1,680
Principal exports (1998): coffee 20.4%
sugar 11.0%; bananas 6.2%; petroleum
2.0% *to:* U.S. 32.2%; Germany 4.3%;
Mexico 4.1%; Japan 2.2%

GUATEMALA

Scale 1: 7,482,000

| 0 | 25 | 50 | 75 mi |
| 0 | 40 | 80 | 120 km |

Language Composition

Mayan languages 35%
Garifuna 0.3%
Spanish 64.7%

The flag was introduced in 1871. It has blue and white stripes
(colors of the former United Provinces of Central America)
and a coat of arms with the quetzal (the national bird), a
scroll, a wreath, and crossed rifles and sabres. Different
artistic variations have been used but on Sept. 12, 1968, the
present pattern was established.

SENEGAL

Mount Tamgué 5,044 ft.

GUINEA-BISSAU

MANDINGUE PLATEAU

MALI

Bamako

Mali

Gaoual

FOUTA DJALLON

Gambia

Boké

Télimélé

Labé

Pita

Tougué

Bafing

Tinkisso

Dinguiraye

Siguiri

Niger

Fatala

Dalaba

Dabola

Kouroussa

Fria

Mamou

Kankan

Sankarani

Cape Verga

Boffa

Kindia

Faranah

Milo

Forécariah

Conakry

ATLANTIC OCEAN

Kolente

SIERRA LEONE

Kissidougou

Kérouané

Guéckédou

Beyla

Freetown

Sewa

Macenta

Nzérékoré

Mount Nimba 6,069 ft.

IVORY COAST

GUINEA

LIBERIA

©2000, Encyclopædia Britannica, Inc.

Scale 1: 11,686,000

0   50   100 mi
0 50 100 150 km

Ethnic Composition

Malinke 25.8%
Other 22.9%
Fulani 40.3%
Susu 11%

Official name: Republic of Guinea
Head of government: President
Official language: French
Monetary unit: Guinean franc
Area: 94,926 sq. mi. (245,857 sq. km.)
Population (2001): 7,614,000
GNP per capita (1999): U.S.$490
Principal exports (1998): bauxite 45.7%;
   gold 17.7%; alumina 14.1% diamonds
   7.2% *to:* U.S. 16.4%; Hong Kong 14.7%;
   Belgium 13.7%; Spain 12.4%;
   Ireland 12.2%

The flag was adopted on Nov. 12, 1958, one month after independence from France. Its simple design was influenced by the French tricolor. The red is said to be a symbol of sacrifice and labor, while the yellow is for mineral wealth, the tropical sun, and justice. Green symbolizes agricultural wealth and the solidarity of the people.

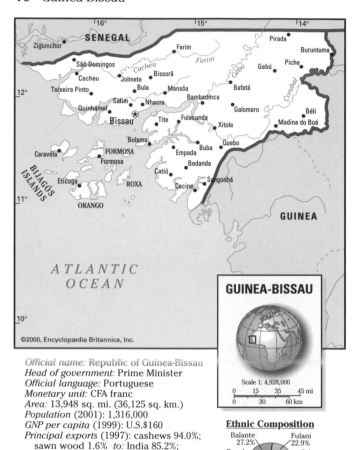

©2000, Encyclopædia Britannica, Inc.

Official name: Republic of Guinea-Bissau
Head of government: Prime Minister
Official language: Portuguese
Monetary unit: CFA franc
Area: 13,948 sq. mi. (36,125 sq. km.)
Population (2001): 1,316,000
GNP per capita (1999): U.S.$160
Principal exports (1997): cashews 94.0%;
   sawn wood 1.6% *to:* India 85.2%;
   other/unspecified 13.1%

GUINEA-BISSAU

Scale 1: 4,928,000
0   15   35   45 mi
0   30   60 km

Ethnic Composition

Balante 27.2%
Fulani 22.9%
Pepel 10%
Other 17.1%
Mandyako 10.6%
Malinke 12.2%

The flag has been used since the declaration of independence
from Portugal on Sept. 24, 1973. The black star on the red
stripe was for African Party leadership, the people, and their
will to live in dignity, freedom, and peace. Yellow was for the
harvest and other rewards of work, and green was for the
nation's vast jungles and agricultural lands.

60° 55°

ATLANTIC OCEAN

Mabaruma
Port Kaituma
VENEZUELA
Charity
Matthews Ridge
Suddie
Cuyuni Parika
Vreed en Hoop **Georgetown**
Mahaicony Village
Bartica New Amsterdam
Linden Rose Hall
Mazaruni
MERUME MTS.
Corriverton
Paramaribo
Kamuda Village
Essequibo
Ituni
Mount Roraima 9,219 ft.
PAKARAIMA MTS.
Orinduik
Mount Makari 1,679 ft.
SURINAME
GUIANA HIGHLANDS
Karasabai
Apotori
Mount Makarapan 3,063 ft.
Kuintaro
Essequibo
Courantyne
Lethem
RUPUNUNI SAVANNA
Isherton
BRAZIL
KAMOA MTS.

5°

0° Equator

©2000, Encyclopædia Britannica, Inc.

GUYANA

Scale 1: 15,337,000
0   60   120 mi
0   80   160 km

Official name: Co-operative Republic of Guyana
Head of government: President
Official language: English
Monetary unit: Guyana dollar
Area: 83,044 sq. mi. (215,083 sq. km.)
Population (2001): 776,000
GNP per capita (1999): U.S.$760
Principal exports (1999): domestic exports 96.1%, of which sugar 25.9%, gold 20.7%, bauxite 14.7%; rice 13.5% *to* (1998): U.S. 24%; Canada 23%; United Kingdom 19%

Religious Affiliation

Hindu 34%
Muslim 9%
Christian 52%
Other 5%

Upon independence from Britain on May 26, 1966, the flag was first hoisted. The green stands for jungles and fields, white suggests the rivers which are the basis for the Indian word guiana ("land of waters"), red is for zeal and sacrifice in nation-building, and black is for perseverance. The flag is nicknamed "The Golden Arrowhead."

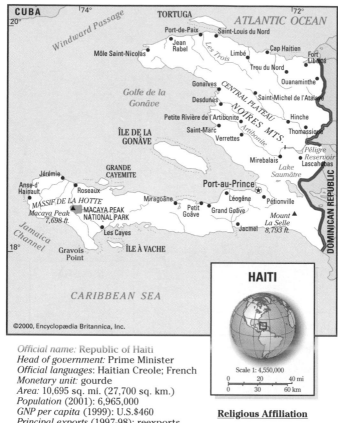

CUBA
20°
TORTUGA
ATLANTIC OCEAN
74°
72°

Windward Passage

Port-de-Paix
Saint-Louis du Nord
Jean Rabel
Limbé
Cap Haïtien
Fort Liberté
Môle Saint-Nicolas
Les Trois
Trou du Nord
Ouanaminthe
Gonaïves
CENTRAL PLATEAU
Saint-Michel de l'Atalaye
Golfe de la Gonâve
Desdunes
NOIRES MTS.
Petite Rivière de l'Artibonite
Hinche
Thomassique
ÎLE DE LA GONÂVE
Saint-Marc
Artibonite
Verrettes
Péligre Reservoir
Mirebalais
Lascahobas
Lake Saumâtre
GRANDE CAYEMITE
Jérémie
Anse-d' Hainault
Roseaux
Port-au-Prince
DOMINICAN REPUBLIC
MASSIF DE LA HOTTE
Miragoâne
Léogâne
Pétionville
Macaya Peak
7,698 ft.
MACAYA PEAK NATIONAL PARK
Petit Goâve
Grand Goâve
Jamaica Channel
18°
Les Cayes
Mount La Selle
8,793 ft.
Jacmel
Gravois Point
ÎLE À VACHE

CARIBBEAN SEA

©2000, Encyclopædia Britannica, Inc.

HAITI

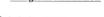

Scale 1: 4,550,000

0   20   40 mi
0   30   60 km

Official name: Republic of Haiti
Head of government: Prime Minister
Official languages: Haitian Creole; French
Monetary unit: gourde
Area: 10,695 sq. mi. (27,700 sq. km.)
Population (2001): 6,965,000
GNP per capita (1999): U.S.$460
Principal exports (1997-98): reexports
  (mostly clothing) 74%; handicrafts,
  (includes paintings, woven sisal
  products) 7%; coffee 7% to (1998):
  U.S. 88%; Belgium 3%; France 3%

Religious Affiliation

Protestant 15.8%
Other 3.9%
Roman Catholic 80.3%

After the French Revolution of 1789 Haiti underwent a slave revolt, but the French tricolor continued in use until 1803. The new blue-red flag represented the black and mulatto populations only. A black-red flag was used by various dictators, including François "Papa Doc" Duvalier and his son, but on Feb. 25, 1986, the old flag was reestablished.

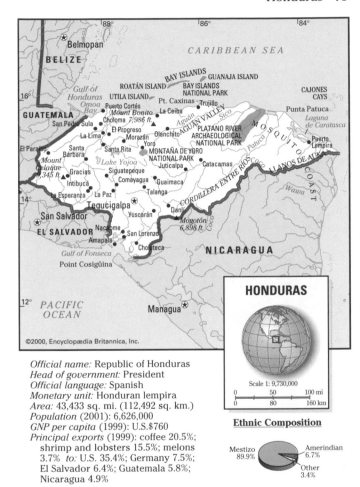

Official name: Republic of Honduras
Head of government: President
Official language: Spanish
Monetary unit: Honduran lempira
Area: 43,433 sq. mi. (112,492 sq. km.)
Population (2001): 6,626,000
GNP per capita (1999): U.S.$760
Principal exports (1999): coffee 20.5%;
 shrimp and lobsters 15.5%; melons
 3.7% *to:* U.S. 35.4%; Germany 7.5%;
 El Salvador 6.4%; Guatemala 5.8%;
 Nicaragua 4.9%

Ethnic Composition

Mestizo 89.9% Amerindian 6.7% Other 3.4%

Since Feb. 16, 1866, the Honduran flag has retained the blue-white-blue design of the flag of the former United Provinces of Central America, but with five central stars symbolizing the states of Honduras, El Salvador, Nicaragua, Costa Rica, and Guatemala. The flag design has often been associated with Central American reunification attempts.

Official name: Republic of Hungary
Head of government: Prime Minister
Official language: Hungarian
Monetary unit: forint
Area: 35,919 sq. mi. (93,030 sq. km.)
Population (2001): 10,190,000
GNP per capita (1999): U.S.$4,640
Principal exports (1999): non-electrical
  machinery 16.8%; office machines and
  computers 13.4%; electrical machinery
  11.0% *to:* Germany 38.4%; Austria
  9.6%; Italy 5.9%

Scale 1: 8,147,000

0   30   60   90 mi
0   40   80   120 km

Religious Affiliation

Protestant 25.1%
Roman Catholic 67.8%
Other 7.1%

The colors of the Hungarian flag were mentioned in a 1608 coronation ceremony, but they may have been used since the 13th century. The tricolor was adopted on Oct. 12, 1957, after the abortive revolution of 1956. The white is said to symbolize Hungary's rivers, the green its mountains, and the red the blood shed in its many battles.

GREENLAND SEA

ATLANTIC OCEAN

©2000, Encyclopædia Britannica, Inc.

ICELAND

Scale 1: 7,540,000

| 0 | 20 | 40 mi |
| 0 | 30 | 60 km |

Official name: Republic of Iceland
Head of government: Prime Minister
Official languages: Icelandic
Monetary unit: krona
Area: 39,699 sq. mi. (102,819 sq. km.)
Population (2001): 284,000
GNP per capita (1999): U.S.$29,540
Principal exports (1999): marine products 61.2%; frozen fish 36.3%; aluminum 15.6%; transportation equipment 4.5% *to:* United Kingdom 19.6%; U.S. 14.7%; The Netherlands 6.0%

Age Breakdown

Under 15 24.6%
15–59 60.4%
60 and over 15%

Approval for an Icelandic flag was given by the king of Denmark on June 19, 1915; it became a national flag on Dec. 1, 1918, when the separate kingdom of Iceland was proclaimed. The flag was retained upon the creation of a republic on June 17, 1944. The design has a typical "Scandinavian cross".

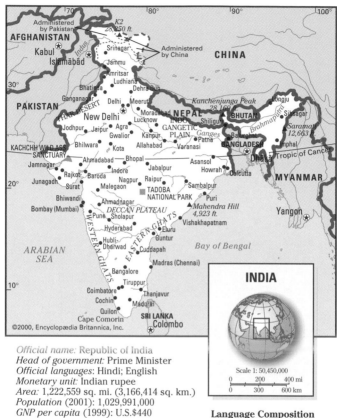

Official name: Republic of India
Head of government: Prime Minister
Official languages: Hindi; English
Monetary unit: Indian rupee
Area: 1,222,559 sq. mi. (3,166,414 sq. km.)
Population (2001): 1,029,991,000
GNP per capita (1999): U.S.$440
Principal exports (1999–2000): cut and
   polished diamonds and jewelry 20.0%;
   cotton ready-made garments 9.2%;
   cotton yarn, fabrics and thread 7.9%
   to: U.S. 22.2%; Hong Kong 6.7%; United
   Kingdom 5.6%

Language Composition

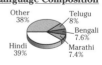

Other 38%
Telugu 8%
Bengali 7.6%
Hindi 39%
Marathi 7.4%

Earlier versions of the flag were used from the 1920s, but the
current flag was hoisted officially on July 22, 1947. The
orange was said to stand for courage and sacrifice, white for
peace and truth, and green for faith and chivalry. The blue
wheel is a chakra, associated with Emperor Asoka's attempts
to unite India in the 3rd century BC.

©2000, Encyclopædia Britannica, Inc.

Official name: Republic of Indonesia
Head of government: President
Official language: Indonesian (Bahasa Indonesia)
Monetary unit: Indonesian rupiah
Area: 741,052 sq. mi. (1,922,570 sq. km.)
Population (2001): 212,195,000
GNP per capita (1999): U.S.$600
Principal exports (1998): crude petroleum 8.3%; natural gas 7.8%; garments 5.4% *to:* Japan 18.7%; U.S. 14.4%; Singapore 10.6%

Scale 1: 88,292,000

| 0 | 400 | 800 mi |
| 0 | 600 | 1200 km |

Language Composition

Indonesian (Malay) 12.1%
Javanese 39.4%
Sundanese 15.8%
Other 32.7%

Indonesia's red and white flag was associated with the Majapahit empire which existed from the 13th to the 16th century. It was adopted on Aug. 17, 1945, and it remained after Indonesia won its independence from The Netherlands in 1949. Red is for courage and white for honesty. The flag is identical, except in dimensions, to the flag of Monaco.

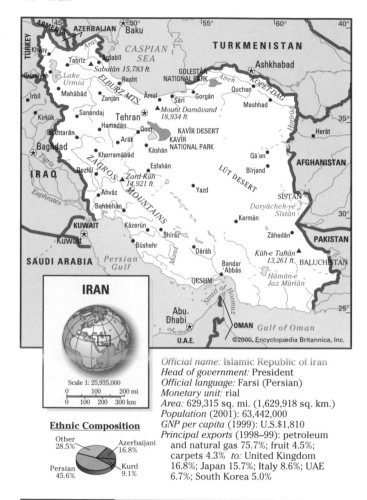

IRAN

Scale 1: 25,935,000

0   100   200 mi
0 100 200 300 km

Ethnic Composition

Other 28.5%
Azerbaijani 16.8%
Persian 45.6%
Kurd 9.1%

Official name: Islamic Republic of Iran
Head of government: President
Official language: Farsi (Persian)
Monetary unit: rial
Area: 629,315 sq. mi. (1,629,918 sq. km.)
Population (2001): 63,442,000
GNP per capita (1999): U.S.$1,810
Principal exports (1998–99): petroleum
  and natural gas 75.7%; fruit 4.5%;
  carpets 4.3% *to:* United Kingdom
  16.8%; Japan 15.7%; Italy 8.6%; UAE
  6.7%; South Korea 5.0%

The tricolor flag was recognized in 1906 but altered after the
revolution of 1979. Along the central stripe are the Arabic
words Allahu akbar ("God is great"), repeated 22 times. The
coat of arms can be read as a rendition of the word Allah, as
a globe, or as two crescents. The green is for Islam, white is
for peace, and red is for valor.

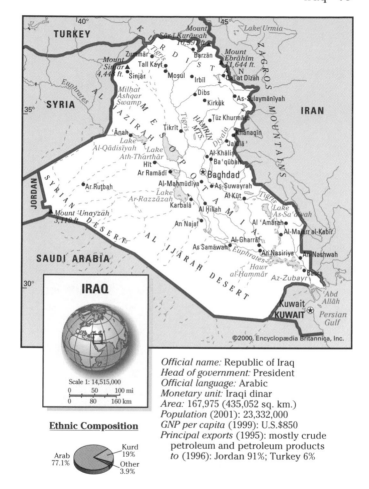

Official name: Republic of Iraq
Head of government: President
Official language: Arabic
Monetary unit: Iraqi dinar
Area: 167,975 (435,052 sq. km.)
Population (2001): 23,332,000
GNP per capita (1999): U.S.$850
Principal exports (1995): mostly crude
petroleum and petroleum products
to (1996): Jordan 91%; Turkey 6%

Scale 1: 14,515,000
0   50   100 mi
0   80   160 km

Ethnic Composition

Arab 77.1%
Kurd 19%
Other 3.9%

Adopted on July 30, 1963, the Iraqi flag is based on the liberation flag first flown in Egypt in 1952. The stars express a
desire to unite with Egypt and Syria. Red is for the willingness
to shed blood, green is for Arab lands, black is for past suffering, and white is for purity. On Jan. 14, 1991, the Arabic
inscription "God is Great" was added.

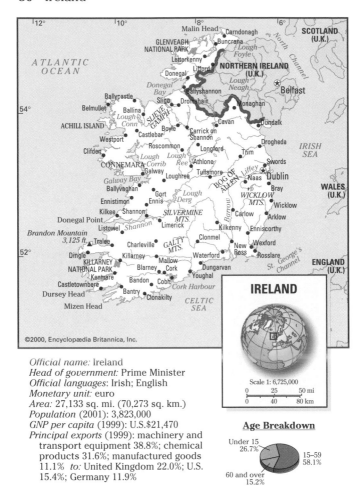

12° 10° 8° 6°

Malin Head · Carndonagh SCOTLAND (U.K.)

GLENVEAGH NATIONAL PARK · Buncrana

Lough Foyle

ATLANTIC OCEAN

Letterkenny

Donegal · Lifford NORTHERN IRELAND (U.K.)

Ballycastle · Donegal Bay · Ballyshannon

Lough Neagh · ⊛ Belfast

54° Belmullet · Sligo · Drumshanbo

Ballina · Monaghan

ACHILL ISLAND · Lough Conn · SLIEVE GAMPH · Boyle · Cavan · Dundalk

Westport · Castlebar · Carrick on Shannon

Roscommon · Longford · Drogheda

Clifden · Lough Corrib · Lough Ree · Athlone · Trim

CONNEMARA · Tullamore · Swords IRISH SEA

Galway · Loughrea · BOG OF ALLEN · Liffey · Dublin

Galway Bay · Ballyvaghan · Naas

Ennistimon · Gort · Ennis · Lough Derg · Bray WALES (U.K.)

Kilkee · Shannon · SILVERMINE MTS. · Barrow · Carlow · Wicklow

Donegal Point · Listowel · Limerick · Arklow

Brandon Mountain 3,125 ft. · Tralee · Charleville · GALTY MTS. · Clonmel · New Ross · Enniscorthy

52° Dingle · Killarney · Mallow · Waterford · Wexford ENGLAND (U.K.)

KILLARNEY NATIONAL PARK · Blarney · Cork · Dungarvan · Rosslare

Castletownbere · Kenmare · Bandon · Cobh · Youghal · St. George's Channel

Dursey Head · Bantry · Clonakilty · Cork Harbour

Mizen Head · CELTIC SEA

©2000, Encyclopædia Britannica, Inc.

Official name: Ireland
Head of government: Prime Minister
Official languages: Irish; English
Monetary unit: euro
Area: 27,133 sq. mi. (70,273 sq. km.)
Population (2001): 3,823,000
GNP per capita (1999): U.S.$21,470
Principal exports (1999): machinery and transport equipment 38.8%; chemical products 31.6%; manufactured goods 11.1% *to:* United Kingdom 22.0%; U.S. 15.4%; Germany 11.9%

IRELAND

Scale 1: 6,725,000

0   25   50 mi
0   40   80 km

Age Breakdown

Under 15 26.7%

15–59 58.1%

60 and over 15.2%

In the 19th century various tricolor flags and ribbons became symbolic of Irish opposition to British rule. Many of them included the colors green (for the Catholics), orange (for the Protestants), and white (for the peace between the two groups). The tricolor in its modern form was recognized by the constitution on Dec. 29, 1937.

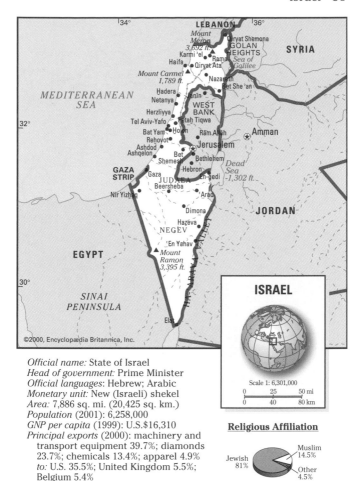

ISRAEL

Scale 1: 6,301,000

0   25   50 mi
0   40   80 km

Official name: State of Israel
Head of government: Prime Minister
Official languages: Hebrew; Arabic
Monetary unit: New (Israeli) shekel
Area: 7,886 sq. mi. (20,425 sq. km.)
Population (2001): 6,258,000
GNP per capita (1999): U.S.$16,310
Principal exports (2000): machinery and
transport equipment 39.7%; diamonds
23.7%; chemicals 13.4%; apparel 4.9%
to: U.S. 35.5%; United Kingdom 5.5%;
Belgium 5.4%

Religious Affiliation

Jewish 81%

Muslim 14.5%

Other 4.5%

Symbolic of the traditional *tallit,* or Jewish prayer shawl, and
including the Star of David, the flag was used from the late
19th century. It was raised when Israel proclaimed independence on May 14, 1948, and the banner was legally recognized on Nov. 12, 1948. A dark blue was also substituted for
the traditional lighter shade of blue.

©2000, Encyclopædia Britannica, Inc.

ITALY

Scale 1: 18,825,000

| 0 | 50 | 100 | 150 mi |
| 0 | 100 | 200 km |

Age Breakdown

Under 15
16.4%

15–59
63%

60 and over
20.6%

Official name: Italian Republic
Head of government: Prime Minister
Official language: Italian
Monetary unit: euro
Area: 116,324 sq. mi. (301,277 sq. km.)
Population (2001): 57,892,000
GNP per capita (1999): U.S.$20,170
Principal exports (1999): machinery and
   transport equipment 41.7%; electrical
   machinery 9.8%; textiles and wearing
   apparel 10.7% *to:* Germany 16.5%;
   France 13.0%; U.S. 9.5%; United
   Kingdom 7.1%; Spain 6.3%

The first Italian national flag was adopted on Feb. 25, 1797, by
the Cispadane Republic. Its stripes were vertically positioned
on May 11, 1798, and thereafter it was honored by all Italian
nationalists. The design was guaranteed by a decree (March
23, 1848) of King Charles Albert of Sardinia, ordering troops
to carry the flag into battle.

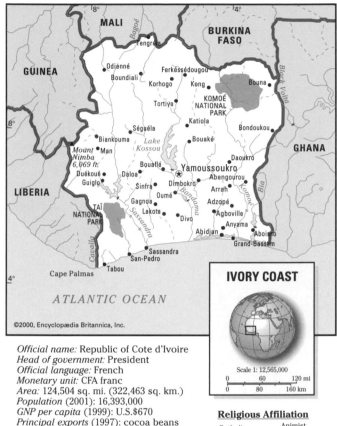

©2000, Encyclopædia Britannica, Inc.

IVORY COAST

Scale 1: 12,565,000

| 0 | 60 | 120 mi |
| 0 | 80 | 160 km |

Official name: Republic of Cote d'Ivoire
Head of government: President
Official language: French
Monetary unit: CFA franc
Area: 124,504 sq. mi. (322,463 sq. km.)
Population (2001): 16,393,000
GNP per capita (1999): U.S.$670
Principal exports (1997): cocoa beans
  and products 33.5%; petroleum
  products 16.8%; coffee and coffee
  products 7.3% *to:* France 17.3%; The
  Netherlands 13.2%; U.S. 7.5%

Religious Affiliation

Catholic 20.8%
Animist 17%
Atheist 13.4%
Muslim 38.7%
Other 10.1%

Adopted on Aug. 7, 1959, the flag of the former French colony
has three stripes corresponding to the national motto (Unity,
Discipline, Labor). The orange is for growth, the white is for
peace emerging from purity and unity, and the green is for
hope and the future. Unofficially the green is for forests and
the orange is for savannas.

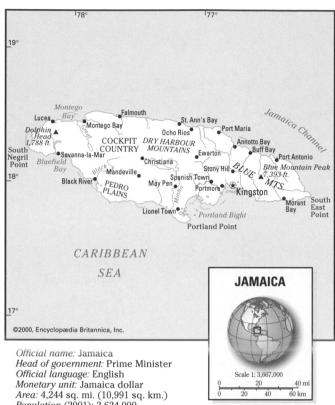

©2000, Encyclopædia Britannica, Inc.

JAMAICA

Scale 1: 3,667,000

0   20   40 mi
0   20   40   60 km

Official name: Jamaica
Head of government: Prime Minister
Official language: English
Monetary unit: Jamaica dollar
Area: 4,244 sq. mi. (10,991 sq. km.)
Population (2001): 2,624,000
GNP per capita (1999): U.S.$2,430
Principal exports (1999): crude materials
   55.7%; food 19.1%; beverages and
   tobacco 4.8%. *to:* U.S. 33.4%; Canada
   14.1%; United Kingdom 13.4%; The
   Netherlands 10.2%

Religious Affiliation

Nonreligious 17%
Other 17%
Roman Catholic 5%
Rastafarian 5%
Protestant 56%

The flag was designed prior to independence from Britain
(Aug. 6, 1962). The black color stood for hardships faced by
the nation, green for agriculture and hope, and yellow for the
natural wealth of Jamaica. This was summed up in the
phrase, "Hardships there are, but the land is green and the
sun shineth."

©2000, Encyclopædia Britannica, Inc.

Official name: Japan
Head of government: Prime Minister
Official language: Japanese
Monetary unit: yen
Area: 145,884 sq. mi. (377,837 sq. km.)
Population (2001): 127,100,000
GNP per capita (1999): U.S.$32,035
Principal exports (1998): electrical
    machinery 23.2%; motor vehicles
    12.9%; chemicals 7.0% *to:* U.S. 30.5%;
    Taiwan 6.6%; Hong Kong 6.5%

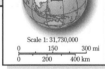

JAPAN

Scale 1: 31,730,000

0   150   300 mi
0   200   400 km

Age Breakdown

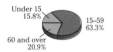

Under 15
15.8%

15–59
63.3%

60 and over
20.9%

The flag features a red sun on a cool white background.
Traditionally, the sun goddess founded Japan in the 7th century BC and gave birth to its first emperor, Jimmu. Even today
the emperor is known as the "Son of the Sun" and the popular
name for the country is "Land of the Rising Sun." The current
flag design was adopted on Aug. 5, 1854.

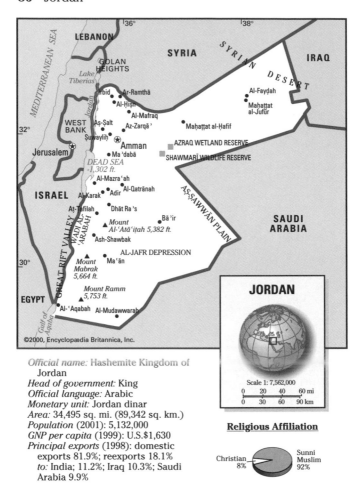

©2000, Encyclopædia Britannica, Inc.

Official name: Hashemite Kingdom of Jordan
Head of government: King
Official language: Arabic
Monetary unit: Jordan dinar
Area: 34,495 sq. mi. (89,342 sq. km.)
Population (2001): 5,132,000
GNP per capita (1999): U.S.$1,630
Principal exports (1998): domestic exports 81.9%; reexports 18.1% *to:* India; 11.2%; Iraq 10.3%; Saudi Arabia 9.9%

JORDAN

Scale 1: 7,562,000

0   20   40   60 mi
0   30   60   90 km

Religious Affiliation

Christian 8%

Sunni Muslim 92%

In 1917 Husayn ibn Ali raised the Arab Revolt flag. With the addition of a white seven-pointed star, this flag was adopted by Transjordan on April 16, 1928, and retained upon the independence of Jordan on March 22, 1946. White is for purity, black for struggle and suffering, red for bloodshed, and green for Arab lands.

Official name: Republic of Kazakhstan
Head of government: President
Official language: Kazakh
Monetary unit: tenge
Area: 1,052,100 sq. mi. (2,724,900 sq. km.)
Population (2001): 14,868,000
GNP per capita (1999): U.S.$1,250
Principal exports (1998): oil and gas
   condensate 28.6%; rolled ferrous metal
   8.9%; refined copper 8.8% *to:* Russia
   28.9%; United Kingdom 9.0%; China
   7.2%; Switzerland 6.1%

Ethnic Composition

Russian 34.8%
Other 14.3%
Kazak 46%
Ukrainian 4.9%

The flag was adopted in June 1992. Light blue is a traditional color of the nomads of Central Asia; it symbolizes peace and well-being. The golden sun and eagle represent freedom and the high ideals of the Kazaks. Along the edge is a band of traditional Kazak ornamentation; the band was originally in red but is now in golden yellow.

KENYA

Scale 1: 17,833,000

0   50   100   150 mi

0   100   200 km

Ethnic Composition

Kamba 9.8%
Other 39.7%
Kalenjin 9.8%
Kikuyu 17.7%
Luo 10.6%
Luhya 12.4%

Official name: Republic of Kenya
Head of government: President
Official languages: Swahili; English
Monetary unit: Kenya shilling
Area: 224,961 sq. mi. (582,646 sq. km.)
Population (2001): 30,766,000
GNP per capita (1999): U.S.$360
Principal exports (1997): tea 20.5%;
   coffee 14.3%; petroleum products
   7.8%; horticulture 7.3% *to:* Uganda
   15.1%; Tanzania 12.9%; United
   Kingdom 11.4%

Upon independence from Britain (Dec. 12, 1963), the Kenyan flag became official. It was based on the flag of the Kenya African National Union. Black is for the people, red for humanity and the struggle for freedom, green for the fertile land, and white for unity and peace. The shield and spears are traditional weapons of the Masai people.

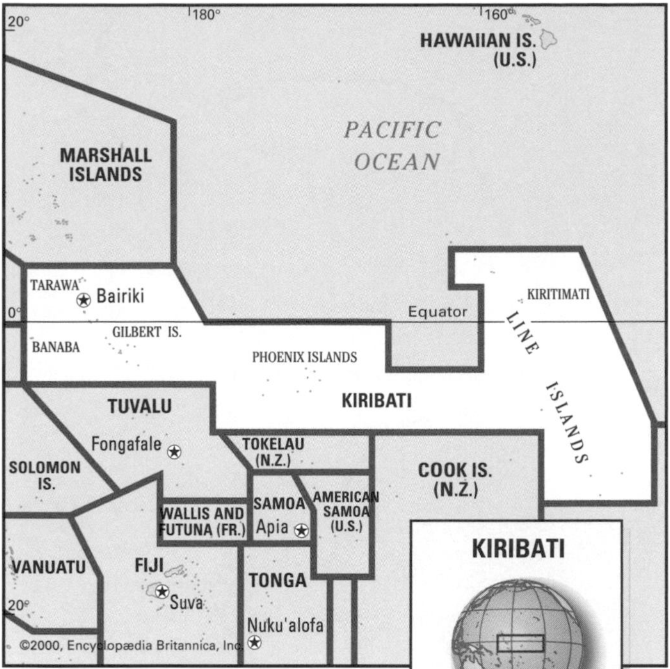

20° | 180° | 160°

HAWAIIAN IS.
(U.S.)

PACIFIC OCEAN

MARSHALL ISLANDS

TARAWA · ⊛ Bairiki

0°

BANABA

GILBERT IS.

KIRITIMATI

Equator

PHOENIX ISLANDS

LINE ISLANDS

KIRIBATI

TUVALU

Fongafale ⊛

TOKELAU
(N.Z.)

SOLOMON IS.

COOK IS.
(N.Z.)

WALLIS AND FUTUNA (FR.)

SAMOA **AMERICAN SAMOA**
Apia ⊛ (U.S.)

VANUATU

FIJI

⊛ Suva

TONGA

20°

Nuku'alofa ⊛

©2000, Encyclopædia Britannica, Inc.

KIRIBATI

Scale 1: 66,436,000

0 — 300 — 600 mi
0 — 400 — 800 km

Official name: Republic of Kiribati
Head of government: President
Official language: English
Monetary unit: Australian dollar
Area: 313 sq. mi. (811 sq. km.)
Population (2001): 94,000
GNP per capita (1999): U.S.$910
Principal exports (1996): domestic
  exports 91.7%, of which copra 62.8%,
  pet fish 11.6%; reexports 8.3%
  to (1994): Japan 32.9%; U.S. 17.1%;
  Hong Kong 12.9%

Age Breakdown

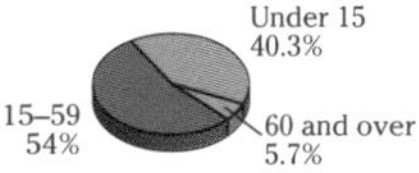

Under 15
40.3%

15–59
54%

60 and over
5.7%

Great Britain acquired the Gilbert and Ellice Islands in the
19th century. In 1975 the Gilbert Islands separated from the
Ellice Islands to form Kiribati, and a new flag was adopted
based on the coat of arms granted to the islands in 1937. It
has waves of white and blue, for the Pacific Ocean, as well as
a yellow sun and a local frigate bird.

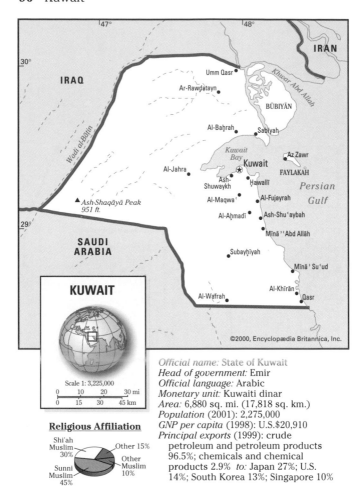

©2000, Encyclopædia Britannica, Inc.

KUWAIT

Scale 1: 3,225,000

| 0 | 10 | 20 | 30 mi |
| 0 | 15 | 30 | 45 km |

Religious Affiliation

Shi'ah Muslim 30%
Sunni Muslim 45%
Other Muslim 10%
Other 15%

Official name: State of Kuwait
Head of government: Emir
Official language: Arabic
Monetary unit: Kuwaiti dinar
Area: 6,880 sq. mi. (17,818 sq. km.)
Population (2001): 2,275,000
GNP per capita (1998): U.S.$20,910
Principal exports (1999): crude
  petroleum and petroleum products
  96.5%; chemicals and chemical
  products 2.9% *to:* Japan 27%; U.S.
  14%; South Korea 13%; Singapore 10%

The red flag of Kuwait, in use since World War I, was replaced by the current flag on Oct. 24, 1961, shortly after independence from Britain. The symbolism is from a poem written over six centuries ago. The green stands for Arab lands, black is for battles, white is for the purity of the fighters, and red is for the blood on their swords.

Official name: Kyrgyz Republic
Head of government: President
Official languages: Kyrgyz; Russian
Monetary unit: som
Area: 77,200 sq. mi. (199,900 sq. km.)
Population (2001): 4,934,000
GNP per capita (1999): U.S.$300
Principal exports (1997): metals 36.3%;
   electricity 13.8%; food prducts 13.2%
   to: Switzerland 26.9%; Uzbekistan
   16.8%; Russian Federation 16.4%

Ethnic Composition

Uzbek
12.9%
Other
13.2%
Kyrgyz
52.4%
Russian
21.5%

The Kyrgyz flag replaced a Soviet-era design on March 3,
1992. The red recalls the flag of the national hero Mansas the
Noble. The central yellow sun has 40 rays, corresponding to
the followers of Mansas and the tribes he united. On the sun
is the stylized view of the roof of a yurt, a traditional nomadic
home that is now seldom used.

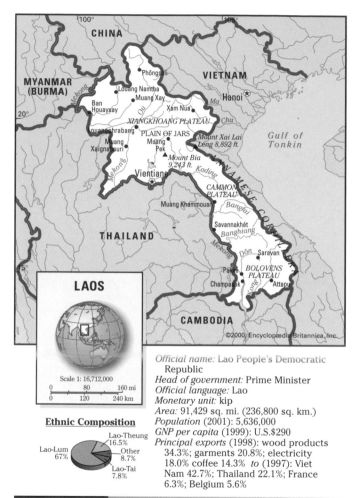

©2000, Encyclopædia Britannica, Inc.

LAOS

Scale 1: 16,712,000

| 0 | 80 | 160 mi |
| 0 | 120 | 240 km |

Ethnic Composition

Lao-Theung 16.5%
Lao-Lum 67%
Other 8.7%
Lao-Tai 7.8%

Official name: Lao People's Democratic Republic
Head of government: Prime Minister
Official language: Lao
Monetary unit: kip
Area: 91,429 sq. mi. (236,800 sq. km.)
Population (2001): 5,636,000
GNP per capita (1999): U.S.$290
Principal exports (1998): wood products 34.3%; garments 20.8%; electricity 18.0% coffee 14.3% *to* (1997): Viet Nam 42.7%; Thailand 22.1%; France 6.3%; Belgium 5.6%

The Lao flag was first used by anticolonialist forces from the mid-20th century. The white disk honored the Japanese who had supported the Lao independence movement, but it also symbolized a bright future. Red was said to stand for the blood of patriots and blue was for the promise of future prosperity. The flag was adopted on Dec. 2, 1975.

Official name: Republic of Latvia
Head of government: Prime Minister
Official language: Latvian
Monetary unit: lats
Area: 24,938 sq. mi. (64,589 sq. km.)
Population (2001): 2,358,000
GNP per capita (1999): U.S.$2,420
Principal exports (1998): wood and paper
products 33.5%; textiles and clothing
16.1% *to:* Germany 15.6%; United
Kingdom 13.5%; Russia 12.1%;
Sweden 10.3%

Ethnic Composition

Latvian 54.8%
Russian 32.8%
Other 8.4%
Belarusian 4%

The basic flag design was used by a militia unit in 1279,
according to a 14th century source. Popularized in the 19th
century among anti-Russian nationalists, the flag flew in 1918
and was legally adopted on Jan. 20, 1923. Under Soviet control the flag was suppressed, but it was again legalized in
1988 and flown officially from Feb. 27, 1990.

94 Lebanon

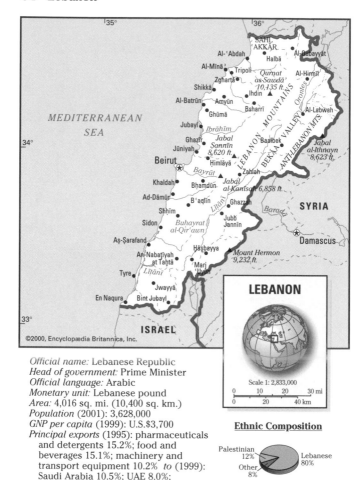

MEDITERRANEAN
SEA

SAHL
AKKĀR
Al-ʿAbdah
Al-Mīnā Tripoli
Zghartā
Shikkā
Al-Batrūn Amyūn
Ghūmā
Jubayl *Ibrāhīm*
Ghazīr *Jabal*
Ṣannīn
Jūniyah *8,620 ft.*
Beirut *Bayrūt*
Himlāyā
Khaldah Bhamdūn *Jabal*
Ad-Dāmūr Bʿaqlīn *al-Kanīsah 6,858 ft.*
Shḥīm *Liṭānī*
Sidon Jubb
Jannīn
As-Ṣarafand *Buhayrat*
al-Qirʿawn
An-Nabaṭīyah Ḥāṣbayyā
at Taḥtā *Mount Hermon*
Tyre *Liṭānī* *9,232 ft.*
Marj
ʿUyūn
En Naqura Jwayyā
Bint Jubayl

Halbā Al-Qubayyāt
Qurnat
as-Sawdāʾ Al-Hirmil
10,135 ft.
Ihdin
Bsharrī
Al-Labwah
Baalbek *Jabal*
Zahlah *al-Ithnayn*
8,623 ft.

LEBANON MOUNTAINS *Orontes*
BEKAA VALLEY
ANTI-LEBANON MTS.

Barada

SYRIA

☆ Damascus

ISRAEL

©2000, Encyclopædia Britannica, Inc.

Official name: Lebanese Republic
Head of government: Prime Minister
Official language: Arabic
Monetary unit: Lebanese pound
Area: 4,016 sq. mi. (10,400 sq. km.)
Population (2001): 3,628,000
GNP per capita (1999): U.S.$3,700
Principal exports (1995): pharmaceuticals
and detergents 15.2%; food and
beverages 15.1%; machinery and
transport equipment 10.2% *to* (1999):
Saudi Arabia 10.5%; UAE 8.0%;
France 7.7%

LEBANON

Scale 1: 2,833,000
0   10   20   30 mi
0   20   40 km

Ethnic Composition

Palestinian
12%
Other
8%
Lebanese
80%

On Sept. 1, 1920, French-administered Lebanon adopted a flag
based on the French tricolor. The current red-white flag was
established by the constitution of 1943, which divided power
among the Muslim and Christian sects. On the central stripe
is a cedar tree, which is a biblical symbol for holiness, peace,
and eternity.

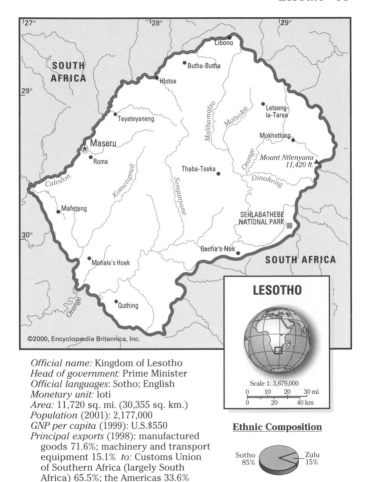

©2000, Encyclopædia Britannica, Inc.

Official name: Kingdom of Lesotho
Head of government: Prime Minister
Official languages: Sotho; English
Monetary unit: loti
Area: 11,720 sq. mi. (30,355 sq. km.)
Population (2001): 2,177,000
GNP per capita (1999): U.S.$550
Principal exports (1998): manufactured
    goods 71.6%; machinery and transport
    equipment 15.1% *to:* Customs Union
    of Southern Africa (largely South
    Africa) 65.5%; the Americas 33.6%

Scale 1: 3,679,000

0   10   20   30 mi
0   20   40 km

Ethnic Composition

Sotho 85%   Zulu 15%

The flag was hoisted on Jan. 20, 1987, after the military overthrew the government of prime minister Leabua Jonathan.
It contains a white triangle (for peace) on which are an
animal-skin shield and traditional weapons used in battles
to preserve Sotho independence. The green triangle is for
prosperity, and the blue stripe is for rain.

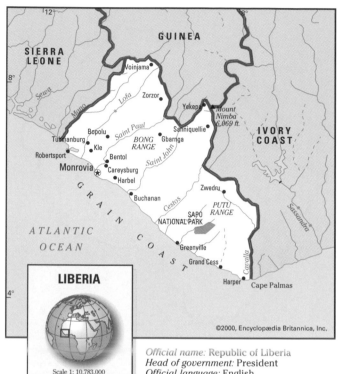

©2000, Encyclopædia Britannica, Inc.

LIBERIA

Scale 1: 10,783,000

0   50   100 mi
0   80   160 km

Religious Affiliation

Traditional beliefs and other 18.5%

Muslim 13.8%

Christian 67.7%

Official name: Republic of Liberia
Head of government: President
Official language: English
Monetary unit: Liberian dollar
Area: 37,743 sq. mi. (97,754 sq. km.)
Population (2001): 3,226,000
GNP per capita (1996): U.S.$490
Principal exports (1999): rubber 56.9%; logs and timber 39.1% *to* (1999): U.S. 54.3%; France 24.3%; Singapore 5.2%; Belgium 4.4%

In the 19th century land was purchased on the African coast by the American Colonization Society, in order to return freed slaves to Africa. On April 9, 1827, a flag based on that of the United States was adopted, featuring a white cross. On Aug. 24, 1847, after independence, the cross was replaced by a star and the number of stripes was reduced.

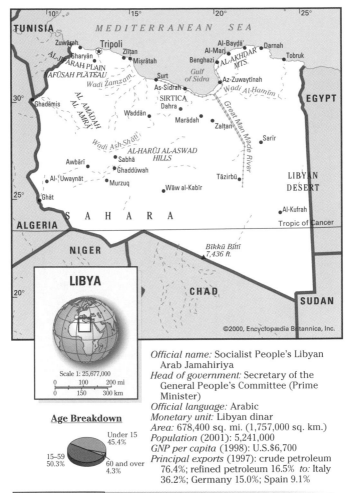

Official name: Socialist People's Libyan
  Arab Jamahiriya
Head of government: Secretary of the
  General People's Committee (Prime
  Minister)
Official language: Arabic
Monetary unit: Libyan dinar
Area: 678,400 sq. mi. (1,757,000 sq. km.)
Population (2001): 5,241,000
GNP per capita (1998): U.S.$6,700
Principal exports (1997): crude petroleum
  76.4%; refined petroleum 16.5% *to:* Italy
  36.2%; Germany 15.0%; Spain 9.1%

LIBYA

Scale 1: 25,677,000

| 0 | 100 | 200 mi |
| 0 | 150 | 300 km |

Age Breakdown

Under 15
45.4%

15–59
50.3%

60 and over
4.3%

After the coup d'état of 1969, Muammar al-Qaddafi adopted a
flag based on the Egyptian flag. When the Egyptian president
Anwar el-Sadat made peace with Israel, however, Qaddafi
broke diplomatic relations and replaced the flag. In November
1977 he established a plain green banner, symbolizing promis-
es of agricultural wealth.

LIECHTENSTEIN

Scale 1: 364,000

0   2   4 mi
0   2   4   6 km

Religious Affiliation

Other 13.1%
Protestant 6.9%
Roman Catholic 80%

Official name: Principality of Liechtenstein
Head of government: Prime Minister
Official language: German
Monetary unit: Swiss franc
Area: 61.8 sq. mi. (160.0 sq. km.)
Population (2001): 33,000
GNP per capita (1996): U.S.$23,000
Principal exports (1997): machinery and transport equipment 49.2%; metal products 15.1%; other finished goods 12.7% *to* (1998): European Union 49.5%

The blue-red flag was given official status in October 1921. At the 1936 Olympics it was learned that this same flag was used by Haiti; thus, in 1937 a yellow crown was added, which symbolizes the unity of the people and their prince. Blue stands for the sky, red for the evening fires in homes. The flag was last modified on Sept. 18, 1982.

©2000, Encyclopædia Britannica, Inc.

LITHUANIA

Scale 1: 7,165,000

0   30   60 mi
0   40   80 km

Ethnic Composition

Lithuanian 81.3%
Russian 8.4%
Polish 7%
Other 3.3%

Official name: Republic of Lithuania
Head of government: Premier
Official language: Lithuanian
Monetary unit: litas
Area: 25,212 sq. mi. (65,300 sq. km.)
Population (2001): 3,691,000
GNP per capita (1999): U.S.$2,640
Principal exports (1998): mineral fuels
   18.6%; textiles and clothing 18.6%;
   food products 12.3%; machinery and
   apparatus 10.8% *to:* Russia 16.5%;
   Germany 13.1%; Latvia 11.1%

The tricolor flag of Lithuania was adopted on Aug. 1, 1922. It
was long suppressed under Soviet rule until its reestablish-
ment on March 20, 1989. The yellow color suggests ripening
wheat and freedom from want. Green is for hope and the
forests of the nation, while red stands for love of country,
sovereignty, and valor in defense of liberty.

Official name: Grand Duchy of
  Luxembourg
Head of government: Prime Minister
Official language: (none)
Monetary unit: euro
Area: 999 sq. mi. (2,586 sq. km.)
Population (2001): 444,000
GNP per capita (1999): U.S.$42.930
Principal exports (1999): fabricated
  metals 28.3%; machinery and
  equipment 20.5%; chemicals and
  chemical products 6.3% *to:* Germany
  25.4%; France 21.1%; Belgium 13.0%

LUXEMBOURG

Scale 1: 1,177,000

0   6   12 mi
0   8   16 km

Ethnic Composition

Other 15.7%
Portuguese 12.1%
Italian 4.8%
Luxemburger 67.4%

In the 19th century the national colors, from the coat of arms
of the dukes of Luxembourg, came to be used in a tricolor of
red-white-blue, coincidentally the same as the flag of The
Netherlands. To distinguish it from the Dutch flag, the propor-
tions were altered and the shade of blue was made lighter. It
was recognized by law on Aug. 16, 1972.

Official name: Republic of Macedonia
Head of government: Prime Minister
Official language: Macedonian
Monetary unit: denar
Area: 9,928 sq. mi. (25,713 sq. km.)
Population (2001): 2,046,000
GNP per capita (1999): U.S.$1,160
Principal exports (1998): manufactured
  products 34.2%; machinery and
  transport equipment 7.5%; food
  products 5.0% to: Germany 21.4%;
  Yugoslavia 18.3%; U.S. 13.3%

Ethnic Composition

Albanian 23.1%
Macedonian 66.4%
Other 10.5%

A "starburst" flag replaced the communist banner on Aug. 11, 1992. The starburst was a symbol of Alexander the Great and his father, Philip of Macedon, but its use by Macedonia was opposed by Greece. Thus on Oct. 6, 1995, the similar "golden sun" flag was chosen instead. The gold and red colors originated in an early Macedonian coat of arms.

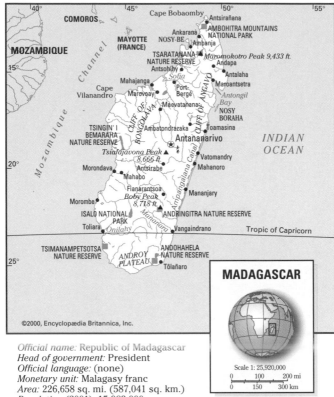

COMOROS

MAYOTTE (FRANCE)

MOZAMBIQUE

Mozambique Channel

Cape Bobaomby
Antsiranana
Ankarana
NOSY-BE
Ambanja
AMBOHITRA MOUNTAINS
NATIONAL PARK
TSARATANANA
NATURE RESERVE
Maromokotro Peak 9,433 ft.
Antsohihy
Andapa
Antalaha
Mahajanga
Sofia
Maroantsetra
Marovoay
Port-
Bergé
Antongil
Bay
NOSY
BORAHA
Cape
Vilanandro
Maevatanana
CLIFF OF ANGAVO
CLIFF OF BONGOLAVA
Ambatondrazaka
Toamasina
TSINGIN' I
BEMARAHA
NATURE RESERVE
Antananarivo
INDIAN
OCEAN
Tsiafajavona Peak
8,666 ft.
Vatomandry
Morondava
Antsirabe
Mahanoro
Mahabo
Ampangalana Canal
Fianarantsoa
Boby Peak
8,718 ft.
Mananjary
Morombe
Mangoro
ANDRINGITRA NATURE RESERVE
ISALO NATIONAL
PARK
Onilahy
Vangaindrano
Tropic of Capricorn
Toliara

TSIMANAMPETSOTSA
NATURE RESERVE
ANDROY
PLATEAU
ANDOHAHELA
NATURE RESERVE
Tôlañaro

©2000, Encyclopædia Britannica, Inc.

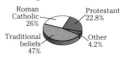

MADAGASCAR

Scale 1: 25,920,000

0   100   200 mi
0   150   300 km

Official name: Republic of Madagascar
Head of government: President
Official language: (none)
Monetary unit: Malagasy franc
Area: 226,658 sq. mi. (587,041 sq. km.)
Population (2001): 15,983,000
GNP per capita (1999): U.S.$250
Principal exports (1998): coffee 17.2%;
    cotton fabrics 14.1%; minerals 11.3%;
    shrimp 6.0% *to* (1998): France 39.4%;
    Mauritius 6.8%; U.S. 5.5%

Religious Affiliation

Roman
Catholic
26%

Protestant
22.8%

Traditional
beliefs
47%

Other
4.2%

The Madagascar flag was adopted on Oct. 16, 1958, by the newly proclaimed Malagasy Republic, formerly a French colony. The flag combines the traditional Malagasy colors of white and red with a stripe of green. The white and red are said to stand for purity and sovereignty, while the green represents the coastal regions and symbolizes hope.

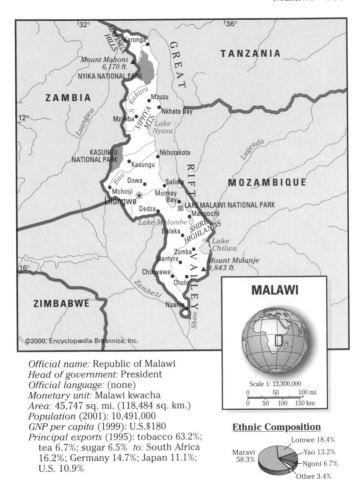

Official name: Republic of Malawi
Head of government: President
Official language: (none)
Monetary unit: Malawi kwacha
Area: 45,747 sq. mi. (118,484 sq. km.)
Population (2001): 10,491,000
GNP per capita (1999): U.S.$180
Principal exports (1995): tobacco 63.2%;
   tea 6.7%; sugar 6.5% *to:* South Africa
   16.2%; Germany 14.7%; Japan 11.1%;
   U.S. 10.9%

Scale 1: 13,300,000

| 0 | 50 | 100 mi |
| 0 | 50 | 100 | 150 km |

Ethnic Composition

Maravi 58.3%
Lomwe 18.4%
Yao 13.2%
Ngoni 6.7%
Other 3.4%

The flag of the Malawi Congress Party was striped black for
the African people, red for the blood of martyrs, and green
for the vegetation and climate. The country's name means
"flaming waters," referring to the setting sun on Lake Malawi.
With independence on July 6, 1964, a new flag was created by
adding the sun symbol to the party flag.

Official name: Malaysia
Head of government: Prime Minister
Official language: Malay
Monetary unit: ringgit
Area: 127,354 sq. mi. (329,845 sq. km.)
Population (2001): 22,602,000
GNP per capita (1999): U.S.$3,390
Principal exports (1998): machinery and
transport equipment 59.2%; basic
manufactures 8.3%; animal and
vegetable oils 7.5% to: U.S. 21.9%;
Singapore 16.5%; Japan 11.6%

Ethnic Composition

Malay and other indigenous 59.9%

Chinese 29.9%

Indian and other 10.2%

The flag hoisted on May 26, 1950, had 11 stripes, a crescent, and an 11-pointed star. The number of stripes and star points was increased to 14 on Sept. 16, 1963. Yellow is a royal color in Malaysia while red, white, and blue indicate connections with the Commonwealth. The crescent is a reminder that the population is mainly Muslim.

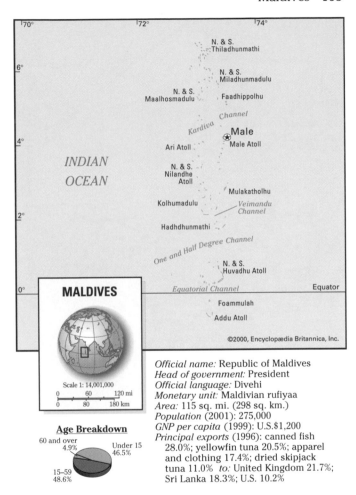

©2000, Encyclopædia Britannica, Inc.

MALDIVES

Scale 1: 14,001,000

0   60   120 mi
0   80   180 km

Age Breakdown

60 and over
4.9%   Under 15
                        46.5%
15–59
48.6%

Official name: Republic of Maldives
Head of government: President
Official language: Divehi
Monetary unit: Maldivian rufiyaa
Area: 115 sq. mi. (298 sq. km.)
Population (2001): 275,000
GNP per capita (1999): U.S.$1,200
Principal exports (1996): canned fish
   28.0%; yellowfin tuna 20.5%; apparel
   and clothing 17.4%; dried skipjack
   tuna 11.0% *to:* United Kingdom 21.7%;
   Sri Lanka 18.3%; U.S. 10.2%

Maldivian ships long used a plain red ensign like those flown
by Arabian and African nations. While a British protectorate
in the early 20th century, the Maldives adopted a flag which
was only slightly altered upon independence (July 26, 1965).
The green panel and white crescent are symbolic of Islam,
progress, prosperity, and peace.

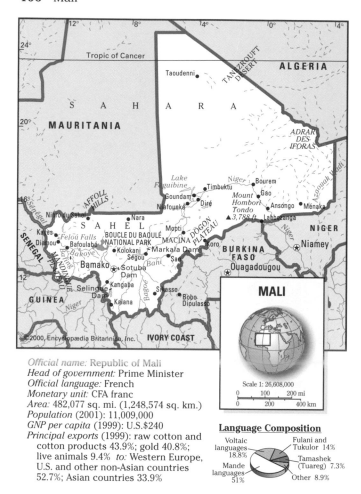

Official name: Republic of Mali
Head of government: Prime Minister
Official language: French
Monetary unit: CFA franc
Area: 482,077 sq. mi. (1,248,574 sq. km.)
Population (2001): 11,009,000
GNP per capita (1999): U.S.$240
Principal exports (1999): raw cotton and
  cotton products 43.9%; gold 40.8%;
  live animals 9.4% *to:* Western Europe,
  U.S. and other non-Asian countries
  52.7%; Asian countries 33.9%

Scale 1: 26,608,000

| 0 | 100 | 200 mi |
| 0 | 200 | 400 km |

Language Composition

Voltaic
languages
18.8%

Mande
languages
51%

Fulani and
Tukulor 14%

Tamashek
(Tuareg) 7.3%

Other 8.9%

Designed for the Mali-Senegal union of 1959, the flag originally
included a human figure, the Kanaga, in its center. In 1960
Senegal and Mali divided. Muslims in Mali objected to the
Kanaga, and on March 1, 1961, the figure was dropped. Green,
yellow, and red are the Pan-African colors and are used by
many former French territories.

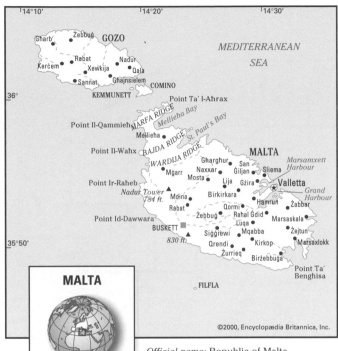

©2000, Encyclopædia Britannica, Inc.

Official name: Republic of Malta
Head of government: Prime Minister
Official languages: Maltese; English
Monetary unit: Maltese lira
Area: 122 sq. mi. (316 sq. km.)
Population (2001): 381,000
GNP per capita (1999): U.S.$9,210
Principal exports (1998): machinery and
transport equipment 64.6%;
manufactured goods 27.7% *to:* France
20.5%; U.S. 19.0%; Singapore 14.3%

Age Breakdown

Under 15
22%

15–59
62.6%

60 and over
15.4%

The Maltese flag was supposedly based on an 11th-century
coat of arms, and a red flag with a white cross was used by
the Knights of Malta from the Middle Ages. The current flag
dates from independence within the Commonwealth (Sept.
21, 1964). The George Cross was granted by the British for
the heroic defense of the island in World War II.

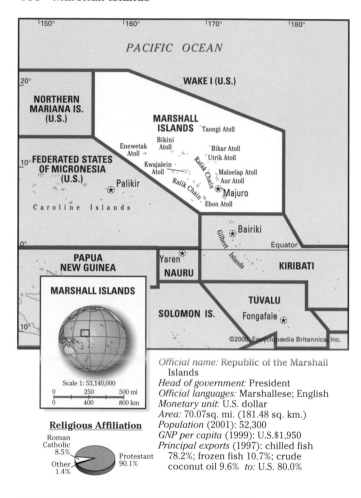

150° 160° 170° 180°

PACIFIC OCEAN

20°

WAKE I (U.S.)

NORTHERN MARIANA IS. (U.S.)

MARSHALL ISLANDS Taongi Atoll

Enewetak Atoll → Bikini Atoll ˙Bikar Atoll Utrik Atoll

10° **FEDERATED STATES OF MICRONESIA (U.S.)**

Kwajalein Atoll *Ratak Chain* ˙Maloelap Atoll Aur Atoll

✪ Palikir *Ralik Chain* ✪ Majuro

C a r o l i n e   I s l a n d s Ebon Atoll

0°

✪ Bairiki

Gilbert Islands Equator

PAPUA NEW GUINEA Yaren ✪ **KIRIBATI**

NAURU

MARSHALL ISLANDS

TUVALU

SOLOMON IS. Fongafale ✪

10° ©2000 Encyclopædia Britannica, Inc.

Scale 1: 53,140,000

0   250   500 mi
0   400   800 km

Religious Affiliation

Roman Catholic 8.5%

Other 1.4%

Protestant 90.1%

Official name: Republic of the Marshall Islands
Head of government: President
Official languages: Marshallese; English
Monetary unit: U.S. dollar
Area: 70.07sq. mi. (181.48 sq. km.)
Population (2001): 52,300
GNP per capita (1999): U.S.$1,950
Principal exports (1997): chilled fish 78.2%; frozen fish 10.7%; crude coconut oil 9.6% *to:* U.S. 80.0%

The island nation hoisted its flag on May 1, 1979. The blue stands for the ocean. The white is for brightness while the orange is for bravery and wealth. The two stripes joined symbolize the Equator, and they increase in width to show growth and vitality. The rays of the star are for the municipalities; its four long rays recall a Christian cross.

Official name: Islamic Republic of
  Mauritania
Head of government: President
Official language: Arabic
Monetary unit: ouguiya
Area: 398,000 sq. mi. (1,030,700 sq. km.)
Population (2001): 2,591,000
GNP per capita (1999): U.S.$390
Principal exports (1997): iron ore 52.4%;
  fish 47.6% *to:* Japan 23.3%; Italy 16.7%;
  France 13.9%; Spain 8.3%

Scale 1: 26,914,000
0   100   200 mi
0   200   400 km

Age Breakdown

Under 15
43.1%

15–59
51.7%

60 and over
5.2%

In 1958 Mauritania was granted autonomous status within the
French Community. The current flag replaced the French tricolor on April 1, 1959, and no changes were made to the
design at independence (Nov. 28, 1960). The green background of the flag and its star and crescent are traditional
Muslim symbols that have been in use for centuries.

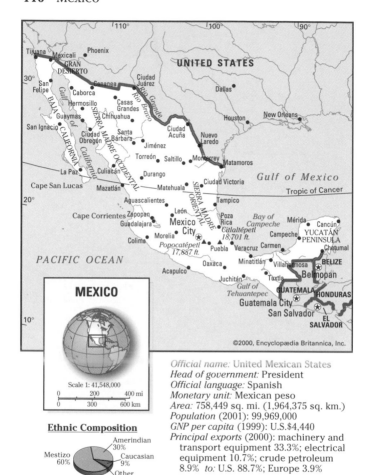

MEXICO

Scale 1: 41,548,000

| 0 | 200 | 400 mi |
| 0 | 300 | 600 km |

Ethnic Composition

Amerindian 30%
Mestizo 60%
Caucasian 9%
Other 1%

Official name: United Mexican States
Head of government: President
Official language: Spanish
Monetary unit: Mexican peso
Area: 758,449 sq. mi. (1,964,375 sq. km.)
Population (2001): 99,969,000
GNP per capita (1999): U.S.$4,440
Principal exports (2000): machinery and
transport equipment 33.3%; electrical
equipment 10.7%; crude petroleum
8.9% *to:* U.S. 88.7%; Europe 3.9%

The green-white-red tricolor was officially established in 1821.
Green is for independence, white for Roman Catholicism, and
red for union. The emblem depicts the scene supposedly wit-
nessed by the Aztecs in 1325: an eagle with a snake in its
beak standing upon a cactus growing out of rocks in the
water. The flag was modified on Sept. 17, 1968.

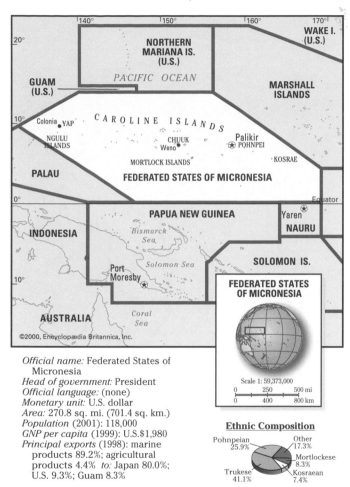

Official name: Federated States of
Micronesia
Head of government: President
Official language: (none)
Monetary unit: U.S. dollar
Area: 270.8 sq. mi. (701.4 sq. km.)
Population (2001): 118,000
GNP per capita (1999): U.S.$1,980
Principal exports (1998): marine
products 89.2%; agricultural
products 4.4% *to:* Japan 80.0%;
U.S. 9.3%; Guam 8.3%

Ethnic Composition

Pohnpeian
25.9%

Other
17.3%

Mortlockese
8.3%

Trukese
41.1%

Kosraean
7.4%

On Nov. 30, 1978, the flag of the former United States trust
territory was approved by an interim congress. Based on the
symbolism of the territory, the flag has stars for the four
states of Micronesia. After sovereignty was granted in 1986, a
dark blue background (for the Pacific Ocean) was substituted
for the original "United Nations blue."

MOLDOVA

Scale 1: 5,251,000

| 0 | 20 | 40 mi |
| 0 | 30 | 60 km |

Ethnic Composition

Moldovan 64.5%
Ukrainian 13.8%
Russian 13%
Gagauz 3.5%
Other 5.2%

Official name: Republic of Moldova
Head of government: Prime Minister
Official language: Romanian
Monetary unit: Moldovan leu
Area: 13,000 sq. mi. (33,700 sq. km.)
Population (2001): 4,431,000
GNP per capita (1999): U.S.$410
Principal exports (1996): food and
  agricultural goods 72.8%; textile
  products 6.2%; machinery 5.3%
  to: Russia 53.6%; Romania 9.4%,
  Ukraine 5.9%

By 1989, Moldovans protested against communist rule, and
the traditional tricolor of blue-yellow-red, which had flown
briefly in 1917–18, became a popular symbol. It replaced the
communist flag in May 1990 and remained after independence
in 1991. The shield has an eagle on whose breast are an
aurochs head, a crescent, a star, and a flower.

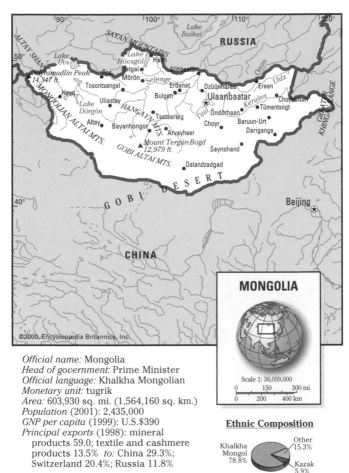

Official name: Mongolia
Head of government: Prime Minister
Official language: Khalkha Mongolian
Monetary unit: tugrik
Area: 603,930 sq. mi. (1,564,160 sq. km.)
Population (2001): 2,435,000
GNP per capita (1999): U.S.$390
Principal exports (1998): mineral
  products 59.0; textile and cashmere
  products 13.5% *to:* China 29.3%;
  Switzerland 20.4%; Russia 11.8%

MONGOLIA

Scale 1: 36,059,000

0   150   300 mi
0   200   400 km

Ethnic Composition

Khalkha
Mongol
78.8%

Other
15.3%

Kazak
5.9%

In 1945, the flag symbolizing communism (red) and Mongol
nationalism (blue) was established. Near the hoist is a *soyon-
ba,* a grouping of philosophical symbols (flame, sun, moon,
yin-yang, triangles, and bars). Yellow traditionally stood for
Lamaist Buddhism. On Jan. 12, 1992, a five-pointed star (for
Communism) was removed from the flag.

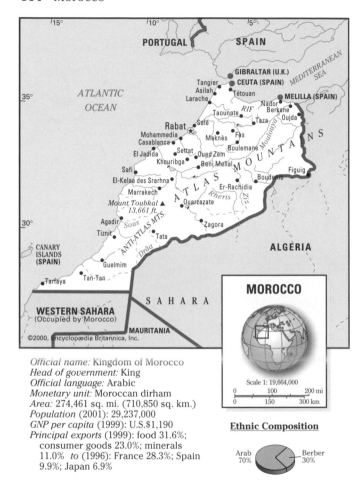

Official name: Kingdom of Morocco
Head of government: King
Official language: Arabic
Monetary unit: Moroccan dirham
Area: 274,461 sq. mi. (710,850 sq. km.)
Population (2001): 29,237,000
GNP per capita (1999): U.S.$1,190
Principal exports (1999): food 31.6%;
consumer goods 23.0%; minerals
11.0% *to* (1996): France 28.3%; Spain
9.9%; Japan 6.9%

MOROCCO

Scale 1: 19,664,000

0   100   200 mi
0   150   300 km

Ethnic Composition

Arab
70%   Berber
30%

After Morocco was subjected to the rule of France and Spain
in the 20th century, the plain red flag, which had been displayed on its ships, was modified on Nov. 17, 1915. To its center was added the ancient pentagram known as the "Seal of
Solomon." The flag continued in use even after the French
granted independence in 1956.

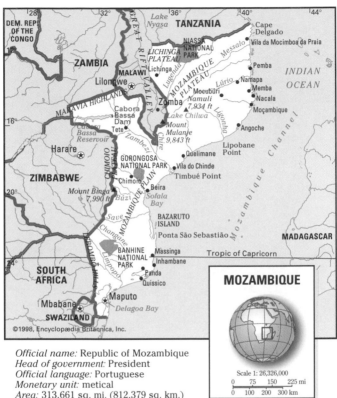

Official name: Republic of Mozambique
Head of government: President
Official language: Portuguese
Monetary unit: metical
Area: 313,661 sq. mi. (812,379 sq. km.)
Population (2001): 19,371,000
GNP per capita (1999): U.S.$220
Principal exports (1996): food and
beverages 66.4%, of which shellfish
38.1%; machinery and transport
equipment 11.5% *to:* European Union
34.7%; South Africa 19.4%; India 11.8%;
U.S. 11.4%

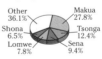

Scale 1: 26,326,000

0   75   150   225 mi
0   100 200 300 km

Language Composition

Other 36.1%
Makua 27.8%
Shona 6.5%
Tsonga 12.4%
Lomwe 7.8%
Sena 9.4%

In the early 1960s, anti-Portuguese groups adopted flags of
green (for forests), black (for the majority population), white
(for rivers and the ocean), gold (for peace and mineral
wealth), and red (for the blood of liberation). The current flag
was readopted in 1983; on its star are a book, a hoe, and an
assault rifle.

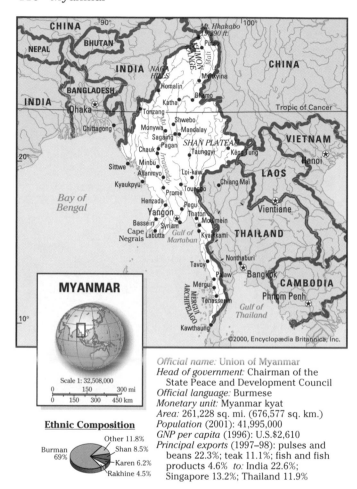

CHINA
NEPAL
BHUTAN
INDIA
BANGLADESH
INDIA
Dhaka
Chittagong
Mt. Hkakabo
19,290 ft.
Putao
KUMON RANGE
NAGA HILLS
Myitkyina
Homalin
Bhamo
Katha
CHINA
Tonzang
Shwebo
Mandalay
Monywa
Sagaing
Chauk
Pagan
SHAN PLATEAU
Taunggyi
Kengtung
VIETNAM
Minbu
Loi-kaw
Hanoi
Sittwe
Allanmyo
Kyaukpyu
Toungoo
Chiang Mai
LAOS
Prome
Bay of Bengal
Henzada
Pegu
Thaton
Yangon
Bassein
Syriam
Moulmein
Vientiane
Cape Negrais
Labutta
Gulf of Martaban
Kyaikkami
THAILAND
Nonthaburi
Tavoy
Palaw
Bangkok
CAMBODIA
Mergui
Tenasserim
Phnom Penh
MERGUI ARCHIPELAGO
Gulf of Thailand
Kawthaung
Tropic of Cancer
Irrawaddy
©2000, Encyclopædia Britannica, Inc.

MYANMAR

Scale 1: 32,508,000
0   150   300 mi
0   150   300   450 km

Ethnic Composition

Burman 69%
Other 11.8%
Shan 8.5%
Karen 6.2%
Rakhine 4.5%

Official name: Union of Myanmar
Head of government: Chairman of the
State Peace and Development Council
Official language: Burmese
Monetary unit: Myanmar kyat
Area: 261,228 sq. mi. (676,577 sq. km.)
Population (2001): 41,995,000
GNP per capita (1996): U.S.$2,610
Principal exports (1997–98): pulses and
beans 22.3%; teak 11.1%; fish and fish
products 4.6% *to:* India 22.6%;
Singapore 13.2%; Thailand 11.9%

The current flag design dates to Jan. 4, 1974. Its 14 stars, for
the states and divisions of Myanmar, form a circle around a
cogwheel, for industrial workers, and ears and leaves of rice,
symbolizing the peasantry. Blue is for truthfulness and
strength; red for bravery, unity, and determination; and white
for truth, purity, and steadfastness.

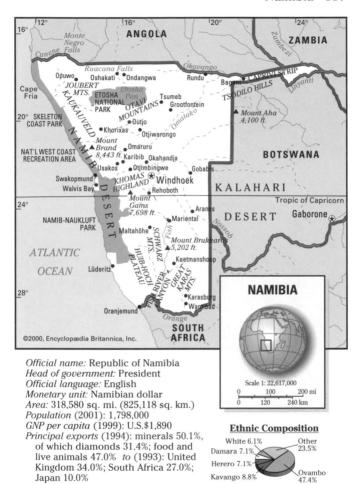

@2000, Encyclopædia Britannica, Inc.

Official name: Republic of Namibia
Head of government: President
Official language: English
Monetary unit: Namibian dollar
Area: 318,580 sq. mi. (825,118 sq. km.)
Population (2001): 1,798,000
GNP per capita (1999): U.S.$1,890
Principal exports (1994): minerals 50.1%,
  of which diamonds 31.4%; food and
  live animals 47.0% *to* (1993): United
  Kingdom 34.0%; South Africa 27.0%;
  Japan 10.0%

NAMIBIA

Scale 1: 22,617,000

0   100   200 mi
0   120   240 km

Ethnic Composition

White 6.1%
Damara 7.1%
Herero 7.1%
Kavango 8.8%
Other 23.5%
Ovambo 47.4%

The flag was adopted on Feb. 2, 1990, and hoisted on independence from South Africa, March 21, 1990. Its colors are
those of the South West Africa People's Organization: blue
(for sky and ocean), red (for heroism and determination), and
green (for agriculture). The gold sun represents life and energy while the white stripes are for water resources.

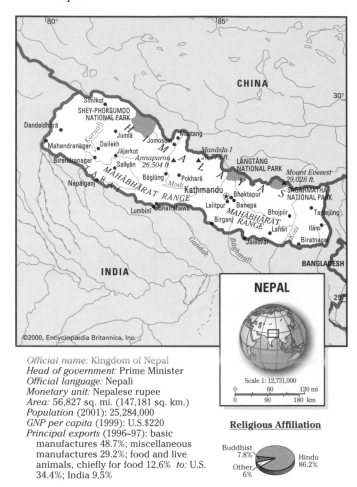

©2000, Encyclopædia Britannica, Inc.

NEPAL

Scale 1: 12,731,000

| 0 | 60 | 120 mi |
| 0 | 90 | 180 km |

Official name: Kingdom of Nepal
Head of government: Prime Minister
Official language: Nepali
Monetary unit: Nepalese rupee
Area: 56,827 sq. mi. (147,181 sq. km.)
Population (2001): 25,284,000
GNP per capita (1999): U.S.$220
Principal exports (1996–97): basic
  manufactures 48.7%; miscellaneous
  manufactures 29.2%; food and live
  animals, chiefly for food 12.6% *to:* U.S.
  34.4%; India 9.5%

Religious Affiliation

Buddhist 7.8%
Hindu 86.2%
Other 6%

Established on Dec. 16, 1962, Nepal's flag consists of two united pennant shapes; it is the only non-rectangular national flag in the world. In the upper segment is a moon with a crescent attached below; in the bottom segment appears a stylized sun. The symbols are for different dynasties and express a hope for the immortality of the nation. The crimson and blue colors are common in Nepali art.

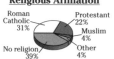

THE NETHERLANDS

Scale 1: 5,169,000

0   20   40 mi
0   30   60 km

Religious Affiliation

Roman Catholic 31%
Protestant 22%
Muslim 4%
Other 4%
No religion 39%

Official name: Kingdom of The Netherlands
Head of government: Prime Minister
Official language: Dutch
Monetary unit: euro
Area: 16,033 sq. mi. (41,526 sq. km.)
Population (2001): 15,968,000
GNP per capita (1999): U.S.$25,140
Principal exports (1999): machinery 27.8%; chemical products 15.3%; food 13.4% *to:* Germany 26.1%; Belgium-Luxembourg 12.2%; France 10.8%; United Kingdom 10.8%

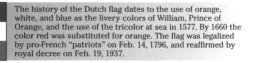

The history of the Dutch flag dates to the use of orange, white, and blue as the livery colors of William, Prince of Orange, and the use of the tricolor at sea in 1577. By 1660 the color red was substituted for orange. The flag was legalized by pro-French "patriots" on Feb. 14, 1796, and reaffirmed by royal decree on Feb. 19, 1937.

Official name: New Zealand
Head of government: Prime Minister
Official languages: English; Maori
Monetary unit: New Zealand dollar
Area: 104,454 sq. mi. (270,534 sq. km.)
Population (2001): 3,861,000
GNP per capita (1999): U.S.$13,990
Principal exports (1998–99): food 47.2%;
  wood and wood products 10.6%;
  machinery 7.7% to: Australia 21.4%;
  U.S. 13.3%; Japan 12.7%

NEW ZEALAND

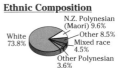

Scale 1: 23,005,000
0   100   200 mi
0   150   300 km

Ethnic Composition

N.Z. Polynesian
(Maori) 9.6%
Other 8.5%
White
73.8%
Mixed race
4.5%
Other Polynesian
3.6%

The Maori of New Zealand accepted British control in 1840,
and a colonial flag was adopted on Jan. 15, 1867. It included
the Union Jack in the canton and the letters "NZ" at the fly
end. Later versions used the Southern Cross. Dominion status
was granted on Sept. 26, 1907, and independence on Nov. 25,
1947, but the flag was unchanged.

NICARAGUA

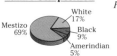

Scale 1: 11,073,000

| 0 | 50 | 100 mi |
| 0 | 80 | 160 km |

Ethnic Composition

Mestizo 69%

White 17%

Black 9%

Amerindian 5%

Official name: Republic of Nicaragua
Head of government: President
Official language: Spanish
Monetary unit: cordoba oro
Area: 50,337 sq. mi. (130,373 sq. km.)
Population (2001): 4,918,000
GNP per capita (1999): U.S.$410
Principal exports (1999): coffee 24.9%;
   manufactured products 19.9%;
   crustaceans 15.4%; beef 7.7%
   to: U.S. 37.7%; El Salvador 12.5%;
   Germany 9.8%

On Aug. 21, 1823, a blue-white-blue flag was adopted by the five member states of the United Provinces of Central America, which included Nicaragua. From the mid-19th century various flag designs were used in Nicaragua, but the old flag was readopted in 1908, with a modified coat of arms, and reaffirmed by law on Aug. 27, 1971.

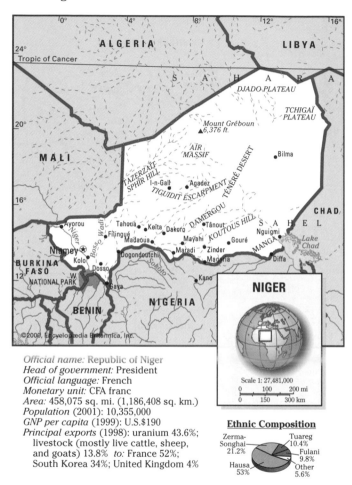

Official name: Republic of Niger
Head of government: President
Official language: French
Monetary unit: CFA franc
Area: 458,075 sq. mi. (1,186,408 sq. km.)
Population (2001): 10,355,000
GNP per capita (1999): U.S.$190
Principal exports (1998): uranium 43.6%;
   livestock (mostly live cattle, sheep,
   and goats) 13.8% *to:* France 52%;
   South Korea 34%; United Kingdom 4%

Ethnic Composition

Zerma-
Songhai
21.2%

Tuareg
10.4%

Fulani
9.8%

Hausa
53%

Other
5.6%

The flag of Niger was chosen on Nov. 23, 1959. The white
color is for purity, innocence, and civic spirit. The orange is
for the Sahara Desert and the heroic efforts of citizens to live
within it, while the orange central disk represents the sun.
The green color stands for agriculture and hope; it is sugges-
tive of the Niger River valley.

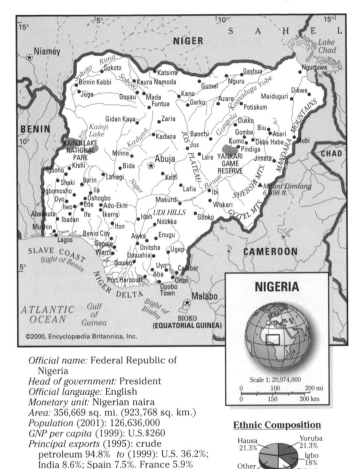

SAHEL

NIGER

Niamey

Lake Chad

Ngurtuwa

Sokoto · Katsina · Gashua

Birnin Kebbi · Kaura Namoda · Gumel · Nguru · Dikwa

Jega · Gusau · Mada · Kano · Azare · Maiduguri

Funtua · Garko · Potiskum

Gidan Kano · Zaria · Dukku · Biu · Asari · Mubi

BENIN

Kaduna · Bauchi · Gombe

Kainji Lake

KAINJI LAKE NATIONAL PARK · Minna · Jos · Kumo · Deba Habe

Igboho · Kishi · Bida · Abuja · Lere · Pindiga · Jimeta

Shaki · Ilorin · Lafiagi · Keffi · YANKARI GAME RESERVE

Ogbomosho · Ila · Lafia · Ibi · Mount Dimlang 6,698 ft.

Oyo · Oshogbo · Makurdi · Wukari

Iwo · Ede · Ado-Ekiti · Gboko

Abeokuta · Ife · Ikerre · Idah · Nsukka

Mushin · Ibadan · Ifon

Benin City · Awka · Enugu

Lagos · Sapele · Onitsha · Ugep

SLAVE COAST · Warri · Umuahia

Bight of Benin · Omoko · Uyo · Calabar

Port Harcourt · Aba · Oron

NIGER DELTA · Opobo Town · Malabo

ATLANTIC OCEAN · Gulf of Guinea · Bight of Biafra

BIOKO (EQUATORIAL GUINEA)

CAMEROON

CHAD

MANDARA MOUNTAINS

SHEBSHI MTS.

GOTEL MTS.

©2000, Encyclopædia Britannica, Inc.

NIGERIA

Scale 1: 20,974,000

0 — 100 — 200 mi
0 — 150 — 300 km

Official name: Federal Republic of Nigeria
Head of government: President
Official language: English
Monetary unit: Nigerian naira
Area: 356,669 sq. mi. (923,768 sq. km.)
Population (2001): 126,636,000
GNP per capita (1999): U.S.$260
Principal exports (1995): crude petroleum 94.8% *to* (1999): U.S. 36.2%; India 8.6%; Spain 7.5%. France 5.9%

Ethnic Composition

Hausa 21.3%
Yoruba 21.3%
Igbo 18%
Fulani 11.2%
Other 28.2%

The Nigerian flag became official upon independence from Britain on Oct. 1, 1960. The flag design is purposefully simple in order not to favor the symbolism of any particular ethnic or religious group. Agriculture is represented by the green stripes while unity and peace are symbolized by the white stripe.

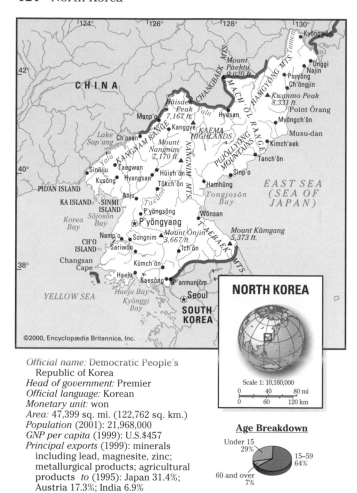

©2000, Encyclopædia Britannica, Inc.

Official name: Democratic People's
  Republic of Korea
Head of government: Premier
Official language: Korean
Monetary unit: won
Area: 47,399 sq. mi. (122,762 sq. km.)
Population (2001): 21,968,000
GNP per capita (1999): U.S.$457
Principal exports (1999): minerals
  including lead, magnesite, zinc;
  metallurgical products; agricultural
  products *to* (1995): Japan 31.4%;
  Austria 17.3%; India 6.9%

NORTH KOREA

Scale 1: 10,160,000

| 0 | 40 | 80 mi |
| 0 | 60 | 120 km |

Age Breakdown

Under 15
29%

15–59
64%

60 and over
7%

The traditional Korean Taeguk flag (still used by South Korea)
was official in North Korea until July 10, 1948, when the current flag was introduced. Its red stripe and star are for the
country's commitment to communism, while blue is said to
stand for a commitment to peace. The white stripes stand for
purity, strength, and dignity.

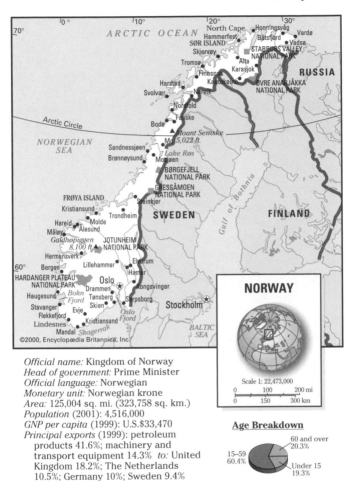

Official name: Kingdom of Norway
Head of government: Prime Minister
Official language: Norwegian
Monetary unit: Norwegian krone
Area: 125,004 sq. mi. (323,758 sq. km.)
Population (2001): 4,516,000
GNP per capita (1999): U.S.$33,470
Principal exports (1999): petroleum
   products 41.6%; machinery and
   transport equipment 14.3% *to:* United
   Kingdom 18.2%; The Netherlands
   10.5%; Germany 10%; Sweden 9.4%

NORWAY

Scale 1: 22,473,000

| 0 | 100 | 200 mi |
| 0 | 150 | 300 km |

Age Breakdown

60 and over
20.3%

15–59
60.4%

Under 15
19.3%

The first distinctive Norwegian flag was created in 1814 while
the country was under Swedish rule. It was based on the red
Danish flag with its white cross. In 1821 the Norwegian parlia-
ment developed the current flag design. From 1844 to 1899,
six years before independence, the official flag included a
symbol of Swedish-Norwegian union.

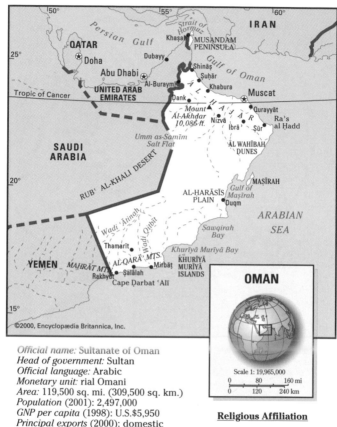

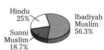

Official name: Sultanate of Oman
Head of government: Sultan
Official language: Arabic
Monetary unit: rial Omani
Area: 119,500 sq. mi. (309,500 sq. km.)
Population (2001): 2,497,000
GNP per capita (1998): U.S.$5,950
Principal exports (2000): domestic
  exports 88.5%, of which petroleum
  82.8%; reexports 11.5% *to:* (non-oil)
  United Arab Emirates 40.1%; Saudi
  Arabia 8.4%; Iran 7.8%

Scale 1: 19,965,000

0   80   160 mi
0   120   240 km

Religious Affiliation

Hindu
25%

Ibadiyah
Muslim
56.3%

Sunni
Muslim
18.7%

The flag dates to Dec. 17, 1970, and it was altered on Nov. 18,
1995. The white is for peace and prosperity, red is for battles,
and green is for the fertility of the land. Unofficially, white
recalls the imamate, red the sultanate, and green Al-Jabal Al-
Akhdar ("The Green Mountain"). The coat of arms has two
swords, a dagger, and a belt.

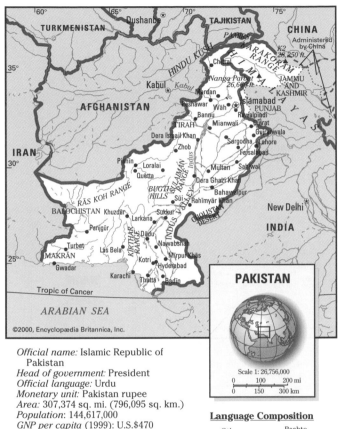

©2000, Encyclopædia Britannica, Inc.

PAKISTAN

Scale 1: 26,756,000

0   100   200 mi
0   150   300 km

Official name: Islamic Republic of Pakistan
Head of government: President
Official language: Urdu
Monetary unit: Pakistan rupee
Area: 307,374 sq. mi. (796,095 sq. km.)
Population: 144,617,000
GNP per capita (1999): U.S.$470
Principal exports (1999–2000): textile fabrics 18.1%; ready-made apparel and made-up articles 14.2%; cotton yarn 12.5% *to* (1998–99): U.S. 21.8%; Hong Kong 7.1%

Language Composition

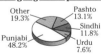

Other 19.3%
Pashto 13.1%
Sindhi 11.8%
Punjabi 48.2%
Urdu 7.6%

On Dec. 30, 1906, the All India Muslim League approved this typically Muslim flag, with its star and crescent. At independence (Aug. 14, 1947) a white stripe was added for minority religious groups. Also symbolized are prosperity and peace by the green and white colors, progress by the crescent, and knowledge and light by the star.

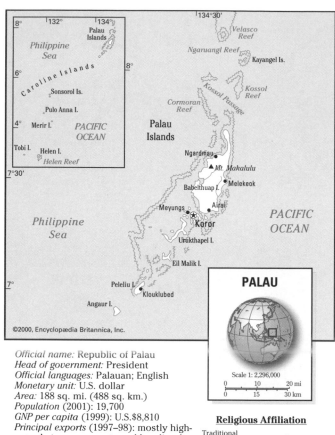

©2000, Encyclopædia Britannica, Inc.

Official name: Republic of Palau
Head of government: President
Official languages: Palauan; English
Monetary unit: U.S. dollar
Area: 188 sq. mi. (488 sq. km.)
Population (2001): 19,700
GNP per capita (1999): U.S.$8,810
Principal exports (1997–98): mostly high-grade tuna; garments and handicrafts
to: mostly Japan

PALAU

Scale 1: 2,296,000
0   10   20 mi
0   15   30 km

Religious Affiliation

Traditional
beliefs
27.1%

Protestant
24.7%

Roman
Catholic
40.7%

Other
7.5%

Approved on Oct. 22, 1980, and hoisted on Jan. 1, 1981, the Palauan flag was left unaltered at independence in 1994. The golden disk represents the full moon, which is said on Palau to be propitious for fishing, planting, and other activities and gives the people "a feeling of warmth, tranquillity, peace, love, and domestic unity."

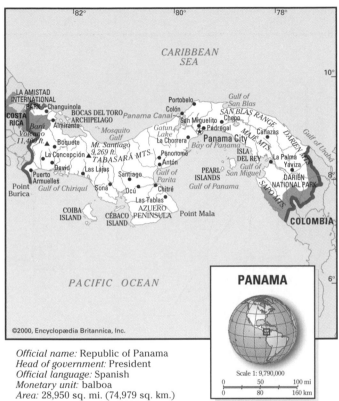

©2000, Encyclopædia Britannica, Inc.

Official name: Republic of Panama
Head of government: President
Official language: Spanish
Monetary unit: balboa
Area: 28,950 sq. mi. (74,979 sq. km.)
Population (2001): 2,903,000
GNP per capita (1999): U.S.$3,080
Principal exports (1998): bananas 19.7%;
   shrimps 19.4%; fish 7.9%; sugar 3.6%;
   clothing 3.6% *to:* U.S. 40.0%; Sweden
   7.2%; Costa Rica 6.6%; Spain 5.4%

Scale 1: 9,790,000
0   50   100 mi
0   80   160 km

Ethnic Composition

Mestizo 64%
Black and Mulatto 14%
White 10%
Amerindian 8%
Asian 4%

The Panamanian flag became official on July 4, 1904, after
independence from Colombia was won through the interven-
tion of the United States, which was determined to construct
the Panama Canal. The flag was influenced by the United
States, and its quartered design was said to symbolize the
power sharing of Panama's two main political parties.

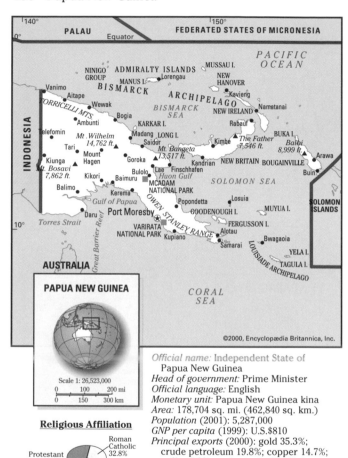

140°

PALAU   Equator   FEDERATED STATES OF MICRONESIA

0°

PACIFIC OCEAN

NINIGO GROUP   ADMIRALTY ISLANDS   MUSSAU I.
Vanimo   MANUS I.   Lorengau   NEW HANOVER
Aitape   BISMARCK   Kavieng
TORRICELLI MTS.   Wewak   ARCHIPELAGO
Bogia   BISMARCK   NEW IRELAND   Namatanai
INDONESIA   Ambunti   SEA
Telefomin   KARKAR I.   Rabaul   BUKA I.
Madang   LONG I.   The Father   Balbi
Mt. Wilhelm   Saidor   7,546 ft.   8,999 ft.
14,762 ft.   Kimbe   Arawa
Tari   Goroka   Mt. Bangeta   Kandrian   BOUGAINVILLE
Kiunga   Mount   13,517 ft.   NEW BRITAIN   Buin
Mt. Bosavi   Hagen   Bulolo   Lae   Finschhafen
7,862 ft.   Kikori   Baimuru   Huon Gulf   SOLOMON SEA
Balimo   MCADAM   Losuia
NATIONAL PARK   SOLOMON
Kerema   Popondetta   MUYUA I.   ISLANDS
Daru   Gulf of Papua   GOODENOUGH I.
Port Moresby   OWEN STANLEY RANGE   FERGUSSON I.
Torres Strait   VARIRATA   Alotau   Bwagaoia
NATIONAL PARK   Kupiano   Samarai
AUSTRALIA   LOUISIADE ARCHIPELAGO   YELA I.
Great Barrier Reef   TAGULA I.

CORAL SEA

©2000, Encyclopædia Britannica, Inc.

PAPUA NEW GUINEA

Scale 1: 26,523,000
0   100   200 mi
0   150   300 km

Religious Affiliation

Protestant 63.8%
Roman Catholic 32.8%
Other 3.4%

Official name: Independent State of
    Papua New Guinea
Head of government: Prime Minister
Official language: English
Monetary unit: Papua New Guinea kina
Area: 178,704 sq. mi. (462,840 sq. km.)
Population (2001): 5,287,000
GNP per capita (1999): U.S.$810
Principal exports (2000): gold 35.3%;
    crude petroleum 19.8%; copper 14.7%;
    coffee 7.0% *to:* Australia 38.1%; Japan
    16.9%; Germany 9.6%; U.S. 6.6%

The formerly German-, British-, and Australian-controlled territory officially recognized its flag on March 11, 1971, and flag usage was extended to ships at independence (Sept. 16, 1975). The colors red and black are shown extensively in local art and clothing. Featured emblems are a bird of paradise and the Southern Cross constellation.

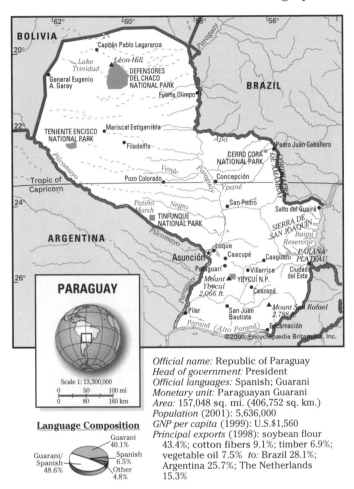

Official name: Republic of Paraguay
Head of government: President
Official languages: Spanish; Guarani
Monetary unit: Paraguayan Guarani
Area: 157,048 sq. mi. (406,752 sq. km.)
Population (2001): 5,636,000
GNP per capita (1999): U.S.$1,560
Principal exports (1998): soybean flour
43.4%; cotton fibers 9.1%; timber 6.9%;
vegetable oil 7.5% *to:* Brazil 28.1%;
Argentina 25.7%; The Netherlands
15.3%

Scale 1: 13,300,000

| 0 | 50 | 100 mi |
| 0 | 80 | 160 km |

Language Composition

Guarani
40.1%

Guarani/
Spanish
48.6%

Spanish
6.5%

Other
4.8%

Under the dictator José Gaspar Rodríguez de Francia
(1814–40) the French colors were adopted for the flag. The
coat of arms (a golden star surrounded by a wreath) is on the
obverse side, but the seal of the treasury (a lion, staff, and
liberty cap, with the motto "Peace and Justice") is on the
reverse; the flag is unique in this respect.

Official name: Republic of Peru
Head of government: President
Official languages: Spanish; Quechua; Aymara
Monetary unit: nuevo sol
Area: 496,225 sq. mi. (1,285,216 sq. km.)
Population (2001): 26,090,000
GNP per capita (1999): U.S.$2,130
Principal exports (1998): gold 16.2%; copper and copper products 13.6%; zinc products 7.8% *to:* U.S. 32.3%; Japan 8.7%; United Kingdom 4.8% Switzerland 4.2%

PERU

Scale 1: 29,277,000
0   100   200 mi
0   150   300 km

Ethnic Composition

Mestizo 32%
White 12%
Aymara 5.4%
Quechua 47.1%
Other 3.5%

Partisans in the early 19th century adopted a red-white-red flag resembling that of Spain, but they soon made its stripes vertical. In 1825 the current design was established. The shield includes figures symbolic of national wealth—the vicuña (a relative of the alpaca), a cinchona tree, and a cornucopia with gold and silver coins.

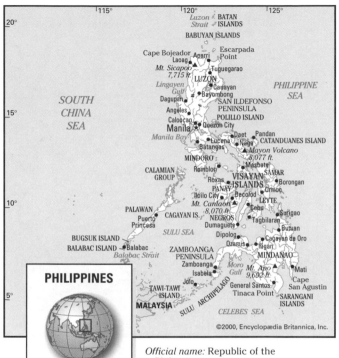

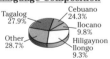

PHILIPPINES

Scale 1: 26,283,000

| 0 | 100 | 200 mi |
| 0 | 150 | 300 km |

Language Composition

Tagalog 27.9%
Cebuano 24.3%
Ilocano 9.8%
Other 28.7%
Hiligaynon Ilongo 9.3%

Official name: Republic of the Philippines
Head of government: President
Official languages: Pilipino; English
Monetary unit: Philippine peso
Area: 115,860 sq. mi. (300,076 sq. km.)
Population (2001): 78,609,000
GNP per capita (1999): U.S.$1,050
Principal exports (1999): electronics 56.2%; garments 6.5%; ignition wiring sets 1.5% *to:* U.S. 29.6%; Japan 13.3%; Taiwan 8.5%; The Netherlands 8.2%

In 1898, during the Spanish-American War, Filipinos established the basic flag in use today; it was officially adopted in 1936. The white triangle is for liberty. The golden sun and stars are for the three main areas of the Philippines: Luzon, the Visayan Islands, and Mindanao. The red color is for courage and the blue color is for sacrifice.

POLAND

Scale 1: 9,837,000

| 0 | 40 | 80 mi |
| 0 | 60 | 120 km |

Age Breakdown

Under 15
22.8%

15–59
61.4%

60 and over
15.8%

Official name: Republic of Poland
Head of government: Prime Minister
Official language: Polish
Monetary unit: zloty
Area: 120,728 sq. mi. (312,685 sq. km.)
Population (2001): 38,647,000
GNP per capita (1999): U.S.$4,070
Principal exports (1999): machinery and
   transport equipment 30.3%; food 8.5%;
   chemicals and chemical products 6.2%
   to: Germany 36.1%; Italy 6.5%; The
   Netherlands 5.3%

The colors of the Polish flag originated in its coat of arms, a
white eagle on a red shield, dating from 1295. The precise
symbolism of the colors is not known, however. Poland's
simple flag of white-red horizontal stripes was adopted on
Aug. 1, 1919. The flag was left unaltered under the Soviet-
allied communist regime (1944 to 1990).

©2000, Encyclopædia Britannica, Inc.

PORTUGAL

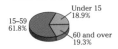

Scale 1: 8,756,000

0	40	80 mi
0	60	120 km

Age Breakdown

Under 15
18.9%

15–59
61.8%

60 and over
19.3%

Official name: Portuguese Republic
Head of government: Prime Minister
Official language: Portuguese
Monetary unit: euro
Area: 35,662 sq. mi. (92,365 sq. km.)
Population (2001): 10,328,000
GNP per capita (1999): U.S.$11,030
Principal exports (1998): machinery and
    transport equipment 32.9%; textiles
    and wearing apparel 25.5%; footwear
    6.6% *to* (1999): Germany 19.8%; Spain
    18.1%; France 13.9%

The central shield includes five smaller shields for a victory
over the Moors in 1139, and a red border with gold castles.
Behind the shield is an armillary sphere (an astronomical
device) recalling world explorations and the kingdom of
Brazil. Red and green were used in many early Portuguese
flags. The current flag dates to June 30, 1911.

136 Qatar

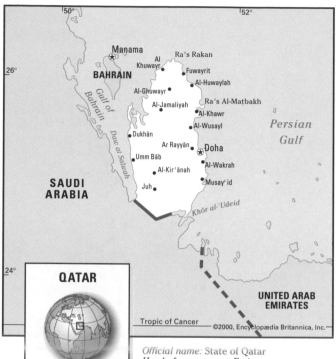

Official name: State of Qatar
Head of government: Emir
Official language: Arabic
Monetary unit: riyal
Area: 4,412 sq. mi. (11,427 sq. km.)
Population (2001): 596,000
GNP per capita (1998): U.S.$11,600
Principal exports (1999): mineral fuels
  and lubricants 81.2%; chemicals and
  chemical products 10.4%;
  manufactured goods 5.9% to (1999):
  Japan 51.0%; South Korea 12.9%;
  Singapore 9.1%

Ethnic Composition

Arab
40%

Other
(Pakistani,
Indian, and
Iranian)
60%

Scale 1: 5,305,000
0   20   40 mi
0   30   60 km

The 1868 treaty between Great Britain and Qatar may have
inspired the creation of the flag. Qataris chose mauve or
maroon instead of red (a more typical color among Arab
countries) perhaps to distinguish it from the flag used in
Bahrain. Passages from the Quran, in Arabic script, have
sometimes been added to the flag.

Official name: Romania
Head of government: Prime Minister
Official language: Romanian
Monetary unit: Romanian leu
Area: 91,699 sq. mi. (237,500 sq. km.)
Population (2001): 22,413,000
GNP per capita (1999): U.S.$2,250
Principal exports (1996): textiles 20.8%;
  mineral products 9.2%; chemicals
  9.0%; machinery 8.0% *to:* Germany
  18.2%; Italy 16.6%; France 5.6%; United
  Kingdom 2.9%

Scale 1: 10,966,000

| 0 | 50 | 100 mi |
| 0 | 80 | 160 km |

Ethnic Composition

Romanian
89.4%

Hungarian
7.1%

Other
3.5%

In 1834 Walachia, an ancient region of Romania, chose a naval ensign with stripes of red, blue, and yellow. The modern Romanian tricolor was created in 1848 and flown for a brief time. In 1867 Romania reestablished the vertical tricolor, and with the fall of the 20th-century communist regime, it was defined on Dec. 27, 1989.

Ethnic Composition

Other
14.7%

Tatar
3.8%

Russian
81.5%

Tsar Peter the Great visited the Netherlands in order to modernize the Russian navy, and in 1699 he chose a Dutch-influenced flag for Russian ships. The flag soon became popular on land as well. After the Russian Revolution it was replaced by the communist red banner, but the tricolor again became official on Aug. 21, 1991.

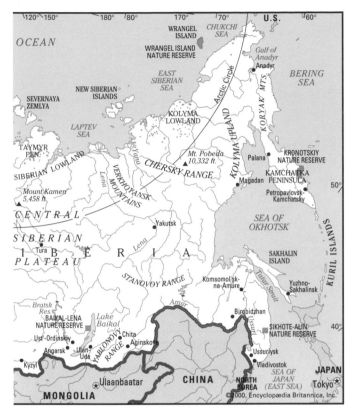

Official name: Russian Federation
Head of government: Prime Minister
Official language: Russian
Monetary unit: ruble
Area: 6,592,800 sq. mi. (17,075,400 sq. km.)
Population (2001): 144,417,000
GNP per capita (1999): U.S.$2,250
Principal exports (1999): fuels and lubricants 43.8%; ferrous and non-ferrous metals 20.5% *to:* U.S. 8.9%; Germany 8.5%; Ukraine 6.6%; Belarus 5.2%

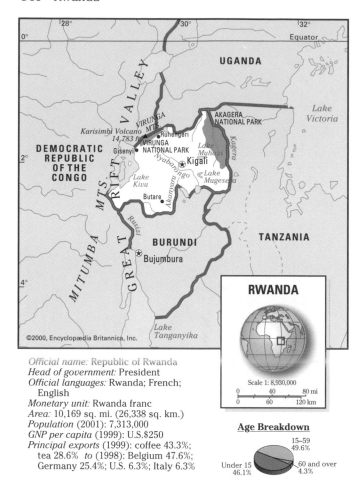

©2000, Encyclopædia Britannica, Inc.

Official name: Republic of Rwanda
Head of government: President
Official languages: Rwanda; French;
  English
Monetary unit: Rwanda franc
Area: 10,169 sq. mi. (26,338 sq. km.)
Population (2001): 7,313,000
GNP per capita (1999): U.S.$250
Principal exports (1999): coffee 43.3%;
  tea 28.6% *to* (1998): Belgium 47.6%;
  Germany 25.4%; U.S. 6.3%; Italy 6.3%

RWANDA

Scale 1: 8,930,000

| 0 | 40 | 80 mi |
| 0 | 60 | 120 km |

Age Breakdown

15–59
49.6%

Under 15
46.1%

60 and over
4.3%

On Jan. 28, 1961, the republic was proclaimed under a tricolor of red, yellow, and green—the Pan African colors. In Rwanda these symbolize the blood shed for liberation, peace and tranquility, and hope and optimism. In 1961 a black "R" was added to distinguish the flag from that of Guinea and to stand for Rwanda, revolution, and referendum.

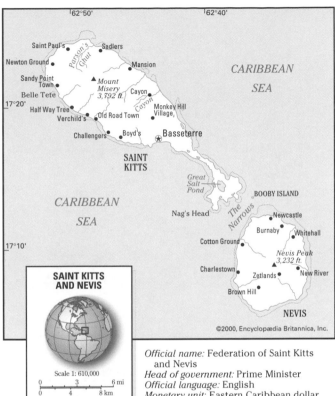

62°50'　62°40'

Saint Paul's　Sadlers
Newton Ground
Parson's Ghut　Mansion
Sandy Point Town
▲ Mount Misery 3,792 ft.　Cayon
Belle Tete
17°20'　Monkey Hill Village
Half Way Tree　Old Road Town
Verchild's
Challengers　Boyd's　★ Basseterre

CARIBBEAN SEA

SAINT KITTS

Great Salt Pond

BOOBY ISLAND

CARIBBEAN SEA

Nag's Head　The Narrows
Newcastle
Burnaby　Whitehall
17°10'
Cotton Ground
Nevis Peak 3,232 ft. ▲
Charlestown　Zetlands　New River
Brown Hill

NEVIS

©2000, Encyclopædia Britannica, Inc.

SAINT KITTS AND NEVIS

Scale 1: 610,000
0　3　6 mi
0　4　8 km

Religious Affiliation

Protestant 76.4%
Other 12.9%
Roman Catholic 10.7%

Official name: Federation of Saint Kitts and Nevis
Head of government: Prime Minister
Official language: English
Monetary unit: Eastern Caribbean dollar
Area: 104.0 sq. mi. (269.4 sq. km.)
Population (2001): 38,800
GNP per capita (1999): U.S.$6,330
Principal exports (1997): food 56.0%; machinery and transportation equipment (mostly electronic goods) 31.7% *to* (1997): U.S. 55.0%; United Kingdom 32.6%

On Sept. 18, 1983, at the time of its independence from Britain, St. Kitts and Nevis hoisted the current flag. It has green (for fertility), red (for the struggle against slavery and colonialism), and black (for African heritage). The yellow flanking stripes are for sunshine, and the two stars, one for each island, are for hope and liberty.

142 Saint Lucia

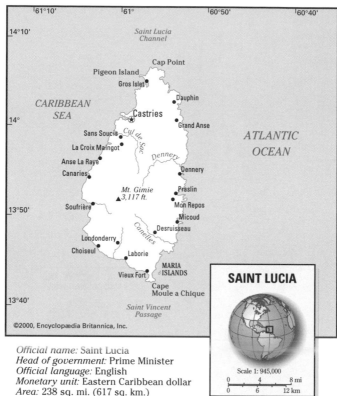

SAINT LUCIA

Scale 1: 945,000

0 ____ 4 ____ 8 mi
0 ____ 6 ____ 12 km

Official name: Saint Lucia
Head of government: Prime Minister
Official language: English
Monetary unit: Eastern Caribbean dollar
Area: 238 sq. mi. (617 sq. km.)
Population (2001): 158,000
GNP per capita (1999): U.S.$3,820
Principal exports (1998): bananas 50.5%;
  clothing 7.5%; paper and paperboard
  5.9% *to:* United Kingdom 60.0%; U.S.
  21.0%; Caricom countries 16.3%

Ethnic Composition

Black 90.5%

Mixed 5.5%

Other 4%

The flag was hoisted on March 1, 1967, when the former colony assumed a status of association with the United Kingdom; it was slightly altered in 1979. The blue represents Atlantic and Caribbean waters. The white and black colors are for racial harmony, while the black triangle also represents volcanoes. The yellow triangle is for sunshine.

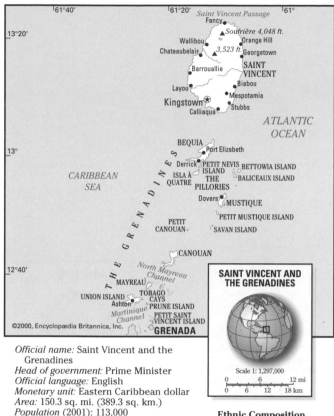

Official name: Saint Vincent and the Grenadines
Head of government: Prime Minister
Official language: English
Monetary unit: Eastern Caribbean dollar
Area: 150.3 sq. mi. (389.3 sq. km.)
Population (2001): 113,000
GNP per capita (1999): U.S.$2,640
Principal exports (1998): domestic exports 94.1%, of which bananas 41.5%; reexports 5.9% *to:* Caricom countries 49.1%; United Kingdom 42.2%

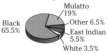

Scale 1: 1,297,000

0   6   12 mi

0   6   12   18 km

Ethnic Composition

Mulatto 19%
Black 65.5%
Other 6.5%
East Indian 5.5%
White 3.5%

At independence from Britain in 1979 a national flag was designed, but it was replaced by the current flag on Oct. 22, 1985. The three green diamonds are arranged in the form of a V. Green is for the rich vegetation and the vitality of the people, yellow is for sand and personal warmth, and blue is for sea and sky.

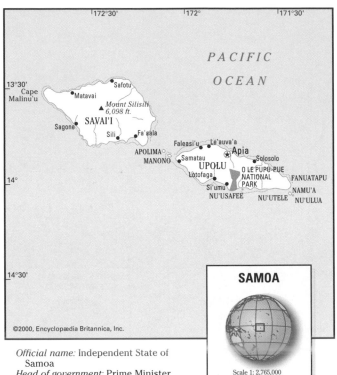

172°30' | 172° | 171°30'

PACIFIC

OCEAN

13°30'
Cape
Malinu'u

Safotu

Matavai

▲ *Mount Silisili*
6,098 ft.

SAVAI'I

Sagone

Sili

Fa'aala

Faleasi'u Le'auva'a
APOLIMA○ ·Apia ⊛
MANONO **UPOLU** Samatau Solosolo

14°
Lotofaga O LE PUPU-PUE NATIONAL PARK FANUATAPU

Si'umu NAMU'A
NU'USAFEE NU'UTELE NU'ULUA

14°30'

©2000, Encyclopædia Britannica, Inc.

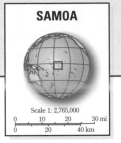

SAMOA

Scale 1: 2,765,000

0   10   20   30 mi
0   20   40 km

Official name: Independent State of
  Samoa
Head of government: Prime Minister
Official languages: Samoan; English
Monetary unit: tala
Area: 1,093 sq. mi. (2,831 sq. km.)
Population (2001): 179,000
GNP per capita (1999): U.S.$1,070
Principal exports (1997): fresh fish 33.0%;
  copra 21.1%; coconut oil 18.1%;
  coconut cream 12.8% *to:* New Zealand
  48.1%; American Samoa (dependency)
  15.3%; Australia 9.2%

Religious Affiliation

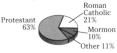

Roman
Catholic
21%

Protestant
63%

Mormon
10%

Other 11%

The first national flag of Samoa may date to 1873. Under
British administration, a version of the current flag was introduced on May 26, 1948. On Feb. 2, 1949, a fifth star was added
to the Southern Cross. White in the flag is said to stand for
purity, blue for freedom, and red for courage. The flag was
left unaltered upon independence in 1962.

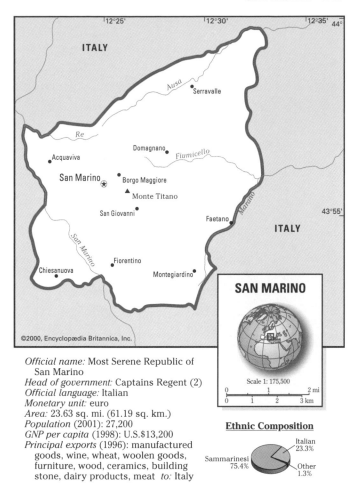

Official name: Most Serene Republic of San Marino
Head of government: Captains Regent (2)
Official language: Italian
Monetary unit: euro
Area: 23.63 sq. mi. (61.19 sq. km.)
Population (2001): 27,200
GNP per capita (1998): U.S.$13,200
Principal exports (1996): manufactured goods, wine, wheat, woolen goods, furniture, wood, ceramics, building stone, dairy products, meat *to:* Italy

SAN MARINO

Scale 1: 175,500

Ethnic Composition

Italian 23.3%
Sammarinesi 75.4%
Other 1.3%

The colors of the flag, blue and white, were first used in the national cockade in 1797. The coat of arms in its present form was adopted on April 6, 1862, when the crown was added as a symbol of national sovereignty. Also in the coat of arms are three towers (Guaita, Cesta, and Montale) from the fortifications on Mount Titano.

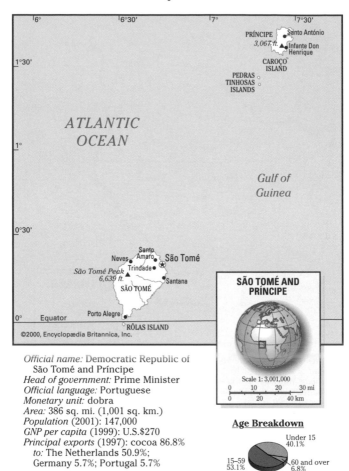

6°   6°30'   7°   7°30'

PRÍNCIPE — Santo António
3,067 ft. ▲ Infante Don Henrique

CAROÇO ISLAND

PEDRAS TINHOSAS ISLANDS

1°30'

ATLANTIC OCEAN

1°

Gulf of Guinea

0°30'

Santo
Neves — Amaro — São Tomé
São Tomé Peak ▲ Trindade
6,639 ft. — Santana
SÃO TOMÉ

Porto Alegre

0°   Equator   RÔLAS ISLAND

©2000, Encyclopædia Britannica, Inc.

Official name: Democratic Republic of São Tomé and Príncipe
Head of government: Prime Minister
Official language: Portuguese
Monetary unit: dobra
Area: 386 sq. mi. (1,001 sq. km.)
Population (2001): 147,000
GNP per capita (1999): U.S.$270
Principal exports (1997): cocoa 86.8%
  to: The Netherlands 50.9%;
  Germany 5.7%; Portugal 5.7%

SÃO TOMÉ AND PRÍNCIPE

Scale 1: 3,001,000

0   10   20   30 mi
0   20   40 km

Age Breakdown

Under 15
40.1%

15–59
53.1%

60 and over
6.8%

The national flag was adopted upon independence from Portugal on July 12, 1975. Its colors are associated with Pan-African independence. The red triangle stands for equality and the nationalist movement. The stars are for the African population living on the nation's two main islands. Green is for vegetation and yellow is for the tropical sun.

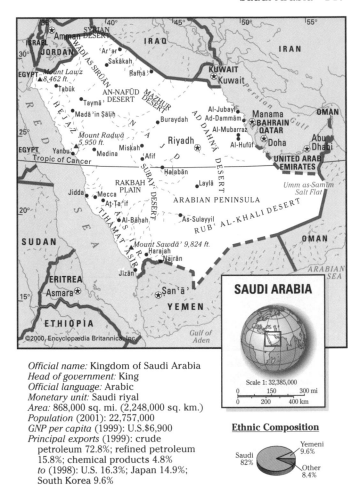

Official name: Kingdom of Saudi Arabia
Head of government: King
Official language: Arabic
Monetary unit: Saudi riyal
Area: 868,000 sq. mi. (2,248,000 sq. km.)
Population (2001): 22,757,000
GNP per capita (1999): U.S.$6,900
Principal exports (1999): crude
petroleum 72.8%; refined petroleum
15.8%; chemical products 4.8%
to (1998): U.S. 16.3%; Japan 14.9%;
South Korea 9.6%

Ethnic Composition

Saudi 82%
Yemeni 9.6%
Other 8.4%

The Saudi flag, made official in 1932 but altered in 1968, originated in the military campaigns of Muhammad. The color green is associated with Fatima, the Prophet's daughter, and the Arabic inscription is translated as "There is no God but Allah and Muhammad is the Prophet of Allah." The saber symbolizes the militancy of the faith.

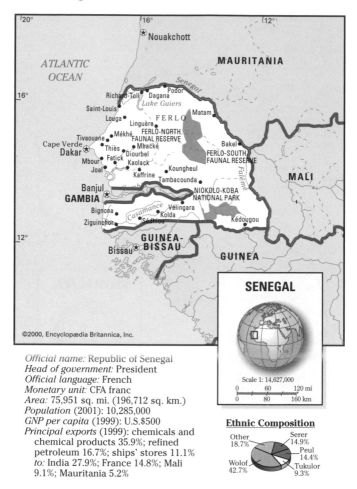

©2000, Encyclopædia Britannica, Inc.

Official name: Republic of Senegal
Head of government: President
Official language: French
Monetary unit: CFA franc
Area: 75,951 sq. mi. (196,712 sq. km.)
Population (2001): 10,285,000
GNP per capita (1999): U.S.$500
Principal exports (1999): chemicals and chemical products 35.9%; refined petroleum 16.7%; ships' stores 11.1% *to:* India 27.9%; France 14.8%; Mali 9.1%; Mauritania 5.2%

Scale 1: 14,627,000

0   60   120 mi
0   80   160 km

Ethnic Composition

Other 18.7%
Serer 14.9%
Peul 14.4%
Tukulor 9.3%
Wolof 42.7%

In a federation with French Sudan (now Mali) on April 4, 1959, Senegal used a flag with a human figure in the center. After the federation broke up in August 1960, Senegal substituted a green star for the central figure. Green is for hope and religion, yellow is for natural riches and labor, and red is for independence, life, and socialism.

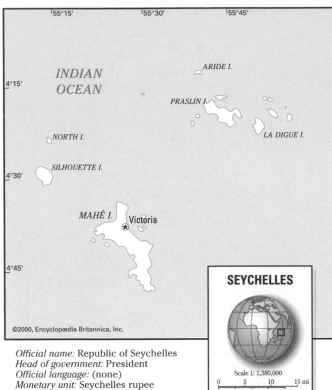

```
                    55°15'        55°30'        55°45'

    INDIAN                              ARIDE I.
    OCEAN
                                  PRASLIN I.
  4°15'
          NORTH I.                              LA DIGUE I.

        SILHOUETTE I.
  4°30'

        MAHÉ I.    Victoria

  4°45'

  ©2000, Encyclopædia Britannica, Inc.
```

Official name: Republic of Seychelles
Head of government: President
Official language: (none)
Monetary unit: Seychelles rupee
Area: 176 sq. mi. (455 sq. km.)
Population (2001): 80,600
GNP per capita (1999): U.S.$6,500
Principal exports (1999): canned tuna
   70.2%; petroleum products 21.9%;
   other fish, including dried shark fins
   1.9%; *to* (1997): France 29.2%;
   Germany 27.3%; Italy 24.0

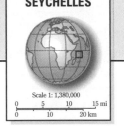

SEYCHELLES

Scale 1: 1,380,000
0   5   10   15 mi
0   10   20 km

Age Breakdown

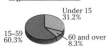

Under 15
31.2%

15–59
60.3%

60 and over
8.3%

The former British colony underwent a revolution in 1977.
The government was democratized in 1993, and on Jan. 8,
1996, a new flag was designed. The blue color is for sky and
sea, yellow is for the sun, red is for the people and their work
for unity and love, white is for social justice and harmony,
and green is for the land and natural environment.

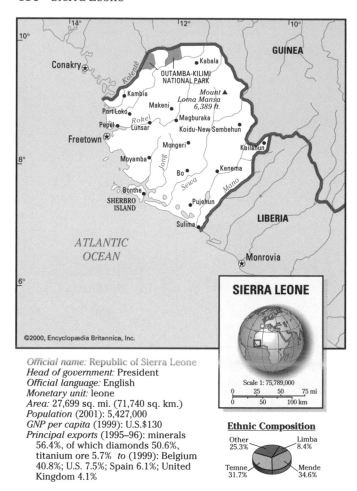

©2000, Encyclopædia Britannica, Inc.

Official name: Republic of Sierra Leone
Head of government: President
Official language: English
Monetary unit: leone
Area: 27,699 sq. mi. (71,740 sq. km.)
Population (2001): 5,427,000
GNP per capita (1999): U.S.$130
Principal exports (1995–96): minerals 56.4%, of which diamonds 50.6%, titanium ore 5.7% *to* (1999): Belgium 40.8%; U.S. 7.5%; Spain 6.1%; United Kingdom 4.1%

SIERRA LEONE

Scale 1: 75,789,000

Ethnic Composition

Other 25.3%
Limba 8.4%
Temne 31.7%
Mende 34.6%

Under British colonial control Sierra Leone was founded as a home for freed slaves. With independence on April 27, 1961, the flag was hoisted. Its stripes stand for agriculture and the mountains (green); unity and justice (white); and the aspiration to contribute to world peace, especially through the use of the natural harbor at Freetown (blue).

©2000, Encyclopædia Britannica, Inc.

Official name: Republic of Singapore
Head of government: Prime Minister
Official languages: Chinese; Malay; Tamil;
    English
Monetary unit: Singapore dollar
Area: 263.6 sq. mi. (682.7 sq. km.)
Population (2001): 3,322,000
GNP per capita (1999): U.S.$29,660
Principal exports (2000): office machines
    22.6%; petroleum products 7.2%;
    telecommunications apparatus 5.5%
    to (1999): U.S. 19.2%; Malaysia 16.6%;
    Hong Kong 7.7%; Japan 7.4%

SINGAPORE

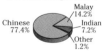

Scale 1: 740,000

0   4   8 mi

0   6   12 km

Ethnic Composition

Malay
14.2%

Chinese
77.4%

Indian
7.2%

Other
1.2%

On Dec. 3, 1959, the flag was acquired, and it was retained
after separation from Malaysia on Aug. 9, 1965. The red and
white stripes stand for universal brotherhood, equality, purity, and virtue. The crescent symbolizes the growth of a young
country, while the five stars are for democracy, peace,
progress, justice, and equality.

©2000, Encyclopædia Britannica, Inc.

Official name: Slovak Republic
Head of government: Prime Minister
Official language: Slovak
Monetary unit: Slovak koruna
Area: 18,933 sq. mi. (49,035 sq. km.)
Population (2001): 5,410,000
GNP per capita (1999): U.S.$3,770
Principal exports (2000): machinery and
  transport equipment 39.5%;
  manufactured goods 27.3% *to* (2000):
  Germany 26.7%; Czech Republic
  20.0%; Italy 9.1%

SLOVAKIA

Scale 1: 6,249,000

0 — 30 — 60 mi
0 — 40 — 80 km

Ethnic Composition

Slovak
85.7%

Hungarian
10.6%

Other
3.7%

In 1189 the kingdom of Hungary (including Slovakia) introduced a double-barred cross in its coat of arms; this symbol
was altered in 1848-49 by Slovak nationalists. After a period of
communist rule, the tricolor was made official in 1989. On
Sept. 3, 1992, the shield was added to the white-blue-red flag
to differentiate it from the flag of Russia.

©2000, Encyclopædia Britannica, Inc.

Official name: Republic of Slovenia
Head of government: Prime Minister
Official language: Slovene
Monetary unit: Slovene tolar
Area: 7,827 sq. mi. (20,273 sq. km.)
Population (2001): 1,991,000
GNP per capita (1999): U.S.$10,000
Principal exports (2000): machinery and
   transport equipment 36.0%;
   manufactured goods 27.3%;
   to: Germany 27.2%; Italy 13.6%;
   Croatia 7.9%; Austria 7.5%;
   France 7.1%

SLOVENIA

Scale 1: 4,314,000

| 0 | 20 | 40 mi |
| 0 | 30 | 60 km |

Age Breakdown

60 and over
18.3%

15–59
63.9%

Under 15
17.8%

Under the current flag Slovenia proclaimed independence on
June 25, 1991, but it was opposed for a time by the Yugoslav
army. The flag is the same as that of Russia and Slovakia
except for the coat of arms. It depicts the peaks of Triglav
(the nation's highest mountain), the waves of the Adriatic
coast, and three stars on a blue background.

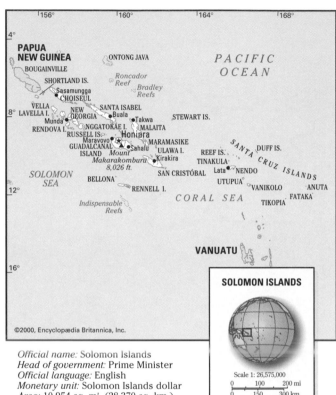

©2000, Encyclopædia Britannica, Inc.

SOLOMON ISLANDS

Scale 1: 26,575,000

0 — 100 — 200 mi
0 — 150 — 300 km

Official name: Solomon Islands
Head of government: Prime Minister
Official language: English
Monetary unit: Solomon Islands dollar
Area: 10,954 sq. mi. (28,370 sq. km.)
Population (2001): 480,000
GNP per capita (1999): U.S.$750
Principal exports (1996): timber products
   60.6%; fish products 18.3%; palm oil
   products 10.9% *to:* Japan 40.1%; South
   Korea 19.4%; United Kingdom 18.4%;
   Thailand 3.8%

Age Breakdown

Under 15
43.7%

15–59
52%

60 and over
4.3%

The flag was introduced on Nov. 18, 1977, eight months
before independence from Britain. The yellow stripe stands
for the sun. The green triangle is for the trees and crops of
the fertile land, while the blue triangle symbolizes rivers,
rain, and the ocean. The five stars represented the original
five districts of the island.

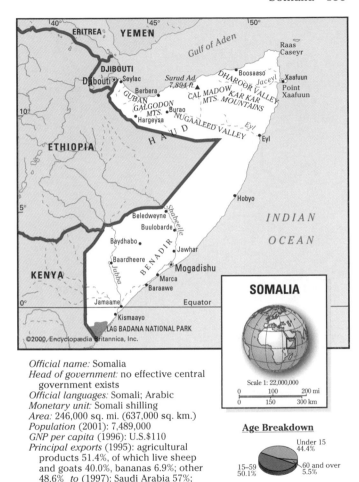

©2000, Encyclopædia Britannica, Inc.

Official name: Somalia
Head of government: no effective central
  government exists
Official languages: Somali; Arabic
Monetary unit: Somali shilling
Area: 246,000 sq. mi. (637,000 sq. km.)
Population (2001): 7,489,000
GNP per capita (1996): U.S.$110
Principal exports (1995): agricultural
  products 51.4%, of which live sheep
  and goats 40.0%, bananas 6.9%; other
  48.6% *to* (1997): Saudi Arabia 57%;
  United Arab Emirates 15%

SOMALIA

Scale 1: 22,000,000

| 0 | 100 | 200 mi |
| 0 | 150 | 300 km |

Age Breakdown

Under 15
44.4%

15–59
50.1%

60 and over
5.5%

From the mid-19th century, areas in the Horn of Africa with
Somali populations were divided between Ethiopia, France,
Britain, and Italy. On Oct. 12, 1954, with the partial unifica-
tion of these areas, the flag was adopted with a white star,
each point referring to a Somali homeland. The colors were
influenced by the colors of the United Nations.

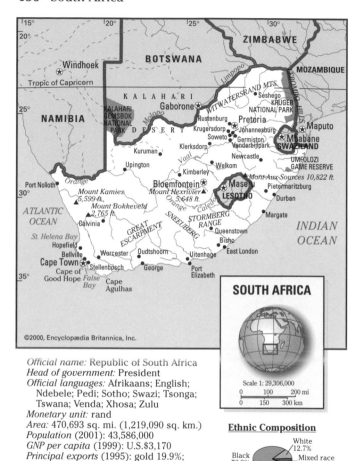

Tropic of Capricorn

NAMIBIA

BOTSWANA

ZIMBABWE

MOZAMBIQUE

• Windhoek

KALAHARI

Gaborone

WITWATERSRAND MTS.

• Sesego

KRUGER
NATIONAL PARK

Rustenburg

Pretoria

• Maputo

Krugersdorp

Johannesburg

• Mbabane

Soweto

Germiston

SWAZILAND

Klerksdorp

Vanderbijlpark

• Kuruman

Newcastle

UMFOLOZI
GAME RESERVE

Upington

Welkom

Mont-Aux-Sources 10,822 ft.

Kimberley

Port Nolloth

Orange

Bloemfontein

Maseru

Pietermaritzburg

Mount Kamies
5,599 ft.

Mount Hexrivier
5,648 ft.

LESOTHO

Durban

ATLANTIC
OCEAN

Mount Bokkeveld
2,765 ft.

STORMBERG
RANGE

Margate

Calvinia

GREAT
ESCARPMENT

SNEEUBERG

Queenstown

INDIAN
OCEAN

St. Helena Bay

Hopefield

Worcester

Oudtshoorn

Bisho

Bellville

Uitenhage

East London

Cape Town

Stellenbosch

George

Port
Elizabeth

Cape of
Good Hope

False
Bay

Cape
Agulhas

©2000, Encyclopædia Britannica, Inc.

SOUTH AFRICA

Scale 1: 29,306,000

0   100   200 mi

0   150   300 km

Official name: Republic of South Africa
Head of government: President
Official languages: Afrikaans; English;
  Ndebele; Pedi; Sotho; Swazi; Tsonga;
  Tswana; Venda; Xhosa; Zulu
Monetary unit: rand
Area: 470,693 sq. mi. (1,219,090 sq. km.)
Population (2001): 43,586,000
GNP per capita (1999): U.S.$3,170
Principal exports (1995): gold 19.9%;
  metal products 15.4%; gem diamonds
  9.8% *to* (1999): United Kingdom 8.3%;
  U.S. 8.2%; Germany 7.0%

Ethnic Composition

White
12.7%

Black
76.3%

Mixed race
8.5%

Asian
2.5%

With the decline of apartheid, the flag was hoisted on April
27, 1994, and confirmed in 1996. Its six colors collectively represent Zulus, English or Afrikaners, Muslims, supporters of
the African National Congress, and other groups. The Y-sym-
bol stands for "merging history and present political realities"
into a united and prosperous future.

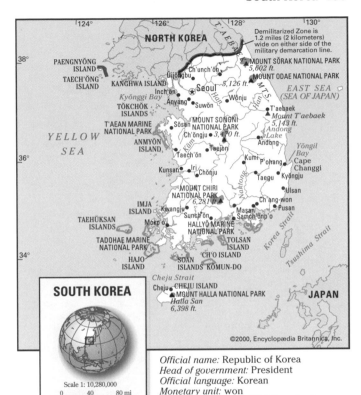

124° 126° 128° 130°

NORTH KOREA

Demilitarized Zone is 1.2 miles (2 kilometers) wide on either side of the military demarcation line.

38°

PAENGNYŎNG ISLAND
TAECH'ŎNG ISLAND

KANGHWA ISLAND
Ŭijŏngbu
Ch'unch'ŏn
MOUNT SŎRAK NATIONAL PARK 5,602 ft.
MOUNT ODAE NATIONAL PARK

Kyŏnggi Bay
Inch'ŏn
Seoul
5,126 ft.
EAST SEA (SEA OF JAPAN)

TŎKCHŎK ISLANDS
Anyang
Suwŏn
Wŏnju

T'AEAN MARINE NATIONAL PARK
Sŏsan
MOUNT SONGNI NATIONAL PARK
Ch'ŏngju • 3,470 ft.
T'aebaek
Mount T'aebaek 5,143 ft.

YELLOW SEA
ANMYŎN ISLAND
Taejŏn
Andong Lake
Andong
Yŏngil Bay

36°
Taech'ŏn
Kŭm
Kumi
P'ohang
Cape Changgi

Kunsan
Iri
Chŏnju
Taegu
Kyŏngju

MOUNT CHIRI NATIONAL PARK 6,281 ft.
Ulsan
Ch'ang-wŏn

IMJA ISLAND
Kwangju
Masan
Pusan

TAEHŬKSAN ISLANDS
Mokp'o
Sunch'ŏn
Samch'ŏnp'o

HALLYŎ MARINE NATIONAL PARK
Korea Strait

TADOHAE MARINE NATIONAL PARK
TOLSAN ISLAND

34°
HAJO ISLAND
SOAN ISLANDS
'CH'O ISLAND
KŎMUN-DO

Cheju Strait

SOUTH KOREA

Cheju
CHEJU ISLAND
MOUNT HALLA NATIONAL PARK
Halla San 6,398 ft.

JAPAN

©2000, Encyclopædia Britannica, Inc.

Scale 1: 10,280,000
0   40   80 mi
0   60   120 km

Age Breakdown

Under 15 23.2%
15–59 67.8%
60 and over 9%

Official name: Republic of Korea
Head of government: President
Official language: Korean
Monetary unit: won
Area: 38,402 sq. mi. (99,461 sq. km.)
Population (2001): 47,676,000
GNP per capita (1999): U.S.$8,490
Principal exports (2000): electric and electronic products 36.0%; machinery and transport equipment 18.2%; chemicals 7.0% *to:* U.S. 21.8%; Japan 11.9%; China 10.7%

The flag was adopted in August 1882. Its white background is for peace, while the central emblem represents yin-yang (Korean: *um-yang*), the duality of the universe. The black bars recall sun, moon, earth, heaven and other Confucian principles. Outlawed under Japanese rule, the flag was revived in 1945 and slightly modified in 1950 and 1984.

©2000, Encyclopædia Britannica, Inc.

Official name: Kingdom of Spain
Head of government: Prime Minister
Official language: Castilian Spanish
Monetary unit: euro
Area: 195,364 sq. mi. (505,990 sq. km.)
Population (2001): 40,144,000
GNP per capita (1999): U.S.$14,800
Principal exports (2000): transport
  equipment 19.5%; agricultural
  products 12.9%; machinery 7.9%
  to: France 19.4%; Germany 12.4%;
  Portugal 9.4%; Italy 8.8%

SPAIN

Scale 1: 16,741,000

0   75   150 mi
0   100   200 km

Language Composition

Catalan 16.9%
Galician 6.4%
Spanish 74.4%
Other 2.3%

The colors of the flag have no official symbolic meaning.
Introduced in 1785 by King Charles III, the flag was changed
only under the Spanish Republic (1931–39). Under different
regimes, however, the coat of arms has been altered. The current design dates from Dec. 18, 1981, with the death of
Francisco Franco and the resurgence of democracy.

©2000, Encyclopædia Britannica, Inc.

Official name: Democratic Socialist
Republic of Sri Lanka
Head of government: President
Official languages: Sinhala; Tamil
Monetary unit: Sri Lanka rupee
Area: 25,332 sq. mi. (65,610 sq. km.)
Population (2001): 19,399,000
GNP per capita (1998): U.S.$810
Principal exports (1999): clothing and
accessories 52.7%; tea 13.5%; gems
4.7% *to:* U.S. 39.6%; United Kingdom
13.3%; Germany 4.8%; Japan 3.5%

SRI LANKA

Scale 1: 7,798,000

0   30   60 mi
0   50   100 km

Ethnic Composition

Tamil
8.9%
Sinhalese
82.7%
Sri Lankan
Moor
7.7%
Other
0.7%

From the 5th century BC the Lion flag was a symbol of the
Sinhalese people. The flag was replaced by the Union Jack in
1815 but readopted upon independence in 1948. The stripes
of green (for Muslims) and orange (for Hindus) were added in
1951. In 1972 four leaves of the Bo tree were added as a symbol of Buddhism; the leaves were altered in 1978.

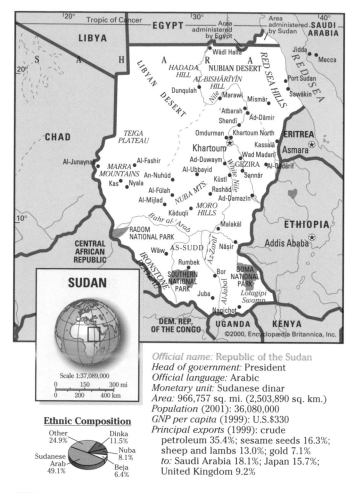

Official name: Republic of the Sudan
Head of government: President
Official language: Arabic
Monetary unit: Sudanese dinar
Area: 966,757 sq. mi. (2,503,890 sq. km.)
Population (2001): 36,080,000
GNP per capita (1999): U.S.$330
Principal exports (1999): crude petroleum 35.4%; sesame seeds 16.3%; sheep and lambs 13.0%; gold 7.1% *to:* Saudi Arabia 18.1%; Japan 15.7%; United Kingdom 9.2%

Ethnic Composition

Other 24.9%
Dinka 11.5%
Nuba 8.1%
Beja 6.4%
Sudanese Arab 49.1%

The flag was first hoisted on May 20, 1970. It uses Pan-Arab colors. Black is for al-Mahdi (a leader in the 1800s) and the name of the country (sudan in Arabic means black); white recalls the revolutionary flag of 1924 and suggests peace and optimism; red is for patriotic martyrs, socialism, and progress; and green is for prosperity and Islam.

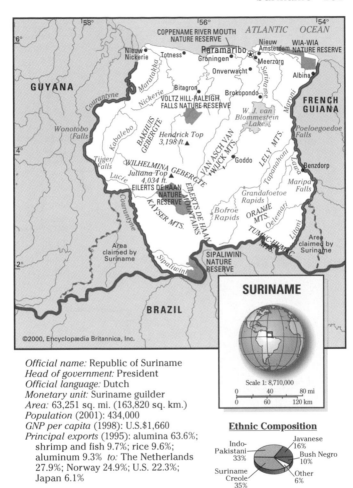

©2000, Encyclopædia Britannica, Inc.

Official name: Republic of Suriname
Head of government: President
Official language: Dutch
Monetary unit: Suriname guilder
Area: 63,251 sq. mi. (163,820 sq. km.)
Population (2001): 434,000
GNP per capita (1998): U.S.$1,660
Principal exports (1995): alumina 63.6%;
  shrimp and fish 9.7%; rice 9.6%;
  aluminum 9.3% *to:* The Netherlands
  27.9%; Norway 24.9%; U.S. 22.3%;
  Japan 6.1%

SURINAME

Scale 1: 8,710,000

| 0 | 40 | 80 mi |
| 0 | 60 | 120 km |

Ethnic Composition

Indo-
Pakistani
33%

Javanese
16%

Bush Negro
10%

Other
6%

Suriname
Creole
35%

Adopted on Nov. 21, 1975, four days before independence
from the Dutch, the flag of Suriname features green stripes for
jungles and agriculture, white for justice and freedom, and
red for the progressive spirit of a young nation. The yellow
star is symbolic of the unity of the country, its golden future,
and the people's spirit of sacrifice.

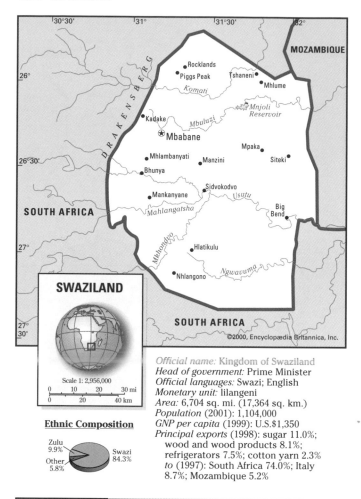

©2000, Encyclopædia Britannica, Inc.

SWAZILAND

Scale 1: 2,956,000

0   10   20   30 mi
0   20   40 km

Ethnic Composition

Zulu 9.9%
Other 5.8%
Swazi 84.3%

Official name: Kingdom of Swaziland
Head of government: Prime Minister
Official languages: Swazi; English
Monetary unit: lilangeni
Area: 6,704 sq. mi. (17,364 sq. km.)
Population (2001): 1,104,000
GNP per capita (1999): U.S.$1,350
Principal exports (1998): sugar 11.0%;
   wood and wood products 8.1%;
   refrigerators 7.5%; cotton yarn 2.3%
   to (1997): South Africa 74.0%; Italy
   8.7%; Mozambique 5.2%

The flag dates to the creation of a military banner in 1941,
when Swazi troops were preparing for the Allied invasion of
Italy. On April 25, 1967, it was hoisted as the national flag.
The crimson stripe stands for past battles, yellow for mineral
wealth, and blue for peace. Featured are a Swazi war shield,
two spears, and a "fighting stick."

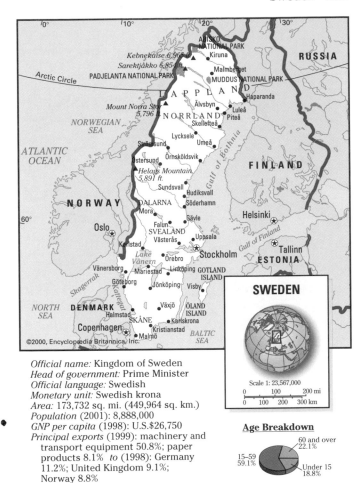

Official name: Kingdom of Sweden
Head of government: Prime Minister
Official language: Swedish
Monetary unit: Swedish krona
Area: 173,732 sq. mi. (449,964 sq. km.)
Population (2001): 8,888,000
GNP per capita (1998): U.S.$26,750
Principal exports (1999): machinery and
  transport equipment 50.8%; paper
  products 8.1% *to* (1998): Germany
  11.2%; United Kingdom 9.1%;
  Norway 8.8%

Scale 1: 23,567,000

| 0 | 100 | 200 mi |
| 0 | 100 | 200 | 300 km |

Age Breakdown

60 and over
22.1%

15–59
59.1%

Under 15
18.8%

From the 14th century the coat of arms of Sweden had a blue
field with three golden crowns, and the earlier Folkung
dynasty used a shield of blue and white wavy stripes with a
gold lion. The off-center "Scandinavian cross" was influenced
by the flag of the rival kingdom of Denmark. The current flag
law was adopted on July 1, 1906.

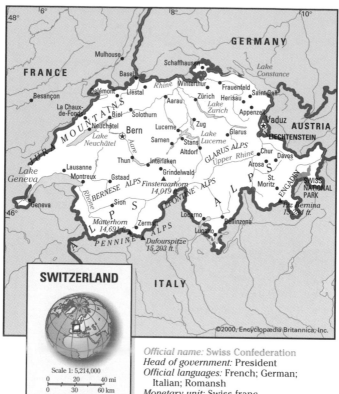

©2000, Encyclopædia Britannica, Inc.

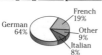

SWITZERLAND

Scale 1: 5,214,000

```
0      20      40 mi
0    30      60 km
```

Language Composition

French
19%

German
64%

Other
9%

Italian
8%

Official name: Swiss Confederation
Head of government: President
Official languages: French; German;
  Italian; Romansh
Monetary unit: Swiss franc
Area: 15,940 sq. mi. (41,284 sq. km.)
Population (2001): 7,222,000
GNP per capita (1999): U.S.$38,380
Principal exports (2000): machinery
  29.3%; chemical products 28.4%;
  precision instruments, watches, and
  jewelry 16.2% *to:* Germany 22.2%; U.S.
  11.6%; France 9.0%

The Swiss flag is ultimately based on the war flag of the Holy Roman
Empire. Schwyz, one of the original three cantons of the Swiss
Confederation, placed a narrow white cross in the corner of its flag in
1240. This was also used in 1339 at the Battle of Laupen. Following the
1848 constitution, the flag was recognized by the army, and it was
established as the national flag on land on Dec. 12, 1889.

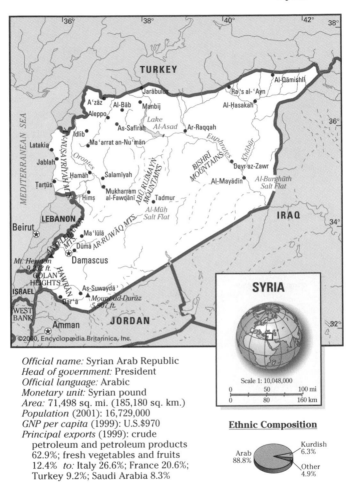

Official name: Syrian Arab Republic
Head of government: President
Official language: Arabic
Monetary unit: Syrian pound
Area: 71,498 sq. mi. (185,180 sq. km.)
Population (2001): 16,729,000
GNP per capita (1999): U.S.$970
Principal exports (1999): crude
    petroleum and petroleum products
    62.9%; fresh vegetables and fruits
    12.4% *to:* Italy 26.6%; France 20.6%;
    Turkey 9.2%; Saudi Arabia 8.3%

Ethnic Composition

Arab
88.8%

Kurdish
6.3%

Other
4.9%

In 1918 the Arab Revolt flag flew over Syria, which joined
Egypt in the United Arab Republic in 1958 and based its new
flag on that of the Egyptian revolution of 1952; its stripes
were red-white-black, with two green stars for the constituent
states. In 1961 Syria broke from the union, but it readopted
the flag on March 29, 1980.

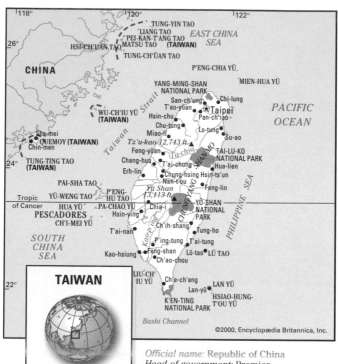

Official name: Republic of China
Head of government: Premier
Official language: Mandarin Chinese
Monetary unit: New Taiwan dollar
Area: 13,969 sq. mi. (36,188 sq. km.)
Population (2001): 22,340,000
GNP per capita (2000): U.S.$14,220
Principal exports (2000): electronics and
  other machinery 55.7%; textile
  products 10.3%; plastic articles 6.1%
  to: U.S. 23.5%; Hong Kong 21.1%; Japan
  11.2%; Singapore 3.7%

Religious Affiliation

Buddhist
43%

Christian
7.4%

Chinese
folk-religionist
48.5%

Other
1.1%

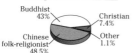

Under Chiang Kai-shek, a new Chinese national flag was
adopted on Oct. 28, 1928, and it was carried to Taiwan in
1949–50 when the Nationalists fled the mainland. The three
colors stand for the "Three Principles of the People" of the
Nationalist (Kuomintang) Party—nationalism, democracy, and
socialism.

Official name: Republic of Tajikistan
Head of government: Prime Minister
Official language: Tajik
Monetary unit: somoni
Area: 55,300 sq. mi. (143,100 sq. km.)
Population (2001): 6,252,000
GNP per capita (1999): U.S.$280
Principal exports (1998): aluminum
 39.9%; cotton fiber 19.1%; electricity
 17.6% *to* (1996): The Netherlands
 28.3%; Uzbekistan 24.8%; Switzerland
 10.8%; Russia 10.2%

Following independence from the Soviet Union in 1991,
Tajikistan developed a new flag on Nov. 24, 1992. The green
stripe is for agriculture, while red is for sovereignty. White is
for the main crop—cotton. The central crown contains seven
stars representing unity among workers, peasants, intellectuals, and other social classes.

©2000, Encyclopædia Britannica, Inc.

TANZANIA

Scale 1: 21,031,000

| 0 | 100 | 200 mi |
| 0 | 150 | 300 km |

Religious Affiliation

Traditional beliefs 35%

Muslim 35%

Christian 30%

Official name: United Republic of Tanzania
Head of government: President
Official languages: Swahili; English
Monetary unit: Tanzania shilling
Area: 364,017 sq. mi. (942,799 sq. km.)
Population (2001): 36,232,000
GNP per capita (1999): U.S.$260
Principal exports (1999): cashew nuts 18.3%; coffee 14.2%; minerals 13.2% *to:* India 19.5%; United Kingdom 17.0%; Japan 8.0%; The Netherlands 5.7%

In April 1964 Tanganyika and Zanzibar united, and in July their flag traditions melded to create the current design. The black stripe is for the majority population, while green is for the rich agricultural resources of the land. Mineral wealth is reflected in the yellow fimbriations (narrow borders), while the Indian Ocean is symbolized by blue.

©2000, Encyclopædia Britannica, Inc.

THAILAND

Scale 1: 24,526,000

0   100   200 mi

0   150   300 km

Official name: Kingdom of Thailand
Head of government: Prime Minister
Official language: Thai
Monetary unit: Thai baht
Area: 198,115 sq. mi. (513,115 sq. km.)
Population (2001): 61,251,000
GNP per capita (1999): U.S.$2,010
Principal exports (1998): electrical
  machinery 18.9%; power generating
  equipment 18.6%; garments 6.1%
  to: U.S. 22.3%; Japan 13.7%;
  Singapore 8.6%

Ethnic Composition

Chinese 12.1%
Malay 3.7%
Other 4.7%
Thai 79.5%

In the 17th century, the flag of Thailand was plain red, and
Thai ships in 1855 displayed a flag with a central white elephant as a symbol of good fortune. The Thai king replaced the
elephant with two white stripes in 1916 and added the blue
stripe on Sept. 28, 1917. Red symbolizes the blood of patriots,
white is for Buddhism, and blue is for royal guidance.

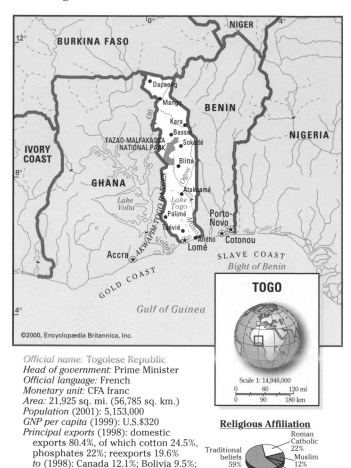

BURKINA FASO
NIGER
Dapaong
Mango
BENIN
Kara
Bassar
FAZAO-MALFAKASSA NATIONAL PARK
Sokodé
NIGERIA
IVORY COAST
Blitta
GHANA
Atakpamé
Lake Volta
Lake Togo
Palimé
Porto-Novo
Tsévié
Aného
Cotonou
Accra
Lomé
SLAVE COAST
Bight of Benin
GOLD COAST
Gulf of Guinea

©2000, Encyclopædia Britannica, Inc.

TOGO

Scale 1: 14,946,000
0   60   120 mi
0   90   180 km

Official name: Togolese Republic
Head of government: Prime Minister
Official language: French
Monetary unit: CFA franc
Area: 21,925 sq. mi. (56,785 sq. km.)
Population (2001): 5,153,000
GNP per capita (1999): U.S.$320
Principal exports (1998): domestic exports 80.4%, of which cotton 24.5%, phosphates 22%; reexports 19.6% *to* (1998): Canada 12.1%; Bolivia 9.5%; Nigeria 7.4%

Religious Affiliation

Roman Catholic 22%
Muslim 12%
Traditional beliefs 59%
Protestant 7%

On April 27, 1960, Togo became independent from France under the current flag. Its stripes correspond to the administrative regions and symbolize that the population depends on the land for its sustenance (green) and its own labor for development (yellow). The red is for love, fidelity, and charity, while the white star is for purity and unity.

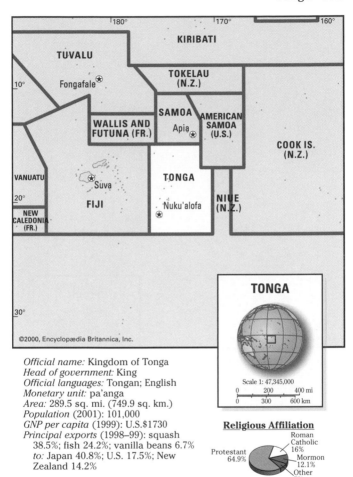

KIRIBATI

TUVALU

180°   170°   160°

10°   Fongafale ⊛

TOKELAU (N.Z.)

SAMOA

WALLIS AND FUTUNA (FR.)   Apia ⊛

AMERICAN SAMOA (U.S.)

COOK IS. (N.Z.)

VANUATU

Suva ⊛

TONGA

NIUE (N.Z.)

20°

FIJI   Nuku'alofa ⊛

NEW CALEDONIA (FR.)

30°

©2000, Encyclopædia Britannica, Inc.

TONGA

Scale 1: 47,345,000

0   200   400 mi
0   300   600 km

Official name: Kingdom of Tonga
Head of government: King
Official languages: Tongan; English
Monetary unit: pa'anga
Area: 289.5 sq. mi. (749.9 sq. km.)
Population (2001): 101,000
GNP per capita (1999): U.S.$1730
Principal exports (1998–99): squash
   38.5%; fish 24.2%; vanilla beans 6.7%
   to: Japan 40.8%; U.S. 17.5%; New
   Zealand 14.2%

Religious Affiliation

Roman Catholic 16%
Protestant 64.9%
Mormon 12.1%
Other 7%

The colors red and white were popular in the Pacific long
before the arrival of Europeans. The Tonga constitution (Nov.
4, 1875) established the flag, which was created by King
George Tupou I with the advice of a missionary. The cross
was chosen as a symbol of the widespread Christian religion,
and the color red was related to the blood of Jesus.

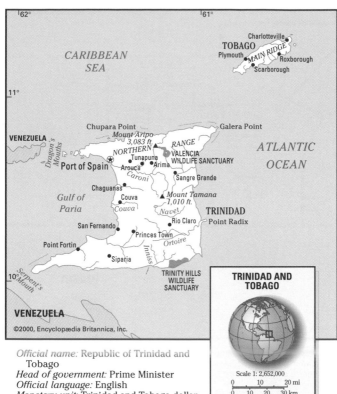

©2000, Encyclopædia Britannica, Inc.

Official name: Republic of Trinidad and Tobago
Head of government: Prime Minister
Official language: English
Monetary unit: Trinidad and Tobago dollar
Area: 1,980 sq. mi. (5,128 sq. km.)
Population (2001): 1,298,000
GNP per capita (1999): U.S.$4,750
Principal exports (1998): petroleum 40.2%; *to* (1999): U.S. 39.3%; Caricom countries 26.1%, of which Jamaica 8.7%, Barbados 5.3%

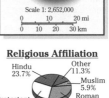

TRINIDAD AND TOBAGO

Scale 1: 2,652,000

| 0 | 10 | 20 mi |
| 0 | 10 | 20 | 30 km |

Religious Affiliation

Hindu 23.7%
Other 11.3%
Muslim 5.9%
Roman Catholic 29.4%
Protestant 29.7%

Hoisted on independence day, Aug. 31, 1962, the flag symbolizes earth, water, and fire as well as past, present, and future. Black also is a symbol of unity, strength, and purpose. White recalls the equality and purity of the people and the sea that unites them. Red is for the sun, the vitality of the people and nation, friendliness, and courage.

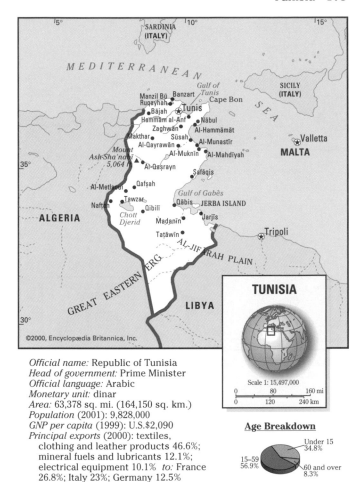

Official name: Republic of Tunisia
Head of government: Prime Minister
Official language: Arabic
Monetary unit: dinar
Area: 63,378 sq. mi. (164,150 sq. km.)
Population (2001): 9,828,000
GNP per capita (1999): U.S.$2,090
Principal exports (2000): textiles,
   clothing and leather products 46.6%;
   mineral fuels and lubricants 12.1%;
   electrical equipment 10.1% *to:* France
   26.8%; Italy 23%; Germany 12.5%

Age Breakdown

Under 15
34.8%

15–59
56.9%

60 and over
8.3%

The Tunisian flag, established in 1835, contains the crescent
and moon, a symbol used by the Ottoman Empire but dating
from the ancient Egyptians and Phoenicians. More as a cultur-
al than a religious symbol, the crescent and star came to be
associated with Islam because of its widespread adoption in
Muslim nations.

Official name: Republic of Turkey
Head of government: Prime Minister
Official language: Turkish
Monetary unit: Turkish lira
Area: 300,948 sq. mi. (779,452 sq. km.)
Population (2001): 66,229,000
GNP per capita (1999): U.S.$2,900
Principal exports (2000): textiles and
   clothing 22.6%; electrical and
   electronic machinery 7.1%
   to: Germany 18.8%; U.S. 11.2%; Russia
   and Eastern Europe 10.8%

Scale 1: 24,576,000

Religious Affiliation

Sunni
Muslim
80%

Other
Muslim
20%

In June 1793 the flag was established for the navy, although
its star had eight points instead of the current five (since
about 1844). This design was reconfirmed in 1936 following
the revolution led by Ataturk. Various myths are associated
with the symbolism of the red color and the star and crescent, but none really explains their origins.

©2000, Encyclopædia Britannica, Inc.

Scale 1: 19,553,000

0   80   160 mi
0   120   240 km

Ethnic Composition

Russian
9.8%

Uzbek
9%

Other
7.9%

Turkmen
73.3%

Official name: Turkmenistan
Head of government: President
Official language: Turkmen
Monetary unit: manat
Area: 188,500 sq. mi. (488,100 sq. km.)
Population (2001): 5,462,000
GNP per capita (1999): U.S.$670
Principal exports (1998): natural gas and
  oil products 54.6%; cotton 22.0%
  to: Iran 24.1%; Turkey 18.3%;
  Azerbaijan 6.9%

The flag was introduced on Feb. 19, 1992. Its stripe contains
intricate designs for five Turkmen tribes. Its green background is for Islam, and its crescent symbolizes faith in a
bright future. The stars are for the human senses and the
states of matter (liquid, solid, gas, crystal, and plasma). On
Feb. 19, 1997, an olive wreath was added to the stripe.

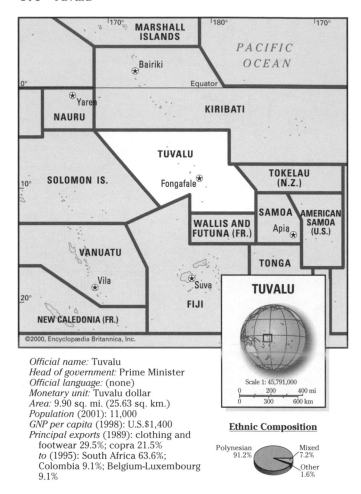

Official name: Tuvalu
Head of government: Prime Minister
Official language: (none)
Monetary unit: Tuvalu dollar
Area: 9.90 sq. mi. (25.63 sq. km.)
Population (2001): 11,000
GNP per capita (1998): U.S.$1,400
Principal exports (1989): clothing and
   footwear 29.5%; copra 21.5%
to (1995): South Africa 63.6%;
   Colombia 9.1%; Belgium-Luxembourg
   9.1%

Ethnic Composition

Polynesian
91.2%

Mixed
7.2%

Other
1.6%

On Oct. 1, 1978, three years after separating from the Gilbert
Islands, Tuvalu became independent under the current flag.
The stars represent the atolls and islands of the country. The
Union Jack recalls links with Britain and the Commonwealth.
Replaced by supporters of republicanism on Oct. 1, 1995, the
flag was reinstated on April 11, 1997.

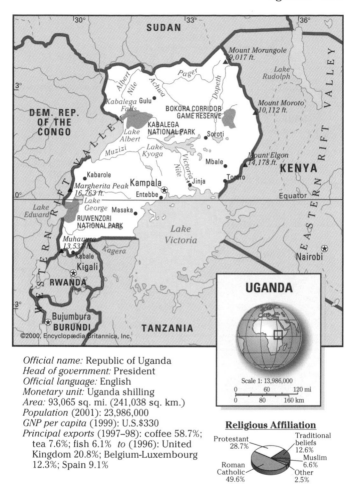

Official name: Republic of Uganda
Head of government: President
Official language: English
Monetary unit: Uganda shilling
Area: 93,065 sq. mi. (241,038 sq. km.)
Population (2001): 23,986,000
GNP per capita (1999): U.S.$330
Principal exports (1997–98): coffee 58.7%;
  tea 7.6%; fish 6.1% *to* (1996): United
  Kingdom 20.8%; Belgium-Luxembourg
  12.3%; Spain 9.1%

Scale 1: 13,986,000

0   60   120 mi
0   80   160 km

Religious Affiliation

Protestant 28.7%
Traditional beliefs 12.6%
Muslim 6.6%
Roman Catholic 49.6%
Other 2.5%

The crested crane symbol was selected by the British for
Uganda. The flag, established for independence on Oct. 9,
1962, was based on the flag of the ruling Uganda People's
Congress (which has three black-yellow-red stripes), with the
addition of the crane in the center. Black stands for the people, yellow for sunshine, and red for brotherhood.

©2000, Encyclopædia Britannica, Inc.

UKRAINE

Scale 1: 19,690,000

| 0 | 80 | 160 mi |
| 0 | 120 | 240 km |

Ethnic Composition

Ukrainian 72.6%

Russian 22.2%

Other 5.2%

Official name: Ukraine
Head of government: Prime Minister
Official language: Ukrainian
Monetary unit: hryvnya
Area: 233,100 sq. mi. (603,700 sq. km.)
Population (2001): 48,767,000
GNP per capita (1999): U.S.$840
Principal exports (1999): ferrous and
    nonferrous metals 39.1%; food and
    raw materials 11.4% *to:* Russia 19.2%;
    China 5.9%; Turkey 5.4%

The first national flag of Ukraine, adopted in 1848, had equal
stripes of yellow over blue and was based on the coat of arms
of the city of Lviv. In 1918 the stripes were reversed to reflect
the symbolism of blue skies over golden wheat fields. A red
Soviet banner flew from 1949, but it was replaced by the blue-
yellow bicolor on Jan. 28, 1992.

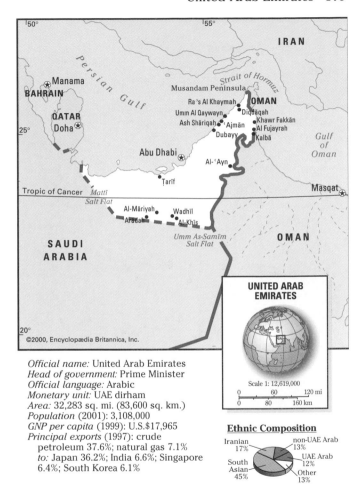

©2000, Encyclopædia Britannica, Inc.

Official name: United Arab Emirates
Head of government: Prime Minister
Official language: Arabic
Monetary unit: UAE dirham
Area: 32,283 sq. mi. (83,600 sq. km.)
Population (2001): 3,108,000
GNP per capita (1999): U.S.$17,965
Principal exports (1997): crude
  petroleum 37.6%; natural gas 7.1%
  to: Japan 36.2%; India 6.6%; Singapore
  6.4%; South Korea 6.1%

Ethnic Composition

Iranian 17%
non-UAE Arab 13%
UAE Arab 12%
Other 13%
South Asian 45%

On Dec. 2, 1971, six small Arab states formed the United Arab Emirates, and a seventh state joined on Feb. 11, 1972. The flag took its colors from the Arab Revolt flag of 1917. The colors are included in a 13th-century poem which speaks of green Arab lands defended in black battles by blood-red swords of Arabs whose deeds are pure white.

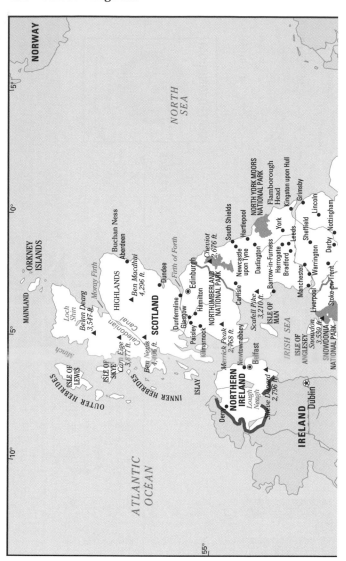

NORWAY

ORKNEY ISLANDS

MAINLAND

NORTH SEA

ATLANTIC OCEAN

ISLE OF LEWIS

OUTER HEBRIDES

The Minch

ISLE OF SKYE

Loch Shin

Ben Dearg 3,547 ft.

Moray Firth

HIGHLANDS

Ben Macdhui 4,296 ft.

Buchan Ness

Aberdeen

Carn Eige 3,877 ft.

Caledonian Canal

Ben Nevis 4,406 ft.

INNER HEBRIDES

ISLAY

SCOTLAND

Dundee

Firth of Forth

Dunfermline

Edinburgh

Glasgow

Hamilton

Paisley

Kilmarnock

Merrick Peak 2,768 ft.

Newtownabbey

Belfast

NORTHERN IRELAND

Derry

Lough Neagh

Slieve Donard 2,796 ft.

IRELAND

Dublin

IRISH SEA

ISLE OF MAN

ISLE OF ANGLESEY

Snowdon 3,559 ft.

SNOWDONIA NATIONAL PARK

Cheviot 2,676 ft.

NORTHUMBERLAND NATIONAL PARK

Carlisle

Newcastle upon Tyne

South Shields

Hartlepool

Darlington

Scafell Pike 3,210 ft.

Barrow-in-Furness

Harrogate

Bradford

Leeds

York

Manchester

Warrington

Liverpool

Sheffield

Derby

Stoke on Trent

Nottingham

NORTH YORK MOORS NATIONAL PARK

Flamborough Head

Kingston upon Hull

Grimsby

Lincoln

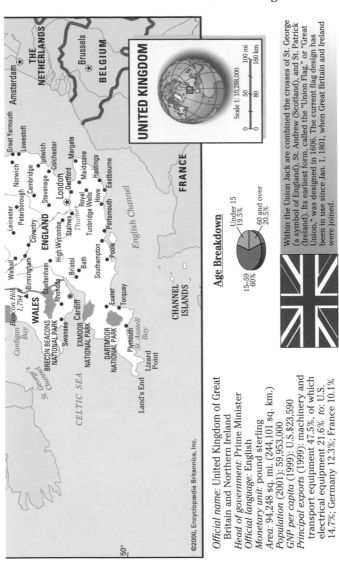

©2000, Encyclopædia Britannica, Inc.

Official name: United Kingdom of Great
Britain and Northern Ireland
Head of government: Prime Minister
Official language: English
Monetary unit: pound sterling
Area: 94,248 sq. mi. (244,101 sq. km.)
Population (2001): 59,953,000
GNP per capita (1999): U.S.$23,590
Principal exports (1999): machinery and
transport equipment 47.5%, of which
electrical equipment 21.6% *to:* U.S.
14.7%; Germany 12.3%; France 10.1%

Age Breakdown

Under 15
19.5%

60 and over
20.5%

15–59
60%

Within the Union Jack are combined the crosses of St. George (a symbol of England), St. Andrew (Scotland), and St. Patrick (Ireland). Its earliest form, called the "Union Flag," or "Great Union," was designed in 1606. The current flag design has been in use since Jan. 1, 1801, when Great Britain and Ireland were joined.

UNITED KINGDOM

Scale 1: 10,288,000

0   50   100 mi
0 80   160 km

Official name: United States of America
Head of government: President
Official language: (none)
Monetary unit: dollar
Area: 3,675,031 sq. mi. (9,518,323 sq. km.)
Population (2001): 286,067,000
GNP per capita (2000): U.S.$35,040
Principal exports (1999): Machinery and transport equipment 47.1%;
  chemicals, chemical products 8.1%; food 5.3% *to:* Canada 23.9%;
  Mexico 12.2%; Japan 8.3%

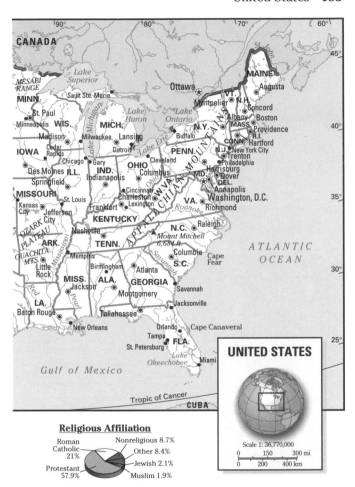

CANADA

90° 80° 70° 60°

45°

St. John

MAINE

Lake Superior

Sault Ste. Marie

Ottawa ★

Augusta

MINN.

MESABI RANGE

Montpelier **VT.** **N.H.**

St. Paul

Lake Huron

Lake Ontario

Concord

Minneapolis

WIS.

MICH.

Albany **MASS.** Boston

Madison

Milwaukee Lansing

Buffalo

N.Y. **R.I.** Providence

Lake Michigan

Lake Erie

CONN. Hartford

IOWA

Cedar Rapids

Chicago Gary

Detroit

PENN.

New York City

Des Moines **ILL.** **IND.** **OHIO**

Cleveland

Trenton **N.J.**

Springfield

Indianapolis Columbus

Philadelphia

MISSOURI

Cincinnati

Ohio **W.VA.** Harrisburg

MD. Dover **DEL.**

Kansas City

St. Louis

Charleston

Lexington

VA. Washington, D.C.

Annapolis

Jefferson City

Frankfort

OZARK

KENTUCKY

Roanoke Richmond

35°

ARK.

PLATEAU

Nashville

Mississippi

TENN.

APPALACHIAN MTS.

Raleigh

N.C.

▲ Mount Mitchell 6,684 ft.

ATLANTIC OCEAN

OUACHITA MTS.

Memphis

Savannah

Columbia

Cape Fear

Little Rock

Birmingham

Atlanta

S.C.

MISS. **ALA.**

GEORGIA

30°

Jackson

Red

Pearl

Montgomery

Savannah

LA.

Tallahassee

Jacksonville

Baton Rouge

New Orleans

Orlando Cape Canaveral

Tampa

St. Petersburg **FLA.**

Lake Okeechobee Miami

25°

Gulf of Mexico

Tropic of Cancer

CUBA

UNITED STATES

Scale 1: 36,770,000

0   150   300 mi
0   200   400 km

Religious Affiliation

Roman Catholic 21%

Nonreligious 8.7%

Other 8.4%

Jewish 2.1%

Protestant 57.9%

Muslim 1.9%

The Stars and Stripes has white stars corresponding to the states of the union (50 since July 4, 1960), as well as stripes for the 13 original states. The first unofficial national flag, hoisted on Jan. 1, 1776, had the British Union flag in the canton. The official flag dates to June 14, 1777; its design was standardized in 1912 and 1934.

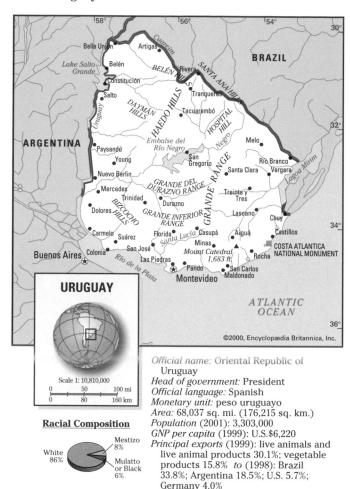

©2000, Encyclopædia Britannica, Inc.

URUGUAY

Scale 1: 10,810,000

| 0 | 50 | 100 mi |
| 0 | 80 | 160 km |

Official name: Oriental Republic of Uruguay
Head of government: President
Official language: Spanish
Monetary unit: peso uruguayo
Area: 68,037 sq. mi. (176,215 sq. km.)
Population (2001): 3,303,000
GNP per capita (1999): U.S.$6,220
Principal exports (1999): live animals and live animal products 30.1%; vegetable products 15.8% *to* (1998): Brazil 33.8%; Argentina 18.5%; U.S. 5.7%; Germany 4.0%

Racial Composition

White 86%
Mestizo 8%
Mulatto or Black 6%

The flag adopted on Dec. 16, 1828, combined symbols of Argentina with the flag pattern of the United States. It was last altered on July 11, 1830. On the canton is the golden "Sun of May," which was seen on May 25, 1810, as a favorable omen for anti-Spanish forces in Buenos Aires, Arg. The stripes are for the original Uruguayan departments.

©2000, Encyclopædia Britannica, Inc.

Official name: Republic of Uzbekistan
Head of government: President
Official language: Uzbek
Monetary unit: sum
Area: 172,700 sq. mi. (447,400 sq. km.)
Population (2001): 25,155,000
GNP per capita (1999): U.S.$720
Principal exports (1998): cotton fiber
   41.5%; energy 22.7%; gold 6%
   to: Western Europe 33.7%; Russia
   22.6%; Asia 11.6%; Ukraine 5.4%

Scale 1: 23,163,000

0   100   200 mi
0   100   200   300 km

Ethnic Composition

Other
14.5%
Russian
7.7%
Tajik
4.8%
Uzbek
73%

The flag of the former Soviet republic was legalized on Nov. 18, 1991. The blue is for water but also recalls the 14th-century ruler Timur. The green is for nature, fertility, and new life. The white is for peace and purity; red is for human life force. The stars are for the months and the Zodiac, while the moon is for the new republic and Islam.

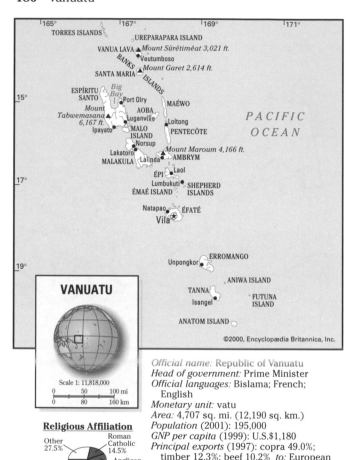

165° 167° 169° 171°

TORRES ISLANDS

UREPARAPARA ISLAND

VANUA LAVA ▲ *Mount Sürétiméat 3,021 ft.*
Veutumboso
BANKS
SANTA MARIA ▲ *Mount Garet 2,614 ft.*
ISLANDS

ESPÍRITU   *Big*
SANTO   *Bay*   Port Olry
                            MAÉWO
Mount   AOBA
Tabwemasana ▲   Luganville
6,167 ft.   Loltong
Ipayato   MALO   PENTECÔTE
             ISLAND
             Norsup
Lakatoro   *Mount Maroum 4,166 ft.*
MALAKULA Lalinda   AMBRYM
           ÉPI
                Laol
          Lumbukuti • SHEPHERD
ÉMAÉ ISLAND   ISLANDS

       Natapao • ÉFATÉ
          Vila ★

                      ERROMANGO
          Unpongkor

                      ANIWA ISLAND

          TANNA   · FUTUNA
          Isangel   ISLAND

       ANATOM ISLAND

15°

17°

19°

PACIFIC
OCEAN

©2000, Encyclopædia Britannica, Inc.

VANUATU

Scale 1: 11,818,000
0   50   100 mi
0   80   160 km

Religious Affiliation

Other
27.5%

Roman
Catholic
14.5%

Anglican
14%

Seventh-day
Adventist
8.2%

Presbyterian
35.8%

Official name: Republic of Vanuatu
Head of government: Prime Minister
Official languages: Bislama; French;
  English
Monetary unit: vatu
Area: 4,707 sq. mi. (12,190 sq. km.)
Population (2001): 195,000
GNP per capita (1999): U.S.$1,180
Principal exports (1997): copra 49.0%;
  timber 12.3%; beef 10.2% *to:* European
  Union 45.9%; Bangladesh 12.6%;
  Japan 10.4%

The flag was hoisted upon independence from France and
Britain, on July 30, 1980. Black is for the soil and the people,
green for vegetation, and red for local religious traditions
such as the sacrifice of pigs. On the triangle are two crossed
branches and a full-round pig's tusk, a holy symbol. The horizontal "Y" is for peace and Christianity.

VENEZUELA

Scale 1: 24,004,000

| 0 | 100 | 200 mi |
| 0 | 150 | 300 km |

Ethnic Composition

White 21%
Mestizo 67%
Black 10%
Indian 2%

Official name: Bolivarean Republic of Venezuela
Head of government: President
Official language: Spanish
Monetary unit: bolivar
Area: 353,841 sq. mi. (916,445 sq. km.)
Population (2001): 24,632,000
GNP per capita (1999): U.S.$3,680
Principal exports (1998): crude petroleum and petroleum products 69.8%; basic and precious metals 6.6% *to:* U.S. 48.5%; Andean Pact countries 11.1%; Canada 2.1%

The Venezuelan flag was adopted on March 18, 1864. Yellow was originally said to stand for the gold of the New World, separated by the blue of the Atlantic Ocean from "bloody Spain," symbolized by red. The stars are for the original seven provinces. In the upper hoist corner, the national arms are added to flags which serve the government.

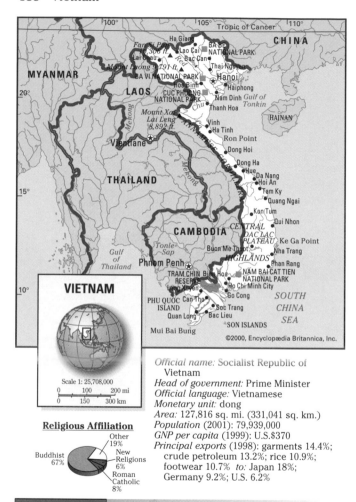

@2000, Encyclopædia Britannica, Inc.

VIETNAM

Scale 1: 25,708,000

0   100   200 mi
0   150   300 km

Religious Affiliation

Buddhist 67%

Other 19%

New Religions 6%

Roman Catholic 8%

Official name: Socialist Republic of Vietnam
Head of government: Prime Minister
Official language: Vietnamese
Monetary unit: dong
Area: 127,816 sq. mi. (331,041 sq. km.)
Population (2001): 79,939,000
GNP per capita (1999): U.S.$370
Principal exports (1998): garments 14.4%; crude petroleum 13.2%; rice 10.9%; footwear 10.7% *to:* Japan 18%; Germany 9.2%; U.S. 6.2%

On Sept. 29, 1945, Vietnamese communists adopted the red flag in use today. On July 4, 1976, following the defeat of the American-sponsored government in the south, the flag became official throughout the nation. The five points of the star are said to stand for the proletariat, peasantry, military, intellectuals, and petty bourgeoisie.

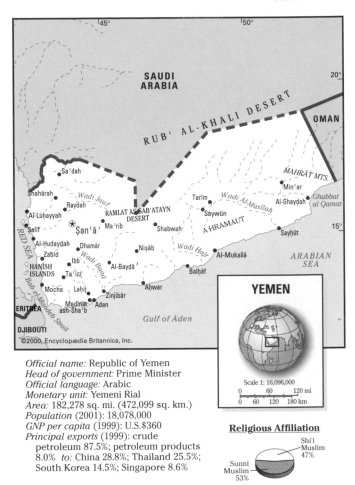

©2000, Encyclopædia Britannica, Inc.

Official name: Republic of Yemen
Head of government: Prime Minister
Official language: Arabic
Monetary unit: Yemeni Rial
Area: 182,278 sq. mi. (472,099 sq. km.)
Population (2001): 18,078,000
GNP per capita (1999): U.S.$360
Principal exports (1999): crude
petroleum 87.5%; petroleum products
8.0% *to:* China 28.8%; Thailand 25.5%;
South Korea 14.5%; Singapore 8.6%

YEMEN

Scale 1: 16,096,000

0   60   120 mi
0   60   120   180 km

Religious Affiliation

Shi'i
Muslim
47%

Sunni
Muslim
53%

Revolutions broke out in North Yemen in 1962 and in South
Yemen in 1967. In 1990 the two states unified, and that May 23
the tricolor was adopted, its design influenced by the former
United Arab Republic. The black is for the dark days of the
past, white for the bright future, and red for the blood shed
for independence and unity.

©2000, Encyclopædia Britannica, Inc.

Official name: Federal Republic of
  Yugoslavia
Head of government: Prime Minister
Official language: Serbian
Monetary unit: Yugoslav dinar
Area: 39,449 sq. mi. (102,173 sq. km.)
Population (2001): 10,677,000
GNP per capita (1999): U.S.$1,742
Principal exports (1998): manufactured
  goods 38.5%; machinery and transport
  equipment 14.2% *to:* Italy 11.6%;
  Macedonia 10.8%; Germany 8.9%;
  Russia 8.6%

YUGOSLAVIA

Scale 1: 8,452,000

0   40   80 mi
0   60   120 km

Ethnic Composition

Serb
62.6%

Albanian
16.5%

Other
15.9%

Montenegrin
5%

The Pan-Slavic colors (blue, white, and red) have been in the
flag from Oct. 31, 1918. A central star was introduced after
World War II, under the leadership of Josip Broz Tito. In 1991
the country broke up, leaving only Serbia and Montenegro
united, and the constitution of April 27, 1992, maintained the
tricolor but omitted the star.

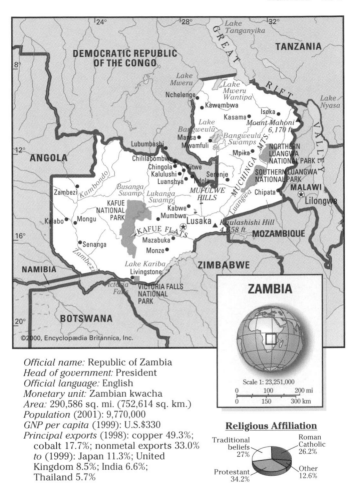

©2000, Encyclopædia Britannica, Inc.

Official name: Republic of Zambia
Head of government: President
Official language: English
Monetary unit: Zambian kwacha
Area: 290,586 sq. mi. (752,614 sq. km.)
Population (2001): 9,770,000
GNP per capita (1999): U.S.$330
Principal exports (1998): copper 49.3%;
   cobalt 17.7%; nonmetal exports 33.0%
   to (1999): Japan 11.3%; United
   Kingdom 8.5%; India 6.6%;
   Thailand 5.7%

ZAMBIA

Scale 1: 23,251,000

| 0 | 100 | 200 mi |
| 0 | 150 | 300 km |

Religious Affiliation

Traditional beliefs 27%
Roman Catholic 26.2%
Protestant 34.2%
Other 12.6%

Zambia separated from Britain on Oct. 24, 1964. Its flag, based on the flag of the United National Independence Party, has a green background for agriculture, red for the freedom struggle, black for the African people, and orange for copper. The orange eagle appeared in the colonial coat of arms of 1939. It symbolizes freedom and success.

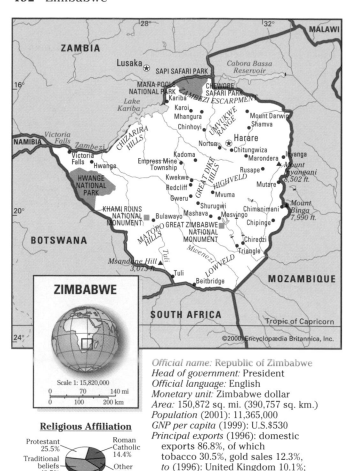

ZIMBABWE

Scale 1: 15,820,000

| 0 | 70 | 140 mi |
| 0 | 100 | 200 km |

Religious Affiliation

Protestant 25.5%
Roman Catholic 14.4%
Traditional beliefs 40.5%
Other 19.6%

Official name: Republic of Zimbabwe
Head of government: President
Official language: English
Monetary unit: Zimbabwe dollar
Area: 150,872 sq. mi. (390,757 sq. km.)
Population (2001): 11,365,000
GNP per capita (1999): U.S.$530
Principal exports (1996): domestic exports 86.8%, of which tobacco 30.5%, gold sales 12.3%, *to* (1996): United Kingdom 10.1%; South Africa 9.6%; Germany 7.9%

On April 18, 1980, elections brought the black majority to power under the current flag. The black color is for the ethnic majority, while red is for blood, green for agriculture, yellow for mineral wealth, and white for peace and progress. At the hoist is a red star (for socialism) and the ancient "Zimbabwe Bird" from the Great Zimbabwe ruins.

States
of the
United States

ALABAMA

Official name: State of Alabama
Nickname: Heart of Dixie
State Capital: Montgomery
State flower: Camellia
Motto: We Dare Defend Our Rights
Admitted to the Union: 1819 (22nd)
Total area: 51,705 sq. mi. (133,916 sq. km.) (ranks 29th)
Population (2000): 4,447,100. (ranks 23rd)

Chief cities: Birmingham, Huntsville, Mobile, Montgomery
Chief products/industries: Corn, soybeans, peanuts, livestock, coal, iron ore, limestone, petroleum, iron and steel, chemicals, textiles, historically notable cotton production.
Highest point: Cheaha Mountain 2407 ft. (734 m.)

State History

Original inhabitants were American Indians whose settlement sites and burial mounds are in evidence; the major groups were Cherokees, Chickasaws, Choctaws, and Creeks when area first explored by Spaniards, notably by Hernando de Soto 1539–40; first permanent settlement established 1711 by French at site of Mobile on Mobile Bay; became English 1763; southern part included in West Florida, retroceded to Spain in 1783 and claimed by U.S. as part of Louisiana Purchase 1803; rest of Alabama became part of U.S. 1783, with dividing line under dispute until 1795 when Spain ceded claim north of 31°; parts included in Territory South of the Ohio River 1790 and Mississippi Territory 1798 ff.; organized as a territory 1817; southern tip formally ceded to U.S. 1819; first constitutional convention July 1819; admitted to Union Dec. 14, 1819; 2nd constitutional convention Jan. 7–Mar. 20, 1861 passed ordinance of secession Jan. 11, 1861; government of Confederate States of America organized at Montgomery Feb. 4, 1861; 3rd constitutional convention Sept. 12–30, 1865 declared secession null and void, and abolished slavery; readmitted to Union 1868; present constitution, formulated by 6th constitutional convention, adopted 1901.

After the Civil War, the design chosen for a state flag was white with a red saltire. No explanation of the symbolism was given, but the intent was clear. The square shape in which the flag was normally represented was a subtle reference to the Battle Flag of the Confederate States of America.

TENNESSEE

35°

Florence • Athens • Huntsville
Tuscumbia • Decatur • Scottsboro
Russellville • Moulton • Fort Payne
Guntersville
Cullman
Hamilton • Centre
Double Springs • Gadsden
Jasper • Oneonta
34°
Vernon • Ashville • Heflin
Berry • Pell City • Anniston
Birmingham • Talladega
Carrollton
Tuscaloosa • Columbiana • Ashland • Wedowee
33°
Centreville • Rockford • Lafayette
Eutaw • Clanton • Dadeville
Greensboro • Wetumpka • Opelika
Livingston • Marion • Prattville • Tuskegee • Phenix City
Linden • Selma • ⊛ Montgomery
Butler • Hayneville • Union Springs
32°
Camden • Clayton
Grove Hill • Greenville • Luverne • Troy • Abbeville
Monroeville • Elba • Ozark
Chatom • Evergreen • Dothan
Andalusia
Brewton • Geneva
31°
Bay Minette
Mobile • FLORIDA
Mobile Bay • Pensacola Bay • Choctawhatchee Bay
Perdido Bay
30° • Gulf of Mexico

MISSISSIPPI

GEORGIA

0   20   40 mi
0   30   60 km

© 2003 Encyclopædia Britannica, Inc.

ALASKA

Official name: State of Alaska
Nickname: The Last Frontier
State Capital: Juneau
State flower: Forget-me-not
Motto: North to the Future
  (unofficial)
Admitted to the Union: 1959 (49th)
Total area: 591,004 sq. mi. (1,530,700
  sq. km.) (ranks 1st)
Population (2000): 626,932
  (ranks 48th)
Chief cities: Anchorage, Fairbanks,
  Juneau

Principal products/industries: Oil extraction, quarrying (sand and gravel),
  fishing, timber, tourism
Highest point: Mt. McKinley 20,320 ft. (6194 m.)

State History

Original inhabitants (American Indians and Inuits) thought to have im-
migrated over Beringia as well as from the Arctic area. Explored by
Russian voyages, especially of Vitus Bering 1741; their first permanent
settlement on Kodiak Island 1792; visited by British explorers James
Cook, George Vancouver, and Sir Alexander Mackenzie and by Hudson
Bay traders 1778–1847; under trade monopoly of Russian-American Fur
Company 1799–1861, first managed by Aleksandr Baranov; ownership
claimed by Russia; region south to 54°40′ ceded by Russia to U.S. for
$7,200,000 by treaty of 1867 negotiated by Secretary of State William H.
Seward (hence early nickname of Alaska, "Seward's Folly"); organized
1884; received final U.S. territorial status 1912; gold discoveries, including Klondike 1896; disputed boundary with British Columbia arbitrated
in favor of U.S. 1903; restriction of seal fisheries by treaties with Great
Britain, Russia, and Japan 1911; in WWII Aleutian islands of Attu and
Kiska occupied by Japanese June 1942–Aug. 1943; present constitution
adopted 1956; was granted statehood 1959; suffered severe earthquake
damage 1964; large oil reserves discovered 1968; crude-oil pipeline
south from North Slope to Valdez begun 1975, opened 1977.

Alaska held a territorial flag design competition in 1926, and the
winning design was created by 13-year-old Benny Benson, who
lived in an orphanage. The dark blue represents the Alaskan
sky and the Big Dipper points to the North Star, for Alaska's
being the northernmost part of the U.S.

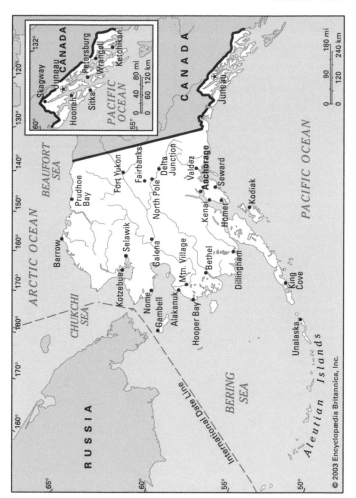

© 2003 Encyclopædia Britannica, Inc.

ARIZONA

Official name: State of Arizona
Nickname: Grand Canyon State
State Capital: Phoenix
State Flower: Saguaro cactus
Motto: Ditat Deus (God Enriches)
Admitted to the Union: 1912 (48th)
Total area: 114,006 sq. mi. (295,276 sq. km.) (ranks 6th)
Population (2000): 5,130,632 (ranks 20th)
Chief Cities: Glendale, Mesa, Phoenix, Scottsdale, Tempe, Tucson
Principal products/industries: Cotton, citrus fruit, copper, molybdenum, gold, electronic equipment, food processing, tourism
Highest point: Humphreys Peak 12,633 ft. (3850 m.)

State History

Inhabited probably from 25,000 B.C. Notable early cultures Hohokum 300 B.C.–1400 A.D. and Anasazi after 100 A.D. Apache and Navajo came later c. 1300. Spanish exploration began with expedition of Franciscan friar Marcos de Niza 1539; Coronado followed 1540; ruled by Spain as part of New Spain 1598–1821; inauguration of Spanish missions to Hopis 1638; region acquired by U.S. by Treaty of Guadalupe Hidalgo 1848 and Gadsden Purchase 1853; included in New Mexico Territory 1850; organized as territory of Arizona 1863; Apache wars continued up to latter part of 19th century until Geronimo finally surrendered 1886; with New Mexico refused statehood 1906; submitted a constitution for congressional approval 1911; congressional resolution accepting this constitution vetoed by President William Howard Taft chiefly because of provision allowing recall of judges by popular vote; after objectionable matter withdrawn from constitution, admitted to Union Feb. 14, 1912; by state constitutional amendment restored the provision allowing recall of judges Nov. 1912.

Five years after attaining statehood, Arizona adopted its state flag. The rays suggest a colorful Arizona sunset over a desert in shadow, and the central star represents the state as a rich copper-producing area. The red and yellow are colors from the Spanish flag, recalling early explorers; the red and blue suggest the Stars and Stripes.

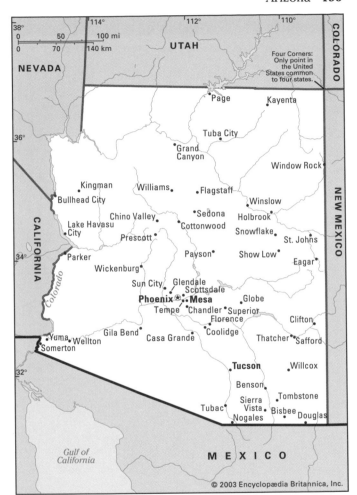

NEVADA

UTAH

COLORADO

Four Corners:
Only point in
the United
States common
to four states.

38°
0   50   100 mi
0   70   140 km

114°   112°   110°

36°

•Page   •Kayenta

•Tuba City

•Grand
Canyon   •Window Rock

•Kingman   •Williams   •Flagstaff   •Winslow

Bullhead City   •Sedona   Holbrook
                                    •
        •Chino Valley   •Cottonwood   Snowflake•
Lake Havasu   •St. Johns
•City
        •Prescott

34°

•Parker   •Payson   Show Low•   Eagar•

        •Wickenburg

        Sun City   •Glendale
        •   Scottsdale•
        Phoenix✪ •**Mesa**   •Globe
        Tempe•• •Chandler   •Superior   •Clifton
        Florence•
•Yuma   Gila Bend•   •Coolidge   Thatcher•Safford
Somerton •Wellton   Casa Grande•

32°

                Tucson   •Willcox

                Benson•
                        •Tombstone
                Sierra
Tubac•   Vista• •Bisbee Douglas•
        Nogales•

CALIFORNIA

Colorado

NEW MEXICO

Gulf of
California

M E X I C O

© 2003 Encyclopædia Britannica, Inc.

ARKANSAS

Official name: State of Arkansas
Nickname: The Natural State
State Capital: Little Rock
State Flower: Apple blossom
Motto: Regnat Populus (The People Rule)
Admitted to the Union: 1836 (25th)
Total area: 53,187 sq. mi. (137,754 sq. km.) (ranks 27th)
Population (2000): 2,673,400 (ranks 33rd)

Chief Cities: Fort Smith, Little Rock, North Little Rock, Pine Bluff
Principal products/industries: Soybeans, cotton, rice, livestock, bauxite, machinery, food processing
Highest point: Magazine Mountain 2753 ft. (839 m.)

State History

Early inhabitants, American Indians c. 500 A.D.; among first European explorers, Hernando de Soto 1541, Jacques Marquette and Louis Joliet 1673, Sieur de La Salle and Henry de Tonti 1682; Arkansas Post first permanent settlement (1686); in region claimed by France and yielded to Spain 1762; retroceded to France 1800; included in Louisiana Purchase 1803, Louisiana Territory 1805, and Missouri Territory 1812; Arkansas Territory organized 1819, which included current state plus most of what is now Oklahoma (except a strip along the northern boundary), and which was reduced to the current state's boundaries by 1828; adopted first constitution 1836 and admitted to Union June 15 of same year; seceded 1861; capture of Arkansas Post from Confederates 1863; readmitted into Union 1868; implementation of strict Jim Crow laws ensued; federal troops sent to Little Rock 1957 to enforce school desegregation laws.

The three stars originally appearing in the center recalled that Arkansas was the third state created from the Louisiana Territory and that it had been ruled by three different countries (France, Spain, and the U.S.). The flag was modified in 1923 by the addition of a fourth star to stand for the Confederate States of America.

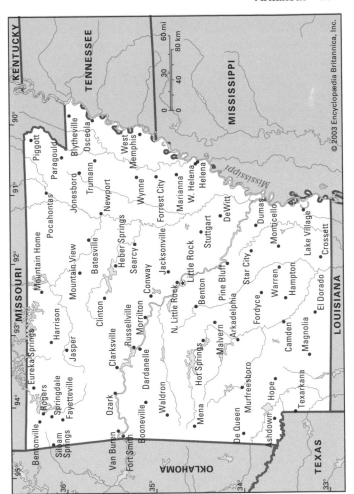

CALIFORNIA

Official name: State of California
Nickname: Golden State
State Capital: Sacramento
State Flower: Golden poppy
Motto: Eureka (I Have Found It)
Admitted to the Union: 1850 (31st)
Total area: 158,706 sq. mi. (411,048 sq. km.) (ranks 3rd)
Population (2000): 33,871,648 (ranks 1st)
Chief Cities: Anaheim, Fresno, Long Beach, Los Angeles, Oakland, Sacramento, San Diego, San Francisco, San Jose, Santa Ana
Principal products/industries: Tomatoes, lettuce, broccoli, strawberries, grapes, oranges, and other fruits and vegetables, cotton, rice, flowers, oil, natural gas, gypsum, transportation equipment, electrical machinery, electronics, movie and television industries, tourism
Highest point: Mt. Whitney 14,494 ft. (4418 m.)

State History

Inhabited originally by American Indians; first European coastal exploration by voyage of Spanish emissaries Juan Rodríguez Cabrillo and Bartolomé Ferrelo who established Spanish claim to region 1542–43; coast reached by English mariner Sir Francis Drake 1579; first Franciscan mission established by Junípero Serra at San Diego 1769; remained under Spanish control and later under Mexican control until conquered by U.S. forces during Mexican War (1846–47); ceded to U.S. by Treaty of Guadalupe Hidalgo 1848; settlement by Americans begun in 1841, greatly accelerated after discovery of gold at Coloma (Sutter's Mill) in 1848 which brought influx of miners and adventurers; admitted to Union Sept. 9, 1850 as a free state under Missouri Compromise; present constitution (many times amended) drawn up by constitutional convention 1878–79, ratified by people, and in force Jan. 1, 1880; with an already expanding population, state in 20th century grew even more with advent of the automobile; has more miles of freeway than any other state in U.S.; economy largest of all states in U.S.; subject to earthquakes, state suffered severe ones in north around San Francisco especially 1906 and 1989 and in south around Los Angeles 1994.

In the Bear Flag Revolt of 1846, in the Mexican-American War, a group of American settlers in the Mexican-ruled territory of California proclaimed independence and hoisted the original Bear Flag (June 14, 1846). In 1911 the California legislature recognized the flag of the short-lived California Republic as the official state flag.

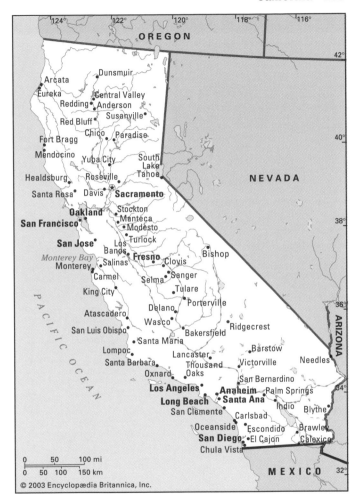

COLORADO

Official name: State of Colorado
Nickname: Centennial State
State Capital: Denver
State Flower: Columbine
Motto: Nil Sine Numine (Nothing
  Without Providence)
Admitted to the Union: 1876 (38th)
Total area: 104,247 sq. mi. (270,000
  sq. km.) (ranks 8th)
Population (2000): 4,301,261 (ranks
  24th)

Chief Cities: Aurora, Colorado Springs, Denver
Principal products/industries: Wheat, sugar beets, corn, livestock, oil,
  molybdenum, coal, food processing, printing, tourism, outdoor recreation
Highest point: Mt. Elbert 14,433 ft. (4399 m.)

State History

In early times, southwestern part of state inhabited by the Anasazi;
when Europeans arrived, plains inhabited primarily by the Arapaho,
Cheyenne, Comanche, and Kiowa; mountains inhabited mainly by the
Utes; explored chiefly by 18th century Spaniards; claimed by Spain and
also France; eastern part acquired by U.S. in Louisiana Purchase 1803,
rest in territory yielded by Mexico 1845–48; explored for U.S. government by Zebulon Pike 1806, Stephen Long 1820, and John Frémont
1842; additional exploration by a host of fur trappers and traders;
parts included in Louisiana, Missouri, Utah, New Mexico, Kansas, and
Nebraska territories 1805–61; gold, discovered at Cherry Creek (in
present-day Denver) in 1858, attracted American settlers; organized as
territory of Colorado 1861; admitted as state Aug. 1, 1876; constitution
adopted 1876.

The red C stands not only for the name of the state but also for
the state flower (columbine) and the state nickname ("Centennial State"). Colorado became a state in 1876, when the
country was celebrating the centennial of its independence.
The red, white, and blue suggest the U.S. flag; the blue, yellow,
and white, the columbine colors.

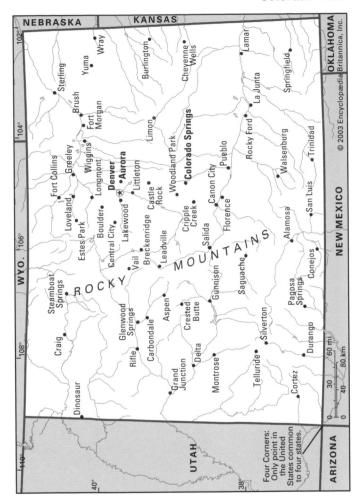

NEBRASKA

KANSAS

OKLAHOMA

WYO.

NEW MEXICO

UTAH

ARIZONA

© 2003 Encyclopædia Britannica, Inc.

102°

104°

106°

108°

110°

40°

38°

Wray

Yuma

Sterling

Burlington

Cheyenne
Wells

Lamar

Springfield

Brush

Fort
Morgan

La Junta

Wiggins

Limon

Colorado Springs

Rocky Ford

Walsenburg

Trinidad

Fort Collins

Greeley

Longmont

Denver

Aurora

Littleton

Woodland Park

Pueblo

Loveland

Boulder

Central City

Lakewood

Castle
Rock

Canon City

Florence

San Luis

Estes
Park

Breckenridge

Cripple
Creek

Salida

Alamosa

Vail

Leadville

M O U N T A I N S

Saguache

Conejos

Gunnison

Steamboat
Springs

R O C K Y

Glenwood
Springs

Aspen

Crested
Butte

Pagosa
Springs

Craig

Rifle

Carbondale

Delta

Silverton

Durango

Dinosaur

Grand
Junction

Montrose

Telluride

Cortez

60 mi

80 km

30

40

0

0

Four Corners:
Only point in
the United
States common
to four states.

CONNECTICUT

Official name: State of Connecticut
Nicknames: Constitution State, Nutmeg
  State
State Capital: Hartford
State Flower: Mountain laurel
Motto: Qui Transtulit Sustinet (He Who
  Transplanted Still Sustains)
Admitted to the Union: 1788; 5th of the
  original 13 colonies to ratify the U.S.
  Constitution

Total area: 5018 sq. mi. (12,997 sq. km.) (ranks 48th)
Population (2000): 3,405,565 (ranks 29th)
Chief Cities: Bridgeport, Hartford, New Haven, Stamford, Waterbury
Principal products/industries: Dairy products, shade-grown tobacco for
  cigar wrappers, jet engines, helicopters, submarines, guns and ammuni-
  tion, insurance
Highest point: Mt. Frissell 2380 ft. (725 m.)

State History

Originally inhabited by the Algonquin Indians. Connecticut River
explored 1614 by Dutch navigator Adriaen Block, and again 1632 by
Edward Winslow of Plymouth; posts established 1633 by the Dutch at
Hartford and by a Plymouth contingent at Windsor; a 3rd post established at Wethersfield 1634 following 1633 exploration of the area by
John Oldham of Massachusetts Bay Colony; permanent settlements
established at the three river towns of Hartford, Windsor, and Wethersfield 1635–36, primarily by colonists from Massachusetts Bay; Saybrook
Colony established 1635; Pequot tribe nearly extinguished in Pequot
War 1636–37; New Haven Colony established 1638; three river towns
formed Connecticut Colony and adopted Fundamental Orders, considered by some to be the first American constitution based on the consent of the governed, 1638–39; in New England Confederation 1643–84;
Connecticut Colony absorbed Saybrook Colony 1644; received charter
1662 which united Connecticut and New Haven colonies and granted
strip of land extending to Pacific; included in Dominion of New England,
the government of Connecticut was briefly taken over by British colonial governor Sir Edmund Andros 1687–89; relinquished claims to western lands 1786 except for Western Reserve (situated in what is now
Ohio) to which it abandoned jurisdiction 1800; participated in Hartford
Convention 1814–15; adopted state constitution 1818, in force until
1965, when it was replaced by another.

The coat of arms is based on the 1711 seal of the colony of
Connecticut. Its three grapevines are thought to represent
either the colonies of Connecticut, New Haven, and Saybrook or
the first three area towns established by Europeans (Hartford,
Wethersfield, and Windsor).

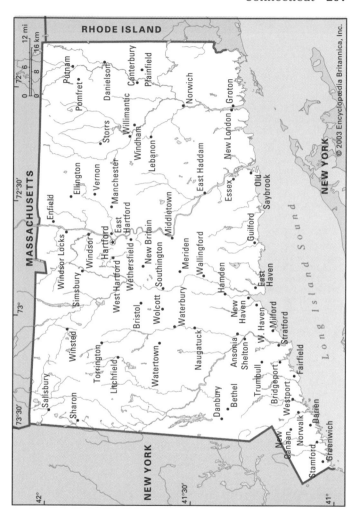

RHODE ISLAND

MASSACHUSETTS

NEW YORK

NEW YORK

Long Island Sound

© 2003 Encyclopædia Britannica, Inc.

12 mi
16 km

72°

73°

72°30′

73°30′

42°

41°30′

41°

Putnam
Pomfret
Danielson
Canterbury
Plainfield
Norwich
Groton
Willimantic
Storrs
Windham
Lebanon
New London
Ellington
Vernon
Manchester
East Haddam
Essex
Old Saybrook
Enfield
East Hartford
Middletown
Guilford
Windsor Locks
Hartford
New Britain
Windsor
Wethersfield
Southington
Meriden
Wallingford
Simsbury
West Hartford
Hamden
East Haven
Bristol
Wolcott
Waterbury
New Haven
W. Haven
Milford
Winsted
Stratford
Torrington
Watertown
Naugatuck
Ansonia
Shelton
Fairfield
Salisbury
Litchfield
Trumbull
Bridgeport
Westport
Sharon
Danbury
Bethel
Norwalk
Darien
New Canaan
Stamford
Greenwich

DELAWARE

Official name: State of Delaware
Nicknames: First State, Diamond
State
State Capital: Dover
State Flower: Peach blossom
Motto: Liberty and Independence
Admitted to the Union: 1787; 1st of
the original 13 colonies to ratify
the U.S. Constitution
Total area: 2057 sq. mi. (5328 sq.
km.) (ranks 49th)

Population (2000): 783,600 (ranks 45th)
Chief Cities: Dover, Newark, Wilmington
Principal products/industries: Chemicals, food processing, poultry, fishing,
soybeans, corn
Highest point: Centerville 442 ft. (135 m.)

State History

Region originally inhabited by several Algonquian tribes; earliest
European settlements made by Dutch 1631 at present site of Lewes; first
permanent settlements made by Swedes 1638; New Sweden captured by
Dutch 1655 and, as part of New Netherland, by English 1664; part of New
York until it became part of a grant made to William Penn 1682; in 1704
received right to separate legislative assembly, but remained under governor of Pennsylvania until 1776; active in American Revolution; formulated first state constitution 1776, adopted present constitution 1897;
remained in Union during Civil War.

The diamond shape may represent the nickname "Diamond
State." The coat of arms incorporates symbols appropriate for
the late 18th century—a soldier, a farmer, agricultural produce
(a sheaf of wheat and an ear of corn), an ox, and a ship.

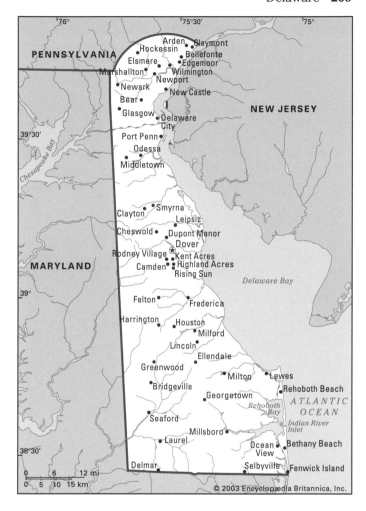

© 2003 Encyclopædia Britannica, Inc.

FLORIDA

Official name: State of Florida
Nickname: Sunshine State
State Capital: Tallahassee
State Flower: Orange blossom
Motto: In God We Trust
Admitted to the Union: 1845 (27th)
Total area: 58,664 sq. mi. (151,940 sq. km.) (ranks 22nd)
Population (2000): 15,982,378 (ranks 4th)

Chief Cities: Fort Lauderdale, Hialeah, Jacksonville, Miami, Orlando, St. Petersburg, Tampa
Principal products/industries: Citrus fruits, vegetables, dairy products, cattle, phosphates, electronic equipment, tourism
Highest point: 345 ft. (105 m.)

State History

Spanish Florida, which included southeastern part of present U.S., sighted and explored by Juan Ponce de León 1513; St. Augustine settled 1565; following Seven Years' War, ceded to England by Spain in exchange for Havana 1763; divided into two provinces (known as the Floridas), East and West Florida; retroceded to Spain 1783; West Florida claimed by U.S. as part of Louisiana Purchase 1803; border crossed by Gen. Andrew Jackson who captured Pensacola 1814 and 1818; purchased for $5,000,000 by U.S. under Adams-Onís Treaty 1819; organized as territory of Florida 1822; most Seminole natives relocated to Indian Territory (now Oklahoma) following war (1835–42); admitted to Union as slave state Mar. 3, 1845; passed ordinance of secession Jan. 10, 1861; annulled ordinance of secession Oct. 28, 1865 and abolished slavery; readmitted to Union 1868; present constitution adopted 1885, much amended 1968.

After the Civil War, Florida designated the state seal to appear in the center of a white flag; the design showed an American Indian woman on a promontory extending into water where a steamboat was sailing. Later, a red saltire (similar to that of the Confederate Battle Flag) was added so that it would not resemble a flag of surrender.

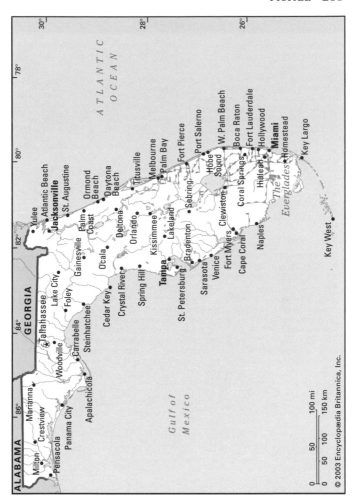

© 2003 Encyclopædia Britannica, Inc.

GEORGIA

Official name: State of Georgia
Nicknames: Empire State of the South, Peach State
State Capital: Atlanta
State Flower: Cherokee rose
Motto: Wisdom, Justice, Moderation
Admitted to the Union: 1788; 4th of the original 13 colonies to ratify the U.S. Constitution
Total area: 58,910 sq. mi. (152,577 sq. km.) (ranks 21st)
Population (2000): 8,186,453 (ranks 10th)
Chief Cities: Albany, Atlanta, Augusta, Columbus, Macon, Savannah
Principal products/industries: Processed foods, peanuts, pecans, peaches, tobacco, poultry, livestock, clays, textiles, pulp, carpets and rugs, automobile assembly
Highest point: Brasstown Bald 4784 ft. (1458 m.)

State History

Inhabited by Creek and Cherokee peoples when explored by Spanish and penetrated by Spanish missions 16th century; English colony, last of original 13 colonies to be founded, chartered 1732 and settled 1733 at Savannah by English philanthropist James E. Oglethorpe as refuge for debtors and as buffer state between Spanish Florida and the Carolinas; surrendered charter to crown 1752; became royal colony 1754; Savannah held by British 1778–82; chartered University of Georgia 1785, the oldest state university; first southern state to ratify U.S. Constitution Jan. 2, 1788; ceded claims to western lands (now Alabama and Mississippi) 1802; Creek and Cherokee tribes forcibly removed to Indian Territory 1830s; seceded from Union Jan. 19, 1861; scene of battle of Chickamauga 1863, campaign between Chattanooga and Atlanta, and Gen. William T. Sherman's "March to the Sea" 1864; ordinance of secession repealed Oct. 30, 1865 and slavery abolished; last state to be readmitted to Union July 15, 1870; adopted present constitution 1945.

In 2001, Georgia changed the design of the state flag, removing from prominence the Confederate Battle Flag, a major feature of the flag for nearly 50 years. The current flag has the state seal surrounded by 13 white stars and a banner underneath featuring 2 American flags and 3 state flags from Georgia's past.

TENNESSEE

NORTH CAROLINA

SOUTH
CAROLINA

ALABAMA

Dalton
Blue Ridge
Clayton
Ellijay
Blairsville
La Fayette
Cleveland
Calhoun
Dahlonega
Jasper
Toccoa
Summerville
Dawsonville
Homer
Hartwell
Rome
Cartersville
Canton
Gainesville
Cedartown
Roswell
Jefferson
Elberton
Winder
Athens
Smyrna
Marietta
Lexington
Lincolnton
Buchanan
Atlanta⊛
Decatur
Monroe
Washington
Carrollton
East Point
Madison
Greensboro
Martinez
Augusta
Newnan
Covington
Thomson
La Grange
Griffin
Jackson
Eatonton
Sparta
Waynesboro
Zebulon
Barnesville
Gray
Milledgeville
Thomaston
Macon
Sandersville
Louisville
Talbotton
Irwinton
Wrightsville
Sylvania
Columbus
Butler
Warner Robins
Swainsboro
Cusseta
Buena
Vista
Fort Valley
Dublin
Statesboro
Andersonville
Oglethorpe
Perry
Cochran
Metter
Springfield
Lumpkin
Americus
Vienna
Eastman
Vidalia
Lyons
Claxton
Savannah
Cuthbert
Cordele
Abbeville
McRae
Reidsville
Hinesville
Dawson
Leesburg
Fitzgerald
Hazlehurst
Fort
Gaines
Albany
Sylvester
Douglas
Baxley
Jesup
Ludowici
Newton
Tifton
Alma
Darien
Colquitt
Camilla
Moultrie
Nashville
Pearson
Blackshear
Brunswick
Bainbridge
Adel
Waycross
Nahunta
Cairo
Thomasville
Lakeland
Homerville
Woodbine
Quitman
Valdosta
Folkston
Statenville

Savannah River

FLORIDA

ATLANTIC
OCEAN

Gulf of
Mexico

0   20   40 mi
0   30   60 km

© 2003 Encyclopædia Britannica, Inc.

HAWAII

Official name: State of Hawaii
Nickname: Aloha State
State Capital: Honolulu
State Flower: Yellow hibiscus
Motto: Ua Mau Ke Ea O Ka Aina I Ka
    Pono (The Life of the Land is
    Perpetuated in Righteousness)
Admitted to the Union: 1959 (50th)
Total area: 6471 sq. mi. (16,760 sq.
    km.) (ranks 47th)
Population (2000): 1,211,537 (ranks
    42nd)

Chief Cities/settlements: Hilo (on
    island of Hawaii), Honolulu (on island of Oahu), Lihue (on island of
    Kauai), Wailuku (on island of Maui)
Principal products/industries: Sugarcane production, food processing,
    tourism, military bases
Highest point: Mauna Kea 13,796 ft. (4205 m.) on island of Hawaii

State History

Original settlers came from the Marquesas Islands c. 400 A.D.; groups
from Tahiti arrived c. 900–1000 A.D.; first European encounter 1778 with
English Capt. James Cook who named it the Sandwich Islands and was
killed here 1779; most of island group united under rule (1795–1819) of
King Kamehameha I; frequented by American whalers from early 19th
century; first visited by Christian missionaries from New England 1820;
recognized as independent by U.S., Great Britain, and France 1840s;
secured reciprocity treaty with U.S. 1875; Queen Liliuokalani over-
thrown and provisional government established with U.S. assistance
1893; declared republic 1894; annexed to U.S. by joint resolution 1898;
established as U.S. territory 1900; scene of Japanese attack on Pearl
Harbor Dec. 7, 1941; admitted as a state Aug. 21, 1959.

In 1793 Captain George Vancouver from Great Britain presented
the Union Jack to the conquering king Kamehameha I, who was
then uniting the islands into a single state; the Union Jack flew
unofficially as the flag of Hawaii until 1816, when red, white, and
blue stripes were added.

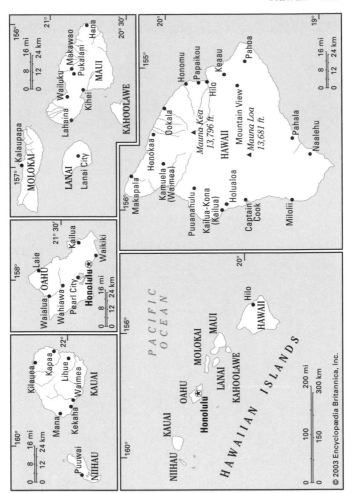

© 2003 Encyclopædia Britannica, Inc.

IDAHO

Official name: State of Idaho
Nickname: Gem State
State Capital: Boise
State Flower: Syringa
Motto: Esto Perpetua (Let It Be Perpetual)
Admitted to the Union: 1890 (43rd)
Total area: 83,557 sq. mi. (216,413 sq. km.) (ranks 13th)
Population (2000): 1,293,953 (ranks 39th)

Chief Cities: Boise, Idaho Falls, Lewiston, Nampa, Pocatello, Twin Falls
Principal products/industries: Potatoes, sugar beets, wheat, cattle, antimony, silver, phosphates, lead, wood products, chemicals, food products, fishing, hunting, outdoor recreation
Highest point: Borah Peak, 12,662 ft. (3859 m.)

State History

First inhabited by American Indians; explored by Lewis and Clark expedition 1805; part of Oregon Country; ceded to U.S. by British 1846; included in Oregon Territory 1848; became part of Washington Territory in 1850s, and part of Idaho Territory 1863; gold discovered 1860; crossed by Oregon Trail; admitted to Union July 3, 1890.

On March 5, 1866, Idaho Territory adopted its first official seal, representing mountains below a new moon, a steamer on the Shoshone River, figures of Liberty and Peace, an elk's head, and agricultural produce. A similar seal was adopted for the new state on March 14, 1891.

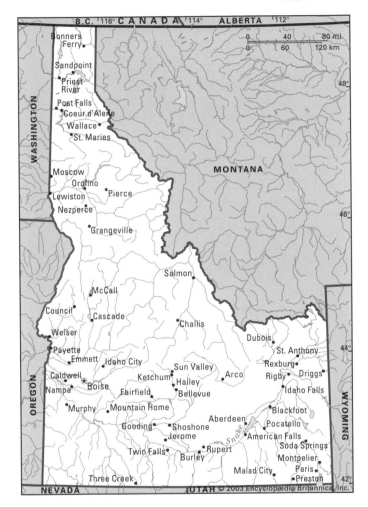

ILLINOIS

Official name: State of Illinois
Nickname: Prairie State
State Capital: Springfield
State Flower: Violet
Motto: State Sovereignty—National
  Union
Admitted to the Union: 1818 (21st)
Total area: 56,400 sq. mi. (146,076 sq.
  km.) (ranks 24th)
Population (2000): 12,419,293 (ranks
  5th)

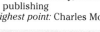

Chief Cities: Aurora, Chicago, Peoria, Rockford, Springfield
Principal products/industries: Corn, soybeans, dairy products, livestock, oil,
  coal, machinery, chemicals, metal products, food products, printing and
  publishing
Highest point: Charles Mound, 1235 ft. (376 m.)

State History

Explored by Père Jacques Marquette and Louis Jolliet 1673 and by René-Robert Cavelier de La Salle who erected Fort Crèvecœur on Illinois River 1680; included in French Louisiana; ceded by France to England 1763 and by England to U.S. 1783; Virginia claims to territory given up by 1786; part of Northwest Territory 1787, of Indiana Territory 1800, and of Illinois Territory 1809; admitted to the Union Dec. 3, 1818 with capital at Kaskaskia (capital transferred to Vandalia 1820 and to Springfield 1837); adopted present constitution 1970.

ILLINOIS

On July 6, 1915, the legislature adopted a flag that had been developed in a contest. The flag showed design elements from the state seal—a rock on a stretch of land with water and the rising sun behind it, plus a shield bearing the national stars and stripes in the claws of a bald eagle.

INDIANA

Official name: State of Indiana
Nickname: Hoosier State
State Capital: Indianapolis
State Flower: Peony
Motto: The Crossroads of America
Admitted to the Union: 1816 (19th)
Total area: 36,291 sq. mi. (93,994 sq.
  km.) (ranks 38th)
Population (2000): 6,080,485 (ranks
  14th)
Chief Cities: Evansville, Fort Wayne,
  Gary, Indianapolis, South Bend

Principal products/industries: Corn, soybeans, wheat, livestock, coal, building stone, steel, machinery, chemicals
Highest point: Franklin township 1257 ft. (383 m.)

State History

Inhabited early perhaps by Mound Builders; the Miami, among other
American Indians in area when Europeans first arrived; French settlement at Vincennes c. 1700; included in territory ceded by France to
England 1763; ceded by England to U.S. by Treaty of Paris 1783; included in Northwest Territory 1787 and Indiana Territory 1800; admitted to
the Union Dec. 11, 1816; capital removed from Corydon to Indianapolis
1825; adopted present constitution 1851.

In 1916, the centennial of Indiana statehood, a flag design competition was held. The winning design contained a torch, symbolic of
enlightenment and liberty, with rays spreading outward from its
flames, and 19 stars ringing the torch, recalling that the state was
the 19th to join the Union.

IOWA

Official name: State of Iowa
Nickname: Hawkeye State
State Capital: Des Moines
State Flower: Wild rose
Motto: Our Liberties We Prize, and
   Our Rights We Will Maintain
Admitted to the Union: 1846 (29th)
Total area: 56,275 sq. mi. (145,752 sq.
   km.) (ranks 25th)
Population (2000): 2,926,324 (ranks
   30th)

Chief Cities: Cedar Rapids, Davenport, Des Moines, Sioux City, Waterloo
Principal products/industries: Corn, soybeans, oats, hay, cattle, hogs,
   cement, food products, farm machinery, chemicals
Highest point: Ocheyedan Mound 1670 ft. (509 m.)

State History

Traces found of early inhabitation by Mound Builders, among others;
French explorers Louis Jolliet and Jacques (Père) Marquette among
first Europeans to visit 1673; became part of U.S. by Louisiana Purchase
1803; part of Louisiana Territory 1805, of Missouri Territory 1812, unorganized territory c. 1821–34, of Michigan Territory 1834, of Wisconsin
Territory 1836, and of Iowa Territory 1838; first permanent settlement
made 1833 at Dubuque; held first constitutional convention 1844; present constitution dates from 1857. Admitted to Union Dec. 28, 1846; capital moved from Iowa City to Des Moines 1857.

IOWA

In 1921 the legislature approved a state banner—rather than a
state flag—with a blue stripe along the hoist and a red stripe in
the fly, recalling the French Tricolor, which had flown over Iowa
before the Louisiana Purchase of 1803. In the center is a flying
bald eagle and a ribbon emblazoned with the state motto.

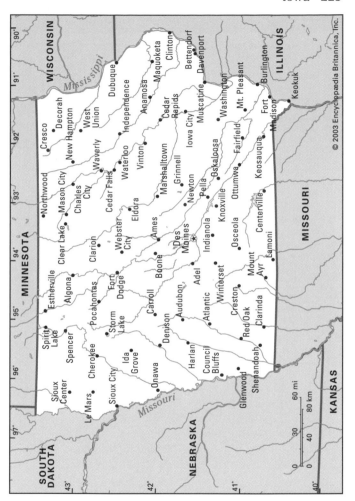

© 2003 Encyclopædia Britannica, Inc.

KANSAS

Official name: State of Kansas
Nickname: Sunflower State
State Capital: Topeka
State Flower: Sunflower
Motto: Ad Astra per Aspera (To the
   Stars Through Difficulty)
Admitted to the Union: 1861 (34th)
Total area: 82,277 sq. mi. (213,097 sq.
   km.) (ranks 14th)
Population (2000): 2,688,418 (ranks
   32nd)

Chief Cities: Kansas City, Overland Park, Topeka, Wichita
Principal products/industries: Wheat, sorghum, corn, cattle, oil, salt, trans-
   portation equipment, machinery, chemicals
Highest point: Mt. Sunflower 4039 ft. (1231 m.)

State History

Before coming of Europeans, inhabited sparsely by both nomadic and
settled American Indians, among them, the Kansa; probably entered by
Spanish explorer Francisco de Coronado's expedition 1541; came to U.S.
as part of Louisiana Purchase 1803; included in Louisiana Territory 1805
and Missouri Territory 1812; southwestern corner lost to Spanish in
1819 treaty; in unorganized territory c. 1821–54; regained southwestern
corner with annexation of Texas 1845; by Kansas-Nebraska Act 1854,
Kansas Territory organized, including Kansas and central portion of
eastern Colorado; admitted to Union with present boundaries as free
state Jan. 29, 1861.

KANSAS

Kansas had a number of banner and flag designs before the current design was approved in 1961. It shows the name of the
state under a state seal, which has a scene that includes a
homesteader's cabin and five bison.

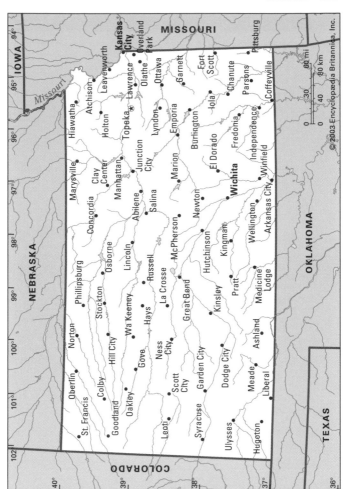

MISSOURI

IOWA

94°

95°

96°

97°

98°

99°

100°

101°

102°

Missouri

NEBRASKA

COLORADO

OKLAHOMA

TEXAS

© 2003 Encyclopædia Britannica, Inc.

60 mi

80 km

30

40

0

0

Kansas City

Overland Park

Pittsburg

Leavenworth

Atchison

Lawrence

Olathe

Ottawa

Garnett

Fort Scott

Chanute

Parsons

Coffeyville

Hiawatha

Holton

Topeka

Lyndon

Emporia

Burlington

Iola

Independence

Fredonia

Marysville

Clay Center

Manhattan

Junction City

Marion

El Dorado

Wichita

Winfield

Concordia

Abilene

Salina

Newton

Arkansas City

Phillipsburg

Osborne

Lincoln

Russell

McPherson

Hutchinson

Kingman

Wellington

Norton

Stockton

Wa Keeney

Hays

La Crosse

Great Bend

Pratt

Medicine Lodge

Kinsley

Oberlin

Hill City

Gove

Ness City

Ashland

Colby

Oakley

Scott City

Garden City

Dodge City

Meade

Liberal

St. Francis

Goodland

Leoti

Syracuse

Ulysses

Hugoton

40°

39°

38°

37°

36°

KENTUCKY

Official name: Commonwealth of Kentucky
Nickname: Bluegrass State
State Capital: Frankfort
State Flower: Goldenrod
Motto: United We Stand, Divided We Fall
Admitted to the Union: 1792 (15th)
Total area: 40,395 sq. mi. (104,623 sq. km.) (ranks 37th)
Population (2000): 4,041,769 (ranks 25th)

Chief Cities: Bowling Green, Covington, Lexington, Louisville, Owensboro
Principal products/industries: Tobacco, corn, wheat, thoroughbred horses, cattle, hogs, oil, natural gas, coal, bourbon whiskey, farm equipment, chemicals
Highest point: Black Mt. 4145 ft. (1263 m.)

State History

Inhabited by American Indian peoples before arrival of European explorers; entered by American explorer Thomas Walker 1750; included in territory ceded by French 1763; explored by expeditions under American pioneer Daniel Boone from 1769; first permanent English settlement at Boonesborough made by Transylvania Company 1775; because of its many Indian wars known as the "Dark and Bloody Ground"; organized as county of Virginia 1776; included in territory of U.S. by Treaty of Paris 1783; received consent of Virginia to statehood 1789; admitted to Union June 1, 1792; as border state during Civil War torn between North and South, providing troops to both sides; despite an attempt to be neutral, invaded by Confederate troops 1862; suffered skirmishes thereafter but remained in Union; adopted present constitution 1891.

At the time of its admission to the Union in 1792, Kentucky was considered the nation's western frontier, and this was reflected in the symbolism of the state seal: two men embracing, one a frontiersman in buckskins and the other a gentleman in formal frock coat, suggesting Westerners and Easterners in national unity.

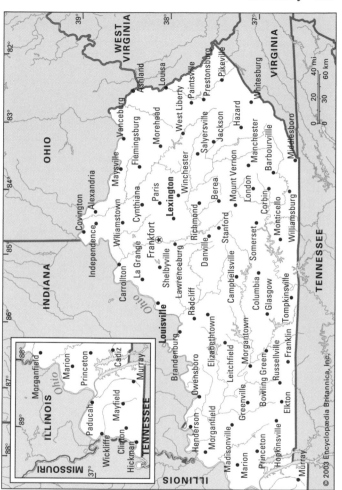

LOUISIANA

Official name: State of Louisiana
Nickname: Pelican State
State Capital: Baton Rouge
State Flower: Magnolia
Motto: Union, Justice, Confidence
Admitted to the Union: 1812 (18th)
Total area: 48,523 sq. mi. (125,674 sq. km.) (ranks 31st)
Population (2000): 4,468,976 (ranks 22nd)

Chief Cities: Baton Rouge, New Orleans, Shreveport
Principal products/industries: Rice, soybeans, cotton, sugarcane, seafood, oil, natural gas, sulfur, salt, chemicals, transportation equipment, lumber, tourism
Highest point: Driskill Mt. 535 ft. (163 m.)

State History

Inhabited by native peoples for thousands of years prior to European exploration, which began in the 16th century; name "Louisiana" originally applied to entire Mississippi River basin, claimed for France by explorer René-Robert Cavelier, Sieur de La Salle 1682; Natchitoches, first settlement within area of present state, founded 1714; New Orleans founded 1718; except for New Orleans, region east of Mississippi River ceded by France to Great Britain 1763; West Florida (incl. portion of present state of Louisiana east of Mississippi River north of Lake Pontchartrain) returned to Spain 1783 and claimed by U.S. as part of Louisiana Purchase 1803; New Orleans and region west of Mississippi River ceded to Spain 1762–63; returned to France 1800–03, and sold to U.S. in Louisiana Purchase; Orleans Territory organized 1804 and admitted to Union Apr. 30, 1812 as state of Louisiana, the first to be carved out of Louisiana Purchase; passed ordinance of secession Jan. 26, 1861; abolished slavery 1864; readmitted to Union 1868; present constitution adopted 1974.

A pelican tearing at its breast to feed its young is the central emblem of the flag. Real pelicans never perform this activity, but from the Middle Ages this symbol has represented the spirit of self-sacrifice and dedication to progeny. As early as 1812 the pelican was used as a Louisiana symbol.

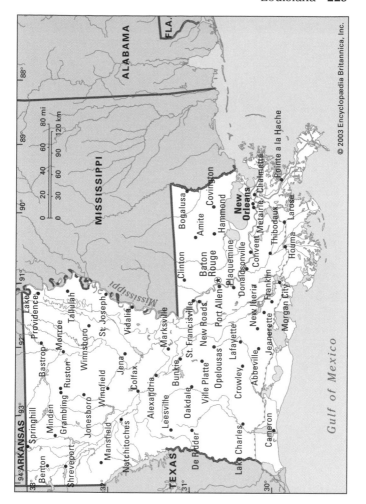

MAINE

Official name: State of Maine
Nickname: Pine Tree State
State Capital: Augusta
State Flower: White pine cone and
    tassel
Motto: Dirigo (I Direct)
Admitted to the Union: 1820 (23rd)
Total area: 33,265 sq. mi. (86,156 sq.
    km.) (ranks 39th)
Population (2000): 1,274,923 (ranks
    40th)
Chief Cities: Auburn, Augusta, Bangor, Biddeford, Lewiston, Portland, South
    Portland
Principal products/industries: Potatoes, blueberries, apples, poultry, gravel,
    tourism, fishing (esp. lobstering), food products, leather goods, paper,
    wood products
Highest point: Mt. Katahdin 5268 ft. (1606 m.)

State History

Evidence of prehistoric inhabitants; inhabited by Algonquians (especially Penobscot and Passamaquoddy tribes) at time of European settlement; claimed and settled by both English and French; included in grant to Plymouth Company 1606; first settlement by English at mouth of the Sagadahoc (Kennebec) 1607 failed, but city of Saco and Monhegan Island were settled c. 1622; through series of grants, beginning in 1622, claimed by Massachusetts Bay Colony and English proprietor Sir Ferdinando Gorges; annexed to Massachusetts (1652) which bought out Gorges's claim 1677; northern parts frequently attacked by French 17th–18th centuries; a district of Massachusetts until 1820; admitted to Union as free state as part of Missouri Compromise Mar. 15, 1820; boundary with Canada settled by treaty with Great Britain 1842.

Until 1820 Maine was a district of Massachusetts, and its early symbols were based on that connection. The pine tree emblem was used for the Massachusetts naval flag in 1776. The current state flag, established in 1909, has its coat of arms showing a moose-and-pine tree emblem on a shield supported by a farmer and a sailor.

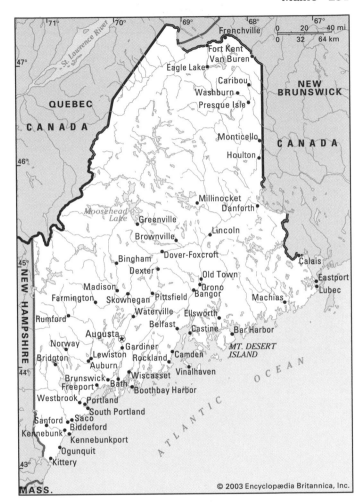

QUEBEC

CANADA

NEW
BRUNSWICK

CANADA

Frenchville
Fort Kent
Van Buren
Eagle Lake
Caribou
Washburn
Presque Isle
Monticello
Houlton
Millinocket
Danforth
Moosehead Lake
Greenville
Lincoln
Brownville
Calais
Bingham
Dover-Foxcroft
Dexter
Old Town
Eastport
Madison
Orono
Lubec
Farmington
Skowhegan
Pittsfield
Bangor
Machias
Rumford
Waterville
Ellsworth
Belfast
Augusta
Castine
Bar Harbor
Norway
Gardiner
MT. DESERT
ISLAND
Bridgton
Lewiston
Rockland
Camden
Auburn
Vinalhaven
Brunswick
Wiscasset
OCEAN
Freeport
Bath
Westbrook
Boothbay Harbor
Portland
Sanford
South Portland
Saco
Biddeford
Kennebunk
Kennebunkport
Ogunquit
Kittery

NEW HAMPSHIRE

ATLANTIC

MASS.

© 2003 Encyclopædia Britannica, Inc.

MARYLAND

Official name: State of Maryland
Nickname: Old Line State
State Capital: Annapolis
State Flower: Black-eyed Susan
Motto: Fatti Maschii, Parole Femine
(Manly Deeds, Womanly Words)
Admitted to the Union: 1788; 7th of
the original 13 colonies to ratify
the U.S. Constitution
Total area: 10,460 sq. mi. (27,091 sq.
km.) (ranks 42nd)

Population (2000): 5,296,486 (ranks 19th)
Chief Cities: Annapolis, Baltimore
Principal products/industries: Dairy products, food products, corn, tobacco,
chickens and other livestock, fishing especially for crabs, stone, sand
and gravel, tourism, primary metals, transportation equipment, chemicals, electrical equipment
Highest point: Backbone Mt. 3360 ft. (1024 m.)

State History

Originally inhabited by American Indians; English first visited early 17th
century; granted to George Calvert (Lord Baltimore) as proprietary
colony 1632; first American colony to achieve religious freedom; first
settled at St. Marys 1634, which was its capital 1634–94; colony under
rule of British crown 1689–1715; its long-standing boundary dispute
with Pennsylvania settled by drawing of Mason-Dixon Line 1760s; first
state constitution adopted 1776; adopted Articles of Confederation
1781; ceded territory for District of Columbia; during Civil War
remained in the Union, but was subjected to suspension of habeas
corpus; invaded by Confederate forces 1862; abolished slavery 1864;
adopted present constitution 1867.

Maryland has a state flag that was flown when the colony was
under British rule: the personal banner of Sir George Calvert,
the first Lord Baltimore. It has six vertical yellow and black
stripes, with a matching diagonal. It is combined with the arms
of the Crossland family (maternal family of Sir George Calvert):
a quartered white-and-red shield.

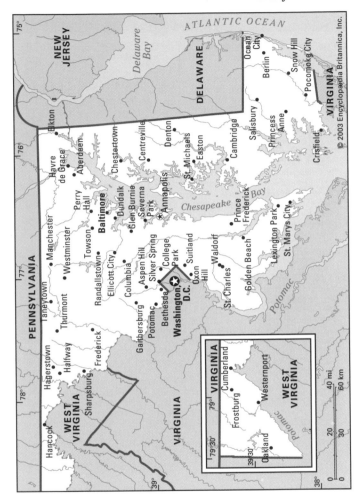

MASSACHUSETTS

Official name: Commonwealth of
    Massachusetts
Nickname: Bay State
State Capital: Boston
State Flower: Mayflower
Motto: Ense Petit Placidam Sub
    Libertate Quietem (By the Sword
    We Seek Peace, but Peace Only
    Under Liberty)
Admitted to the Union: 1788; 6th of
    the original 13 colonies to ratify
    the U.S. Constitution

Total area: 8284 sq. mi. (21,456 sq. km.) (ranks 45th)
Population (2000): 6,349,097 (ranks 13th)
Chief Cities: Boston, Springfield, Worcester
Principal products/industries: Dairy products, cranberries and other fruit,
    vegetables, electronic equipment, electrical equipment, printing and
    publishing, tourism, education, fishing
Highest point: Mt. Greylock 3491 ft. (1064 m.)

State History

Perhaps explored by Norse c. 11th century; coast skirted by Florentine
explorer Giovanni da Verrazano 1524; Cape Cod discovered by English-
man Bartholomew Gosnold 1602 who made first (temporary) European
settlement within present limits of state; at time of European settlement, region inhabited by several Algonquin tribes; Plymouth settled
by Pilgrims 1620; Massachusetts Bay Colony, founded and governed by
Massachusetts Bay Company 1629–84; Harvard College founded 1636;
joined New England Confederation 1643; acquired province of Maine
1652; after loss of first charter 1684, governed as part of Dominion of
New England 1686; by its 2nd charter 1691, received jurisdiction over
Maine and Plymouth colonies; in 18th century, gradually became a center of resistance to imperial colonial policy; British troops withdrawn to
Boston after colonial uprisings at Lexington and Concord 1775; battle of
Bunker Hill 1775; British evacuated Boston 1776; gave up claims to western lands 1785–86; western Massachusetts scene of Shays' Rebellion, an
uprising in protest of harsh government economic policies 1786–87;
eastern Massachusetts early center of American cotton manufacture.
Maine became separate state 1820.

The seal of the Massachusetts Bay Colony of 1629 showed an
Indian and pine trees, and both of these symbols have continued to be used up to the present time. The Indian appears in
gold on a blue shield together with a silver star indicative of
statehood.

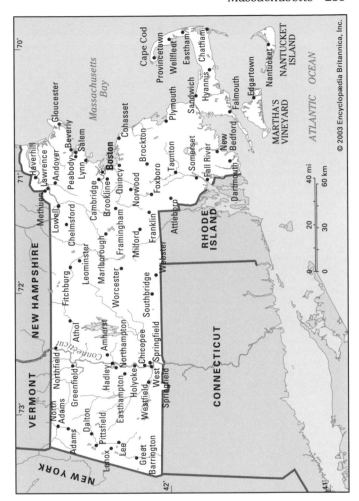

© 2003 Encyclopædia Britannica, Inc.

MICHIGAN

Official name: State of Michigan
Nickname: Wolverine State
State Capital: Lansing
State Flower: Apple blossom
Motto: Si Quaeris Peninsulam
　　Amoenam Circumspice (If You
　　Seek a Beautiful Peninsula, Look
　　Around You)
Admitted to the Union: 1837 (26th)
Total area: 58,527 sq. mi. (151,585 sq.
　km.) (ranks 23rd)
Population (2000): 9,938,444 (ranks 8th)
Chief Cities: Ann Arbor, Detroit, Flint, Grand Rapids, Lansing, Livonia,
　Sterling Heights, Warren
Principal products/industries: Dairy products, fruit, iron ore, limestone, cop-
　per, natural gas, motor vehicles and parts, tourism
Highest point: Mt. Arvon 1979 ft. (604 m.)

State History

Inhabited especially by Algonquian tribes prior to arrival of Europeans;
first European to visit the region was French adventurer Étienne Brulé
in early 17th century; first settled at Sault Sainte Marie by French
explorer and missionary Père Marquette 1668; military post of Detroit
founded 1701; ceded to England 1763 following French and Indian War
and to U.S. 1783; included in Northwest Territory 1787 and in Indiana
Territory 1800, 1803; Michigan Territory organized on the Lower Peninsula, 1805; boundaries extended 1818 to include Upper Peninsula and
beyond; Upper Peninsula briefly included in Wisconsin Territory 1836;
boundary dispute with Ohio (Toledo War) settled by U.S. Congress in
favor of Ohio, with Michigan receiving as compensation the Upper
Peninsula and statehood (admitted as free state Jan. 26, 1837); Lansing
became capital 1847; adopted present constitution 1963.

The bald eagle of the U.S. serves as a crest to the state shield,
while an elk and a moose, supposedly based on the coat of
arms of the Hudson's Bay Company, serve as supporters. The
central design of the shield shows a man with a rifle standing
on a peninsula and the sun setting over surrounding waters.

Eagle River
Calumet
Houghton
47°
L'Anse
Ishpeming
Munising
Crystal Falls
Iron Mountain Gladstone
Escanaba
46°
Menominee

Lake Superior

Grand Marais
Marquette

Newberry
Sault Ste. Marie
Manistique
St. Ignace
Mackinaw City
Cheboygan
Rogers City
Petoskey
Charlevoix
Leland
Bellaire
Gaylord
Alpena
Traverse City
Kalkaska
Atlanta
Frankfort
Beulah
Grayling
Mio
Harrisville
Manistee
Cadillac
Lake City
West Branch
Tawas City
Ludington
Reed City
Clare
Gladwin
Bad Axe
Baldwin
Big Rapids
Harrison
Midland
Hart
Mt. Pleasant
Bay City
Sandusky
Whitehall
Alma
Saginaw
Caro
Muskegon
Grand Rapids
Greenville
Ionia
St. Johns
Owosso
Frankenmuth
Lapeer
Grand Haven
Wyoming
Lansing
Corunna
Flint
Port Huron
Holland
Hastings
Charlotte
East Lansing
Waterford
South Haven
Battle Creek
Ann Arbor
Pontiac
Livonia
Sterling Heights
Warren
Benton Harbor
Kalamazoo
Marshall
Jackson
Detroit
St. Joseph
Portage
Dowagiac
Coldwater
Tecumseh
Monroe
Niles
Three Rivers
Sturgis
Hillsdale
Adrian

CANADA
ONTARIO

Lake Huron

WISCONSIN

Lake Michigan

CANADA
ONTARIO
Lake Erie

ILLINOIS
INDIANA
OHIO

ISLE ROYALE
Lake Superior
48°
89°

Lake Superior
Houghton
Ontonagon
L'Anse
Bessemer
Ironwood
Iron River
WISCONSIN

0   20   40   60   80 mi
0   30   60   90   120 km

© 2003 Encyclopædia Britannica, Inc.

MINNESOTA

Official name: State of Minnesota
Nicknames: North Star State, Gopher State
State Capital: St. Paul
State Flower: Pink and white moccasin flower
Motto: L'étoile du Nord (Star of the North)
Admitted to the Union: 1858 (32nd)
Total area: 84,068 sq. mi. (217,736 sq. km.) (ranks 12th)
Population (2000): 4,919,479 (ranks 21st)
Chief Cities: Bloomington, Duluth, Minneapolis, Rochester, St. Paul
Principal products/industries: Oats, corn, soybeans, sugar beets, wild rice, turkeys, hogs, dairy products, iron ore, granite, limestone, electronic equipment, pulp and paper products, food processing, tourism
Highest point: Eagle Mt. 2301 ft. (701 m.)

State History

Evidence of prehistoric habitation; at time of European arrival, inhabited by Algonquian Ojibwa and Siouan Dakota American Indian tribes; probably visited by French explorers Pierre Radisson and Seigneur Chouart des Groseilliers 1654–60; Upper Mississippi Valley explored by Frenchmen René-Robert, Sieur de La Salle and Louis Hennepin 1680, and became extensive fur-trading region under the French; part northeast of the Mississippi ceded to British 1763 and to U.S. 1783, and included in Northwest Territory 1787; southwestern part acquired by U.S. in Louisiana Purchase 1803; northwestern part ceded to U.S. in border treaty with British 1818; Fort Snelling, first U.S. outpost in the region, established 1819; included in various territories before organization of Minnesota Territory Mar. 3, 1849, which included present Minnesota and the parts of North and South Dakota that lie east of the Missouri River; admitted to Union (with present boundaries) May 11, 1858; Sioux uprising occurred in southern Minnesota 1862; an early center of the Grange movement from 1867 on.

The central design of the flag has the state seal in circular form. Around the seal are 19 gold stars (arranged in 5 groups) symbolizing Minnesota as the 19th state to follow the original 13, and a border of lady's slipper flowers. Inside is a mounted Indian, a representation of St. Anthony Falls, and a setting sun.

MISSISSIPPI

Official name: State of Mississippi
Nickname: Magnolia State
State Capital: Jackson
State Flower: Magnolia
Motto: Virtute et Armis (By Valor and Arms)
Admitted to the Union: 1817 (20th)
Total area: 47,689 sq. mi. (123,514 sq. km.) (ranks 32nd)
Population (2000): 2,844,658 (ranks 31st)
Chief Cities: Biloxi, Greenville, Gulfport, Hattiesburg, Jackson, Meridian,
Principal Products: Cotton, soybeans, grains, livestock, petroleum, natural gas, chemicals, apparel, wood products
Highest point: Woodall Mt. 806 ft. (246 m.)

State History

Evidence of prehistoric inhabitants (Mound Builders); prior to European settlement inhabited by several tribes including the Choctaw, Natchez, and Chickasaw; became part of French-controlled Louisiana; Biloxi settled by French colonist Pierre Le Moyne d'Iberville 1699; except for southern part (British West Florida), region ceded to U.S. 1783; northern section included in Territory South of the Ohio River 1790; southern part included in Mississippi Territory 1798, which was expanded 1804 to include most of current state; western part of the territory admitted to the Union with its present boundaries Dec. 10, 1817 as state of Mississippi, but its southernmost strip of land not formally ceded by Spain until 1819; seceded Jan. 9, 1861; scene of important battles during Civil War; readmitted to Union Feb. 23, 1870; adopted present constitution 1890.

After the Civil War, a new state constitution was adopted, the product of a white majority that wished to minimize the influence in state affairs of local blacks and of the federal government. The new flag, still in use, has three stripes that recall the Stars and Bars of the Confederacy, and the Confederate Battle Flag as its canton.

MISSOURI

Official name: State of Missouri
Nickname: Show Me State
State Capital: Jefferson City
State Flower: Hawthorn
Motto: Salus Populi Suprema Lex
  Esto (Let the Welfare of the People
  Be the Supreme Law)
Admitted to the Union: 1821 (24th)
Total area: 69,697 sq. mi. (180,515 sq.
  km.) (ranks 19th)
Population (2000): 5,595,211 (ranks
  17th)

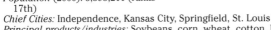

Chief Cities: Independence, Kansas City, Springfield, St. Louis
Principal products/industries: Soybeans, corn, wheat, cotton, livestock,
  cement, lead, iron ore, coal, transportation and aerospace equipment,
  chemicals, fabricated metal products
Highest point: Taum Sauk Mt. 1772 ft. (540 m.)

State History

Evidence of prehistoric inhabitants (Mound Builders); prior to European settlement inhabited by several Algonquian and Siouan tribes,
including the Osage and the Missouri; visited by French explorers Père
Marquette 1673 and Louis Jolliet 1683; probably first settled by French
at Ste. Genevieve 1735; part of Louisiana Purchase 1803; included in
Louisiana Territory 1805, and in Missouri Territory 1812; Missouri's
application for admission as slave state 1817 caused bitter controversy
which was settled by Missouri Compromise 1820 (Missouri admitted as
slave state Aug. 10, 1821, Maine as free, no slavery above 36°30′—later
repealed); did not secede from Union 1861; scene of fighting during Civil
War 1861–64; adopted present constitution 1945.

The flag has the state coat of arms, which is divided vertically,
with the arms of the United States on one side and a crescent
and bear on the other. The crescent, a traditional symbol in her-
aldry of a 2nd son, was intended to indicate that Missouri was
the 2nd state carved out of the Louisiana Territory.

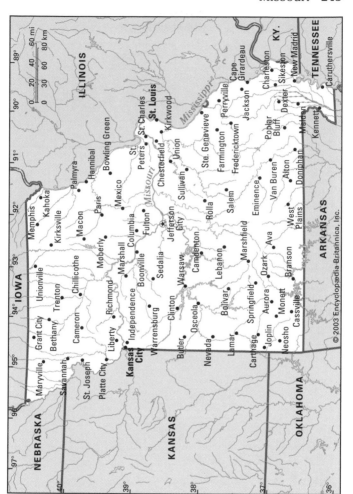

MONTANA

Official name: State of Montana
Nickname: Treasure State
State Capital: Helena
State Flower: Bitterroot
Motto: Oro y Plata (Gold and Silver)
Admitted to the Union: 1889 (41st)
Total area: 147,046 sq. mi. (380,849 sq. km.) (ranks 4th)
Population (2000): 902,195 (ranks 44th)
Chief Cities: Billings, Bozeman, Butte, Great Falls, Helena, Missoula
Principal products/industries: Wheat, barley, sugar beets, corn, livestock, copper, petroleum, phosphate rock, food processing, lumber, primary metals
Highest point: Granite Peak 12,799 ft. (3901 m.)

State History

Inhabited by several native tribes prior to European settlement, including Blackfoot, Cheyenne, Arapaho, and Flathead Indians; all except a small area in northwest was part of Louisiana Purchase 1803; crossed by American explorers Meriwether Lewis and William Clark 1805–06; its boundary with Canada settled by treaties 1818 and 1846; part west of the Rocky Mountains acquired in Oregon Country; parts included in various territories of the U.S. prior to organization of territory of Montana 1864; first crossed by rail (Northern Pacific) 1883; admitted to Union Nov. 8, 1889; adopted new state constitution 1972.

MONTANA

The state flag has at its center a seal that includes a representation of the Rocky Mountains, fundamental to the state's topography and to its name, from the Spanish montaña ("mountain"). The seal also depicts a river and forests and Great Falls, a distinctive landmark.

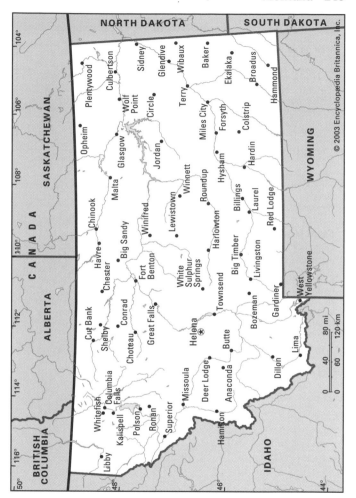

NEBRASKA

Official name: State of Nebraska
Nickname: Cornhusker State
State Capital: Lincoln
State Flower: Goldenrod
Motto: Equality Before the Law
Admitted to the Union: 1867 (37th)
Total area: 77,355 sq. mi. (200,349 sq. km.) (ranks 15th)
Population (2000): 1,711,263 (ranks 38th)
Chief Cities: Lincoln, Omaha
Principal products/industries: Corn, wheat, livestock, oil, food processing, machinery, fabricated metal products
Highest point: Johnson Township 5426 ft. (1654 m.)

State History

Part of Louisiana Purchase 1803, of Louisiana Territory 1805, and of Missouri Territory 1812; part of unorganized U.S. territory c. 1821–54; part of Nebraska Territory organized 1854 as result of Kansas-Nebraska Act; territory reduced to area of present state by 1863; held first constitutional convention 1866; admitted to Union Mar. 1, 1867; established one-house legislature, the nation's only one, 1937.

In 1925, Nebraska became the last of the conterminous 48 states to adopt a flag of its own. In the design is the seal, which shows the Missouri River with a steamboat, a blacksmith in the foreground, a settler's cabin surrounded by wheat sheaves and growing corn, and a railroad train heading toward the Rocky Mountains.

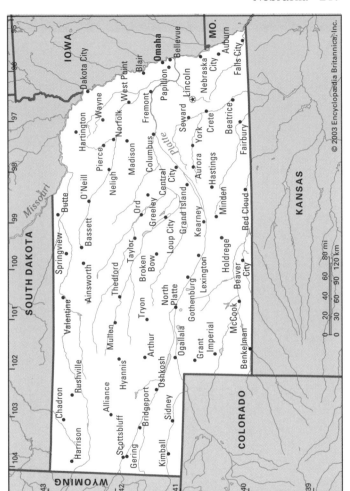

IOWA

MO.

Omaha

Bellevue

Auburn

Dakota City

Falls City

Blair

West Point

Papillion

Nebraska City

Wayne

Fremont

Lincoln

Hartington

Norfolk

Seward

Crete

York

Beatrice

Pierce

Columbus

Platte

Madison

Fairbury

Central City

Aurora

O'Neill

Neligh

Hastings

Butte

Ord

Greeley

Grand Island

Minden

Bassett

Loup City

Kearney

Red Cloud

Springview

Taylor

Broken Bow

Holdrege

Ainsworth

Thedford

North Platte

Lexington

Beaver City

Valentine

Tryon

Gothenburg

McCook

Mullen

Arthur

Ogallala

Imperial

Benkelman

Rushville

Hyannis

Oshkosh

Grant

Chadron

Alliance

Bridgeport

Sidney

Scottsbluff

Harrison

Gering

Kimball

SOUTH DAKOTA

Missouri

KANSAS

COLORADO

WYOMING

© 2003 Encyclopædia Britannica, Inc.

0   20   40   60   80 mi
0 30 60 90 120 km

95   96   97   98   99   100   101   102   103   104

43   42   41   40   39

NEVADA

Official name: State of Nevada
Nickname: Silver State; Sagebrush State
State Capital: Carson City
State Flower: Sagebrush
Motto: All For Our Country
Admitted to the Union: 1864 (36th)
Total area: 110,561 sq. mi. (286,353 sq. km.) (ranks 7th)
Population (2000): 1,998,257 (ranks 35th)
Chief Cities: Carson City, Las Vegas, Reno
Principal products/industries: Wheat, livestock, gold, barite, mercury, lumber and wood products, chemicals, tourism and gambling
Highest point: Boundary Peak 13,140 ft. (4005 m.)

State History

Evidence of prehistoric inhabitants in the region (since about 20,000 years ago) includes projectile points, rock art, and dwelling remains; some Anasazi sites in southeast; at time of European contact (c. 18th century) region inhabited by several Indian tribes including Shoshoni and Paiute; some exploration by Spanish (18th century), fur traders (1820s), and others; major exploration and mapping by John C. Frémont and Kit Carson 1843–45; included in region ceded by Mexico to U.S. 1848; included in Utah Territory 1850–61; first permanent settlement made c. 1850 at Mormon Station (now Genoa); settlement increased after discovery of Comstock Lode 1859; organized as Territory of Nevada 1861; admitted to Union as state Oct. 31, 1864; enlarged slightly 1866 to present boundaries.

An early state flag, honoring the mining industry in the state, had silver and gold stars and the words "silver," "Nevada," and "gold" on a blue field. Today's flag features a wreath of sagebrush surrounding a silver star and the motto "Battle Born," honoring Nevada's admission to the Union during the Civil War.

CALIFORNIA

ORE.

IDAHO

UTAH

ARIZONA

Vya
Orovada
Mountain City
Tuscarora
Montello
Wells
Winnemucca
Gerlach
Carlin
Elko
Spring Creek
Imlay
Battle Mountain
Lee
Lovelock
Sun Valley
Fernley
Eureka
McGill
Reno
Sparks
Fallon
Ruth
Ely
Crystal Bay
Virginia City
Austin
Baker
Carson City
Lake Tahoe
Gabbs
Duckwater
Gardnerville
Yerington
Babbitt
Hawthorne
Mina
Mount Montgomery
Tonopah
Pioche
Dyer
Panaca
Goldfield
Caliente
Alamo
Beatty
Mesquite
Logandale
North Las Vegas
Overton
Pahrump
Sunrise Manor
Las Vegas
Henderson
Paradise
Boulder City
Colorado

0   20   40   60   80 mi
0   30   60   90 120 km

© 2003 Encyclopædia Britannica, Inc.

NEW HAMPSHIRE

Official name: State of New
  Hampshire
Nickname: Granite State
State Capital: Concord
State Flower: Purple lilac
Motto: Live Free Or Die
Admitted to the Union: 1788; 9th of
  the original 13 colonies to ratify
  the U.S. Constitution
Total area: 9279 sq. mi. (24,033 sq.
  km.) (ranks 44th)

Population (2000): 1,235,786 (ranks 41st)
Chief Cities: Concord, Manchester, Nashua
Principal products/industries: Dairy products, apples, maple syrup, vegetables, nursery plants, tourism, electrical products, electronic equipment, paper products, leather goods, once an important center of granite quarrying
Highest point: Mt. Washington 6288 ft. (1917 m.)

State History

Prior to European settlement, inhabited by numerous Algonquin tribes, especially of the Pennacook confederacy; coast explored by several English explorers early 17th century; area east of the Merrimack River included in grant to John Mason and Sir Ferdinando Gorges 1622 and in New Hampshire grant to Mason 1629; first settled by English near Portsmouth 1623; controlled by Massachusetts 1641–79; made a separate royal province 1679 but under same governor as Massachusetts 1699–1741; area of Vermont settled under New Hampshire jurisdiction, which New York disputed; area of Vermont awarded 1764 by royal order to jurisdiction of New York (final claims to area not relinquished by New Hampshire until 1782); first colony to declare independence from Great Britain 1776; adopted first constitution 1776, present constitution 1784 which later was frequently amended; Dartmouth College case decided 1819 in U.S. Supreme Court, confirming right of private corporations against excessive state regulation.

The 1909 flag law provided for the state seal in the center, framed by a wreath of laurel with nine stars interspersed, signifying the rank of New Hampshire as the ninth state to ratify the U.S. Constitution. The seal, modified in 1931, features the frigate Raleigh being built at Portsmouth in 1776.

73°

72°

71°

CANADA

QUEBEC

45°

Pittsburg

Errol

0   20   40 mi

0   30   60 km

Stratford

West Milan

Groveton

Lancaster

Berlin

MAINE

Whitefield

Littleton

Lisbon

Woodsville

North
Woodstock

Glen

44°

VERMONT

Conway

Connecticut

Plymouth

Hanover

Ossipee

Lake
Winnipesaukee

Lebanon

Enfield

Meredith

Laconia

Franklin

Belmont

Newport

New
London

Farmington

Claremont

Sutton

Rochester

Somersworth

Merrimack

Concord

Dover

Hillsborough

Pembroke

Allenstown

Walpole

Hooksett

Portsmouth

43°

Antrim

Manchester

Exeter

Keene

Peterborough

Hampton

Derry

ATLANTIC
OCEAN

Troy

Milford

Salem

Winchester

Nashua

MASSACHUSETTS

© 2003 Encyclopædia Britannica, Inc.

NEW JERSEY

Official name: State of New Jersey
Nickname: Garden State
State Capital: Trenton
State Flower: Violet
Motto: Liberty and Prosperity
Admitted to the Union: 1787; 3rd of the original 13 colonies to ratify the U.S. Constitution
Total area: 7787 sq. mi. (20,168 sq. km.) (ranks 46th)
Population (2000): 8,414,350 (ranks 9th)

Chief Cities: Elizabeth, Jersey City, Newark, Paterson
Principal products/industries: Corn, cranberries, peppers, tomatoes, nursery plants, chemicals, electronic equipment, apparel, electrical machinery
Highest point: High Point 1803 ft. (550 m.)

State History

Prior to European colonization, region inhabited especially by Delaware tribes; sighted by Florentine navigator Giovanni da Verrazano 1524 and English navigator Henry Hudson 1609; first settled by Dutch and along Delaware River by Swedes; ceded to English as part of New Netherland 1664 and given the Latin name of Nova Caesarea; its eastern and northern part (East Jersey) became a proprietary colony regranted by Duke of York to Sir George Carteret and was sold to William Penn and associates 1682; its western and southern part (West Jersey), or the lower counties on Delaware River, held by William Penn 1676–1702; became royal province 1702; governed by governor of New York until 1738; declared independence from England and adopted first state constitution 1776; scene of numerous battles during the Revolutionary War, especially the important battles at Trenton, Princeton, and Monmouth; delegates to Constitutional Convention 1787 forwarded New Jersey Plan for small states; Trenton became state capital 1790; adopted new state constitution 1844 which included several democratic reforms; present constitution adopted 1947.

The state flag was adopted in 1896. The coat of arms depicts three plows that stand for agriculture, which is also represented by the goddess Ceres (one of the supporters). The other supporter is Liberty. The horse's head in the crest was shown on early New Jersey coins.

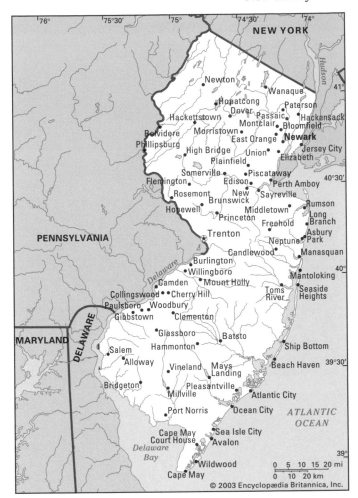

NEW YORK

Newton
Wanaque
Hopatcong
Paterson
Dover
Hackettstown
Passaic
Hackensack
Montclair
Bloomfield
Belvidere
Morristown
East Orange
Newark
Phillipsburg
High Bridge
Union
Jersey City
Plainfield
Elizabeth
Flemington
Somerville
Edison
Piscataway
Perth Amboy
Rosemont
New
Sayreville
Rumson
Brunswick
Hopewell
Middletown
Long
Princeton
Freehold
Branch
Trenton
Neptune
Asbury
Park
Candlewood
Manasquan
Burlington
Willingboro
Mantoloking
Camden
Mount Holly
Toms
Seaside
Collingswood
Cherry Hill
River
Heights
Paulsboro
Woodbury
Gibbstown
Clementon
Glassboro
Batsto
Salem
Hammonton
Ship Bottom
Alloway
Vineland
Mays
Beach Haven
Landing
Bridgeton
Pleasantville
Millville
Atlantic City
Port Norris
Ocean City
ATLANTIC
OCEAN
Cape May
Sea Isle City
Court House
Avalon
Delaware
Bay
Wildwood
Cape May

PENNSYLVANIA

MARYLAND

DELAWARE

Delaware

Hudson

41°

40°30'

40°

39°30'

39°

76°
75°30'
75°
74°30'
74°

0 5 10 15 20 mi
0 10 20 km

© 2003 Encyclopædia Britannica, Inc.

NEW MEXICO

Official name: State of New Mexico
Nickname: Land of Enchantment
State Capital: Santa Fe
State Flower: Yucca
Motto: Crescit Eundo (It Grows As It Goes)
Admitted to the Union: 1912 (47th)
Total area: 121,593 sq. mi. (314,926 sq. km.) (ranks 5th)
Population (2000): 1,819,046 (ranks 36th)
Chief Cities: Albuquerque, Las Cruces, Santa Fe
Principal products/industries: Livestock, oil, natural gas, potash, copper, uranium, food processing, chemicals
Highest point: Wheeler Peak 13,161 ft. (4011 m.)

State History

Evidence of prehistoric inhabitants, especially Mogollon and Anasazi peoples; at time of European arrival inhabited mainly by Pueblo tribes (such as the Zuni) and Athabascan tribes (such as the Apache and the Navajo); first European visitor to area was missionary Marcos de Niza sent from Mexico (New Spain) 1539; explored by Spanish explorer Francisco Vásquez de Coronado's expedition 1540–42; Spanish settlement begun by explorer Juan de Oñate 1598; Santa Fe founded in 1609–10; governed by Mexico after 1821; part east of Rio Grande included in annexation of Texas 1845; rest ceded to U.S. by Mexico 1848 (Treaty of Guadalupe Hidalgo) except for southern strip which was included in Gadsden Purchase 1853; first bid for statehood 1850 denied in favor of organization of New Mexico Territory; territory reduced to area of present state by 1863; held several constitutional conventions before finally being admitted to Union as state Jan. 6, 1912.

The flag was officially adopted in March 1925 as a result of a design competition. The colors are based on the flag of Spain, which had ruled New Mexico until the early 19th century. Today the Zia sun is widely recognized as a state symbol, and the design of the capitol building of New Mexico was influenced by its shape.

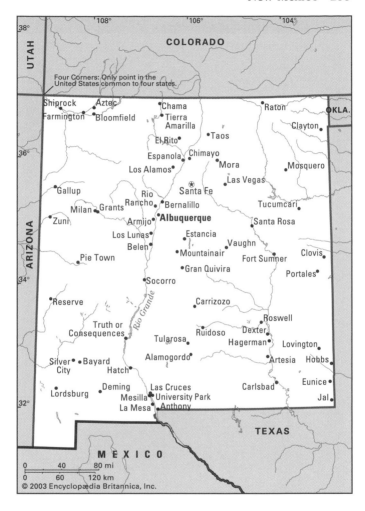

Four Corners: Only point in the
United States common to four states.

© 2003 Encyclopædia Britannica, Inc.

NEW YORK

Official name: State of New York
Nickname: Empire State
State Capital: Albany
State Flower: Rose
Motto: Excelsior (Ever Upward)
Admitted to the Union: 1788; 11th of
the original 13 colonies to ratify
the U.S. Constitution
Total area: 49,576 sq. mi. (128,402 sq.
km.) (ranks 30th)
Population (2000): 18,976,457 (ranks
3rd)

Chief Cities: Albany, Buffalo, New York City, Rochester, Syracuse, Yonkers
Principal products/industries: Vegetables, fruit, dairy products, zinc, gravel,
salt, apparel, primary metals, electrical machinery, chemicals, finance,
printing and publishing, food processing
Highest point: Mt. Marcy 5344 ft. (1629 m.)

State History

Prior to European colonization inhabited by Algonquins (Mahican,
Wappinger) and Iroquois (Mohawk, Oneida, Onondaga, Cayuga, and
Seneca); New York Bay visited by Florentine navigator Giovanni da Verrazano 1524; explored 1609 by English navigator Henry Hudson (Hudson
River) and French explorer Samuel de Champlain (northern New York to
Lake Champlain); Dutch trading posts, established on Manhattan Island
and at Fort Nassau, were taken over by Dutch West India Company
under which early colonization occurred; opened 1629 to patroon colonization for several years; formed part of Dutch colony of New Netherland, surrendered without resistance to English 1664 and renamed New
York after its proprietor, Duke of York; briefly recaptured by Dutch
1673–74; scene of much fighting during French and Indian War, in which
the Iroquois Confederacy became allied with the British; after ratifying
Declaration of Independence, held first state constitutional convention
1776, adopted first state constitution 1777; scene of numerous engagements of the American Revolution including Ticonderoga, Long Island,
White Plains, Saratoga, and Kingston, and also of Benedict Arnold's trea-
son at West Point; ratified U.S. Constitution 1788; state capital moved
1797 from New York City to Albany; Canadian frontier scene of several
engagements during War of 1812; opening of Erie Canal 1825 spurred
development of western New York; adopted present constitution 1894.

The coat of arms features a sun symbol, two supporters, and
the state motto. The scene depicted under the sun is a view of
the Hudson River. The supporters of the shield are Liberty
(with her liberty cap on a staff) and Justice. An American eagle
surmounts the globe at the top.

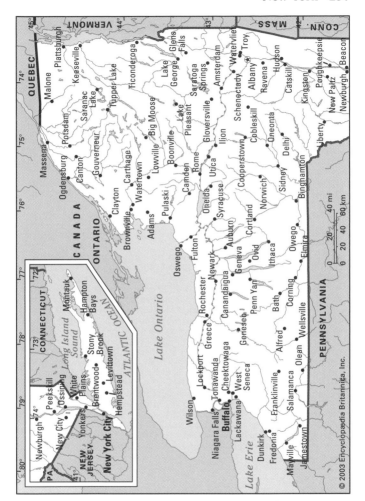

© 2003 Encyclopædia Britannica, Inc.

NORTH CAROLINA

Official name: State of North Carolina
Nicknames: Tar Heel State, Old North
  State
State Capital: Raleigh
State Flower: Dogwood
Motto: To Be Rather Than To Seem
Admitted to the Union: 1789; 12th of
  the original 13 colonies to ratify
  the U.S. Constitution
Total area: 52,669 sq. mi. (136,413 sq.
  km.) (ranks 28th)
Population (2000): 8,049,313 (ranks 11th)
Chief Cities: Charlotte, Durham, Greensboro, Raleigh, Winston-Salem
Principal products/industries: Tobacco, corn, soybeans, peanuts, livestock,
  gravel, feldspar, tourism, textiles, cigarettes, food products, chemicals,
  furniture
Highest point: Mt. Mitchell 6684 ft. (2037 m.)

State History

Inhabited by several Algonquin, Siouan, and Iroquoian tribes prior to
European contact, especially the Cherokee, Catawba, and Tuscarora;
coast explored by Florentine navigator Giovanni da Verrazano (under
French employ) 1524, and others; first English settlement in the New
World established 1585 at Roanoke Island; region of Albemarle Sound
settled mid-17th century by Virginia colonists; formed a part of Carolina
grant given 1663 (expanded 1665) by King Charles II to eight noblemen
of his court; governed largely separately from South Carolina from late
17th century, and officially separated 1712; Regulator movement
(1768–71) against excessive taxation and government corruption suppressed by colonial forces at Alamance 1771; first Revolutionary battle
in the state occurred at "Moores Creek Bridge" Feb. 27, 1776; Provincial
Congress adopted Apr. 12, 1776 the Halifax Resolves that authorized the
delegates for North Carolina to the Continental Congress "to concur
with the delegates of the other colonies in declaring independency"—
the first explicit sanction of independence by an American colony;
adopted state constitution 1776; passed ordinance of secession May 20,
1861; secession ordinance annulled and slavery abolished 1865; new
state constitution 1868; readmitted to Union July 11, 1868; latest state
constitution 1971.

One of the ribbons in the flag has "May 20th, 1775," the date
on which some local citizens were supposedly first to proclaim
their independence from Great Britain. The other ribbon has
"April 12th, 1776," date of the Halifax Resolves, authorizing
North Carolina delegates to approve the U.S. Declaration of
Independence.

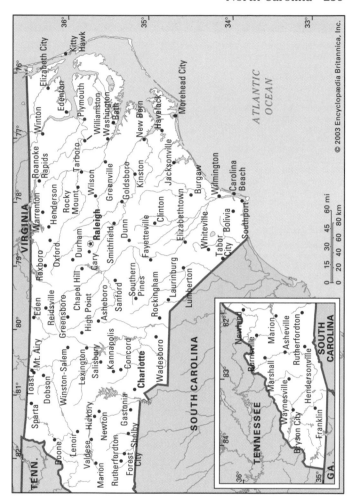

© 2003 Encyclopædia Britannica, Inc.

NORTH DAKOTA

Official name: State of North Dakota
Nicknames: Peace Garden State,
 Flickertail State
State Capital: Bismarck
State Flower: Wild prairie rose
Motto: Liberty and Union, Now and
 Forever, One and Inseparable
Admitted to the Union: 1889 (39th)
Total area: 70,665 sq. mi. (183,022 sq.
 km.) (ranks 17th)
Population (2000): 642,200 (ranks
 47th)
Chief Cities: Bismarck, Fargo, Grand Forks, Minot
Principal products/industries: Wheat, barley, flaxseed, oats, livestock, oil,
 coal, food processing
Highest point: White Butte 3506 ft. (1069 m.)

State History

Evidence of prehistoric inhabitants throughout the state; at time of
European contact was inhabited by native Algonquin (Cheyenne and
Ojibwa), Caddoan (Arikara), and especially Siouan (Assiniboin, Dakota,
Hidatsa, and Mandan) peoples; first visited by La Vérendrye brothers
1742–43; greater part included in Louisiana Purchase 1803; northern
limit of northeast section determined by treaty with Great Britain 1818;
parts included in several U.S. territories 1805–61; Dakota Territory (capital Yankton 1861–83, Bismark 1883–89) organized Mar. 2, 1861 including
North and South Dakota and much of Wyoming and Montana; reduced
in 1868 to area of present two states of North and South Dakota; settlement hastened by discovery of gold c. 1874 in the Black Hills; separated from South Dakota and admitted to Union as state Nov. 2, 1889; constitution passed 1889.

In the late 19th century the Dakota Territorial Guard displayed a
blue flag with the coat of arms of the U.S. in the center. After North
Dakota joined the Union in 1889, a similar design was used by the
state's National Guard. In 1911 the design was approved for the official state flag.

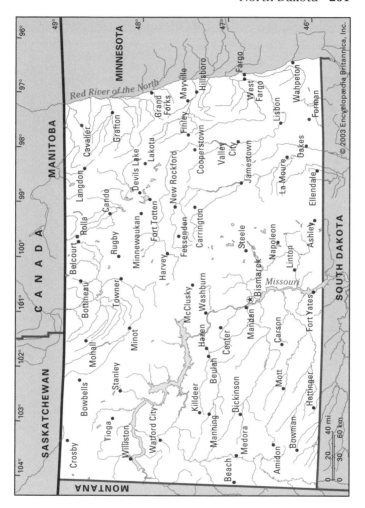

OHIO

Official name: State of Ohio
Nickname: Buckeye State
State Capital: Columbus
State Flower: Scarlet carnation
Motto: With God, All Things Are
  Possible
Admitted to the Union: 1803 (17th)
Total area: 41,222 sq. mi. (106,765 sq.
  km.) (ranks 35th)
Population (2000): 11,353,140 (ranks
  7th)

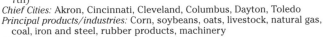

Chief Cities: Akron, Cincinnati, Cleveland, Columbus, Dayton, Toledo
Principal products/industries: Corn, soybeans, oats, livestock, natural gas,
  coal, iron and steel, rubber products, machinery
Highest point: Campbell Hill 1550 ft. (472 m.)

State History

Has many earthwork mounds of prehistoric Mound Builders; inhabited
by various Indian tribes (including Miami, Shawnee, Delaware, and
Wyandot) when Europeans began settling the area; claimed by both
France and Britain in colonial times; ceded to Britain 1763 following
French and Indian War; became part of U.S. by Treaty of Paris 1783 following American Revolution; included 1787 in Northwest Territory;
first permanent white settlement at Marietta 1788; western boundary
with Indian lands determined by Maj. Gen. Anthony Wayne's defeat
of Indians 1794 at Fallen Timbers and by Treaty of Greenville 1795;
Western Reserve incorporated 1800; first constitution 1802; unofficially
entered Union Feb. 19, 1803. In 1953, by resolution of U.S. Congress,
Mar. 1, 1803 declared official day of admission to Union.

The red disk at the hoist end suggests the seed of the buckeye,
the official state tree. The white O is the initial letter of the state
name, while the use of stars and stripes and the colors red,
white, and blue clearly honor the national flag. The 17 stars in
the flag recall that Ohio was the 17th state to join the Union.

CANADA

ONTARIO

MICHIGAN

Lake Erie

PENNSYLVANIA

Conneaut
Ashtabula
Painesville
Jefferson

Wauseon
Bryan
Toledo
Port Clinton
Sandusky
Lorain
Cleveland
Chardon

Napoleon
Bowling Green
Fremont
Elyria
Parma
Warren
Niles

Defiance
New Bavaria
Clyde
Norwalk
Medina
Cuyahoga Falls
Ravenna
Youngstown

Paulding
Findlay
Tiffin
Willard
Barberton
Akron
Alliance
Salem

Van Wert
Ottawa
Upper Sandusky
Bucyrus
Shelby
Ashland
Wooster
Massillon
Lisbon

Delphos
Lima
Kenton
Galion
Mansfield
East Liverpool

Celina
Wapakoneta
Marion
Millersburg
Dover
New Philadelphia

Bellefontaine
Mount Gilead
Cadiz
Steubenville

Sidney
Marysville
Delaware
Mount Vernon
Coshocton
St. Clairsville
Martins Ferry

Greenville
Urbana
Upper Arlington
Newark
Zanesville
Cambridge

Troy
London
Columbus
Grove City
New Lexington
Caldwell
Woodsfield

Dayton
Kettering
Springfield
Lancaster
Circleville
Logan
McConnelsville
Marietta

Xenia
Washington Court House
Chillicothe
McArthur
Athens

Middletown
Lebanon
Wilmington
Waverly
Pomeroy

Hamilton
Fairfield
Hillsboro
Jackson
Gallipolis

Cincinnati
Batavia
Georgetown
West Union
Portsmouth
WEST VIRGINIA

Ohio
Ironton
South Point

KENTUCKY

INDIANA

Ohio River

0   20   40 mi
0   30   60 km

© 2003 Encyclopædia Britannica, Inc.

OKLAHOMA

Official name: State of Oklahoma
Nickname: Sooner State
State Capital: Oklahoma City
State Flower: Mistletoe
Motto: Labor Omnia Vincit (Labor Conquers All Things)
Admitted to the Union: 1907 (46th)
Total area: 69,956 sq. mi. (181,186 sq. km.) (ranks 18th)
Population (2000): 3,450,654 (ranks 27th)
Chief Cities: Oklahoma City, Tulsa

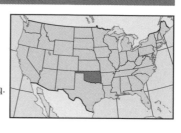

Principal products/industries: Wheat, cotton, sorghum, beef cattle, gas and petroleum, food processing, fabricated-metal products
Highest point: Black Mesa 4973 ft. (1516 m.)

State History

Except for Panhandle, formed part of Louisiana Purchase 1803; southern part nominally included in Arkansas Territory 1819–28; settled by Indians as unorganized Indian Territory c. 1820–40, especially following the 1830 Indian Removal Act and subsequent forced migration of tribes from the East; part opened to white settlement 1889; western part organized as Oklahoma Territory 1890; rest gradually opened to whites; on Nov. 16, 1907, Indian Territory and Oklahoma Territory were merged and admitted to Union as state.

OKLAHOMA

The blue background symbolizes loyalty and devotion; the traditional bison-hide shield of the Osage Indians suggests the defense of the state. The shield has small crosses, standing for stars (common in Native American art), and an olive branch and calumet as emblems of peace for whites and Native Americans.

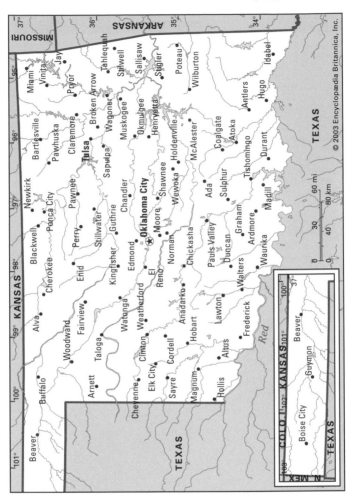

© 2003 Encyclopædia Britannica, Inc.

OREGON

Official name: State of Oregon
Nickname: Beaver State
State Capital: Salem
State Flower: Oregon grape
Motto: Alis Volat Propriis (She Flies
   With Her Own Wings)
Admitted to the Union: 1859 (33rd)
Total area: 97,073 sq. mi. (251,419 sq.
   km.) (ranks 10th)
Population (2000): 3,421,399 (ranks
   28th)
Chief Cities: Eugene, Portland, Salem
Principal products/industries: Wheat, fruit, vegetables, livestock, dairy prod-
   ucts, lumber, fishing, gravel, plywood, primary-metal products, high-tech
   industries, tourism
Highest point: Mt. Hood 11,235 ft. (3424 m.)

State History

Inhabited by numerous American Indian peoples when Europeans
arrived; coast first sighted by Spanish sailors; region claimed for
England by Sir Francis Drake 1579; visited by Capt. James Cook 1778;
Columbia River explored by Capt. Robert Gray of Boston 1792, giving
U.S. a claim to the region; mouth of Columbia River reached by Meriwether Lewis and William Clark's overland expedition 1805; for a time
jointly occupied by England and U.S.; first white settlement founded at
Astoria by American fur trader John Jacob Astor 1811, but lost to British
during War of 1812; region dominated by Britain's Hudson's Bay Company under John McLoughlin (often called "the father of Oregon") 1820s
through 1840s; first permanent settlement in the Willamette Valley
established 1834 by Methodist missionaries; settlement accelerated
from c. 1843 with mass migration of Americans over the Oregon Trail;
Great Britain relinquished claim to region 1846; part of Oregon Territory
1848; admitted to Union with present boundaries Feb. 14, 1859.

The elements in the seal are ships, mountains, and symbols of
agriculture, as well as a pioneer covered wagon and the phrase
"The Union." The 33 stars correspond to Oregon's order of
admission to the Union. A beaver symbol on the reverse recalls
the importance of the animal to early trappers and hunters in
the Pacific Northwest.

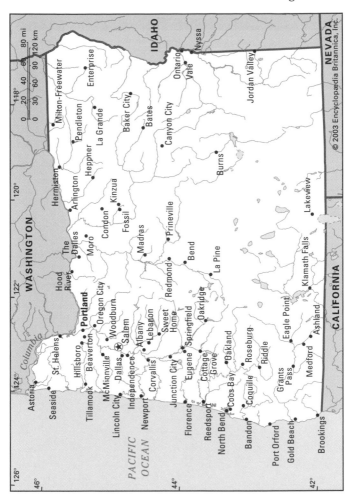

PENNSYLVANIA

Official name: Commonwealth of
Pennsylvania
Nickname: Keystone State
State Capital: Harrisburg
State Flower: Mountain laurel
Motto: Virtue, Liberty, and
Independence
Admitted to the Union: 1787; 2nd of
the original 13 colonies to ratify
the U.S. Constitution
Total area: 45,333 sq. mi. (117,412 sq.
km.) (ranks 33rd)

Population (2000): 12,281,054 (ranks 6th)
Chief Cities: Allentown, Erie, Harrisburg, Philadelphia, Pittsburgh
Principal products/industries: Corn, wheat, oats, dairy products, coal, iron
ore, iron and steel, electrical machinery, apparel, chemicals, transporta-
tion equipment
Highest point: Mt. Davis 3213 ft. (979 m.)

State History

French adventurer Étienne Brulé probably first European to visit this
area 1615–16, inhabited principally by Delaware, Susquehanna, and
Shawnee tribes; first European settlement made by Swedes on Tinicum
Island 1643; rights to land granted by British crown to William Penn,
who established Quaker colony 1682; first hospital in U.S. established
in Philadelphia 1751; Pennsylvania-Maryland boundary line determined
1763–67; Declaration of Independence pronounced in Philadelphia 1776;
delegation headed by Benjamin Franklin represented Pennsylvania in
Constitutional Convention in Philadelphia 1787; ratified U.S. Constitution Dec. 12, 1787; flood disaster at Johnstown May 31, 1889.

Agriculture and commerce are represented in the coat of arms
by the ship and the wheat sheaves, the plow, the wreath of corn
and olive, and the horses in harness. The state motto, "Virtue,
Liberty, and Independence," is inscribed on the ribbon below
the arms.

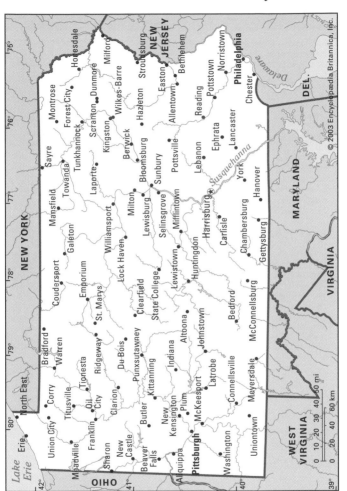

© 2003 Encyclopædia Britannica, Inc.

RHODE ISLAND

Official name: State of Rhode Island and Providence Plantations
Nicknames: Ocean State, Little Rhody
State Capital: Providence
State Flower: Violet
Motto: Hope
Admitted to the Union: 1790; 13th of the original 13 colonies to ratify the U.S. Constitution
Total area: 1212 sq. mi. (3139 sq. km.) (ranks 50th)
Population (2000): 1,048,319 (ranks 43rd)
Chief Cities: Cranston, Newport, Pawtucket, Providence, Warwick
Principal products/industries: Jewelry making, electronics, tourism, historically important textile industry
Highest point: Jerimoth Hill 812 ft. (247 m.)

State History

Originally settled by Narragansett Indians; Narragansett Bay explored by Florentine navigator Giovanni da Verrazano 1524; first permanent nonnative settlement founded by Roger Williams for religious dissenters at Providence 1636; scattered settlements united when charter granted by British King Charles II to Roger Williams 1663; charter provisions continued in effect until Dorr's Rebellion 1842, led by political activist Thomas Dorr, whose attempts to form an alternate government providing for extension of suffrage resulted in new state constitution 1843.

The Rhode Island legislature adopted an anchor for its colonial seal in 1647. The anchor was used on military flags by the time of the American Revolutionary War. The flag's anchor and motto were represented in Rococo style and encircled by stars corresponding to the number of original states in the Union.

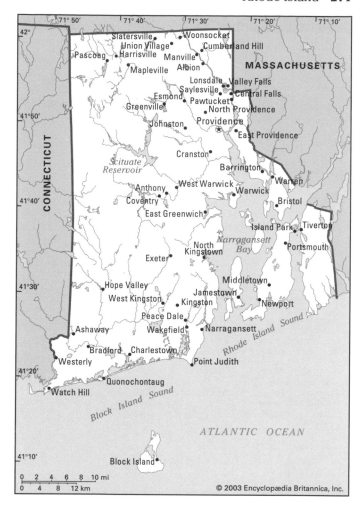

71° 50'   71° 40'   71° 30'   71° 20'   71° 10'

42°

Slatersville   Woonsocket
Union Village   Cumberland Hill
Pascoag   Harrisville   Manville
Mapleville   Albion   **MASSACHUSETTS**

Lonsdale   Valley Falls
Saylesville   Central Falls
Esmond   Pawtucket
41°50'   Greenville   North Providence
Johnston   Providence

CONNECTICUT

East Providence

Cranston

*Scituate
Reservoir*   Barrington

Anthony   West Warwick   Warren
41°40'   Coventry   Warwick
East Greenwich   Bristol

Island Park   Tiverton

*Narragansett
Bay*   Portsmouth

North
Kingstown
Exeter

41°30'   Middletown

Hope Valley   Jamestown
West Kingston   Kingston   Newport
Peace Dale
Ashaway   Wakefield   Narragansett
Bradford   Charlestown   *Rhode Island Sound*
41°20'   Westerly   Point Judith

Quonochontaug
Watch Hill   *Block Island Sound*

ATLANTIC   OCEAN

41°10'

Block Island

0   2   4   6   8   10 mi
0   4   8   12 km

© 2003 Encyclopædia Britannica, Inc.

SOUTH CAROLINA

Official name: State of South
  Carolina
Nickname: Palmetto State
State Capital: Columbia
State Flower: Yellow jassemine
Motto: Dum Spiro, Spero (While
  I Breathe, I Hope)
Admitted to the Union: 1788; 8th of
  the original 13 colonies to ratify
  the U.S. Constitution
Total area: 31,113 sq. mi. (80,583 sq.
  km.) (ranks 40th)
Population (2000): 4,012,012 (ranks 26th)
Chief Cities: Charleston, Columbia
Principal products/industries: Tobacco, cotton, soybeans, fruit, peanuts,
  livestock, lumbering, sand, gravel, stone, textiles, chemicals, paper prod-
  ucts, cement, clothing, tourism
Highest point: Sassafras Mt. 3560 ft. (1085 m.)

State History

Evidence of Mound Builder inhabitants in western part of state; at time
of European contact, inhabited by Siouan, Iroquoian, and Muskogean
Indians; coast explored by Spanish 1521; unsuccessful attempts at settlement made by Spanish and French 16th century; included in Carolina
grant given 1663 by Charles II to eight noblemen of his court; Charleston
founded 1670; English settlements harassed by Spanish and Indians
17th–18th centuries; overthrew proprietary rule 1719 in favor of rule as
a crown province 1729; scene of several engagements during American

Revolution, notably Kings Mountain, Cowpens, Eutaw Springs, Camden,
and Guilford Courthouse; ceded western lands to U.S. 1787; ratified U.S.
Constitution May 23, 1788; first state to secede from Union, passing
ordinance of secession Dec. 20, 1860; Confederate forces attacked Fort
Sumter Apr. 12, 1861, in the initial action of the Civil War; ordinance of
secession repealed and slavery abolished 1865; readmitted to the Union
June 25, 1868; adopted its present constitution 1895.

On September 13, 1775, a blue flag with a white crescent was
raised by anti-British forces at a fort in Charleston Harbor. The
fortification was protected by palmetto logs that caused British
cannonballs to bounce off. Consequently the palmetto was
adopted by South Carolinians as their chief state symbol.

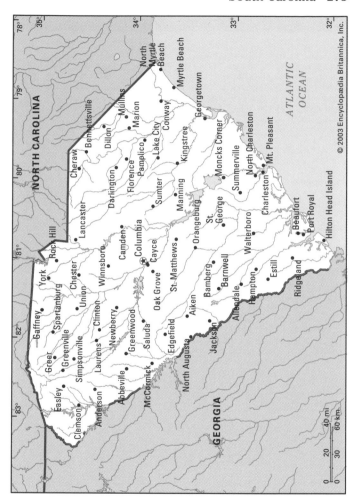

© 2003 Encyclopædia Britannica, Inc.

SOUTH DAKOTA

Official name: State of South Dakota
Nickname: Mount Rushmore State
State Capital: Pierre
State Flower: Pasqueflower
Motto: Under God the People Rule
Admitted to the Union: 1889 (40th)
Total area: 77,116 sq. mi. (199,730 sq. km.) (ranks 16th)
Population (2000): 754,844 (ranks 46th)
Chief Cities: Rapid City, Sioux Falls
Principal products/industries: Corn, wheat, oats, rye, flaxseed, livestock, gold, food processing, lumber and wood products, tourism
Highest point: Harney Peak 7242 ft. (2207 m.)

State History

Evidence of prehistoric Mound Builders' settlements; at time of European contact, inhabited by several Indian tribes, including especially the Arikara, who soon moved north, and several Dakota tribes; explored somewhat by French in 18th century; included in Louisiana Purchase 1803 and traversed by Lewis and Clark expedition 1804, 1806; fur trade with Indians conducted throughout 19th century until outbreak of Civil War; first permanent European settlement founded 1817, on future site of Fort Pierre, as a trading post; after several attempts, organized as part of Dakota Territory 1861 with capital at Yankton; latter 19th century characterized by conflict with Indians, several insect plagues, and Black Hills gold rush (discovery 1874); admitted to Union Nov. 2, 1889 upon division of Dakota Territory into two states; Pierre selected as state capital 1889; state constitution dates from 1889.

The South Dakota seal is represented over a sun in such a way that only the sun's rays are visible. The seal repeats the name of the state and the date of admission to the Union. Around the seal is the state name and nickname. The seal depicts a farmer, cattle, crops, a smelting furnace, and a steamship.

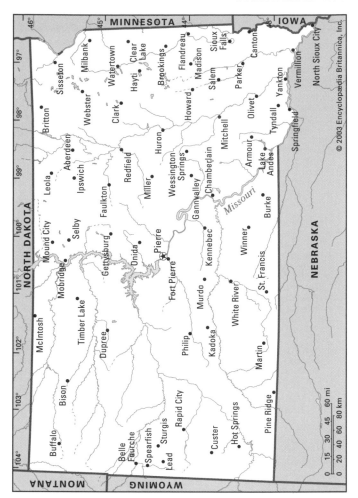

TENNESSEE

Official name: State of Tennessee
Nickname: Volunteer State
State Capital: Nashville
State Flower: Iris
Motto: Agriculture and Commerce
Admitted to the Union: 1796 (16th)
Total area: 42,144 sq. mi. (109,153 sq. km.) (ranks 34th)
Population (2000): 5,689,283 (ranks 16th)
Chief Cities: Chattanooga, Knoxville, Memphis, Nashville
Principal products/industries: Tobacco, soybeans, corn, livestock, coal, phosphate rock, chemicals, textiles, cement, electrical machinery
Highest point: Clingmans Dome 6643 ft. (2025 m.)

State History

Original inhabitants included Chicksaw, Cherokee, and Shawnee, among others; region visited by Spanish explorer Hernando de Soto c. 1540; included in British charter of Carolina and in French Louisiana claim late 17th century; claim to region ceded by France to Great Britain after French and Indian War; first permanent settlements made in Watauga Valley c. 1770; acknowledged by Great Britain as a part of United States after Revolutionary War; temporary state of Franklin formed c. 1784; included in Territory South of the Ohio River after North Carolina relinquished claims 1790; admitted to Union with present boundaries June 1, 1796; passed ordinance of secession June 8, 1861; scene of battles in Civil War, notably Shiloh, Chattanooga, Stones River, Nashville; slavery abolished and ordinance of secession declared null and void 1865; first of seceding states to be reorganized and readmitted to Union (July 24, 1866). Constitution dates from 1870.

The current flag design features three stripes and three stars. These were said by the designer to refer to "the three grand divisions of the State," but they have also been said to represent the three presidents who lived in Tennessee (Andrew Jackson, James Polk, and Andrew Johnson).

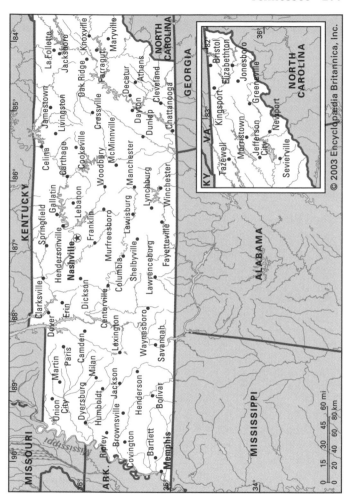

© 2003 Encyclopædia Britannica, Inc.

TEXAS

Official name: State of Texas
Nickname: Lone Star State
Capital: Austin
State flower: Bluebonnet
Motto: Friendship
Admitted to the Union: 1845 (28th)
Total area: 266,807 sq. mi. (691,030 sq. km.) (ranks 2nd)
Population (2000): 20,851,820 (ranks 2nd)
Chief cities: Arlington, Austin, Corpus Christi, Dallas, El Paso, Fort Worth, Houston, San Antonio
Principal products/industries: Cotton, rice, sorghum grain, wheat, livestock, oil, natural gas, sulfur, chemicals, electronics, food processing
Highest point: Guadalupe Peak 8749 ft. (2667 m.)

State History

Originally inhabited by Indians including Apaches, several tribes of the Caddo group, and others; explored by Spaniards early 16th–late 17th centuries; French explorer René-Robert Cavelier, Sieur de La Salle, attempted settlement at Matagorda Bay 1685, laying basis for French claim to region as part of Louisiana; effective Spanish occupation began c. 1700; U.S. acquired French claim in Louisiana Purchase 1803; U.S. claim to Texas relinquished by treaty with Spain 1819; became part of Mexico after Mexico gained independence from Spain 1821; Declaration of Independence from Mexico Mar. 1836; Texan army under commander Sam Houston won decisive battle against Mexican forces at San Jacinto Apr. 1836, gaining independence for the Republic of Texas; sought annexation to U.S. and was admitted to Union Dec. 29, 1845; boundary with Mexico along the Rio Grande fixed after Mexican War by Treaty of Guadalupe Hidalgo 1848; passed ordinance of secession Feb. 1, 1861; readmitted to Union Mar. 30, 1870; adopted constitution 1876.

The first official (though nonnational) Texas flag was based on the green-white-red vertical tricolor of Mexico. The present state flag was originally adopted in 1839 as the second national flag of the Republic of Texas. There was no change when Texas became a state of the United States in 1845.

104° COLO. 102° 100° KANSAS 98° 96° 94° MISSOURI

NEW MEXICO

36°

Dalhart • Spearman • Perryton
• Dumas • Borger • Canadian
• Panhandle • Pampa
Hereford • Amarillo • Wheeler OKLAHOMA ARKANSAS
• Canyon • Wellington
Dimmitt • Tulia • Memphis 34°
Muleshoe • Childress • Quanah
Littlefield • Plainview • Vernon • Wichita Falls Red
Leveland • Lubbock • Benjamin • Gainesville • Denison Paris Texarkana
Brownfield • • Seymour • Denton Sherman New Boston • Atlanta
• Post • Aspermont Haskell Graham Plano Greenville Mt. Pleasant
Seminole • Snyder Sweet- Mineral Wells • **Fort** Garland Tyler • Marshall
Andrews • Lamesa Big water Weatherford **Worth** **Dallas** • Longview
Midland • Spring Abilene Stephenville **Arlington** Athens Nacogdoches Henderson 32°
Kermit • Odessa Robert Lee Coleman Hillsboro Corsicana • Palestine
• Monahans Brownwood Waco Mexia Crockett Lufkin
Pecos Rankin San Angelo Gatesville Marlin Madisonville Jasper
Fort Big Lake Brady Killeen • Temple Bryan Huntsville Woodville
Stockton Ozona Sonora Mason Round Caldwell Conroe Orange 30°
Alpine Llano Rock Brenham Houston Liberty Beaumont
Sanderson Rocksprings Fredericksburg • **Austin** Lockhart Pasadena
Leakey Kerrville San Marcos Missouri City Texas City
Del Rio New Braunfels Seguin Wharton Angleton Galveston
Uvalde Hondo **San** Victoria Lake Jackson
Eagle Pass Crystal **Antonio** El Campo Bay City
City Pearsall Pleasanton Refugio Port Lavaca 28°
Carrizo Springs Cotulla Beeville Sinton
Laredo Alice **Corpus Christi**
Hebbronville Kingsville Gulf of
Falfurrias Mexico
Zapata PADRE
Rio Grande Edinburg ISLAND 26°
City McAllen Harlingen
Brownsville

0 60 120 mi
0 80 160 km

106° N.M. 104°
El Paso
Mentone
Sierra Pecos
Blanco • Van Horn
Rio Grande Fort Davis
29°30' Marfa Alpine

MEXICO

© 2003 Encyclopædia Britannica, Inc.

UTAH

Official name: State of Utah
Nickname: Beehive State
State Capital: Salt Lake City
State Flower: Sego lily
Motto: Industry
Admitted to the Union: 1896 (45th)
Total area: 84,899 sq. mi. (219,888 sq. km.) (ranks 11th)
Population (2000): 2,233,169 (ranks 34th)
Chief Cities: Ogden, Orem, Provo, Salt Lake City, Sandy, West Valley City

Principal products/industries: Wheat, hay, livestock, turkeys, dairy products, copper, gold, silver, molybdenum, high-tech products, food products, tourism
Highest point: Kings Peak 13,528 ft. (4123 m.)

State History

Originally inhabited by American Indian peoples including the Shoshoni, Ute, and Paiute. Possibly explored by Spaniards sent out by explorer Francisco Vásquez de Coronado 1540; visited by Spanish missionaries 1776; Great Salt Lake discovered by American pioneer James Bridger 1824; acquired by U.S. from Mexico in Treaty of Guadalupe Hidalgo 1848; first permanent white settlers were Mormons, led to valley of Great Salt Lake by Brigham Young, head of Mormon Church, in 1847; part of Utah Territory organized 1850; territory reduced to area of present state by 1868; conflict between Mormon authorities and U.S. government, known as Utah War (1857–58); admitted to Union Jan. 4, 1896.

The design carries the state seal, which features a bald eagle over a beehive and crossed U.S. flags to indicate the protection of the U.S. and Utah's loyalty to the nation. The dates 1847 and 1896 refer to the settlement of the original Mormon community at Salt Lake City and the achievement of statehood.

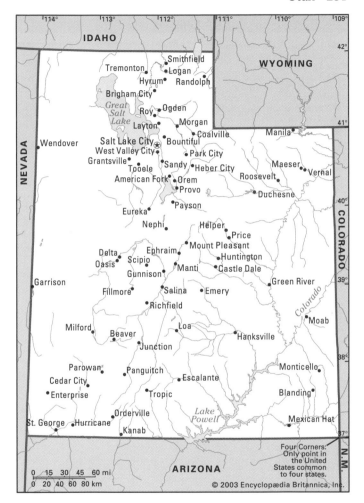

IDAHO

WYOMING

Smithfield
Tremonton • Logan
Hyrum • Randolph
Brigham City
Great Salt Lake
Roy • Ogden
Layton • Morgan
NEVADA
Wendover
Salt Lake City ⊛ Bountiful Coalville Manila
West Valley City • Park City
Grantsville • Sandy • Heber City Maeser • Vernal
Tooele • American Fork • Orem Roosevelt
• Provo Duchesne
Payson
Eureka •
Nephi • Helper
• Price
Delta Ephraim • Mount Pleasant
Oasis Scipio • Huntington
Gunnison • Manti • Castle Dale
Garrison Fillmore • Salina • Emery Green River
• Richfield *Colorado*
Milford • Loa
Beaver • Hanksville Moab
Junction
Parowan • Panguitch Monticello
Cedar City • Escalante
• Enterprise • Tropic Blanding
Lake Powell
Orderville Mexican Hat
St. George • Hurricane Kanab
COLORADO
N.M.
ARIZONA

0 15 30 45 60 mi
0 20 40 60 80 km

Four Corners:
Only point in
the United
States common
to four states.

© 2003 Encyclopædia Britannica, Inc.

VERMONT

Official name: State of Vermont
Nickname: Green Mountain State
State Capital: Montpelier
State Flower: Red clover
Motto: Freedom and Unity
Admitted to the Union: 1791 (14th)
Total area: 9609 sq. mi. (24,887 sq. km.) (ranks 43rd)
Population (2000): 608,827 (ranks 49th)
Chief Cities/Towns: Burlington, Essex, Rutland

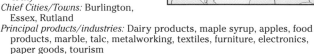

Principal products/industries: Dairy products, maple syrup, apples, food products, marble, talc, metalworking, textiles, furniture, electronics, paper goods, tourism
Highest point: Mt. Mansfield 4393 ft. (1339 m.)

State History

Inhabited originally by American Indians, the Abnaki; explored 1609 by French expedition led by Samuel de Champlain, who discovered the lake now bearing his name; temporary settlement by French at Fort Ste. Anne on Isle La Motte 1666; English established Fort Dummer near site of present Brattleboro 1724; disputes arose between New Hampshire and New York concerning jurisdiction of area, New Hampshire having awarded grants to settlers; Green Mountain Boys organized by Ethan Allen 1770 to repel encroachers from west, New York having won its appeal to crown for rights to settle; when Revolutionary War intervened, Allen and Green Mountain Boys fighting for colonies captured Fort Ticonderoga from British 1775; declared itself independent republic 1777; claims to the region later dropped by New Hampshire and New York; admitted to Union Mar. 4, 1791; present constitution adopted 1793 (since amended).

The flag design has the Vermont coat of arms which shows a pastoral scene with the Green Mountains in the background, a large pine tree in the foreground, wheat sheaves, and a cow. The inscription "Freedom and Unity," the word "Vermont," a wreath, and the head of a deer as the crest complete the design.

QUEBEC C A N A D A

Alburg

Swanton

Richford

Derby

Newport

North Hero

Island Pond

Lake Champlain

St. Albans

Barton

Milton

Hyde Park

Guildhall

Winooski

Essex Junction

Hardwick

Lyndonville

Burlington

Stowe

South Burlington

Richmond

St. Johnsbury

Waterbury

Montpelier

Waitsfield

Barre

South Barre

Vergennes

Northfield

Graniteville

Bristol

Middlebury

Chelsea

NEW YORK

Randolph

Bethel

Sharon

NEW HAMPSHIRE

Pittsford

White River Junction

Proctor

Rutland

Woodstock

Fair Haven

Poultney

Windsor

Connecticut

Dorset

Springfield

Manchester

Bellows Falls

Hudson

North Bennington

Newfane

Bennington

Brattleboro

Pownal

MASSACHUSETTS

© 2003 Encyclopædia Britannica, Inc.

0 5 10 15 20 mi
0   10   20 km

VIRGINIA

Official name: Commonwealth of
Virginia
Nickname: Old Dominion
State Capital: Richmond
State Flower: American dogwood
Motto: Sic Semper Tyrannis (Thus
Always to Tyrants)
Admitted to the Union: 1788; 10th of
the original 13 colonies to ratify
the U.S. Constitution
Total area: 40,767 sq. mi. (105,586 sq.
km.) (ranks 36th)
Population (2000): 7,078,515 (ranks 12th)
Chief Cities: Norfolk, Richmond, Virginia Beach
Principal products/industries: Dairy products, tobacco, vegetables, live-
stock, coal, chemicals, food products, transportation equipment, electri-
cal equipment, textiles, federal-government employment
Highest point: Mt. Rogers 5729 ft. (1746 m.)

State History

Originally inhabited by American Indians when futile attempts were
made by English navigator Sir Walter Raleigh to found settlements
1584–87; first royal charter to London (Virginia) Company followed by
first permanent settlement, made by colonists sent out by this company,
at Jamestown 1607; first popular assembly in America convened 1619;
colony finally thrived primarily on successful tobacco cultivation introduced to settlers by Indians; one of the first colonies to express resistance to the Stamp Act and other British taxes 1765; active in movement
for independence during the Revolution; scene of surrender of British
Lord Charles Cornwallis at Yorktown 1781; northwestern part of western
lands ceded to U.S. 1784; southern part admitted to the Union as the
state of Kentucky 1792; ratified the U.S. Constitution June 25, 1788;
although slavery had been outlawed, it continued to be important part
of economy; tensions heightened between slaveholders and abolition-
ists during first half of 19th century; passed ordinance of secession 1861;
western counties remained loyal to the Union, separated from Virginia
1861 and admitted to the Union as the state of West Virginia 1863; scene
of many battles of the Civil War, among them Bull Run (first and second),
Fair Oaks, Chancellorsville, Fredericksburg, the Wilderness, Cold
Harbor, and many engagements in Shenandoah Valley; readmitted to
Union Jan. 26, 1870. New constitution promulgated 1902, revised 1971.

The design of the seal features a woman personifying virtue and
dressed as an Amazon. She wears a helmet and holds a spear
and sword above the Latin motto "Sic semper tyrannis" ("Thus
always to tyrants"). She is standing on the prostrate figure of a
fallen king, his crown lying to one side.

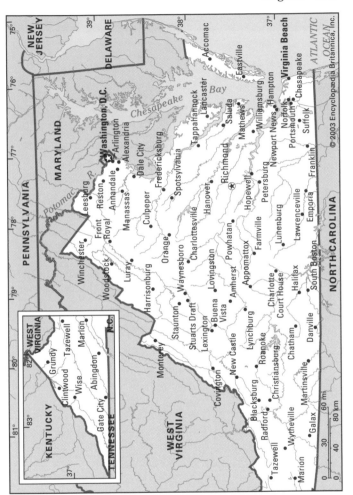

© 2003 Encyclopædia Britannica, Inc.

WASHINGTON

Official name: State of Washington
Nickname: Evergreen State
State Capital: Olympia
State Flower: Rhododendron
Motto: Alki (By and By)
Admitted to the Union: 1889 (42nd)
Total area: 68,192 sq. mi. (176,617 sq. km.) (ranks 20th)
Population (2000): 5,894,121 (ranks 15th)
Chief Cities: Seattle, Spokane, Tacoma

Principal products/industries: Wheat, fruit, dairy products, fishing, zinc, lead, gravel, aircraft and other transportation equipment, lumber, chemicals
Highest point: Mt. Rainier 14,410 ft. (4392 m.)

State History

Area inhabited by Pacific coast Indians when region visited by Spanish, Russian, British, and French explorers 1543–1792 (short-lived settlement 1791 at Neah Bay); explored by Lewis and Clark, who sailed down Columbia River 1805; part of Oregon Country; occupied jointly by Great Britain and U.S. 1818–46; first permanent settlement at Tumwater 1845; by treaty with Great Britain 1846 northern boundary set at 49th parallel; part of Oregon Territory 1848; settlement at Seattle 1851, at Tacoma 1852; became part of Washington Territory 1853; territory reduced to area of present state 1863; admitted to Union as state Nov. 11, 1889.

The flag contains the state seal with the name of the state, the date of its admission to the Union, and a bust of George Washington. In 1915 a background of green for the flag of the "Evergreen State" was chosen.

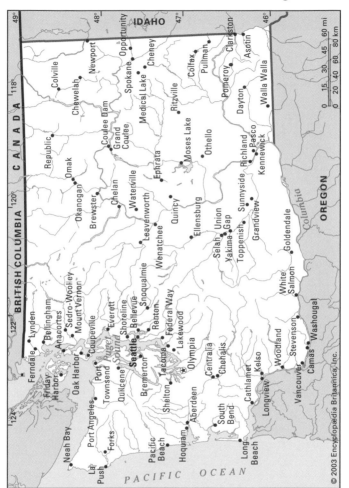

© 2003 Encyclopædia Britannica, Inc.

WEST VIRGINIA

Official name: State of West Virginia
Nickname: Mountain State
State Capital: Charleston
State Flower: Rhododendron
Motto: Montani Semper Liberi
(Mountaineers Are Always Free)
Admitted to the Union: 1863 (35th)
Total area: 24,181 sq. mi. (62,629 sq. km.) (ranks 41st)
Population (2000): 1,808,344 (ranks 37th)
Chief Cities: Charleston, Huntington
Principal products/industries: Corn, tobacco, apples, dairy products, cattle, coal, stone, primary metals, chemicals, recreation
Highest point: Spruce Knob 4861 ft. (1482 m.)

State History

Inhabited originally by Mound Builders and later by other American Indian peoples; European arrival 17th–18th centuries brought conflicts among French, British, and Indians; although part of Virginia, rugged terrain restricted settlement; after American Revolution, concerns of inhabitants who were less likely to have slaves differed from those in eastern Virginia; dissatisfaction with Virginia government grew, as did sentiment for separation from eastern part of state; with outbreak of Civil War, residents from western Virginia voted against ordinance of secession May 1861; government loyal to U.S. federal government organized at Wheeling June 1861; population voted to create new state 1861 and a state constitution ratified 1862; admitted to Union June 20, 1863; state constitution adopted 1872 (since amended).

The farmer and the miner in the coat of arms flank a rock inscribed with the date of West Virginia statehood, June 20, 1863. The cap of liberty and crossed rifles in the foreground are symbolic of the Latin motto below: "Montani Semper Liberi" ("Mountaineers Are Always Free").

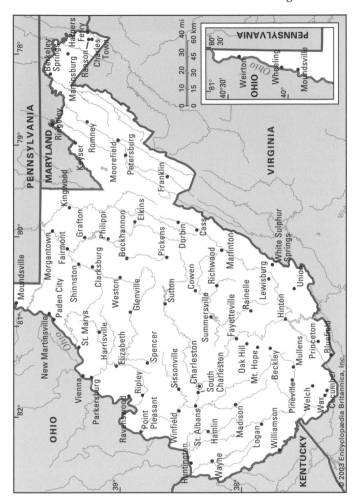

WISCONSIN

Official name: State of Wisconsin
Nickname: Badger State (unofficial)
State Capital: Madison
State Flower: Violet
Motto: Forward
Admitted to the Union: 1848 (30th)
Total area: 56,154 sq. mi. (145,439 sq. km.) (ranks 26th)
Population (2000): 5,363,675 (ranks 18th)
Chief Cities: Green Bay, Kenosha, Madison, Milwaukee, Racine
Principal products/industries: Dairy products, corn, cranberries, potatoes, livestock, machinery, paper products, metal products, recreation
Highest point: Timms Hill 1952 ft. (595 m.)

State History

Originally inhabited by prehistoric Mound Builders; by time of European arrival, several different Indian tribes were inhabiting the region; area visited by French explorer Jean Nicolet 1634; first permanent European settlement 1717; French settlement at Green Bay 1745; throughout 18th century some Indian tribes sided with French while others sided with English, provoking general unrest; French claim ceded to Great Britain 1763 after French and Indian War; recognized by Great Britain as part of U.S. 1783; claims relinquished during 1780s by Virginia, Massachusetts, and Connecticut; part of Northwest Territory 1787, Indiana Territory 1800, Illinois Territory 1809, and Michigan Territory 1818; conflicts between Indians and settlers continued into 19th century culminating in Black Hawk War 1832, in which Indians suffered massacre; included in Wisconsin Territory 1836; admitted to Union May 29, 1848; constitution ratified 1848 (since amended).

WISCONSIN
1848

The flag features the U.S. motto and national shield in the center, surrounded by symbols of typical 19th-century occupations—farming, mining, manufacturing, and shipping. A miner and sailor serve as supporters to the shield, above which appears a badger as a crest honoring "the Badger State," a nickname referring to early miners.

MINNESOTA

Lake
Superior

MICHIGAN

Washburn
Superior
Ashland
Hurley

Hayward

Eagle River
Florence

Grantsburg
Shell Lake
Phillips
Rhinelander
Crandon

Balsam
Lake
Rice Lake
Ladysmith

Barron

New Richmond
Medford
Merrill
Antigo
Peshtigo
Marinette
Sturgeon
Bay

Hudson
Chippewa Falls
Wausau
Keshena
Oconto

Menomonie
Eau Claire
Marshfield
Shawano
Green Bay
Algoma

Ellsworth
Neillsville
Wisconsin
Rapids
Stevens Point
Kewaunee

Durand
Whitehall
Plover
Appleton
De Pere

Alma
Black River Falls
Kaukauna
Two Rivers

Sparta
Tomah
Wautoma
Oshkosh
Neenah
Manitowoc

La Crosse
Mauston
Berlin
Ripon
Fond
du Lac
Sheboygan

Viroqua
Reedsburg
Wisconsin
Dells
Portage
Waupun
West
Bend
Plymouth

Baraboo
Columbus
Beaver
Dam
Port
Washington

Richland Center
Watertown
Menomonee Falls

Spring Green
Madison
Waukesha
Milwaukee

Prairie
du Chien
Dodgeville
Stoughton
Jefferson
West Allis

IOWA
Lancaster
Platteville
Janesville
Whitewater
Elkhorn
Racine

Monroe
Beloit
Lake
Geneva
Kenosha

Lake
Michigan

MINNESOTA

Mississippi River

Green
Bay

ILLINOIS

0   40   80 mi
0   50   100 km
© 2003 Encyclopædia Britannica, Inc.

WYOMING

Official name: State of Wyoming
Nicknames: Equality State, Cowboy
  State
State Capital: Cheyenne
State Flower: Indian paintbrush
Motto: Equal Rights
Admitted to the Union: 1890 (44th)
Total area: 97,914 sq. mi. (253,597 sq.
  km.) (ranks 9th)
Population (2000): 493,782 (ranks
  50th)

Chief Cities: Casper, Cheyenne, Laramie
Principal products/industries: Sugar beets, beans, barley, hay, wheat, live-
  stock, oil, natural gas, uranium, coal, oil refining, tourism
Highest point: Gannett Peak 13,804 ft. (4207 m.)

State History

Inhabited by Plains Indians when first visited by white explorers during
18th century; originally a part of Louisiana region claimed by France;
greater part acquired by U.S. in Louisiana Purchase 1803; remainder
acquired with annexation of Texas 1845, British cession of Oregon
Country 1846, and cession of Mexican territory to U.S. 1848; included in
several U.S. territories prior to organization of Wyoming 1868; adopted
women's suffrage, first instance in U.S., 1869; admitted to Union July 10,
1890; constitution adopted 1890; Nellie Tayloe Ross governor 1925–27,
first woman governor of a U.S. state.

The winning design in a 1916 flag competition features the
national colors, the white silhouette of a bison, the Wyoming
state seal, and the state motto, "Equal Rights," recalling that in
1869 Wyoming's constitution was the first in the modern world
to give equal voting and office-holding rights to women.

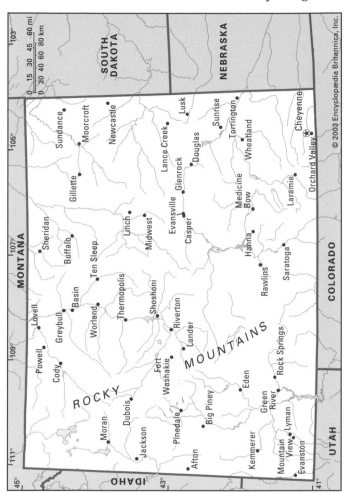

List of
Selected Cities

AFGHANISTAN ....pg. 1

Adraskan	33°39' N,	062°16' E
Almār	35°50' N,	064°32' E
Anār Darreh	32°46' N,	061°39' E
Andkhvoy	36°56' N,	065°08' E
Āqchah	36°56' N,	066°11' E
Baghlān	36°13' N,	068°46' E
Bāghrān	33°04' N,	065°05' E
Bagrām	34°58' N,	069°17' E
Bālā Bolūk	32°38' N,	062°28' E
Bāmīān (Bāmyān)	34°50' N,	067°50' E
Barg-e Matāl	35°40' N,	071°21' E
Bāzār-e Panjvā'i	31°32' N,	065°28' E
Chaghcharān	34°31' N,	065°15' E
Chahār Borjak	30°17' N,	062°03' E
Chakhānsūr	31°10' N,	062°04' E
Delārām	32°11' N,	063°25' E
Do Qal'eh	32°08' N,	061°27' E
Dowlātabād	36°26' N,	064°55' E
Dūrāj	37°56' N,	070°43' E
Eslām Qal'eh	34°40' N,	061°04' E
Farāh (Farrah, Ferah)	32°22' N,	062°07' E
Feyzābād (Faizābād)	37°06' N,	070°34' E
Ghaznī	33°33' N,	068°26' E
Ghūrīān	34°21' N,	061°30' E
Gīzāb	33°23' N,	066°16' E
Golestān	32°37' N,	063°39' E
Golrān	35°06' N,	061°41' E
Gowmal Kalay	32°31' N,	068°51' E
Herāt (Harāt)	34°20' N,	062°12' E
Jabal os Sarāj	35°07' N,	069°14' E
Jalālābād	34°26' N,	070°28' E
Jaldak	31°58' N,	066°43' E
Jawand	35°04' N,	064°09' E
Kabul	34°31' N,	069°12' E
Kajakī	32°16' N,	065°03' E
Kandahār (Qandahār)	31°35' N,	065°45' E
Khadīr	33°55' N,	065°56' E
Khānābād	36°41' N,	069°07' E
Kholm	36°42' N,	067°41' E
Khowst	33°22' N,	069°57' E
Kondūz (Qonduz)	36°45' N,	068°51' E
Koshk	34°57' N,	062°15' E
Kūhestānāt	35°49' N,	065°52' E
Lashkar Gāh (Bust)	31°35' N,	064°21' E
Maḥmūd-e Rāqī	35°01' N,	069°20' E
Mazār-e Sharif	36°42' N,	067°06' E
Nāvor	33°53' N,	067°57' E
Orgūn	32°57' N,	069°11' E
Orūzgān	32°56' N,	066°38' E
Owbeh	34°22' N,	063°10' E
Palālak	30°14' N,	062°54' E
Pol-e 'Alam	33°59' N,	069°02' E

Porchaman	33°08' N,	063°51' E
Qalāt	32°07' N,	066°54' E
Qal'eh-ye Now	34°59' N,	063°08' E
Sar-e Pol	36°14' N,	065°55' E
Sayghān	35°11' N,	067°42' E
Shāh Jūy	32°31' N,	067°25' E
Shahrak	34°06' N,	064°18' E
Shīndand (Sabzevār)	33°18' N,	062°08' E
Shīr Khān	37°11' N,	068°36' E
Yangī Qal'eh	37°28' N,	069°36' E
Zaranj	30°58' N,	061°53' E

ALBANIA ....pg. 2

Berat	40°42' N,	019°57' E
Burrel	41°36' N,	020°01' E
Cërrik	41°02' N,	019°57' E
Çorovodë	40°30' N,	020°13' E
Durrës	41°19' N,	019°26' E
Elbasan	41°06' N,	020°05' E
Ersekë	40°22' N,	020°40' E
Fier	40°43' N,	019°34' E
Gjirokastër	40°05' N,	020°10' E
Gramsh	40°52' N,	020°11' E
Himarë	40°07' N,	019°44' E
Kavajë	41°11' N,	019°33' E
Korçë (Koritsa)	40°37' N,	020°46' E
Krujë	41°30' N,	019°48' E
Kukës	42°05' N,	020°24' E
Laç	41°38' N,	019°43' E
Lezhë	41°47' N,	019°39' E
Librazhd	41°11' N,	020°19' E
Lushnje	40°56' N,	019°42' E
Patos	40°38' N,	019°39' E
Përmet	40°14' N,	020°21' E
Peshkopi	41°41' N,	020°25' E
Pogradec	40°54' N,	020°39' E
Pukë	42°03' N,	019°54' E
Rrëshen	41°47' N,	019°54' E
Sarandë	39°52' N,	020°00' E
Shkodër (Scutari)	42°05' N,	019°30' E
Tepelenë	40°19' N,	020°01' E
Tiranë (Tirana)	41°20' N,	019°50' E
Vlorë	40°27' N,	019°30' E
Vorë	41°23' N,	019°40' E

ALGERIA ....pg. 3

Adrar (Timmi)	27°54' N,	000°17'W
Aïn Beïda (Daoud)	35°48' N,	007°24' E
Algiers (or Al-Jaza'ir)	36°47' N,	003°03' E
Annaba (Bone)	36°54' N,	007°46' E
Batna	35°34' N,	006°11' E
Béchar (Colomb-Bechar)	31°37' N,	002°13' W
Bejaïa (Bougie)	36°45' N,	005°05' E
Beni Abbès	30°08' N,	002°10' W
Biskra (Beskra)	34°51' N,	005°44' E
Bordj Bou Arréridj	36°04' N,	004°47' E

Chlef (El-Asnam or
   Orleansville) . . . . 36°10' N, 001°20' E
Constantine (Qacentina) . . 36°22' N, 006°37' E
Djelfa . . . . 34°40' N, 003°15' E
El-Oued . . . . 33°20' N, 006°53' E
Ghardaïa . . . . 32°29' N, 003°40' E
In Salah (Aïn Salah) . . . . . 27°13' N, 002°28' E
Kenadsa. . . . . 31°34' N, 002°26' E
Médéa (Lemdiyya) . . . . 36°16' N, 002°45' E
Mostaganem
   (Mestghanem) . . . . 35°56' N, 000°05' E
Oran (Wahran) . . . . 35°42' N, 000°38' W
Ouargla (Warqla) . . . . 31°57' N, 005°20' E
Saïda . . . . 34°50' N, 000°09' E
Sétif (Stif) . . . . 36°12' N, 005°24' E
Sidi Bel Abbés. . . . . 35°12' N, 000°38' W
Skikda (Philippeville) . . . . 36°52' N, 006°54' E
Souk-Ahras . . . . 36°17' N, 007°57' E
Tamanrasset
   (Fort Laperrine). . . . . . . 22°47' N, 005°31' W
Tébessa (Tbessa or
   Theveste) . . . . 35°24' N, 008°07' E
Tiaret
   (Tihert or Tagdempt) . . . 35°22' N, 001°19' E
Tindouf . . . . 27°42' N, 008°09' W
Tlemcen (Tlemsen) . . . . . . 34°52' N, 001°19' W
Touggourt . . . . 33°06' N, 006°04' E

ANDORRA . . . . pg. 4

Andorra la Vella . . . . 42°30' N, 001°30' E
Canillo . . . . 42°34' N, 001°35' E
Encamp . . . . 42°32' N, 001°35' E
La Massana . . . . 42°33' N, 001°31' E
Les Escaldes . . . . 42°30' N, 001°32' E
Ordino . . . . 42°34' N, 001°30' E
Sant Julià de Lòria . . . . . . 42°28' N, 001°30' E
Soldeu . . . . 42°35' N, 001°40' E

ANGOLA . . . . pg. 5

Benguela (São Félipe
   de Benguela) . . . . 12°35' S, 013°24' E
Caála (Robert Williams) . . 12°51' S, 015°34' E
Cabinda . . . . 05°33' S, 012°12' E
Cacolo . . . . 10°08' S, 019°16' E
Caconda . . . . 13°44' S, 015°04' E
Caluquembe . . . . 13°52' S, 014°26' E
Camacupa (General
   Machado). . . . . 12°01' S, 017°29' E
Cangamba . . . . 13°41' S, 019°52' E
Catumbela. . . . . 12°26' S, 013°33' E
Cubal . . . . 13°02' S, 014°15' E
Cuchi . . . . 14°39' S, 016°54' E
Damba . . . . 06°41' S, 015°08' E
Gabela . . . . 10°51' S, 014°22' E
Ganda (Mariano
   Machado). . . . . 13°01' S, 014°38' E
Huambo (Nova Lisboa) . . . 12°46' S, 015°44' E
Kuito (Silva Porto) . . . . . . 12°23' S, 016°56' E

Lobito . . . . 12°21' S, 013°33' E
Luanda (São Paulo de
   Luanda) . . . . 08°49' S, 013°15' E
Luau . . . . 10°42' S, 022°14' E
Lubango (Sá da Bandeira) . 14°55' S, 013°30' E
Lucapa . . . . 08°25' S, 020°45' E
Luena (Vila Luso) . . . . 11°47' S, 019°55' E
Malanje . . . . 09°32' S, 016°20' E
Mavinga . . . . 15°48' S, 020°21' E
M'banza Congo
   (São Salvador) . . . . 06°16' S, 014°15' E
Menongue (Serpa Pinto) . . 14°40' S, 017°42' E
Namibe (Moçâmedes,
   or Mossamedes) . . . . 15°10' S, 012°09' E
N'dalatando
   (Dalatando, or Salazar). . 09°18' S, 014°55' E
Negage. . . . . 07°46' S, 015°16' E
Nóqui. . . . . 05°51' S, 013°26' E
Ondjiva . . . . 17°04' S, 015°44' E
Porto Amboin . . . . 10°44' S, 013°45' E
Quimbele. . . . . 06°31' S, 016°13' E
Saurimo
   (Henrique de Carvalho) . 09°39' S, 020°24' E
Soyo. . . . . 06°08' S, 012°22' E
Sumbe (Novo Redondo). . . 11°12' S, 013°50' E
Tombua (Porto
   Alexandre) . . . . 15°48' S, 011°51' E
Uíge (Carmona). . . . . 07°37' S, 015°03' E
Waku Kungo
   (Santa Comba). . . . . 11°21' S, 015°07' E

ANTIGUA AND BARBUDA . . . . pg. 6

Codrington . . . . 17°38' N, 061°50' W
St. John's . . . . 17°06' N, 061°51' W

ARGENTINA . . . . . . pg. 7

Avellaneda. . . . . 29°07' S, 059°40' W
Bahía Blanca . . . . 38°43' S, 062°17' W
Buenos Aires. . . . . 34°36' S, 058°27' W
Comodoro Rivadavia . . . . 45°52' S, 067°30' W
Concordia . . . . 31°24' S, 058°02' W
Córdoba . . . . 31°24' S, 064°11' W
Corrientes . . . . 27°28' S, 058°50' W
Formosa . . . . 26°11' S, 058°11' W
La Plata . . . . 34°55' S, 057°57' W
La Rioja . . . . 29°26' S, 066°51' W
Luján . . . . 34°34' S, 059°07' W
Mar del Plata. . . . . 38°00' S, 057°33' W
Mercedes. . . . . 33°40' S, 065°28' W
Neuquén . . . . 38°57' S, 068°04' W
Paraná . . . . 31°44' S, 060°32' W
Posadas. . . . . 27°23' S, 055°53' W
Rawson . . . . 43°18' S, 065°06' W
Resistencia . . . . 27°27' S, 058°59' W
Río Gallegos . . . . 51°38' S, 069°13' W

Salta	24°47' S,	065°25' W
San Miguel de Tucumán	26°49' S,	065°13' W
San Rafael	34°36' S,	068°20' W
Santa Fe	31°38' S,	060°42' W
Santa Rosa	36°37' S,	064°17' W
Santiago del Estero	27°47' S,	064°16' W
Tandil	37°19' S,	059°09' W
Tigre	34°25' S,	058°34' W
Ushuaia	54°48' S,	068°18' W
Viedma	40°48' S,	063°00' W
Villa María	32°25' S,	063°15' W

ARMENIA . . . . pg. 8

Abovyan	40°15' N,	044°35' E
Alaverdi	41°08' N,	044°39' E
Ararat	39°50' N,	044°42' E
Artashat (Artaxata)	39°57' N,	044°33' E
Artik	40°37' N,	043°59' E
Charentsavan	40°24' N,	044°38' E
Dilijan	40°44' N,	044°52' E
Ejmiadzin (Echmiadzin)	40°10' N,	044°18' E
Goris (Geryusy)	39°30' N,	046°23' E
Gyumri (Kumayri, Alexandropol, or Leninakan)	40°48' N,	043°50' E
Hoktemberyan (Oktemberyan)	40°09' N,	044°02' E
Hrazdan (Razdan)	40°29' N,	044°46' E
Ijevan	40°51' N,	045°09' E
Kamo (Nor-Bayazet)	40°21' N,	045°08' E
Kapan	39°12' N,	046°24' E
Sevan	40°32' N,	044°56' E
Spitak	40°49' N,	044°16' E
Stepanavan	41°01' N,	044°23' E
Vanadzor	40°48' N,	044°30' E
Yerevan (Erevan)	40°11' N,	044°30' E

AUSTRALIA . . . . . . pg. 9

Adelaide	34°56' S,	138°36' E
Alice Springs	23°42' S,	133°53' E
Bowral	34°28' S,	150°25' E
Brisbane	27°30' S,	153°01' E
Broken Hill	31°57' S,	141°26' E
Bunbury	33°20' S,	115°38' E
Bundaberg	24°51' S,	152°21' E
Cairns	16°55' S,	145°46' E
Canberra	35°20' S,	149°10' E
Darwin	12°28' S,	130°50' E
Devonport	41°10' S,	146°21' E
Geelong	38°09' S,	144°21' E
Geraldton	28°46' S,	114°36' E
Gladstone	23°51' S,	151°15' E
Gold Coast	28°06' S,	153°27' E
Goulburn	34°45' S,	149°43' E
Hobart	42°55' S,	147°20' E
Kalgoorlie-Boulder	30°45' S,	121°28' E
Lismore	28°48' S,	153°16' E
Mackay	21°09' S,	149°12' E

Maryborough	25°32' S,	152°42' E
Melbourne	37°50' S,	145°00' E
Mount Gambier	37°50' S,	140°46' E
Mount Isa	20°44' S,	139°30' E
Newcastle	32°55' S,	151°45' E
Perth	31°56' S,	115°50' E
Port Macquarie	31°26' S,	152°55' E
Rockingham	32°17' S,	115°43' E
Sydney	33°53' S,	151°12' E
Toowoomba	27°33' S,	151°58' E
Warrnambool	38°23' S,	142°29' E
Whyalla	33°02' S,	137°35' E
Wollongong	34°25' S,	150°54' E

AUSTRIA . . . . pg. 10

Amstetten	48°07' N,	014°52' E
Baden	48°01' N,	016°14' E
Branau [am Inn]	48°16' N,	013°02' E
Bregenz	47°30' N,	009°46' E
Bruck [an der Leitha]	47°25' N,	015°17' E
Dornbirn	47°25' N,	009°44' E
Eisenstadt	47°51' N,	016°31' E
Feldkirch	47°14' N,	009°36' E
Freistadt	48°30' N,	014°30' E
Fürstenfeld	47°03' N,	016°05' E
Gmünd	48°46' N,	014°59' E
Gmunden	47°55' N,	013°48' E
Graz	47°04' N,	015°27' E
Hallein	47°41' N,	013°06' E
Innsbruck	47°16' N,	011°24' E
Kapfenberg	47°26' N,	015°18' E
Klagenfurt	46°38' N,	014°18' E
Klosterneuburg	48°18' N,	016°19' E
Köflach	47°04' N,	015°05' E
Krems an der Donau	48°25' N,	015°36' E
Kufstein	47°35' N,	012°10' E
Laa [an der Thaya]	48°43' N,	016°23' E
Landeck	47°08' N,	010°34' E
Leibnitz	46°46' N,	015°32' E
Leoben (Donawitz)	47°23' N,	015°06' E
Leonding	48°16' N,	014°15' E
Liezen	47°34' N,	014°14' E
Linz	48°18' N,	014°18' E
Neunkirchen	47°43' N,	016°05' E
Oberwart	47°17' N,	016°12' E
Radenthein	46°48' N,	013°43' E
Salzburg	47°48' N,	013°02' E
Sankt Pölten	48°12' N,	015°38' E
Schrems	48°47' N,	015°04' E
Steyr	48°03' N,	014°25' E
Telfs	47°18' N,	011°04' E
Ternitz	47°43' N,	016°02' E
Traun	48°13' N,	014°14' E
Trofaiach	47°25' N,	015°00' E
Vienna (Wien)	48°12' N,	016°22' E
Villach	46°36' N,	013°50' E
Vöcklabruck	48°01' N,	013°39' E
Völkermarkt	46°39' N,	014°38' E
Weiner Neustadt	47°48' N,	016°15' E
Wolfsberg	46°50' N,	014°50' E

AZERBAIJAN .....pg. 11

Ağcabädi	40°02' N,	047°28' E
Ağdam	39°59' N,	046°57' E
Ağstafa	41°07' N,	045°27' E
Ağsu	40°34' N,	048°24' E
Äli-Bayramli	39°55' N,	048°56' E
Astara	38°26' N,	048°53' E
Baku (Bakı)	40°23' N,	049°51' E
Balakän	41°43' N,	046°24' E
Bärdä	40°24' N,	047°10' E
Daïkäsän	40°32' N,	046°07' E
Däväçi	41°12' N,	048°59' E
Füzuli	39°36' N,	047°09' E
Gäncä (Gyandzha, Gandzha, Kirovabad, or Yelizavetpol)	40°41' N,	046°22' E
Göyçay	40°39' N,	047°45' E
İmişli	40°47' N,	048°09' E
İsmayıllı	40°47' N,	048°09' E
Kürdämir	40°21' N,	048°11' E
Länkäran	38°45' N,	048°50' E
Masallı	39°03' N,	048°40' E
Mingäçevir (Mingechaur)	40°45' N,	047°03' E
Nakhichevan (Naxcivan)	39°12' N,	045°24' E
Neftçala	39°23' N,	049°16' E
Ordubad	38°54' N,	046°01' E
Qäbälä (Kutkashen)	40°58' N,	047°52' E
Qax	41°25' N,	046°55' E
Qazax	41°05' N,	045°22' E
Qazimämmäd	40°03' N,	048°56' E
Şäki (Sheki, Nukha)	41°12' N,	047°12' E
Salyan	39°35' N,	048°59' E
Şamaxı	40°38' N,	048°39' E
Şämkir	40°50' N,	046°02' E
Siyäzän	41°04' N,	049°02' E
Sumqayit	40°36' N,	049°38' E
Tovuz	40°59' N,	045°36' E
Ucar	40°31' N,	047°39' E
Xaçmaz	41°28' N,	048°48' E
Xankändi (Stepanakert)	39°50' N,	046°46' E
Xudat	41°38' N,	048°41' E
Yevlax	40°37' N,	047°09' E
Zaqatala	41°38' N,	046°39' E

BAHAMAS, THE .pg. 12

Dunmore Town	25°30' N,	076°39' W
Freeport	26°32' N,	078°42' W
Matthew Town	20°57' N,	073°40' W
Nassau	25°05' N,	077°21' W
Old Bight	24°15' N,	075°21' W
West End	26°41' N,	078°58' W

BAHRAIN ....pg. 13

Ad Dūr	25°59' N,	050°37' E
Al-Ḥadd	26°15' N,	050°39' E
Al Jasrah	26°10' N,	050°27' E
Al Mālikīyah	37°10' N,	042°08' E
Al-Muharraq	26°16' N,	050°37' E
Ar-Rifa'	26°07' N,	050°33' E
Ar-Rifā'ash-Sharqī	26°07' N,	050°34' E
Ar-Rumaythah	25°55' N,	050°33' E
'Awāli	26°05' N,	050°33' E
Bārbaār	26°14' N,	050°29' E
Madīnat Ḥamad	26°08' N,	050°30' E
Madīnat 'Īsā	26°10' N,	050°33' E
Manama	26°13' N,	050°35' E

BANGLADESH ....pg. 14

Azmiriganj	24°33' N,	091°14' E
Bāgerhāt	22°40' N,	089°48' E
Bājitpur	24°13' N,	090°57' E
Barisāl	22°42' N,	090°22' E
Bhairab Bāzār	24°04' N,	090°58' E
Bogra	24°51' N,	089°22' E
Brāhmanbāria	23°59' N,	091°07' E
Chālna Port (Mongla Port)	22°28' N,	089°35' E
Chāndpur	23°13' N,	090°39' E
Chaumuhāni (Chowmohani)	22°56' N,	091°07' E
Chittagong	22°20' N,	091°50' E
Chuadānga	23°38' N,	088°51' E
Comilla (Kumillā)	23°27' N,	091°12' E
Cox's Bāzār	21°26' N,	091°59' E
Dhaka (Dacca or Dhakal)	23°43' N,	090°25' E
Dinājpur	25°38' N,	088°38' E
Farīdpur	23°36' N,	089°50' E
Gopālpur	24°50' N,	090°06' E
Ishurdi (Ishurda)	24°08' N,	089°05' E
Jamālpur	24°55' N,	089°56' E
Jessore	23°10' N,	089°13' E
Jhenida	23°33' N,	089°10' E
Khulna	22°48' N,	089°33' E
Kishorganj	24°26' N,	090°46' E
Kurigrām	25°49' N,	089°39' E
Kushtia	23°55' N,	089°07' E
Lākshām	23°14' N,	091°08' E
Lakshmipur	22°57' N,	090°50' E
Lālmanir Hāt (Lalmonirhat)	25°54' N,	089°27' E
Mādārīpur	23°10' N,	090°12' E
Mymensingh (Nasirābād)	24°45' N,	090°24' E
Naogaon	24°47' N,	088°56' E
Nārāyanganj	23°37' N,	090°30' E
Narsinghdi (Narsingdi)	23°55' N,	090°43' E
Nawābganj	24°36' N,	088°17' E
Noākhāli (Sudhárám)	22°49' N,	091°06' E
Pābna (Pubna)	24°00' N,	089°15' E
Patuākhāli	22°21' N,	090°21' E
Rājshāhi	24°22' N,	088°36' E
Rāngāmāti	22°38' N,	092°12' E
Rangpur	25°45' N,	089°15' E
Saidpur	25°47' N,	088°54' E
Sātkhira	22°43' N,	089°06' E
Sherpur	24°41' N,	089°25' E

Sherpur . . . . 25°01' N, 090°01' E
Sirajganj (Seraganj) . . . . . . 24°27' N, 089°43' E
Sylhet. . . . . 24°54' N, 091°52' E
Tangail. . . . . 24°15' N, 089°55' E

BARBADOS . . . . . . .pg. 15

Bennetts . . . . 13°10' N, 059°36' W
Bridgetown . . . . 13°06' N, 059°37' W
Holetown. . . . . 13°11' N, 059°39' W
Marchfield. . . . . 13°07' N, 059°28' W
Massiah . . . . 13°10' N, 059°29' W
Oistins. . . . . 13°04' N, 059°32' W
Portland . . . . 13°16' N, 059°36' W
Prospect . . . . 13°08' N, 059°36' W
Speightstown . . . . 13°15' N, 059°39' W
Westmoreland. . . . . 13°13' N, 059°37' W

BELARUS . . . . .pg. 16

Baranovichi. . . . . 53°08' N, 026°02' E
Beloözersk
  (Beloozyorsk) . . . . 52°28' N, 025°10' E
Bobruysk. . . . . 53°09' N, 029°14' E
Borisov (Barysaw) . . . . . . 54°15' N, 028°30' E
Braslav . . . . 55°38' N, 027°02' E
Brest (Brest-Litovsk) . . . . . 52°06' N, 023°42' E
Bykhov . . . . 53°31' N, 030°15' E
Chashniki . . . . 54°52' N, 029°10' E
Cherikov . . . . 53°34' N, 031°23' E
Cherven. . . . . 53°42' N, 028°26' E
Dobrush . . . . 52°25' N, 031°19' E
Dokshitsy . . . . 54°54' N, 027°46' E
Drogichin. . . . . 52°11' N, 025°09' E
Dyatlovo . . . . 53°28' N, 025°24' E
Dzerzhinsk . . . . 53°41' N, 027°08' E
Gantsevichi. . . . . 52°45' N, 026°26' E
Glubokoye . . . . 55°08' N, 027°41' E
Gorki . . . . 54°17' N, 030°59' E
Gorodok . . . . 55°28' N, 029°59' E
Grodno (Hrodna) . . . . 53°41' N, 023°50' E
Homyel' (Gomel). . . . . 52°25' N, 031°00' E
Kletsk. . . . . 53°04' N, 026°38' E
Klimovichi. . . . . 53°37' N, 031°58' E
Kobrin . . . . 52°13' N, 024°21' E
Kossovo. . . . . 52°45' N, 025°09' E
Kostyukovichi. . . . . 53°20' N, 032°03' E
Lepel . . . . 54°53' N, 028°42' E
Lida . . . . 53°53' N, 025°18' E
Luninets . . . . 52°15' N, 026°48' E
Mahilyow
  (Mogilyov, Mahilyou) . . . 53°54' N, 030°21' E
Malorita. . . . . 51°47' N, 024°05' E
Minsk (Mensk) . . . . 53°54' N, 027°34' E
Molodechno
  (Maladzyechna). . . . . . . 54°19' N, 026°51' E
Mosty. . . . . 53°25' N, 024°32' E
Mozyr (Mazyr) . . . . 52°03' N, 029°16' E
Mstislavl . . . . 54°02' N, 031°44' E
Narovlya . . . . 51°48' N, 029°30' E
Nesvizh . . . . 53°13' N, 026°40' E

Novolukomi. . . . . 54°39' N, 029°13' E
Orsha. . . . . 54°31' N, 030°26' E
Oshmyany . . . . 54°25' N, 025°56' E
Osipovichi. . . . . 53°18' N, 028°38' E
Petrikov. . . . . 52°08' N, 028°30' E
Pinsk . . . . 52°07' N, 026°07' E
Polotsk (Polatsk) . . . . 55°29' N, 028°47' E
Pruzhany . . . . 52°33' N, 024°28' E
Rechitsa (Rechytsa) . . . . . . 52°22' N, 030°23' E
Slutsk. . . . . 53°01' N, 027°33' E
Soligorsk (Salihorsk) . . . . 52°48' N, 027°32' E
Starye Dorogi . . . . 53°02' N, 028°16' E
Stolbtsy . . . . 53°29' N, 026°44' E
Stolin . . . . 51°53' N, 026°51' E
Svetlogorsk
  (Svetlahorsk). . . . . 52°38' N, 029°46' E
Verkhnedvinsk . . . . 55°47' N, 027°56' E
Vetka . . . . 52°33' N, 031°10' E
Vileyka. . . . . 54°30' N, 026°55' E
Vitebsk (Vitsyebsk) . . . . . . 55°12' N, 030°11' E
Volkovysk . . . . 53°10' N, 024°28' E
Vysokoye. . . . . 52°22' N, 023°22' E
Yelsk . . . . 51°48' N, 029°09' E
Zaslavl. . . . . 54°00' N, 027°17' E
Zhitkovichi . . . . 52°14' N, 027°52' E
Zhodino . . . . 54°06' N, 028°21' E

BELGIUM . . . . .pg. 17

Aalst (Alost) . . . . 50°56' N, 004°02' E
Aalter. . . . . 51°05' N, 003°27' E
Antwerp (Antwerpen,
  Anvers) . . . . 51°13' N, 004°25' E
Arlon (Aarlen). . . . . 49°41' N, 005°49' E
Ath . . . . 50°38' N, 003°47' E
Athus . . . . 49°34' N, 005°50' E
Bastogne . . . . 50°00' N, 005°43' E
Bouillon. . . . . 49°48' N, 005°04' E
Boussu. . . . . 50°26' N, 003°48' E
Braine-l'Alleud. . . . . 50°41' N, 004°22' E
Brecht . . . . 51°21' N, 004°38' E
Bree . . . . 51°08' N, 005°36' E
Brugge (Bruges) . . . . 51°13' N, 003°14' E
Brussels (Brussel,
  Bruxelles). . . . . 50°50' N, 004°20' E
Charleroi . . . . 50°25' N, 004°26' E
Ciney . . . . 50°18' N, 005°06' E
Couvin . . . . 50°03' N, 004°29' E
Dinant . . . . 50°16' N, 004°55' E
Eeklo . . . . 51°11' N, 003°34' E
Enghien (Edingen) . . . . . . 50°42' N, 004°02' E
Eupen . . . . 50°38' N, 006°02' E
Florenville . . . . 49°42' N, 005°18' E
Geel (Gheel) . . . . 51°10' N, 005°00' E
Genk (Genck) . . . . 50°58' N, 005°30' E
Ghent (Gand, Gent) . . . . . 51°03' N, 003°43' E
Hasselt. . . . . 50°56' N, 005°20' E
Ixelles (Elsene) . . . . 50°50' N, 004°22' E
Kapellen . . . . 51°19' N, 004°26' E
Kortrijk (Courtrai) . . . . . . 50°50' N, 003°16' E
La Louviere . . . . 50°28' N, 004°11' E

Liège (Luttich)	50°38' N,	005°34' E
Louvain (Leuven)	50°53' N,	004°42' E
Marche-en-Famenne	50°12' N,	005°20' E
Mechelen (Malines)	51°02' N,	004°28' E
Mons (Bergen)	50°27' N,	003°56' E
Mouscron (Moeskroen)	50°44' N,	003°13' E
Namur (Namen)	50°28' N,	004°52' E
Neerpelt	51°13' N,	005°25' E
Ostend (Oostende)	51°13' N,	002°55' E
Peer	51°08' N,	005°28' E
Péruwelz	50°31' N,	003°35' E
Philippeville	50°12' N,	004°32' E
Riemst	50°48' N,	005°36' E
Roeselare (Roulers)	50°57' N,	003°08' E
Saint-Hubert	50°01' N,	005°23' E
Schaerbeek (Schaarbeek)	50°51' N,	004°23' E
Seraing	50°36' N,	005°29' E
Sint-Niklaas	51°10' N,	004°08' E
Spa	50°30' N,	005°52' E
Spy	50°29' N,	004°42' E
Staden	50°59' N,	003°01' E
Tessenderlo	51°04' N,	005°05' E
Thuin	50°20' N,	004°17' E
Tienen	50°48' N,	004°57' E
Torhout	51°04' N,	003°06' E
Tournai (Doornik)	50°36' N,	003°23' E
Turnhout	51°19' N,	004°57' E
Uccle (Ukkel)	50°48' N,	004°19' E
Verviers	50°35' N,	005°52' E
Wanze	50°32' N,	005°13' E
Waremme	50°41' N,	005°15' E
Waterloo	50°43' N,	004°23' E
Zwijndrecht	51°13' N,	004°20' E

BELIZE .... pg. 18

Belize City	17°30' N,	088°12' W
Belmopan	17°15' N,	088°46' W
Benque Viejo	17°05' N,	089°08' W
Bermudian Landing	17°33' N,	088°31' W
Corozal	18°24' N,	088°24' W
Dangriga (Stann Creek)	16°58' N,	088°13' W
Monkey River	16°22' N,	088°29' W
Orange Walk	18°06' N,	088°33' W
Pembroke Hall	18°17' N,	088°27' W
Punta Gorda	16°07' N,	088°48' W
San Ignacio (El Cavo)	17°10' N,	89°04' W

BENIN .... pg. 19

Abomey	07°11' N,	001°59' E
Cotonou	06°21' N,	002°26' E
Djougou	09°42' N,	001°40' E
Kandi	11°08' N,	002°56' E
Natitingou	10°19' N,	001°22' E
Parakou	09°21' N,	002°37' E
Porto-Novo	06°29' N,	002°37' E
Savalou	07°56' N,	001°58' E
Savé	08°02' N,	002°29' E

BHUTAN .... pg. 20

Bumthang (Byakar or Jakar)	27°32' N,	090°43' E
Chhukha	27°04' N,	089°35' E
Chima Kothi	27°03' N,	089°35' E
Chirang	27°04' N,	090°06' E
Dagana (Taga)	27°03' N,	089°55' E
Deothang (Dewangiri)	26°52' N,	091°28' E
Domphu (Damphu)	27°01' N,	090°08' E
Gaylegphug (Gelekphu, Hatisar or Hatsar)	26°51' N,	090°29' E
Ha	27°22' N,	089°17' E
Kanglung (Kanglum)	27°16' N,	091°30' E
Lhuntsi	27°39' N,	091°09' E
Mongar	27°15' N,	091°12' E
Paro	27°26' N,	089°25' E
Pema Gatsel	26°59' N,	091°26' E
Phuntsholing	26°52' N,	089°26' E
Punakha	27°37' N,	089°52' E
Samchi (Tori Bari)	26°53' N,	089°07' E
Samdrup Jongkhar	26°47' N,	091°30' E
Shemgang	27°12' N,	090°38' E
Shompangkha (Sarbhang)	26°52' N,	090°16' E
Sibsoo	27°01' N,	088°55' E
Tashigang	27°20' N,	091°32' E
Thimphu	27°28' N,	089°38' E
Tongsa	27°31' N,	090°30' E
Wangdü Phodrang	27°29' N,	089°54' E

BOLIVIA .... pg. 21

Apolo	14°43' S,	068°31' W
Benavides	12°38' S,	067°20' W
Bermejo	22°44' S,	064°21' W
Camargo	20°39' S,	065°13' W
Camiri	20°03' S,	063°31' W
Caranavi	15°46' S,	067°36' W
Chulumani	16°24' S,	067°31' W
Cobija	11°02' S,	068°44' W
Cochabamba	17°24' S,	066°09' W
Concepción	16°15' S,	062°04' W
Copacabana	16°10' S,	069°05' W
Corocoro	17°12' S,	068°29' W
Cuevo	20°27' S,	063°32' W
El Carmen	18°49' S,	058°33' W
Fortaleza	10°37' S,	066°13' W
Guayaramerin	10°48' S,	065°23' W
Huacaya	20°45' S,	063°43' W
Huachacalla	18°45' S,	068°17' W
Ixiamas	13°45' S,	068°09' W
La Esperanza	14°34' S,	062°10' W
La Horquilla	12°34' S,	064°25' W
La Paz	16°30' S,	068°09' W
Llallagua	18°25' S,	066°38' W
Llica	19°52' S,	068°16' W
Loreto	15°13' S,	064°40' W
Magdalena	13°20' S,	064°08' W
Monteagudo	19°49' S,	063°59' W
Montero	17°20' S,	063°15' W

Oruro................. 17°59′ S, 067°09′ W
Porvenir .... 11°15′ S, 068°41′ W
Potosí .... 19°35′ S, 065°45′ W
Puerto Acosta .... 15°32′ S, 069°15′ W
Puerto Rico .... 11°05′ S, 067°38′ W
Punata .... 17°33′ S, 065°50′ W
Quetena.............. 22°10′ S, 067°25′ W
Quillacollo........... 17°26′ S, 066°17′ W
Reyes................ 14°19′ S, 067°23′ W
Riberalta .... 10°59′ S, 066°06′ W
Roboré............... 18°20′ S, 059°45′ W
Samaipata .... 18°09′ S, 063°52′ W
San Ignacio .... 16°23′ S, 060°59′ W
San José.............. 17°51′ S, 060°47′ W
San Matías........... 16°22′ S, 058°24′ W
San Pablo .... 15°41′ S, 063°15′ W
San Ramón .... 13°17′ S, 064°43′ W
Santa Cruz........... 17°48′ S, 063°10′ W
Santiago............. 19°22′ S, 060°51′ W
Siglo Veinte .... 18°22′ S, 066°38′ W
Sucre................ 19°02′ S, 065°17′ W
Tarabuco............. 19°10′ S, 064°57′ W
Tarija............... 21°31′ S, 064°45′ W
Tiahuanacu (Tiwanacu)... 16°33′ S, 068°42′ W
Trinidad............. 14°47′ S, 064°47′ W
Tupiza .... 21°27′ S, 065°43′ W
Uyuni............... 20°28′ S, 066°50′ W
Villazón .... 22°06′ S, 065°36′ W
Yacuiba .... 22°02′ S, 063°45′ W

BOSNIA AND HERZEGOVINA ...pg. 22

Banja Luka........... 44°46′ N, 017°10′ E
Bihać .... 44°49′ N, 015°52′ E
Bijeljina .... 44°45′ N, 019°13′ E
Bosanska Gradiška ...... 45°09′ N, 017°15′ E
Bosanski Šamac .... 45°04′ N, 018°28′ E
Brčko............... 44°52′ N, 018°49′ E
Derventa .... 44°59′ N, 017°55′ E
Goražde............. 43°40′ N, 018°59′ E
Jablanica .... 43°39′ N, 017°45′ E
Jajce................ 44°21′ N, 017°17′ E
Kladanj .... 44°14′ N, 018°42′ E
Ključ .... 44°32′ N, 016°47′ E
Konjic .... 43°39′ N, 017°58′ E
Mostar.............. 43°21′ N, 017°49′ E
Prijedor............. 44°59′ N, 016°42′ E
Sanski Most.......... 44°46′ N, 016°40′ E
Sarajevo............. 43°50′ N, 018°25′ E
Srebrenica........... 44°06′ N, 019°18′ E
Travnik .... 44°14′ N, 017°40′ E
Tuzla............... 44°33′ N, 018°41′ E
Vareš............... 44°10′ N, 018°20′ E
Zenica .... 44°13′ N, 017°55′ E

BOTSWANA ......pg. 23

Francistown .... 21°13′ S, 027°31′ E

Gaborone.............. 24°40′ S, 025°54′ E
Ghanzi .... 21°34′ S, 021°47′ E
Kanye................ 24°59′ S, 025°21′ E
Kasane............... 17°49′ S, 025°09′ E
Letlhakane............ 21°25′ S, 025°35′ E
Lobatse .... 25°13′ S, 025°40′ E
Mahalapye............ 23°04′ S, 026°50′ E
Maun .... 19°59′ S, 023°25′ E
Mochudi .... 24°25′ S, 026°09′ E
Orapa................ 21°17′ S, 025°22′ E
Palapye
  (Palapye Road) .... 22°33′ S, 027°08′ E
Ramotswa .... 24°52′ S, 025°49′ E
Selebi-Phikwe .... 22°01′ S, 027°50′ E
Serowe............... 22°23′ S, 026°43′ E
Shashe............... 21°26′ S, 027°27′ E
Tlokweng............. 24°32′ S, 025°58′ E
Tshabong .... 26°03′ S, 022°27′ E
Tshane............... 24°05′ S, 021°54′ E

BRAZIL ....pg. 24

Aracaju .... 10°55′ S, 037°04′ W
Belém (Para)........... 01°27′ S, 048°29′ W
Belo Horizonte .... 19°55′ S, 043°56′ W
Boa Vista............. 02°49′ N, 060°30′ W
Brasília .... 15°47′ S, 047°55′ W
Campina Grande........ 07°13′ S, 035°53′ W
Campo Grande .... 20°27′ S, 054°37′ W
Canoas............... 29°56′ S, 051°11′ W
Caxias do Sul.......... 29°10′ S, 051°11′ W
Curitiba .... 25°25′ S, 049°15′ W
Duque de Caxias........ 22°47′ S, 043°18′ W
Florianópolis.......... 27°35′ S, 048°34′ W
Fortaleza .... 03°43′ S, 038°30′ W
Goiânia .... 16°40′ S, 049°16′ W
Itabuna .... 14°48′ S, 039°16′ W
João Pessoa........... 07°07′ S, 034°52′ W
Macapá .... 00°02′ N, 051°03′ W
Maceió............... 09°40′ S, 035°43′ W
Manaus .... 03°08′ S, 060°01′ W
Natal .... 05°47′ S, 035°13′ W
Nova Iguaçu .... 22°45′ S, 043°27′ W
Novo Hamburgo .... 29°41′ S, 051°08′ W
Passo Fundo .... 28°15′ S, 052°24′ W
Pôrto Alegre .... 30°04′ S, 051°11′ W
Pôrto Velho........... 08°46′ S, 063°54′ W
Recife................ 08°03′ S, 034°54′ W
Rio Branco .... 09°58′ S, 067°48′ W
Rio de Janeiro......... 22°54′ S, 043°14′ W
Rio Grande .... 32°02′ S, 052°05′ W
Salvador .... 12°59′ S, 038°31′ W
Santarém .... 02°26′ S, 054°42′ W
Santo André .... 23°40′ S, 046°31′ W
São Gonçalo .... 22°51′ S, 043°04′ W
São José do Rio Prêto .. 20°48′ S, 049°23′ W
São Luís .... 02°31′ S, 044°16′ W
São Paulo............. 23°32′ S, 046°37′ W
Tefé .... 03°22′ S, 064°42′ W
Teresina .... 05°05′ S, 042°49′ W
Vitória .... 20°19′ S, 040°21′ W

BRUNEI . . . . pg. 25

Badas. . . . . 04°36' N, 114°27' E
Bandar Seri Begawan
(Brunei) . . . . 04°53' N, 114°56' E
Bangar. . . . . 04°43' N, 115°04' E
Kuala Belait. . . . . 04°36' N, 114°14' E
Labi. . . . . 04°23' N, 114°27' E
Labu. . . . . 04°45' N, 115°11' E
Muara . . . . 05°02' N, 115°04' E
Seria. . . . . 04°37' N, 114°19' E
Sukang. . . . . 04°19' N, 114°37' E
Tutong. . . . . 04°48' N, 114°39' E

BULGARIA . . . . pg. 26

Balchik. . . . . 43°25' N, 028°10' E
Berkovitsa. . . . . 43°14' N, 023°07' E
Blagoevgrad . . . . 42°01' N, 023°06' E
Burgas. . . . . 42°30' N, 027°28' E
Dimitrovgrad. . . . . 42°03' N, 025°36' E
Dobrich (Tolbukhin) . . . . . 43°34' N, 027°50' E
Dulovo . . . . 43°49' N, 027°09' E
Gabrovo. . . . . 42°52' N, 025°19' E
Grudovo . . . . 42°21' N, 027°10' E
Kazanlŭk . . . . 42°37' N, 025°24' E
Khaskovo. . . . . 41°56' N, 025°33' E
Kŭrdzhali. . . . . 41°39' N, 025°22' E
Kyustendil . . . . 42°17' N, 022°41' E
Lom . . . . 43°49' N, 023°14' E
Lovech. . . . . 43°08' N, 024°43' E
Montana
(Mikhaylovgrad) . . . . 43°25' N, 023°13' E
Nikopol . . . . 43°42' N, 024°54' E
Pazardzhik. . . . . 42°12' N, 024°20' E
Pernik (Dimitrovo) . . . . 42°36' N, 023°02' E
Petrich. . . . . 41°24' N, 023°13' E
Pleven . . . . 43°25' N, 024°37' E
Plovdiv . . . . 42°09' N, 024°45' E
Razgrad. . . . . 43°32' N, 026°31' E
Ruse. . . . . 43°50' N, 025°57' E
Shumen (Kolarovgrad). . . . 43°16' N, 026°55' E
Silistra . . . . 44°07' N, 027°16' E
Sliven. . . . . 42°40' N, 026°19' E
Sofia. . . . . 42°41' N, 023°19' E
Stara Zagora . . . . 42°25' N, 025°38' E
Troyan. . . . . 42°53' N, 024°43' E
Varna . . . . 43°13' N, 027°55' E
Veliko Tŭrnovo . . . . 43°04' N, 025°39' E
Velingrad. . . . . 42°01' N, 024°00' E
Vidin . . . . 43°59' N, 022°52' E
Vratsa (Vraca) . . . . 43°12' N, 023°33' E
Vrŭv . . . . 44°11' N, 022°44' E
Yambol . . . . 42°29' N, 026°30' E

BURKINA FASO . . pg. 27

Banfora . . . . 10°38' N, 004°46' W
Bobo-Dioulasso. . . . . 11°12' N, 004°18' W

Boulsa . . . . 12°39' N, 000°34' W
Dédougou . . . . 12°28' N, 003°28' W
Diébougou. . . . . 10°58' N, 003°15' W
Dori . . . . 14°02' N, 000°02' W
Fada Ngourma. . . . . 12°04' N, 000°21' W
Faramana. . . . . 12°03' N, 004°40' W
Gaoua . . . . 10°20' N, 003°11' W
Kaya. . . . . 13°05' N, 001°05' W
Koudougou . . . . 12°15' N, 002°22' W
Koupéla . . . . 12°11' N, 000°21' W
Léo . . . . 11°06' N, 002°06' W
Nouna . . . . 12°44' N, 003°52' W
Orodara . . . . 10°59' N, 004°55' W
Ouagadougou . . . . 12°22' N, 001°31' W
Ouahigouya . . . . 13°35' N, 002°25' W
Pô. . . . . 11°10' N, 001°09' W
Réo. . . . . 12°19' N, 002°28' W
Tenkodogo . . . . 11°47' N, 000°22' W
Yako. . . . . 12°58' N, 002°16' W

BURUNDI . . . . pg. 28

Bubanza. . . . . 03°06' S, 029°23' E
Bujumbura . . . . 03°23' S, 029°22' E
Bururi . . . . 03°57' S, 029°37' E
Gitega . . . . 03°26' S, 029°56' E
Muramvya . . . . 03°16' S, 029°37' E
Ngozi . . . . 02°54' S, 029°50' E
Nyanza-Lac . . . . 04°21' S, 029°36' E

CAMBODIA . . . . . . pg. 29

Ânlóng Vêng . . . . 14°14' N, 104°05' E
Bā Kêv . . . . 13°42' N, 107°12' E
Battambang
(Batdambang) . . . . 13°06' N, 103°12' E
Chbar. . . . . 12°46' N, 107°10' E
Chŏăm Khsant . . . . 14°13' N, 104°56' E
Chŏng Kal . . . . 13°57' N, 103°35' E
Kâmpóng Cham . . . . 12°00' N, 105°27' E
Kâmpóng Chhnăng . . . . . . 12°15' N, 104°40' E
Kâmpóng Kdei. . . . . 13°07' N, 104°21' E
Kâmpóng Saôm
(Sihanoukville) . . . . 10°38' N, 103°30' E
Kâmpóng Spoe . . . . 11°27' N, 104°32' E
Kâmpóng Thum . . . . 12°42' N, 104°54' E
Kâmpot (Kâmpôt) . . . . 10°37' N, 104°11' E
Krâchéh (Kratie). . . . . 12°29' N, 106°01' E
Krâkôr . . . . 12°32' N, 104°12' E
Krŏng Kaôh Kŏng . . . . 11°37' N, 102°59' E
Lumphăt (Lomphat) . . . . . . 13°30' N, 106°59' E
Mémót . . . . 11°49' N, 106°11' E
Moŭng Roessei . . . . 12°46' N, 103°27' E
Ŏdŏngk . . . . 11°48' N, 104°45' E
Péam Prus. . . . . 12°19' N, 103°09' E
Phnom Penh (Phnum Penh
or Pnom Penh) . . . . 11°33' N, 104°55' E
Phnum Tbêng Méanchey . . 13°49' N, 104°58' E
Phsar Réam (Ream) . . . . . . 10°30' N, 103°37' E

Prey Vêng . . . . 11°29' N, 105°19' E
Pursat (Poŭthĭsăt) . . . . 12°32' N, 103°55' E
Rôviĕng Tbong . . . . 13°21' N, 105°07' E
Sândăn. . . . . 12°42' N, 106°01' E
Senmonorom. . . . . 12°27' N, 107°12' E
Siĕmpang. . . . . 14°07' N, 106°23' E
Siem Reap (Siĕmréab) . . . . 13°22' N, 103°51' E
Sisŏphŏn . . . . 13°35' N, 102°59' E
Stoeng Trêng
   (Stung Treng) . . . . 13°31' N, 105°58' E
Svay Chék . . . . 13°48' N, 102°58' E
Takêv (Takéo). . . . . 10°59' N, 104°47' E
Tăng Krāsăng . . . . 12°34' N, 105°03' E
Virôchey . . . . 13°59' N, 106°49' E

CAMEROON . . . . . . pg. 30

Bafang . . . . 05°09' N, 010°11' E
Bafia. . . . . 04°45' N, 011°14' E
Bafoussam . . . . 05°28' N, 010°25' E
Bamenda . . . . 05°56' N, 010°10' E
Banyo . . . . 06°45' N, 011°49' E
Batibo . . . . 05°50' N, 009°52' E
Batouri. . . . . 04°26' N, 014°22' E
Bertoua . . . . 04°35' N, 013°41' E
Bétaré-Oya . . . . 05°36' N, 014°05' E
Douala . . . . 04°03' N, 009°42' E
Ebolowa . . . . 02°54' N, 011°09' E
Edéa. . . . . 03°48' N, 010°08' E
Eséka . . . . 03°39' N, 010°46' E
Foumban . . . . 05°43' N, 010°55' E
Garoua. . . . . 09°18' N, 013°24' E
Guider . . . . 09°56' N, 013°57' E
Kaélé . . . . 10°07' N, 014°27' E
Kribi. . . . . 02°57' N, 009°55' E
Kumba . . . . 04°38' N, 009°25' E
Loum . . . . 04°43' N, 009°44' E
Mamfe . . . . 05°46' N, 009°17' E
Maroua . . . . 10°36' N, 014°20' E
Mbalmayo . . . . 03°31' N, 011°30' E
Meiganga . . . . 06°31' N, 014°18' E
Mora . . . . 11°03' N, 014°09' E
Ngaoundéré. . . . . 07°19' N, 013°35' E
Nkambe . . . . 06°38' N, 010°40' E
Nkongsamba . . . . 04°57' N, 009°56' E
Obala . . . . 04°10' N, 011°32' E
Sangmélima . . . . 02°56' N, 011°59' E
Tcholliré . . . . 08°24' N, 014°10' E
Tibati . . . . 06°28' N, 012°38' E
Wum . . . . 06°23' N, 010°24' E
Yagoua. . . . . 10°20' N, 015°14' E
Yaoundé . . . . 03°52' N, 011°31' E
Yokadouma. . . . . 03°31' N, 015°03' E

CANADA . . . . pg. 31

Amos . . . . 48°35' N, 078°07' W
Arctic Bay . . . . 73°02' N, 085°11' W
Baie-Comeau . . . . 49°13' N, 068°09' W
Baker Lake. . . . . 64°15' N, 096°00' W

Banff . . . . 51°10' N, 115°34' W
Barrie. . . . . 44°24' N, 079°40' W
Battleford . . . . 52°44' N, 108°19' W
Beauport . . . . 46°52' N, 071°11' W
Bonavista . . . . 48°39' N, 053°07' W
Brandon. . . . . 49°50' N, 099°57' W
Bridgewater. . . . . 44°23' N, 064°31' W
Brooks . . . . 50°35' N, 111°53' W
Buchans. . . . . 48°49' N, 056°52' W
Burlington . . . . 43°19' N, 079°47' W
Burnaby. . . . . 49°16' N, 122°57' W
Calgary . . . . 51°03' N, 114°05' W
Cambridge Bay . . . . 69°03' N, 105°05' W
Camrose . . . . 53°01' N, 112°50' W
Carbonear. . . . . 47°44' N, 053°13' W
Carmacks. . . . . 62°05' N, 136°17' W
Charlesbourg . . . . 46°51' N, 071°16' W
Charlottetown . . . . 46°14' N, 063°08' W
Chatham . . . . 42°24' N, 082°11' W
Chibougamau . . . . 49°55' N, 074°22' W
Chicoutimi. . . . . 48°26' N, 071°04' W
Churchill . . . . 58°46' N, 094°10' W
Churchill Falls. . . . . 53°33' N, 064°01' W
Cranbrook . . . . 49°30' N, 115°46' W
Dartmouth. . . . . 44°40' N, 063°34' W
Dauphin. . . . . 51°09' N, 100°03' W
Dawson . . . . 64°04' N, 139°26' W
Dawson Creek. . . . . 55°46' N, 120°14' W
Duck Lake . . . . 52°49' N, 106°14' W
Edmonton . . . . 53°33' N, 113°28' W
Elliot Lake . . . . 46°23' N, 082°42' W
Enderby. . . . . 50°33' N, 119°09' W
Eskimo Point . . . . 61°07' N, 094°03' W
Esterhazy . . . . 50°39' N, 102°05' W
Estevan . . . . 49°08' N, 102°59' W
Faro . . . . 62°14' N, 133°20' W
Fernie. . . . . 49°30' N, 115°04' W
Flin Flon . . . . 54°46' N, 101°53' W
Fogo. . . . . 49°43' N, 054°17' W
Fort Liard . . . . 60°15' N, 123°28' W
Fort MacLeod . . . . 49°43' N, 113°25' W
Fort McMurray . . . . 56°44' N, 111°23' W
Fort McPherson . . . . 67°27' N, 134°53' W
Fort Qu'Appelle. . . . . 50°46' N, 103°48' W
Fort St. John . . . . 56°15' N, 120°51' W
Fort Smith . . . . 60°00' N, 111°53' W
Fredericton . . . . 45°58' N, 066°39' W
Gagnon . . . . 51°53' N, 068°10' W
Gander. . . . . 48°57' N, 054°37' W
Gaspe. . . . . 48°50' N, 064°29' W
Glace Bay . . . . 46°12' N, 059°57' W
Granby . . . . 45°24' N, 072°43' W
Grand Bank . . . . 47°06' N, 055°46' W
Grande Prairie. . . . . 55°10' N, 118°48' W
Grand Falls . . . . 48°56' N, 055°40' W
Grimshaw . . . . 56°11' N, 117°36' W
Grise Fiord . . . . 76°25' N, 082°55' W
Haines Junction . . . . 60°45' N, 137°30' W
Halifax . . . . 44°39' N, 063°36' W
Hamilton . . . . 43°15' N, 079°51' W
Happy Valley-Goose Bay . . 53°19' N, 060°20' W

Harbour Grace	47°42' N, 053°13' W
Hay River.	60°49' N, 115°47' W
Inuvik.	68°21' N, 133°43' W
Iqaluit (Frobisher Bay). . . .	63°45' N, 068°31' W
Iroquois Falls	48°46' N, 080°41' W
Jasper	52°53' N, 118°05' W
Joliette.	46°01' N, 073°27' W
Jonquiere	48°25' N, 071°13' W
Kamloops	50°40' N, 120°19' W
Kapuskasing	49°25' N, 082°26' W
Kelowna.	49°53' N, 119°29' W
Kenora.	49°47' N, 094°29' W
Kindersley	51°28' N, 109°10' W
Kirkland Lake	48°09' N, 080°02' W
Kitchener.	43°27' N, 080°29' W
Kuujjuaq (Fort-Chimo) . . .	58°06' N, 068°25' W
La Baie.	48°20' N, 070°52' W
Labrador City	52°57' N, 066°55' W
La Tuque	47°26' N, 072°47' W
Lethbridge.	49°42' N, 112°49' W
Lewisporte	49°14' N, 055°03' W
Liverpool.	44°02' N, 064°43' W
Lloydminster	53°17' N, 110°00' W
London	42°59' N, 081°14' W
Longueuil.	45°32' N, 073°30' W
Lynn Lake	56°51' N, 101°03' W
Maple Creek	49°55' N, 109°29' W
Marystown	47°10' N, 055°09' W
Mayo	63°36' N, 135°54' W
Medicine Hat.	50°03' N, 110°40' W
Mississauga.	43°35' N, 079°39' W
Moncton	46°07' N, 064°48' W
Montmagny	46°59' N, 070°33' W
Montreal	45°30' N, 073°36' W
Moose Jaw	50°24' N, 105°32' W
Mount Pearl	47°31' N, 052°47' W
Nanaimo	49°10' N, 123°56' W
Nelson	49°30' N, 117°17' W
Nepean	45°16' N, 075°46' W
New Liskeard	47°30' N, 079°40' W
Niagara Falls	43°06' N, 079°04' W
Nickel Centre	46°34' N, 080°49' W
Nipawin	53°22' N, 104°00' W
North Battleford	52°47' N, 108°17' W
North Bay	46°19' N, 079°28' W
North West River	53°32' N, 060°08' W
Old Crow	67°34' N, 139°50' W
Oshawa	43°54' N, 078°51' W
Ottawa.	45°25' N, 075°42' W
Pangnirtung.	66°08' N, 065°43' W
Parry Sound	45°21' N, 080°02' W
Peace River	56°14' N, 117°17' W
Perce	48°32' N, 064°13' W
Peterborough	44°18' N, 078°19' W
Pine Point	60°50' N, 114°28' W
Portage la Prairie	49°59' N, 098°18' W
Port Alberni	49°14' N, 124°48' W
Port Hawkesbury	45°37' N, 061°21' W
Prince Albert	53°12' N, 105°46' W
Prince George.	53°55' N, 122°45' W
Prince Rupert	54°19' N, 130°19' W
Quebec	46°49' N, 071°14' W
Quesnel	53°00' N, 122°30' W
Rae-Edzo	62°50' N, 116°03' W
Rankin Inlet	62°49' N, 092°05' W
Red Deer	52°16' N, 113°48' W
Regina	50°27' N, 104°37' W
Resolute Bay	74°41' N, 094°54' W
Revelstoke.	50°59' N, 118°12' W
Rimouski	48°26' N, 068°33' W
Roberval	48°31' N, 072°13' W
Ross River	61°59' N, 132°26' W
Sachs Harbour	72°00' N, 125°13' W
Saint Albert	53°38' N, 113°38' W
Sainte-Foy	46°47' N, 071°17' W
Saint John	45°16' N, 066°03' W
Saint John's	47°34' N, 052°43' W
Saskatoon	52°07' N, 106°38' W
Sault Ste. Marie.	46°31' N, 084°20' W
Scarborough	43°47' N, 079°15' W
Schefferville	54°48' N, 066°50' W
Selkirk	50°09' N, 096°52' W
Senneterre.	48°23' N, 077°14' W
Sept-Îles	50°12' N, 066°23' W
Shawinigan	46°33' N, 072°45' W
Shelburne	43°46' N, 065°19' W
Sherbrooke	45°25' N, 071°54' W
Snow Lake	54°53' N, 100°02' W
Springdale.	49°30' N, 056°04' W
Sturgeon Falls	46°22' N, 079°55' W
Sudbury.	46°30' N, 081°00' W
Surrey	49°06' N, 122°47' W
Swan River	52°07' N, 101°16' W
Sydney.	46°09' N, 060°11' W
Teslin.	60°10' N, 132°43' W
The Pas	53°50' N, 101°15' W
Thompson.	55°45' N, 097°52' W
Thunder Bay	48°24' N, 089°19' W
Timmins	48°28' N, 081°20' W
Toronto	43°39' N, 079°23' W
Trois-Rivieres	46°21' N, 072°33' W
Truro	45°22' N, 063°16' W
Tuktoyaktuk	69°27' N, 133°02' W
Val-d'Or	48°06' N, 077°47' W
Vancouver.	49°15' N, 123°07' W
Vernon.	50°16' N, 119°16' W
Victoria.	48°26' N, 123°22' W
Wabush	52°55' N, 066°52' W
Watson Lake	60°04' N, 128°42' W
Weyburn	49°40' N, 103°51' W
Whitehorse	60°43' N, 135°03' W
Williams Lake	52°08' N, 122°09' W
Windsor.	42°18' N, 083°01' W
Windsor.	44°59' N, 064°08' W
Winnipeg.	49°53' N, 097°09' W
Yarmouth	43°50' N, 066°07' W
Yellowknife	62°27' N, 114°22' W
Yorkton	51°13' N, 102°28' W

CAPE VERDE . . . . . pg. 32

Mindelo	16°53' N, 025°00' W

Porto Novo	17°01' N,	025°04' W
Praia	14°55' N,	023°31' W
São Filipe	14°54' N,	024°31' W

CENTRAL AFRICAN REPUBLIC........pg. 33

Alindao	05°02' N,	021°13' E
Baboua	05°48' N,	014°49' E
Bambari	05°45' N,	020°40' E
Bangassou	04°44' N,	022°49' E
Bangui	04°22' N,	018°35' E
Batangafo	07°18' N,	018°18' E
Berbérati	04°16' N,	015°47' E
Bimbo	04°18' N,	018°33' E
Birao	10°17' N,	022°47' E
Boda	04°19' N,	017°28' E
Bossangoa	06°29' N,	017°27' E
Bossembélé	05°16' N,	017°39' E
Bouar	05°57' N,	015°36' E
Bouca	06°30' N,	018°17' E
Bozoum	06°19' N,	016°23' E
Bria	06°32' N,	021°59' E
Carnot	04°56' N,	015°52' E
Dekóa	06°19' N,	019°04' E
Ippy	06°15' N,	021°12' E
Kaga Bandoro	06°59' N,	019°11' E
Mbaïki	03°53' N,	018°00' E
Mobaye	04°19' N,	021°11' E
Mouka	07°16' N,	021°52' E
Ndélé	08°24' N,	020°39' E
Nola	03°32' N,	016°04' E
Obo	05°24' N,	026°30' E
Ouadda	08°04' N,	022°24' E
Ouanda Djallé	08°54' N,	022°48' E
Sibut	05°44' N,	019°05' E
Zinga	03°43' N,	018°35' E

CHAD............pg. 34

Abéché	13°49' N,	020°49' E
Adre	13°28' N,	022°12' E
Am Dam	12°46' N,	020°29' E
Am Timan	11°02' N,	020°17' E
Am Zoer	14°13' N,	021°23' E
Aozou	21°49' N,	017°25' E
Arada	15°01' N,	020°40' E
Ati	13°13' N,	018°20' E
Biltine	14°32' N,	020°55' E
Bol	13°28' N,	014°43' E
Bongor	10°17' N,	015°22' E
Doba	08°39' N,	016°51' E
Gélengdeng	10°56' N,	015°32' E
Goré	07°55' N,	016°38' E
Goz Beïda	12°13' N,	021°25' E
Koro Toro	16°05' N,	018°30' E
Laï	09°24' N,	016°18' E
Largeau (Faya-Largeau)	17°55' N,	019°07' E
Mao	14°07' N,	015°19' E

Massenya	11°24' N,	016°10' E
Mongo	12°11' N,	018°42' E
Moundou	08°34' N,	016°05' E
N'Djamena (Fort Lamy)	12°07' N,	015°03' E
Pala	09°22' N,	014°54' E
Sarh (Fort-Archambault)	09°09' N,	018°23' E

CHILE ....pg. 35

Antofagasta	23°39' S,	070°24' W
Arica	18°29' S,	070°20' W
Castro	42°29' S,	073°46' W
Chillán	36°36' S,	072°07' W
Chuquicamata	22°19' S,	068°56' W
Coihaique	45°34' S,	072°04' W
Concepción	36°50' S,	073°03' W
Copiapó	27°22' S,	070°20' W
Coquimbo	29°58' S,	071°21' W
Iquique	20°13' S,	070°10' W
La Serena	29°54' S,	071°16' W
Porvenir	53°18' S,	070°22' W
Potrerillos	26°26' S,	069°29' W
Puerto Aisén	45°24' S,	072°42' W
Puerto Montt	41°28' S,	072°57' W
Punta Arenas	53°09' S,	070°55' W
Purranque	40°55' S,	073°10' W
San Pedro	33°54' S,	071°28' W
Santiago	33°27' S,	070°40' W
Talca	35°26' S,	071°40' W
Talcahuano	36°43' S,	073°07' W
Temuco	38°44' S,	072°36' W
Tocopilla	22°05' S,	070°12' W
Valdivia	39°48' S,	073°14' W
Valparaíso	33°02' S,	071°38' W
Viña del Mar	33°02' S,	071°34' W

CHINA ....pg. 36-7

Anshan	41°07' N,	122°57' E
Beijing	39°56' N,	116°24' E
Changchun	43°52' N,	125°21' E
Changsha	28°12' N,	112°58' E
Chengdu	30°40' N,	104°04' E
Chongqing (locally Yuzhou)	29°34' N,	106°35' E
Dalian (Lüda)	38°55' N,	121°39' E
Fushun	41°52' N,	123°53' E
Fuzhou	26°05' N,	119°18' E
Guangzhou	23°07' N,	113°15' E
Guiyang	26°35' N,	106°43' E
Haikou	20°03' N,	110°19' E
Hangzhou	30°15' N,	120°10' E
Harbin	45°45' N,	126°39' E
Hefei	31°51' N,	117°17' E
Hohhot	40°47' N,	111°37' E
Jinan	36°40' N,	117°00' E
Kunming	25°04' N,	102°41' E
Lanzhou	36°03' N,	103°41' E
Lhasa	29°39' N,	091°06' E
Nanchang	28°41' N,	115°53' E

COLOMBIA . . . . . . .pg. 38

COMOROS . . . . . .pg. 39

CONGO, DEMOCRATIC REPUBLIC OF THE . . . . . . .pg. 40

CONGO, REPUBLIC OF THE .... .pg. 41

Brazzaville. . . . . 04°16' S, 015°17' E
Djambala . . . . 02°33' S, 014°45' E
Gamboma . . . . 01°53' S, 015°51' E
Impfondo . . . . 01°37' N, 018°04' E
Kayes . . . . 04°25' S, 011°41' E
Liranga . . . . 00°40' S, 017°36' E
Loubomo . . . . 04°12' N, 012°41' E
Madingou . . . . 04°09' S, 013°34' E
Makabana . . . . 02°48' S, 012°29' E
Makoua . . . . 00°01' N, 015°39' E
Mossendjo. . . . . 02°57' S, 012°44' E
Mpouya . . . . 02°37' S, 16°013' E
Nkayi . . . . 04°11' S, 013°18' E
Ouesso. . . . . 01°37' N, 016°04' E
Owando . . . . 00°29' S, 015°55' E
Pointe-Noire . . . . 04°48' S, 011°51' E
Sibiti . . . . 03°41' S, 013°21' E
Souanké . . . . 02°05' N, 014°03' E
Zanaga. . . . . 02°15' S, 013°50' E

COSTA RICA .... .pg. 42

Alajuela . . . . 10°01' N, 084°13' W
Cañas. . . . . 10°26' N, 085°06' W
Desamparados . . . . 09°54' N, 084°05' W
Golfito . . . . 08°39' N, 083°09' W
Heredia . . . . 10°00' N, 084°07' W
Ipís. . . . . 09°58' N, 084°01' W
La Cruz . . . . 11°04' N, 085°38' W
Liberia . . . . 10°38' N, 085°26' W
Miramar. . . . . 10°06' N, 084°44' W
Nicoya . . . . 10°09' N, 085°27' W
Puerto Limón (Limón) . . . . 10°00' N, 083°02' W
Puntarenas . . . . 09°58' N, 084°50' W
Quesada . . . . 10°20' N, 084°26' W
San Isidro . . . . 09°23' N, 083°42' W
San José. . . . . 09°56' N, 084°05' W
San Ramón . . . . 10°05' N, 084°28' W
Santa Cruz. . . . . 10°16' N, 085°35' W
Siquirres . . . . 10°06' N, 083°31' W
Tilarán . . . . 10°28' N, 084°58' W

CROATIA . . . . .pg. 43

Bjelovar. . . . . 45°54' N, 016°51' E
Đakovo . . . . 45°19' N, 018°25' E
Dubrovnik . . . . 42°39' N, 018°07' E
Jasenovac . . . . 45°16' N, 016°54' E
Karlovac . . . . 45°29' N, 015°33' E
Knin . . . . 44°02' N, 016°12' E
Makarska . . . . 43°18' N, 017°02' E
Nin . . . . 44°14' N, 015°11' E
Opatija. . . . . 45°20' N, 014°19' E
Osijek. . . . . 45°33' N, 018°42' E

Ploče . . . . 43°04' N, 017°26' E
Pula . . . . 44°52' N, 013°50' E
Sesvete . . . . 45°50' N, 016°10' E
Rijeka. . . . . 45°21' N, 014°24' E
Sisak . . . . 45°29' N, 016°22' E
Slavonski Brod . . . . 45°09' N, 018°02' E
Slavonska Požega
(Požega) . . . . 45°20' N, 017°41' E
Split . . . . 43°31' N, 016°26' E
Trogir . . . . 43°32' N, 016°15' E
Varaždin . . . . 46°18' N, 016°20' E
Vinkovci . . . . 45°17' N, 018°49' E
Vukovar. . . . . 45°21' N, 019°00' E
Zadar. . . . . 44°07' N, 015°15' E
Zagreb . . . . 45°48' S, 016°00' E

CUBA . . . . .pg. 44

Banes. . . . . 20°58' N, 075°43' W
Baracoa . . . . 20°21' N, 074°30' W
Bayamo . . . . 20°23' N, 076°39' W
Camagüey . . . . 21°23' N, 077°55' W
Cárdenas. . . . . 23°02' N, 081°12' W
Ciego de Avila. . . . . 21°51' N, 078°46' W
Cienfuegos . . . . 22°09' N, 080°27' W
Colón . . . . 22°43' N, 080°54' W
Florida . . . . 21°32' N, 078°14' W
Guantánamo . . . . 20°08' N, 075°12' W
Güines . . . . 22°50' N, 082°02' W
Havana (La Habana) . . . . 23°08' N, 082°22' W
Holguín . . . . 20°53' N, 076°15' W
Jagüey Grande . . . . 22°32' N, 081°08' W
Jovellanos . . . . 22°48' N, 081°12' W
Las Tunas . . . . 20°58' N, 076°57' W
Manzanillo. . . . . 20°21' N, 077°07' W
Matanzas. . . . . 23°03' N, 081°35' W
Mayarí . . . . 20°40' N, 075°41' W
Morón . . . . 22°06' N, 078°38' W
Nueva Gerona . . . . 21°53' N, 082°48' W
Nuevitas . . . . 21°33' N, 077°16' W
Palma Soriano. . . . . 20°13' N, 076°00' W
Pinar del Río . . . . 22°25' N, 083°42' W
Placetas . . . . 22°19' N, 079°40' W
Puerto Padre. . . . . 21°12' N, 076°36' W
Sagua la Grande . . . . 22°49' N, 080°05' W
San Antonio
de los Baños . . . . 22°53' N, 082°30' W
Sancti Spíritus. . . . . 21°56' N, 079°27' W
Santa Clara . . . . 22°24' N, 079°58' W
Santa Cruz del Sur . . . . . . 20°43' N, 078°00' W
Santiago de Cuba . . . . 20°01' N, 075°49' W

CYPRUS . . . . .pg. 45

Akanthou. . . . . 35°22' N, 033°45' E
Akrotiri . . . . 34°36' N, 032°57' E
Athna . . . . 35°03' N, 033°47' E
Ayios Amvrosios. . . . . 35°20' N, 033°35' E
Ayios Theodhoros . . . . . . 34°48' N, 033°23' E
Famagusta. . . . . 35°07' N, 033°57' E

Kalokhorio	34°55' N,	033°32' E
Kouklia	34°42' N,	032°34' E
Kyrenia	35°20' N,	033°19' E
Larnaca	34°55' N,	033°38' E
Laxia	35°06' N,	033°22' E
Leonarisso	35°28' N,	034°08' E
Limassol	34°40' N,	033°02' E
Livadhia	35°24' N,	034°02' E
Liveras	35°23' N,	032°57' E
Mari	34°44' N,	033°18' E
Morphou	35°12' N,	032°59' E
Nicosia (Lefkosia)	35°10' N,	033°22' E
Ora	34°51' N,	033°12' E
Ormidhia	34°59' N,	033°47' E
Pakhna	34°46' N,	032°48' E
Pano Lakatamia	35°06' N,	033°18' E
Paphos	34°45' N,	032°25' E
Paralimni	35°02' N,	033°59' E
Patriki	35°22' N,	033°59' E
Perivolia	34°49' N,	033°35' E
Pomos	35°09' N,	032°33' E
Prastio	35°10' N,	033°45' E
Trikomo	35°17' N,	033°52' E
Tsadha	34°50' N,	032°28' E
Varosha	35°06' N,	033°57' E
Vroisha	35°04' N,	032°40' E
Yialoussa	35°32' N,	034°11' E

CZECH REPUBLIC
............pg. 46

Břeclav	48°46' N,	016°53' E
Brno	49°12' N,	016°38' E
Česká Lípa	50°41' N,	014°33' E
České Budějovice	48°59' N,	014°28' E
Český Těšín	49°45' N,	018°37' E
Cheb	50°04' N,	012°22' E
Chomutov	50°27' N,	013°26' E
Děčín	50°47' N,	014°13' E
Frýdek Místek	49°41' N,	018°21' E
Havířov	49°47' N,	018°22' E
Havlíčkův Brod	49°37' N,	015°35' E
Hodonín	48°52' N,	017°08' E
Hradec Králové	50°13' N,	015°50' E
Jablonec	50°43' N,	015°11' E
Jihlava	49°24' N,	015°35' E
Karlovy Vary	50°13' N,	012°54' E
Karviná	49°52' N,	018°33' E
Kladno	50°09' N,	014°06' E
Kolín	50°02' N,	015°12' E
Krnov	50°06' N,	017°43' E
Kroměříž	49°18' N,	017°24' E
Liberec	50°47' N,	015°03' E
Litvínov	50°36' N,	013°37' E
Mladá Boleslav	50°25' N,	014°54' E
Most	50°32' N,	013°39' E
Nový Jičín	49°36' N,	018°01' E
Olomouc	49°35' N,	017°15' E
Opava	49°57' N,	017°55' E
Orlová	49°51' N,	018°25' E

Ostrava	49°50' N,	018°17' E
Pardubice	50°02' N,	015°47' E
Písek	49°18' N,	014°09' E
Plzeň	49°45' N,	013°22' E
Prague (Praha)	50°05' N,	014°28' E
Přerov	49°27' N,	017°27' E
Příbřam	49°42' N,	014°01' E
Prostějov	49°28' N,	017°07' E
Šumperk	49°58' N,	016°58' E
Tábor	49°25' N,	014°40' E
Teplice	50°38' N,	013°50' E
Třebíč	49°13' N,	015°53' E
Trinec	49°41' N,	018°39' E
Trutnov	50°34' N,	015°54' E
Uherské Hradiště	49°04' N,	017°27' E
Ústí nad Labem	50°40' N,	014°02' E
Valašské Meziříčí	49°28' N,	017°58' E
Vsetín	49°20' N,	018°00' E
Žd'ár nad Sázavou	49°35' N,	015°56' E
Zlín	49°13' N,	017°40' E
Znojmo	48°51' N,	016°03' E

DENMARK ....pg. 47

Ålborg (Aalborg)	57°03' N,	009°56' E
Århus (Aarhus)	56°09' N,	010°13' E
Års	56°48' N,	009°32' E
Brønderslev	57°16' N,	009°58' E
Brørup	55°29' N,	009°01' E
Copenhagen (København)	55°40' N,	012°35' E
Esbjerg	55°28' N,	008°27' E
Fakse	55°15' N,	012°08' E
Fredericia	55°35' N,	009°46' E
Frederiksberg	55°41' N,	012°32' E
Frederikshavn	57°26' N,	010°32' E
Gilleleje	56°07' N,	012°19' E
Give	55°51' N,	009°15' E
Grenå	56°25' N,	010°53' E
Hadsund	56°43' N,	010°07' E
Helsingør	56°02' N,	012°37' E
Herning	56°08' N,	008°59' E
Hillerød	55°56' N,	012°19' E
Hirtshals	57°35' N,	009°58' E
Hjørring	57°28' N,	009°59' E
Holstebro	56°21' N,	008°38' E
Hornslet	56°19' N,	010°20' E
Horsens	55°52' N,	009°52' E
Jyderup	55°40' N,	011°26' E
Klarup	57°01' N,	010°03' E
Køge	55°27' N,	012°11' E
Kolding	55°29' N,	009°29' E
Lemvig	56°32' N,	008°18' E
Løgstør	56°58' N,	009°15' E
Næstved	55°14' N,	011°46' E
Nakskov	54°50' N,	011°09' E
Nykøbing	54°46' N,	011°53' E
Nykøbing	55°55' N,	011°41' E
Nykøbing	56°48' N,	008°52' E
Odense	55°24' N,	010°23' E
Ølgod	55°49' N,	008°37' E

Otterup	55°31' N, 010°24' E
Padborg	54°49' N, 009°22' E
Randers	56°28' N, 010°03' E
Ribe	55°21' N, 008°46' E
Ringkøbing	56°05' N, 008°15' E
Rønne	55°06' N, 014°42' E
Roskilde	55°39' N, 012°05' E
Rudkøbing	54°56' N, 010°43' E
Skagen	57°44' N, 010°36' E
Skive	56°34' N, 009°02' E
Skjern	55°57' N, 008°30' E
Slagelse	55°24' N, 011°22' E
Sønderborg	54°55' N, 009°47' E
Struer	56°29' N, 008°37' E
Svendborg	55°03' N, 010°37' E
Thisted	56°57' N, 008°42' E
Tilst	56°12' N, 010°07' E
Toftlund	55°11' N, 009°04' E
Tønder	54°56' N, 008°54' E
Varde	55°38' N, 008°29' E
Vejle	55°42' N, 009°32' E
Viborg	56°26' N, 009°24' E
Vodskov	57°06' N, 010°02' E
Vordingborg	55°01' N, 011°55' E

DJIBOUTI . . . . .pg. 48

Ali Sabih	11°10' N, 042°42' E
Dikhil	11°06' N, 042°23' E
Djibouti	11°36' N, 043°09' E
Tadjoura	11°47' N, 042°53' E

DOMINICA . . . . . . .pg. 49

Castle Bruce	15°26' N, 061°16' W
Colihaut	15°30' N, 061°29' W
La Plaine	15°20' N, 061°15' W
Marigot	15°32' N, 061°18' W
Portsmouth	15°35' N, 061°28' W
Rosalie	15°22' N, 061°16' W
Roseau	15°18' N, 061°24' W
Saint Joseph	15°24' N, 061°26' W
Salibia	15°29' N, 061°16' W
Soufrière	15°13' N, 061°22' W
Vieille Case	15°36' N, 061°24' W

DOMINICAN REPUBLIC . . . . .pg. 50

Azua	18°27' N, 070°44' W
Baní	18°17' N, 070°20' W
Barahona	18°12' N, 071°06' W
Bayaguana	18°58' N, 069°00' W
Bonao	18°56' N, 070°25' W
Cotuí	19°03' N, 070°09' W
Dajabón	19°33' N, 071°42' W
Duvergé	18°22' N, 071°31' W

El Seibo	18°46' N, 069°02' W
Enriquillo	17°54' N, 071°14' W
Higüey	18°37' N, 068°42' W
Jimaní	18°28' N, 071°51' W
La Romana	18°25' N, 068°58' W
La Vega	19°13' N, 070°31' W
Las Matas	18°52' N, 071°31' W
Mao	19°34' N, 071°05' W
Miches	18°59' N, 069°03' W
Moca	19°24' N, 070°31' W
Montecristi	19°52' N, 071°39' W
Nagua (Julia Molina)	19°23' N, 069°50' W
Neiba	18°28' N, 071°25' W
Pedernales	18°02' N, 071°45' W
Puerto Plata	19°48' N, 070°41' W
Sabaneta	19°28' N, 071°20' W
Salcedo	19°23' N, 070°25' W
Samaná	19°13' N, 069°19' W
San Cristóbal	18°25' N, 070°06' W
San Francisco de Macorís	19°18' N, 070°15' W
San Juan	18°48' N, 071°14' W
San Pedro de Macorís	18°27' N, 069°18' W
Sánchez	19°14' N, 069°36' W
Santiago	19°27' N, 070°42' W
Santo Domingo	18°28' N, 069°54' W

ECUADOR . . . . . . .pg. 51

Ambato	01°15' S, 078°37' W
Azogues	02°44' S, 078°50' W
Babahoyo	01°49' S, 079°31' W
Balzar	01°22' S, 079°54' W
Cuenca	02°53' S, 078°59' W
Esmeraldas	00°59' N, 079°42' W
General Leonidas Plaza Gutiérrez	02°58' S, 078°25' W
Girón	03°10' S, 079°08' W
Guayaquil	02°10' S, 079°54' W
Huaquillas	03°29' S, 080°14' W
Ibarra	00°21' N, 078°07' W
Jipijapa	01°20' S, 080°35' W
Latacunga	00°56' S, 078°37' W
Loja	04°00' S, 079°13' W
Macará	04°23' S, 079°57' W
Macas	02°19' S, 078°07' W
Machala	03°16' S, 079°58' W
Manta	00°57' S, 080°44' W
Milagro	02°07' S, 079°36' W
Muisne	00°36' N, 080°02' W
Naranjal	02°40' S, 079°37' W
Otavalo	00°14' N, 078°16' W
Pasaje	03°20' S, 079°49' W
Piñas	03°40' S, 079°39' W
Portoviejo	01°03' S, 080°27' W
Puerto Francisco de Orellana (Coca)	00°28' S, 076°58' W
Puyo	01°28' S, 077°59' W
Quevedo	01°02' S, 079°27' W
Quito	00°13' S, 078°30' W
Riobamba	01°40' S, 078°38' W
Salinas	02°13' S, 080°58' W

San Gabriel . . . . 00°36' N, 077°49' W
San Lorenzo . . . . 01°17' N, 078°50' W
Santo Domingo de los
  Colorados (Santo
  Domingo) . . . . 00°15' S, 079°09' W
Tena. . . . . 00°59' S, 077°49' W
Tulcán . . . . 00°48' N, 077°43' W
Valdez . . . . 01°15' N, 079°00' W
Yantzaza . . . . 03°51' S, 078°45' W
Zamora . . . . 04°04' S, 078°58' W
Zaruma . . . . 03°41' S, 079°37' W

EGYPT . . . . pg. 52

Akhmīm. . . . . 26°34' N, 031°44' E
Al-'Arish . . . . 31°08' N, 033°48' E
Alexandria
  (Al-Iskandariyah). . . . . . 31°12' N, 029°54' E
Al-Fayyūm . . . . 29°19' N, 030°50' E
Al-Khārijah . . . . 25°26' N, 030°33' E
Al-Maḥallah Al-Kubrā . . . . 30°58' N, 031°10' E
Al-Manṣūrah . . . . 31°03' N, 031°23' E
Al-Ma'ṣarah. . . . . 25°30' N, 029°04' E
Al-Minyā . . . . 28°06' N, 030°45' E
Aswān . . . . 24°05' N, 032°53' E
Asyut . . . . 27°11' N, 031°11' E
Aṭ-Ṭur . . . . 28°14' N, 033°37' E
Az-Zāqaziq. . . . . 30°35' N, 031°31' E
Banhā . . . . 30°28' N, 031°11' E
Bani Suwayf. . . . . 29°05' N, 031°05' E
Cairo (Al-Qahirah) . . . . 30°03' N, 031°15' E
Damanhūr . . . . 31°02' N, 030°28' E
Damietta (Dumyāt). . . . . . . 31°25' N, 031°48' E
Giza (Al-Jīzah). . . . . 30°01' N, 031°13' E
Jirjā . . . . 26°20' N, 031°53' E
Luxor (Al-Uqsur). . . . . 25°41' N, 032°39' E
Mallawī . . . . 27°44' N, 030°50' E
Matruh. . . . . 31°21' N, 027°14' E
Port Said (Bur Sa'id) . . . . . 31°16' N, 032°18' E
Qinā . . . . 26°10' N, 032°43' E
Sawhāj . . . . 26°33' N, 031°42' E
Shibīn al-Kawm . . . . 30°33' N, 031°01' E
Suez (As-Suways) . . . . 29°58' N, 032°33' E
Ṭanṭā . . . . 30°47' N, 031°00' E

EL SALVADOR . . . pg. 53

Acajutla . . . . 13°35' N, 089°50' W
Chalatenango . . . . 14°02' N, 088°56' W
Chalchuapa. . . . . 13°59' N, 089°41' W
Cojutepeque . . . . 13°43' N, 088°56' W
Ilobasco. . . . . 13°51' N, 088°51' W
Izalco . . . . 13°45' N, 089°40' W
La Unión . . . . 13°20' N, 087°51' W
Nueva San Salvador
  (Santa Tecla) . . . . 13°41' N, 089°17' W
San Francisco
  (San Francisco Gotera) . . 13°42' N, 088°06' W
San Miguel. . . . . 13°29' N, 088°11' W

San Salvador . . . . 13°42' N, 089°12' W
Santa Ana . . . . 13°59' N, 089°34' W
San Vincente . . . . 13°38' N, 088°48' W
Sensuntepeque . . . . 13°52' N, 088°38' W
Sonsonate . . . . 13°43' N, 089°44' W
Usulatán . . . . 13°21' N, 088°27' W
Zacatecoluca. . . . . 13°20' N, 088°52' W

EQUATORIAL GUINEA . . . . .pg. 54

Bata . . . . 01°51' N, 009°45' E
Kogo . . . . 01°05' N, 009°42' E
Malabo (Santa Isabel). . . . . 03°21' N, 008°40' E
Mbini . . . . 01°34' N, 009°37' E
Mikomeseng . . . . 02°08' N, 010°37' E
Niefang . . . . 01°51' N, 010°15' E
San Antonio de Ureca. . . . . 03°16' N, 008°32' E

ERITREA . . . . .pg. 55

Akordat . . . . 15°33' N, 037°53' E
Aseb (Assab). . . . . 13°00' N, 042°44' E
Asmara (Asmera) . . . . 15°20' N, 038°56' E
Keren . . . . 15°47' N, 038°28' E
Massawa (Mitsiwa) . . . . . . 15°36' N, 039°28' E
Nakfa . . . . 16°40' N, 038°29' E

ESTONIA . . . . .pg. 56

Abja-Paluoja . . . . 58°08' N, 025°21' E
Ambla . . . . 59°11' N, 025°51' E
Antsla . . . . 57°50' N, 026°32' E
Haapsalu . . . . 58°56' N, 023°33' E
Järva-Jaani. . . . . 59°02' N, 025°53' E
Järvakandi . . . . 58°47' N, 024°49' E
Jõgeva . . . . 58°45' N, 026°24' E
Käina . . . . 58°50' N, 022°47' E
Kallaste . . . . 58°39' N, 027°09' E
Kärdla . . . . 59°00' N, 022°45' E
Kehra . . . . 59°20' N, 025°20' E
Keila. . . . . 59°18' N, 024°25' E
Kilingi-Nõmme. . . . . 58°09' N, 024°58' E
Kiviõli . . . . 59°21' N, 026°57' E
Kohtla-Järve . . . . 59°24' N, 027°15' E
Kunda . . . . 59°29' N, 026°32' E
Kuressaare (Kingissepa) . . . 58°15' N, 022°28' E
Lavassaare . . . . 58°31' N, 024°22' E
Lihula (Lihula) . . . . 58°41' N, 023°50' E
Loksa . . . . 59°35' N, 025°42' E
Maardu . . . . 59°25' N, 024°59' E
Märjamaa . . . . 58°54' N, 024°26' E
Mõisaküla . . . . 58°06' N, 025°11' E
Mustla . . . . 58°14' N, 025°52' E
Narva . . . . 59°23' N, 028°12' E
Nuia . . . . 58°06' N, 025°33' E
Orissaare. . . . . 58°34' N, 023°05' E

Otepää . . . . 58°03' N, 026°30' E
Paide . . . . 58°54' N, 025°33' E
Paldiski . . . . 59°20' N, 024°06' E
Pärnu . . . . 58°24' N, 024°32' E
Põlva . . . . 58°03' N, 027°03' E
Püssi . . . . 59°22' N, 027°03' E
Rakvere . . . . 59°22' N, 026°20' E
Räpina . . . . 58°06' N, 027°27' E
Rapla . . . . 59°01' N, 024°47' E
Saue . . . . 59°18' N, 024°34' E
Sindi . . . . 58°24' N, 024°40' E
Suure-Jaani . . . . 58°33' N, 025°28' E
Tallinn . . . . 59°25' N, 024°45' E
Tapa . . . . 59°16' N, 025°58' E
Tartu . . . . 58°23' N, 026°43' E
Tootsi . . . . 58°34' N, 024°49' E
Tõrva . . . . 58°00' N, 025°56' E
Türi . . . . 58°48' N, 025°26' E
Valga . . . . 57°47' N, 026°02' E
Viivikonna . . . . 59°19' N, 027°42' E
Viljandi . . . . 58°24' N, 025°36' E
Võsu . . . . 59°35' N, 025°58' E

ETHIOPIA . . . . pg. 57

Addis Ababa (Adis Abeba). 09°02' N, 038°42' E
Adigrat . . . . 14°17' N, 039°28' E
Adwa (Adowa or Aduwa) . . 14°10' N, 038°54' E
Agaro . . . . 07°51' N, 036°39' E
Akaki . . . . 09°05' N, 039°00' E
Aksum . . . . 14°08' N, 038°43' E
Alamata . . . . 12°25' N, 039°33' E
Arba Minch (Arba Mench). 06°02' N, 037°33' E
Bahir Dar . . . . 11°36' N, 037°23' E
Debre Markos . . . . 10°21' N, 037°44' E
Debre Zeyit . . . . 08°45' N, 038°59' E
Dembidollo . . . . 08°32' N, 034°48' E
Dese (Dase) . . . . 11°08' N, 039°38' E
Dire Dawa . . . . 09°35' N, 041°52' E
Finchaa . . . . 09°33' N, 037°21' E
Gonder . . . . 12°36' N, 037°28' E
Gore . . . . 08°09' N, 035°32' E
Harer (Harar) . . . . 09°19' N, 042°07' E
Jijiga . . . . 09°21' N, 042°48' E
Jima (Jimma) . . . . 07°40' N, 036°50' E
Kembolcha (Kombolcha) . . 11°05' N, 039°44' E
Kibre Mengist . . . . 05°53' N, 038°59' E
Lalibela . . . . 12°02' N, 039°02' E
Mekele . . . . 13°30' N, 039°28' E
Metu . . . . 08°18' N, 035°35' E
Nazret . . . . 08°33' N, 039°16' E
Nekemte . . . . 09°05' N, 036°33' E
Sodo . . . . 06°54' N, 037°45' E
Weldya . . . . 11°50' N, 039°41' E
Yirga Alem . . . . 06°45' N, 038°25' E

FIJI . . . . pg. 58

Ba . . . . 17°33' S, 177°41' E

Lami . . . . 18°07' S, 178°25' E
Lautoka . . . . 17°37' S, 177°28' E
Nadi . . . . 17°48' S, 177°25' E
Suva . . . . 18°08' S, 178°25' E

FINLAND . . . . pg. 59

Espoo (Esbo) . . . . 60°13' N, 024°40' E
Forssa . . . . 60°49' N, 023°38' E
Hämeenlinna
   (Tavastehus) . . . . 61°00' N, 024°27' E
Hanko . . . . 59°50' N, 022°57' E
Haukipudas . . . . 65°11' N, 025°21' E
Heinola . . . . 61°13' N, 026°02' E
Helsinki . . . . 60°10' N, 024°58' E
Ilmajoki . . . . 62°44' N, 022°34' E
Ivalo . . . . 68°39' N, 027°36' E
Jämsä . . . . 61°52' N, 025°12' E
Joensuu . . . . 62°36' N, 029°46' E
Jyväskylä . . . . 62°14' N, 025°44' E
Kangasala . . . . 61°28' N, 024°05' E
Kaskinen . . . . 62°23' N, 021°13' E
Kemi . . . . 65°44' N, 024°34' E
Kittilä . . . . 67°40' N, 024°54' E
Kotka . . . . 60°28' N, 026°55' E
Kouvola . . . . 60°52' N, 026°42' E
Kuhmo . . . . 64°08' N, 029°31' E
Kuopio . . . . 62°54' N, 027°41' E
Lahti . . . . 60°58' N, 025°40' E
Lappeenranta
   (Villmanstrand) . . . . 61°04' N, 028°11' E
Lapua . . . . 62°57' N, 023°00' E
Lohja . . . . 60°15' N, 024°05' E
Mariehamn
   (Maarianhamina) . . . . . . 60°06' N, 019°57' E
Mikkeli (Sankt Michel) . . . . 61°41' N, 027°15' E
Nivala . . . . 63°55' N, 024°58' E
Nurmes . . . . 63°33' N, 029°07' E
Oulu (Uleåborg) . . . . 65°01' N, 025°28' E
Pello . . . . 66°47' N, 023°55' E
Pietarsaari . . . . 63°40' N, 022°42' E
Pori (Björneborg) . . . . 61°29' N, 021°47' E
Posio . . . . 66°06' N, 028°09' E
Raahe . . . . 64°41' N, 024°29' E
Rauma . . . . 61°08' N, 021°30' E
Rovaniemi . . . . 66°30' N, 025°43' E
Salla . . . . 66°50' N, 028°40' E
Salo . . . . 60°23' N, 023°08' E
Sotkamo . . . . 64°08' N, 028°25' E
Tampere (Tammerfors) . . . 61°30' N, 023°45' E
Turku (Åbo) . . . . 60°27' N, 022°17' E
Vaasa (Vasa) . . . . 63°06' N, 021°36' E
Vantaa (Vanda) . . . . 60°18' N, 024°51' E

FRANCE . . . . pg. 60

Ajaccio . . . . 41°55' N, 008°44' E
Amiens . . . . 49°54' N, 002°18' E
Angers . . . . 47°28' N, 000°33' W

Annecy	45°54' N,	006°07' E
Auch	43°39' N,	000°35' E
Aurillac	44°55' N,	002°27' E
Auxerre	47°48' N,	003°34' E
Avignon	43°57' N,	004°49' E
Bar-le-Duc	48°47' N,	005°10' E
Bastia	42°42' N,	009°27' E
Beauvais	49°26' N,	002°05' E
Belfort	47°38' N,	006°52' E
Bonifacio	41°23' N,	009°09' E
Bordeaux	44°50' N,	000°34' W
Bourges	47°05' N,	002°24' E
Brest	48°24' N,	004°29' W
Caen	49°11' N,	000°21' W
Cahors	44°26' N,	001°26' E
Calais	50°57' N,	001°50' E
Charleville-Mézières	49°46' N,	004°43' E
Chartres	48°27' N,	001°30' E
Clermont-Ferrand	45°47' N,	003°05' E
Colmar	48°05' N,	007°22' E
Dijon	47°19' N,	005°01' E
Dunkirk (Dunkerque)	51°03' N,	002°22' E
Épinal	48°11' N,	006°27' E
Grenoble	45°10' N,	005°43' E
Guéret	46°10' N,	001°52' E
La Rochelle	46°10' N,	001°09' W
Le Havre	49°30' N,	000°08' E
Le Mans	48°00' N,	000°12' E
Lille	50°38' N,	003°04' E
Limoges	45°45' N,	001°20' E
Lyon	45°45' N,	004°51' E
Marseille	43°18' N,	005°24' E
Metz	49°08' N,	006°10' E
Mont-de-Marsan	43°53' N,	000°30' W
Moulins	46°34' N,	003°20' E
Nancy	48°41' N,	006°12' E
Nantes	47°13' N,	001°33' W
Nevers	46°59' N,	003°10' E
Nice	43°42' N,	007°15' E
Nîmes	43°50' N,	004°21' E
Niort	46°19' N,	000°28' W
Orléans	47°55' N,	001°54' E
Paris	48°52' N,	002°20' E
Pau	43°18' N,	000°22' W
Périgueux	45°11' N,	000°43' E
Perpignan	42°41' N,	002°53' E
Poitiers	46°35' N,	000°20' E
Quimper	48°00' N,	004°06' W
Rennes	48°05' N,	001°41' W
Saint-Brieuc	48°31' N,	002°47' W
Strasbourg	48°35' N,	007°45' E
Tarbes	43°14' N,	000°05' E
Toulon	43°07' N,	005°56' E
Toulouse	43°36' N,	001°26' E
Tours	47°23' N,	000°41' E
Troyes	48°18' N,	004°05' E
Tulle	45°16' N,	001°46' E
Valence	44°56' N,	004°54' E
Vannes	47°40' N,	002°45' W
Versailles	48°48' N,	002°08' E
Vesoul	47°38' N,	006°10' E

GABON . . . . .pg. 61

Bitam	02°05' N,	011°29' E
Booué	00°06' S,	011°56' E
Fougamou	01°13' S,	010°36' E
Franceville	01°38' S,	013°35' E
Kango	00°09' N,	010°08' E
Koula-Moutou	01°08' S,	012°29' E
Lambaréné	00°42' S,	010°13' E
Lastoursville	00°49' S,	012°42' E
Léconi	01°35' S,	014°14' E
Libreville	00°23' N,	009°27' E
Makokou	00°34' N,	012°52' E
Mayumba	03°25' S,	010°39' E
Mekambo	01°01' N,	013°56' E
Mimongo	01°38' S,	011°39' E
Minvoul	02°09' N,	012°08' E
Mitzic	00°47' N,	011°34' E
Mouila	01°52' S,	011°01' E
Ndjolé	00°11' S,	010°45' E
Okondja	00°41' S,	013°47' E
Omboué	01°34' S,	009°15' E
Ovendo	00°17' N,	009°30' E
Oyem	01°37' N,	011°35' E
Port-Gentil	00°43' S,	008°47' E
Setté Cama	02°32' S,	009°45' E
Tchibanga	02°51' S,	011°02' E

GAMBIA, THE . . . .pg. 62

Banjul	13°27' N,	016°35' W
Basse Santa Su	13°19' N,	014°13' W
Brikama	13°16' N,	016°39' W
Georgetown	13°32' N,	014°46' W
Mansa Konko	13°28' N,	015°33' W
Serekunda	13°26' N,	016°34' W
Yundum	13°20' N,	016°41' W

GEORGIA . . . . .pg. 63

Akhalk'alak'i	41°24' N,	043°29' E
Batumi	41°38' N,	041°38' E
Chiat'ura	42°19' N,	043°18' E
Gagra	43°20' N,	040°15' E
Gardabani	41°28' N,	045°05' E
Gori	41°58' N,	044°07' E
Gudaut'a	43°06' N,	040°38' E
Khashuri	41°59' N,	043°36' E
K'obulet'i	41°50' N,	041°45' E
Kutaisi	42°15' N,	042°40' E
Marneuli	41°27' N,	044°48' E
Och'amch'ire	42°43' N,	041°28' E
Pot'i	42°09' N,	041°40' E
Rustari	41°33' N,	045°03' E
Samtredia	42°11' N,	042°20' E
Sokhumi	43°00' N,	041°02' E
Tbilisi (Tiflis)	41°42' N,	044°45' E
T'elavi	41°55' N,	045°28' E

Tqibuli . . . . 42°22' N, 042°59' E
Tqvarch'eli (Tkvarchely) . . 42°51' N, 041°41' E
Ts'khinvali (Staliniri) . . . . . 42°14' N, 043°58' E
Tsqaltubo . . . . 42°20' N, 042°34' E
Zugdidi . . . . 42°30' N, 041°53' E

GERMANY . . . . pg. 64

Aachen . . . . 50°46' N, 006°06' E
Augsburg . . . . 48°22' N, 010°53' E
Aurich . . . . 53°28' N, 007°29' E
Baden-Baden . . . . 48°45' N, 008°15' E
Berlin . . . . 52°30' N, 013°22' E
Bielefeld . . . . 52°02' N, 008°32' E
Bonn . . . . 50°44' N, 007°06' E
Brandenburg . . . . 52°25' N, 012°33' E
Bremen . . . . 53°05' N, 008°48' E
Bremerhaven . . . . 53°33' N, 008°35' E
Chemnitz
  (Karl-Marx-Stadt) . . . . . . 50°50' N, 012°55' E
Cologne (Köln) . . . . 50°56' N, 006°57' E
Cottbus . . . . 51°46' N, 014°20' E
Dessau . . . . 51°50' N, 012°15' E
Dortmund . . . . 51°31' N, 007°27' E
Dresden . . . . 51°03' N, 013°45' E
Duisburg . . . . 51°26' N, 006°45' E
Düsseldorf . . . . 51°13' N, 006°46' E
Erfurt . . . . 50°59' N, 011°02' E
Erlangen . . . . 49°36' N, 011°01' E
Essen . . . . 51°27' N, 007°01' E
Frankfurt am Main . . . . 50°07' N, 008°41' E
Freiburg . . . . 48°00' N, 007°51' E
Göttingen . . . . 51°32' N, 009°56' E
Halle . . . . 51°30' N, 012°00' E
Hamburg . . . . 53°33' N, 010°00' E
Hannover . . . . 52°22' N, 009°43' E
Heidelberg . . . . 49°25' N, 008°42' E
Jena . . . . 50°56' N, 011°35' E
Kassel . . . . 51°19' N, 009°30' E
Kiel . . . . 54°20' N, 010°08' E
Leipzig . . . . 51°18' N, 012°20' E
Lübeck . . . . 53°52' N, 010°42' E
Magdeburg . . . . 52°10' N, 011°40' E
Mainz . . . . 50°00' N, 008°15' E
Mannheim . . . . 49°29' N, 008°28' E
Munich . . . . 48°09' N, 011°35' E
Nürnberg (Nuremberg) . . . . 49°27' N, 011°05' E
Oldenburg . . . . 54°18' N, 010°53' E
Osnabrück . . . . 52°16' N, 008°03' E
Potsdam . . . . 52°24' N, 013°04' E
Regensburg . . . . 49°01' N, 012°06' E
Rostock . . . . 54°05' N, 012°08' E
Saarbrücken . . . . 49°14' N, 007°00' E
Schwerin . . . . 53°38' N, 011°23' E
Siegen . . . . 50°52' N, 008°02' E
Stuttgart . . . . 48°46' N, 009°11' E
Ulm . . . . 48°24' N, 010°00' E
Wiesbaden . . . . 50°05' N, 008°15' E
Würzburg . . . . 49°48' N, 009°56' E
Zwickau . . . . 50°44' N, 012°30' E

GHANA . . . . pg. 65

Accra . . . . 05°33' N, 000°13' E
Anloga . . . . 05°48' N, 000°54' E
Awaso . . . . 06°14' N, 002°16' W
Axim . . . . 04°52' N, 002°14' W
Bawku . . . . 11°03' N, 000°15' W
Bolgatanga . . . . 10°47' N, 000°51' W
Cape Coast . . . . 05°06' N, 001°15' W
Damongo . . . . 09°05' N, 001°49' W
Dunkwa . . . . 05°58' N, 001°47' W
Koforidua . . . . 05°14' N, 001°20' W
Kumasi . . . . 06°41' N, 001°37' W
Mampong . . . . 07°04' N, 001°24' W
Obuasi . . . . 06°12' N, 001°40' W
Prestea . . . . 05°26' N, 002°09' W
Salaga . . . . 08°33' N, 000°31' W
Sekondi-Takoradi . . . . 04°53' N, 001°45' W
Sunyani . . . . 07°20' N, 002°20' W
Swedru . . . . 05°32' N, 000°42' W
Tamale . . . . 09°24' N, 000°50' W
Tarkwa . . . . 05°18' N, 001°59' W
Tema . . . . 05°37' N, 000°01' E
Wa . . . . 10°03' N, 002°29' W
Yendi . . . . 09°26' N, 000°01' W

GREECE . . . . pg. 66

Alexandroúpolis
  (Alexandhroupolis) . . . . . 40°51' N, 025°52' E
Ándros . . . . 37°50' N, 024°56' E
Árgos . . . . 37°38' N, 022°44' E
Árta . . . . 39°09' N, 020°59' E
Áyios Nikólaos . . . . 35°11' N, 025°43' E
Drama . . . . 41°09' N, 024°09' E
Edessa (Edhessa) . . . . 40°48' N, 022°03' E
Ermoúpolis
  (Hermoúpolis) . . . . 37°27' N, 024°56' E
Flórina . . . . 40°47' N, 021°24' E
Hydra (Ídhra) . . . . 37°21' N, 023°28' E
Igoumenítsa . . . . 39°30' N, 020°16' E
Ioánnina (Yannina) . . . . . . 39°40' N, 020°50' E
Ios . . . . 36°44' N, 025°17' E
Iráklion
  (Candia or Heraklion) . . . 35°20' N, 025°08' E
Kalamariá . . . . 40°35' N, 022°58' E
Kalamata (Kalámai) . . . . . . 37°02' N, 022°07' E
Kálimnos . . . . 36°57' N, 026°59' E
Karditsa . . . . 39°22' N, 021°55' E
Kariaí . . . . 40°15' N, 024°15' E
Karpenísion . . . . 38°55' N, 021°47' E
Kateríni . . . . 40°16' N, 022°30' E
Kavála
  (Kaválla or Neapolis) . . . 40°56' N, 024°25' E
Kéa . . . . 37°38' N, 024°21' E
Kérkira . . . . 39°36' N, 019°55' E
Khalkís (Chalcis) . . . . 38°28' N, 023°36' E
Khaniá (Canea) . . . . 35°31' N, 024°02' E
Khíos (Chios) . . . . 38°22' N, 026°08' E

Kilkís	41°00' N,	022°52' E
Komotiní	41°07' N,	025°24' E
Lamía	38°54' N,	022°26' E
Larissa (Lárisa)	39°38' N,	022°25' E
Laurium (Lávrion)	37°43' N,	024°03' E
Mégara	38°00' N,	023°21' E
Mesolóngion (Missolonghi)	38°22' N,	021°26' E
Mitilíni (Mytilene)	39°06' N,	026°33' E
Monemvasía	36°41' N,	023°03' E
Náuplia(Navplion)	37°34' N,	022°48' E
Náxos	37°06' N,	025°23' E
Néa Ionía	38°02' N,	023°45' E
Pátrai	38°15' N,	021°44' E
Piraeus (Piraievs)	37°57' N,	028°38' E
Préveza	38°57' N,	020°45' E
Pylos (Pílos)	36°55' N,	021°42' E
Pyrgos (Pírgos)	37°41' N,	021°27' E
Réthimnon	35°22' N,	024°28' E
Rhodes (Ródhos)	36°26' N,	028°13' E
Sámos	37°45' N,	026°58' E
Samothráki	40°29' N,	025°31' E
Sérrai	41°05' N,	023°33' E
Sparta (Spárti)	37°05' N,	022°26' E
Thásos	40°47' N,	024°43' E
Thebes (Thívai)	38°19' N,	023°19' E
Thessaloníki (Salonika)	40°38' N,	022°56' E
Tríkala	39°33' N,	021°46' E
Trípolis	37°31' N,	022°22' E
Vólos	39°22' N,	022°57' E
Yithion (Githion)	36°45' N,	022°34' E
Xánthi	41°08' N,	024°53' E
Zákinthos	37°47' N,	020°54' E

GRENADA . . . . .pg. 67

Birch Grove	12°07' N,	061°40' W
Concord	12°07' N,	061°44' W
Corinth	12°02' N,	061°40' W
Gouyave	12°10' N,	061°44 W
Grand Anse	12°01' N,	061°45' W
Grenville	12°07' N,	061°37' W
Hillsborough	12°29' N,	061°28' W
La Poterie	12°10' N,	061°36' W
Rose Hill	12°12' N,	061°37' W
St. George's	12°03' N,	061°45' W
Sauteurs	12°14' N,	061°38' W
Victoria	12°12' N,	061°42' W

GUATEMALA . . . . .pg. 68

Amatitlán	14°29' N,	090°37' W
Antigua Guatemala (Antigua)	14°34' N,	090°44' W
Champerico	14°18' N,	091°55' W
Coatepeque	14°42' N,	091°52' W
Cobán	15°29' N,	090°22' W
Cuilapa (Cuajiniquilapa)	14°17' N,	090°18' W

El Estor	15°32' N,	089°21' W
Escuintla	14°18' N,	090°47' W
Esquipulas	14°34' N,	089°21' W
Flores	16°56' N,	089°53' W
Gualán	15°08' N,	089°22' W
Guatemala City (Guatemala)	14°38' N,	090°31' W
Huehuetenango	15°20' N,	091°28' W
Jalapa	14°38' N,	089°59' W
Jutiapa	14°17' N,	089°54' W
Mazatenango	14°32' N,	091°30' W
Poptún	16°21' N,	089°26' W
Pueblo Nuevo Tiquisate	14°17' N,	091°22' W
Puerto Barrios	15°43' N,	088°36' W
Puerto San José	13°55' N,	090°49' W
Quezaltenango	14°50' N,	091°31' W
Salamá	15°06' N,	090°16' W
San Benito	16°55' N,	089°54' W
San Cristóbal Verapaz	15°23' N,	090°24' W
Santa Cruz del Quiché	15°02' N,	091°08' W
Sololá	14°46' N,	091°11' W
Todos Santos Cuchumatán	15°31' N,	091°37' W
Villa Nueva	14°31' N,	090°35' W
Zacapa	14°58' N,	089°32' W
Zunil	14°47' N,	091°29' W

GUINEA . . . . .pg. 69

Beyla	08°41' N,	008°38' W
Boffa	10°10' N,	014°02' W
Boké	10°56' N,	014°18' W
Conakry	09°31' N,	013°43' W
Dabola	10°45' N,	011°07' W
Dalaba	10°42' N,	012°15' W
Dinguiraye	11°18' N,	010°43' W
Faranah	10°02' N,	010°44' W
Forécariah	09°26' N,	013°06' W
Fria	10°27' N,	013°32' W
Gaoual	11°45' N,	013°12' W
Guéckédou	08°33' N,	010°09' W
Kankan	10°23' N,	009°18' W
Kérouané	09°16' N,	009°01' W
Kindia	10°04' N,	012°51' W
Kissidougou	09°11' N,	010°06' W
Kouroussa	10°39' N,	009°53' W
Labé	11°19' N,	012°17' W
Macenta	08°33' N,	009°28' W
Mamou	10°23' N,	012°05' W
Nzérékoré	07°45' N,	008°49' W
Pita	11°05' N,	012°24' W
Siguiri	11°25' N,	009°10' W
Télimélé	10°54' N,	013°02' W
Tougué	11°27' N,	011°41' W

GUINEA-BISSAU . .pg. 70

Bafatá	12°10' N,	014°40' W
Bambadinca	12°02' N,	014°52' W
Bedanda	11°21' N,	015°07' W

Béli . . . . 11°51' N, 013°56' W
Bissau . . . . 11°51' N, 015°35' W
Bissorã . . . . 12°03' N, 015°26' W
Bolama . . . . 11°35' N, 015°28' W
Buba . . . . 11°35' N, 015°00' W
Bula . . . . 12°07' N, 015°43' W
Buruntuma . . . . 12°26' N, 013°39' W
Cacheu . . . . 12°16' N, 016°10' W
Catió . . . . 11°17' N, 015°15' W
Empada . . . . 11°33' N, 015°14' W
Farim . . . . 12°29' N, 015°13' W
Fulacunda . . . . 11°46' N, 015°10' W
Gabú (Nova Lamego) . . . . . 12°17' N, 014°13' W
Galomaro . . . . 11°57' N, 014°38' W
Jolmete . . . . 12°13' N, 015°52' W
Madina do Boé . . . . 11°45' N, 014°13' W
Mansôa . . . . 12°04' N, 015°19' W
Nhacra . . . . 11°58' N, 015°33' W
Piche . . . . 12°20' N, 013°57' W
Pirada . . . . 12°40' N, 014°10' W
Quebo . . . . 11°20' N, 014°56' W
Quinhámel . . . . 11°53' N, 015°51' W
Safim . . . . 11°57' N, 015°39' W
Sangonhá . . . . 11°10' N, 014°53' W
São Domingos . . . . 12°24' N, 016°12' W
Teixeira Pinto . . . . 12°04' N, 016°02' W
Tite . . . . 11°47' N, 015°24' W
Xitole . . . . 11°44' N, 014°49' W

GUYANA . . . . pg. 71

Apoteri . . . . 04°02' N, 058°34' W
Bartica . . . . 06°24' N, 058°37' W
Charity . . . . 07°24' N, 058°36' W
Corriverton . . . . 05°52' N, 057°10' W
Georgetown . . . . 06°48' N, 058°10' W
Isherton . . . . 02°19' N, 059°22' W
Ituni . . . . 05°30' N, 058°14' W
Karasabai . . . . 04°02' N, 059°32' W
Karmuda Village . . . . 05°38' N, 060°18' W
Lethem . . . . 03°23' N, 059°48' W
Linden . . . . 06°00' N, 058°18' W
Mabaruma . . . . 08°12' N, 059°47' W
Mahaicony Village . . . . 06°36' N, 057°48' W
Matthews Ridge . . . . 07°30' N, 060°10' W
New Amsterdam . . . . 06°15' N, 057°31' W
Orinduik . . . . 04°42' N, 060°01' W
Parika . . . . 06°52' N, 058°25' W
Port Kaituma . . . . 07°44' N, 059°53' W
Rose Hall . . . . 06°16' N, 057°21' W
Suddie . . . . 07°07' N, 058°29' W
Vreed en Hoop . . . . 06°48' N, 058°11' W

HAITI . . . . pg. 72

Anse-d'Hainault . . . . 18°30' N, 074°27' W
Cap-Haïtien . . . . 19°45' N, 072°12' W
Desdunes . . . . 19°17' N, 072°39' W
Gonaïves . . . . 19°27' N, 072°41' W
Grand Goâve . . . . 18°26' N, 072°46' W

Hinche . . . . 19°09' N, 072°01' W
Jean Rabel . . . . 18°15' N, 072°40' W
Lascahobas . . . . 18°50' N, 071°56' W
Léogâne . . . . 18°31' N, 072°38' W
Limbé . . . . 19°42' N, 072°24' W
Miragoâne . . . . 18°27' N, 073°06' W
Mirebalais . . . . 18°55' N, 072°06' W
Môle Saint-Nicolas . . . . 19°48' N, 073°23' W
Ouanaminthe . . . . 19°33' N, 071°44' W
Pètionville . . . . 18°31' N, 072°17' W
Petite Rivière de
  l'Artibonite . . . . 19°08' N, 072°29' W
Port-au-Prince . . . . 18°32' N, 072°20' W
Roseaux . . . . 18°36' N, 074°01' W
Saint-Louis du Nord . . . . . . 19°56' N, 072°43' W
Saint-Michel de l'Atalaye . . 19°22' N, 072°20' W
Thomassique . . . . 19°05' N, 071°50' W
Trou du Nord . . . . 19°38' N, 072°01' W
Verrettes . . . . 19°03' N, 072°28' W

HONDURAS . . . . . . pg. 73

Amapala . . . . 13°17' N, 087°39' W
Catacamas . . . . 14°48' N, 085°54' W
Choloma . . . . 15°37' N, 087°57' W
Choluteca . . . . 13°18' N, 087°12' W
Comayagua . . . . 14°27' N, 087°38' W
Danlí . . . . 14°02' N, 086°35' W
El Paraíso . . . . 15°01' N, 088°59' W
El Progreso . . . . 15°24' N, 087°48' W
Gracias . . . . 14°35' N, 088°35' W
Guaimaca . . . . 14°32' N, 086°49' W
Intibucá . . . . 14°19' N, 088°10' W
Juticalpa . . . . 14°39' N, 086°12' W
La Ceiba . . . . 15°47' N, 086°48' W
La Esperanza . . . . 14°18' N, 088°11' W
La Lima . . . . 15°26' N, 087°55' W
La Paz . . . . 14°19' N, 087°41' W
Morazán . . . . 15°19' N, 087°36' W
Nacaome . . . . 13°32' N, 087°29' W
Olanchito . . . . 15°30' N, 086°34' W
Puerto Cortés . . . . 15°50' N, 087°50' W
Puerto Lempira . . . . 15°16' N, 083°46' W
San Lorenzo . . . . 13°25' N, 087°27' W
San Marcos de Colón . . . . . 13°26' N, 086°48' W
San Pedro Sula . . . . 15°30' N, 088°02' W
Santa Bárbara . . . . 14°55' N, 088°14' W
Santa Rita . . . . 15°12' N, 087°53' W
Signatapeque . . . . 14°36' N, 087°57' W
Talanga . . . . 14°24' N, 087°05' W
Tegucigalpa . . . . 14°06' N, 087°13' W
Trujillo . . . . 15°55' N, 86°00' W
Yoro . . . . 15°08' N, 087°08' W
Yuscarán . . . . 13°56' N, 086°51' W

HUNGARY . . . . pg. 74

Baja . . . . 46°11' N, 018°58' E
Balmazújváros . . . . 47°37' N, 021°21' E
Barcs . . . . 45°58' N, 017°28' E

Békéscsaba	46°41' N,	021°06' E
Berettyóújfalu	47°13' N,	021°33' E
Budapest	47°30' N,	019°05' E
Cegléd	47°10' N,	019°48' E
Debrecen	47°32' N,	021°38' E
Dunaújváros		
(Sztálinváros)	46°59' N,	018°56' E
Eger	47°54' N,	020°23' E
Esztergom	47°48' N,	018°45' E
Fertőd (Eszterháza)	47°37' N,	016°52' E
Gyomaendrőd	46°56' N,	020°50' E
Gyöngyös	47°47' N,	019°56' E
Gyor	47°41' N,	017°38' E
Gyula	46°39' N,	021°17' E
Hódmezovásárhely	46°25' N,	020°20' E
Kalocsa	46°32' N,	019°00' E
Kaposvár	46°22' N,	017°48' E
Kazincbarcika	48°15' N,	020°38' E
Kecskemét	46°54' N,	019°42' E
Keszthely	46°46' N,	017°15' E
Kisvárda	48°13' N,	022°05' E
Körmend	47°01' N,	016°36' E
Kőszeg	47°23' N,	016°33' E
Lenti	46°37' N,	016°33' E
Makó	46°13' N,	020°29' E
Marcali	46°35' N,	017°25' E
Miskolc	48°06' N,	020°47' E
Mohács	45°59' N,	018°42' E
Nagyatád	46°13' N,	017°22' E
Nagykanizsa	46°27' N,	016°59' E
Nagykőrös	47°02' N,	019°47' E
Nyirbátor	47°50' N,	022°08' E
Nyíregyháza	47°57' N,	021°43' E
Oroshaza	46°34' N,	020°40' E
Ózd	48°13' N,	020°18' E
Paks	46°38' N,	018°52' E
Pápa	47°20' N,	017°28' E
Pécs	46°05' N,	018°14' E
Salgótarján	48°07' N,	019°49' E
Sarkad	46°45' N,	021°23' E
Sárospatak	48°19' N,	021°35' E
Sátoraljaújhely	48°24' N,	021°40' E
Siklós	45°51' N,	018°18' E
Sopron	47°41' N,	016°36' E
Szeged	46°15' N,	020°10' E
Szeghalom	47°02' N,	021°10' E
Székesfehérvár	47°12' N,	018°25' E
Szekszárd	46°21' N,	018°43' E
Szigetvár	46°03' N,	017°48' E
Szolnok	47°11' N,	020°12' E
Szombathely	47°14' N,	016°37' E
Tamási	46°38' N,	018°17' E
Tatabánya	47°34' N,	018°25' E
Vác	47°47' N,	019°08' E
Veszprém	47°06' N,	017°55' E
Zalaegerszeg	46°50' N,	016°51' E

ICELAND . . . . pg. 75

Akureyri	65°40' N,	018°06' W
Reykjavík	64°09' N,	021°57' W

Vestmannaeyjar	62°26' N,	020°16' W

INDIA . . . . pg. 76

Agra	27°11' N,	078°01' E
Ahmadabad		
(Ahmedabad)	23°02' N,	072°37' E
Ahmadnāgar		
(Ahmednagar)	19°05' N,	074°44' E
Allahabad	25°27' N,	081°51' E
Amritsar	31°35' N,	074°53' E
Āsānsol	23°41' N,	086°59' E
Balurghat	25°13' N,	088°46' E
Bangalore	12°59' N,	077°35' E
Baroda (Vadodara)	22°18' N,	073°12' E
Bathinda (Bhatinda)	30°12' N,	074°57' E
Bhilwara	25°21' N,	074°38' E
Bhiwandi	19°18' N,	073°04' E
Bhopal	23°16' N,	077°24' E
Bombay (Mumbai)	18°58' N,	072°50' E
Calcutta	22°32' N,	088°22' E
Cochin	09°58' N,	076°14' E
Coimbatore	11°00' N,	076°58' E
Cuddapah	14°28' N,	078°49' E
Dehra Dun	30°19' N,	078°02' E
Delhi	28°40' N,	077°13' E
Eluru (Ellore)	16°42' N,	081°06' E
Gangānagar		
(Sri Gangānagar)	29°55' N,	073°53' E
Guntur	16°18' N,	080°27' E
Gwalior	26°13' N,	078°10' E
Howrah (Haora)	22°35' N,	088°20' E
Hubli-Dharwad	15°21' N,	075°10' E
Hyderabad	17°23' N,	078°28' E
Imphal	24°49' N,	093°57' E
Indore	22°43' N,	075°50' E
Jabalpur (Jubbulpore)	23°10' N,	079°57' E
Jaipur	26°55' N,	075°49' E
Jammu	32°44' N,	074°52' E
Jamnagar	22°28' N,	070°04' E
Jodhpur	26°17' N,	073°02' E
Jūnāgadh	21°31' N,	070°28' E
Kanpur (Cawnpore)	26°28' N,	080°21' E
Khambhat (Cambay)	22°18' N,	072°37' E
Kota (Kotah)	25°11' N,	075°50' E
Longju	28°45' N,	093°35' E
Lucknow	26°51' N,	080°55' E
Ludhiana	30°54' N,	075°51' E
Madras (Chennai)	13°05' N,	080°17' E
Madurai (Madura)	09°56' N,	078°07' E
Malegaon	20°33' N,	074°32' E
Meerut	28°59' N,	077°42' E
Nagpur	21°09' N,	079°06' E
New Delhi	28°36' N,	077°12' E
Patna	25°36' N,	085°07' E
Pune (Poona)	18°32' N,	073°52' E
Puri	19°48' N,	085°51' E
Quilon	08°53' N,	076°36' E
Raipur	21°14' N,	081°38' E
Rajkot	22°18' N,	070°47' E
Sambalpur	21°27' N,	083°58' E

Shiliguri (Siliguri) . . . . 26°42' N, 088°26' E
Sholapur (Solapur) . . . . 17°41' N, 075°55' E
Sibsāgar . . . . 26°59' N, 094°38' E
Srinagar . . . . 34°05' N, 074°49' E
Surat . . . . 21°10' N, 072°50' E
Thanjavur (Tanjore) . . . . . . 10°48' N, 079°09' E
Tiruppur (Tirupper) . . . . . . 11°06' N, 077°21' E
Vadodara (Baroda) . . . . 22°18' N, 073°12' E
Vārānasi (Banāras,
   Benares) . . . . 25°20' N, 083°00' E
Vishākhapatnam
   (Visākhāpatam) . . . . 17°42' N, 083°18' E

INDONESIA . . . . . . .pg. 77

Ambon . . . . 03°43' S, 128°12' E
Balikpapan . . . . 01°17' S, 116°50' E
Banda Aceh (Kuta Raja) . . 05°34' N, 095°20' E
Bandung . . . . 06°54' S, 107°36' E
Banjarmasin . . . . 03°20' S, 114°35' E
Cilacap . . . . 07°44' S, 109°00' E
Jakarta . . . . 06°10' S, 106°48' E
Jambi . . . . 01°36' S, 103°37' E
Kendari . . . . 03°57' S, 122°35' E
Kupang . . . . 10°10' S, 123°35' E
Malang . . . . 07°59' S, 112°37' E
Manado . . . . 01°29' N, 124°51' E
Mataram . . . . 08°35' S, 116°07' E
Medan . . . . 03°35' N, 098°40' E
Padang . . . . 00°57' S, 100°21' E
Palembang . . . . 02°55' S, 104°45' E
Palu . . . . 00°53' S, 119°53' E
Samarinda . . . . 00°30' S, 117°09' E
Semarang . . . . 06°58' S, 110°25' E
Surabaya . . . . 07°15' S, 112°45' E
Ujungpandang . . . . 05°07' S, 119°24' E

IRAN . . . . .pg. 78

Ahvāz . . . . 31°19' N, 048°42' E
Āmol . . . . 36°28' N, 052°21' E
Arāk . . . . 34°05' N, 049°41' E
Ardabīl . . . . 38°15' N, 048°18' E
Bakhtarān . . . . 34°19' N, 047°04' E
Bandar 'Abbās . . . . 27°11' N, 056°17' E
Behbahān . . . . 30°35' N, 050°14' E
Bīrjand . . . . 32°53' N, 059°13' E
Būshehr . . . . 28°59' N, 050°50' E
Dārāb . . . . 28°45' N, 054°34' E
Dezfūl . . . . 32°23' N, 048°24' E
Eşfahān . . . . 32°40' N, 051°38' E
Gorgān . . . . 36°50' N, 054°29' E
Hamadān . . . . 34°48' N, 048°30' E
Kāshān . . . . 33°59' N, 051°29' E
Kāzerūn . . . . 29°37' N, 051°38' E
Kermān . . . . 30°17' N, 057°05' E
Khorramābād . . . . 33°30' N, 048°20' E
Khvoy . . . . 38°33' N, 044°58' E
Mahābād . . . . 36°45' N, 045°43' E
Mashhad . . . . 36°18' N, 059°36' E

Orūmīyeh . . . . 37°33' N, 045°04' E
Qā'en . . . . 33°44' N, 059°11' E
Qom . . . . 34°39' N, 050°54' E
Quchan . . . . 37°06' N, 058°30' E
Rafsanjān . . . . 30°24' N, 056°00' E
Rasht . . . . 37°16' N, 049°36' E
Sanandaj . . . . 35°19' N, 047°00' E
Shīrāz . . . . 29°36' N, 052°32' E
Tabrīz . . . . 38°05' N, 046°18' E
Tehran . . . . 35°40' N, 051°26' E
Yazd . . . . 31°53' N, 054°22' E
Zāhedān . . . . 29°30' N, 060°52' E
Zanjān . . . . 36°40' N, 048°29' E

IRAQ . . . . .pg. 79

Ad-Diwaniyah . . . . 31°59' N, 044°56' E
Al-'Amarah . . . . 31°50' N, 047°09' E
Al-Gharrāf . . . . 31°21' N, 046°17' E
Al-Hillah . . . . 32°29' N, 044°25' E
Al-Khāliş . . . . 33°49' N, 044°32' E
Al-Kūt . . . . 32°30' N, 045°49' E
Al-Maḥmūdiya . . . . 33°03' N, 044°21' E
Al-Majarr al-Kabir . . . . 31°34' N, 047°00' E
'Ānah . . . . 34°28' N, 041°56' E
An-Najaf . . . . 31°59' N, 044°20' E
An-Nashwah . . . . 30°49' N, 047°36' E
An-Nasiriyah . . . . 31°02' N, 046°16' E
Ar-Ramādī . . . . 33°25' N, 043°17' E
Ar-Ruţbah . . . . 33°02' N, 040°17' E
As-Samawah . . . . 31°18' N, 045°17' E
As-Sulaymaniyah . . . . 35°33' N, 045°26' E
Aş-Şuwayrah . . . . 32°55' N, 044°47' E
Baghdad . . . . 33°21' N, 044°25' E
Ba'qubah . . . . 33°45' N, 044°38' E
Barzān . . . . 36°55' N, 044°03' E
Basra (Al-Basrah) . . . . 30°30' N, 047°47' E
Dibs . . . . 35°40' N, 044°04' E
Hīt . . . . 33°38' N, 042°49' E
Irbil
   (Arbela, Arbil, or Erbil) . . 36°11' N, 044°01' E
Jalūlā' . . . . 34°16' N, 045°10' E
Karbala' . . . . 32°36' N, 044°02' E
Khānaqin . . . . 34°21' N, 045°22' E
Kirkuk . . . . 35°28' N, 044°23' E
Mosul (Al-Mawsil) . . . . 36°20' N, 043°08' E
Qal'at Dizah . . . . 36°11' N, 045°07' E
Sinjār . . . . 36°19' N, 041°52' E
Tall Kayf . . . . 36°29' N, 043°08' E
Tikrīt . . . . 34°36' N, 043°42' E
Ţūz Khurmātū
   (Touz Hourmato) . . . . . . 34°53' N, 044°38' E
Zummār . . . . 36°47' N, 042°38' E

IRELAND . . . . .pg. 80

Arklow
   (An tinbhear Mor) . . . . . . 52°48' N, 006°09' W
Athlone . . . . 53°26' N, 007°57' W
Ballina . . . . 54°07' N, 009°10' W

Ballycastle. . . . . 54°17' N, 009°22' W
Ballycotton . . . . 51°50' N, 008°01' W
Ballymote . . . . 54°05' N, 008°31' W
Ballyvaghan. . . . . 53°07' N, 009°09' W
Bandon
   (Droichead na Bandan). . 51°45' N, 008°44' W
Bantry . . . . 51°41' N, 009°27' W
Belmullet. . . . . 54°13' N, 010°00' W
Blarney . . . . 51°56' N, 008°34' W
Boyle . . . . 53°58' N, 008°18' W
Bray (Bre) . . . . 53°12' N, 006°06' W
Buncrana. . . . . 55°08' N, 007°27' W
Carlow (Ceatharlach). . . . . 52°50' N, 006°56' W
Carndonagh. . . . . 55°15' N, 007°16' W
Carrick on Shannon . . . . . 53°57' N, 008°05' W
Castlebar. . . . . 53°51' N, 009°18' W
Castletownbere. . . . . 51°39' N, 009°55' W
Cavan (Cabhan, An) . . . . . 54°00' N, 007°22' W
Charleville (Rath Luirc) . . 52°21' N, 008°41' W
Clifden . . . . 53°29' N, 010°01' W
Clonakilty . . . . 51°37' N, 008°53' W
Clonmel (Cluain Meala) . . 52°21' N, 007°42' W
Cobh . . . . 51°51' N, 008°17' W
Cork (Corcaigh) . . . . 51°54' N, 008°28' W
Dingle . . . . 52°08' N, 010°15' W
Donegal . . . . 54°39' N, 008°07' W
Drogheda
   (Droichead Atha) . . . . . . 53°43' N, 006°21' W
Dublin . . . . 53°20' N, 006°15' W
Dundalk (Dun Dealgan) . . 54°00' N, 006°25' W
Dungarvan. . . . . 52°05' N, 007°37' W
Ennis (Inis) . . . . 52°51' N, 008°59' W
Enniscorthy. . . . . 52°30' N, 006°34' W
Ennistimon . . . . 52°56' N, 009°18' W
Galway (Gaillimh). . . . . . . 53°17' N, 009°03' W
Gort . . . . 53°04' N, 008°49' W
Kenmare . . . . 51°53' N, 009°35' W
Kilkee. . . . . 52°41' N, 009°38' W
Kilkenny
   (Cill Chainnigh) . . . . 52°39' N, 007°15' W
Killarney (Cill Airne). . . . . 52°03' N, 009°31' W
Letterkenny. . . . . 54°57' N, 007°44' W
Lifford . . . . 54°50' N, 007°29' W
Limerick (Luimneach) . . . 52°40' N, 008°37' W
Listowel. . . . . 52°27' N, 009°29' W
Longford . . . . 53°44' N, 007°48' W
Loughrea. . . . . 53°12' N, 008°34' W
Mallow. . . . . 52°08' N, 008°38' W
Monaghan . . . . 54°15' N, 006°58' W
Naas (Nas, An) . . . . 53°13' N, 006°40' W
New Ross (Ros Mhic
   Thriuin) . . . . 52°23' N, 006°56' W
Portlaoise (Maryborough,
   Portlaoighise) . . . . 53°02' N, 007°18' W
Portumna . . . . 53°05' N, 008°13' W
Roscommon . . . . 53°38' N, 008°11' W
Rosslare. . . . . 52°17' N, 006°23' W
Shannon . . . . 52°42' N, 008°52' W
Sligo. . . . . 54°16' N, 008°29' W
Swords. . . . . 53°27' N, 006°13' W
Tralee . . . . 52°16' N, 009°43' W

Trim. . . . . 53°33' N, 006°48' W
Tullamore . . . . 53°16' N, 007°29' W
Waterford (Port Lairge) . . . 52°15' N, 007°06' W
Westport . . . . 53°48' N, 009°31' W
Wexford (Loch Garman) . . 52°20' N, 006°28' W
Wicklow (Cill Mhantain). . 52°59' N, 006°03' W
Youghal . . . . 51°57' N, 007°51' W

ISRAEL . . . . .pg. 81

'Arad . . . . 31°15' N, 035°13' E
Ashdod . . . . 31°49' N, 034°39' E
Ashqelon. . . . . 31°40' N, 034°35' E
Bat Yam. . . . . 32°01' N, 034°45' E
Beersheba
   (Be'er Sheva') . . . . 31°14' N, 034°47' E
Bet She'an . . . . 32°30' N, 035°30' E
Bet Shemesh . . . . 31°45' N, 035°00' E
Dimona . . . . 31°04' N, 035°02' E
Elat. . . . . 29°33' N, 034°57' E
'En Yahav . . . . 30°38' N, 035°11' E
Hadera. . . . . 32°26' N, 034°55' E
Haifa (Hefa) . . . . 32°50' N, 035°00' E
Hazeva. . . . . 30°48' N, 035°15' E
Herzliyya . . . . 32°10' N, 034°51' E
Holon. . . . . 32°01' N, 034°46' E
Jerusalem
   (Yerushalayim) . . . . 31°46' N, 035°14' E
Karmi'el. . . . . 32°55' N, 035°18' E
Nazareth (Nazerat). . . . . . . 32°42' N, 035°18' E
Netanya . . . . 32°20' N, 034°51' E
Nir Yizhaq. . . . . 31°14' N, 034°22' E
Petah Tiqwa . . . . 32°05' N, 034°53' E
Qiryat Ata . . . . 32°48' N, 035°06' E
Qiryat Shemona . . . . 33°13' N, 035°34' E
Rama . . . . 32°56' N, 035°22' E
Rehovot. . . . . 31°54' N, 034°49' E
Tel Aviv-Yafo. . . . . 32°04' N, 034°46' E

ITALY . . . . .pg. 82

Agrigento (Girgenti) . . . . . 37°19' N, 013°34' E
Ancona . . . . 43°38' N, 013°30' E
Aosta . . . . 45°44' N, 007°20' E
Arezzo . . . . 43°25' N, 011°53' E
Bari . . . . 41°08' N, 016°51' E
Bologna . . . . 44°29' N, 011°20' E
Bolzano . . . . 46°31' N, 011°22' E
Brescia. . . . . 45°33' N, 010°15' E
Cagliari . . . . 39°13' N, 009°07' E
Catania . . . . 37°30' N, 015°06' E
Catanzaro . . . . 38°54' N, 016°35' E
Crotone . . . . 39°05' N, 017°08' E
Cuneo (Coni). . . . . 44°23' N, 007°32' E
Fermo . . . . 43°09' N, 013°43' E
Florence (Firenze or
   Florentia) . . . . 43°46' N, 011°15' E
Foggia . . . . 41°27' N, 015°34' E
Genoa (Genova) . . . . 44°25' N, 008°57' E
Grosseto . . . . 42°46' N, 011°08' E

Iglesias	39°19' N,	008°32' E
Latina	41°28' N,	012°52' E
Manfredonia	41°38' N,	015°55' E
Marsala	37°48' N,	012°26' E
Milan (Milano)	45°28' N,	009°12' E
Naples (Napoli or Neapolis)	40°50' N,	014°15' E
Oristano	39°54' N,	008°36' E
Padua (Padova)	45°25' N,	011°53' E
Palermo	38°07' N,	013°22' E
Perugia (Perusia)	43°08' N,	012°22' E
Pescara	42°28' N,	014°13' E
Piombino	42°55' N,	010°32' E
Pisa	43°43' N,	010°23' E
Porto Torres	40°50' N,	008°24' E
Potenza	40°38' N,	015°48' E
Ragusa	36°55' N,	014°44' E
Ravenna	44°25' N,	012°12' E
Rome (Roma)	41°54' N,	012°29' E
Salerno	40°41' N,	014°47' E
San Remo	43°49' N,	007°46' E
Sassari	40°43' N,	008°34' E
Siena	43°19' N,	011°21' E
Syracuse (Siracusa)	37°04' N,	015°18' E
Taranto (Taras or Tarentum)	40°28' N,	017°14' E
Trapani	38°01' N,	012°29' E
Trento	46°04' N,	011°08' E
Trieste	45°40' N,	013°46' E
Turin (Torino)	45°03' N,	007°40' E
Udine	46°03' N,	013°14' E
Venice (Venezia)	45°27' N,	012°21' E
Verona	45°27' N,	011°00' E

IVORY COAST . . . . pg. 83

Abengourou	06°44' N,	003°29' W
Abidjan	05°19' N,	004°02' W
Aboisso	05°28' N,	003°12' W
Adzopé	06°06' N,	003°52' W
Agboville	05°56' N,	004°13' W
Anyama	05°30' N,	004°03' W
Arrah	06°40' N,	003°58' W
Biankouma	07°44' N,	007°37' W
Bondoukou	08°02' N,	002°48' W
Bouaflé	06°59' N,	005°45' W
Bouaké	07°41' N,	005°02' W
Bouna	09°16' N,	003°00' W
Boundiali	09°31' N,	006°29' W
Daloa	06°53' N,	006°27' W
Daoukro	07°03' N,	003°58' W
Dimbokro	06°39' N,	004°42' W
Divo	05°50' N,	005°22' W
Duékoué	06°45' N,	007°21' W
Ferkéssédougou	09°36' N,	005°12' W
Gagnoa	06°08' N,	005°56' W
Grand-Bassam	05°12' N,	003°44' W
Guiglo	06°33' N,	007°29' W
Katiola	08°08' N,	005°06' W
Kong	09°09' N,	004°37' W
Korhogo	09°27' N,	005°38' W

Lakota	05°51' N,	005°41' W
Man	07°24' N,	007°33' W
Odienné	09°30' N,	007°34' W
Oumé	06°23' N,	005°25' W
San-Pédro	04°44' N,	006°37' W
Sassandra	04°57' N,	006°05' W
Séguéla	07°57' N,	006°40' W
Sinfra	06°37' N,	005°55' W
Tabou	04°25' N,	007°21' W
Tengréla	10°26' N,	006°20' W
Tortiya	08°46' N,	005°41' W
Yamoussoukro	06°49' N,	005°17' W

JAMAICA . . . . pg. 84

Annotto Bay	18°16' N,	076°46' W
Kingston	17°58' N,	076°48' W
Lucea	18°27' N,	078°10' W
Mandeville	18°02' N,	077°30' W
May Pen	17°58' N,	077°14' W
Montego Bay	18°28' N,	077°55' W
Port Antonio	18°11' N,	076°28' W
St. Ann's Bay	18°26' N,	077°08' W
Savanna-la-Mar	18°13' N,	078°08' W
Spanish Town	17°59' N,	076°57' W

JAPAN . . . . pg. 85

Akita	39°43' N,	140°07' E
Aomori	40°49' N,	140°45' E
Asahikawa	43°46' N,	142°22' E
Chiba	35°36' N,	140°07' E
Fukui	36°04' N,	136°13' E
Fukuoka	33°35' N,	130°24' E
Fukushima	37°45' N,	140°28' E
Funabashi	35°42' N,	139°59' E
Gifu	35°25' N,	136°45' E
Hachinohe	40°30' N,	141°29' E
Hakodate	41°45' N,	140°43' E
Hiroshima	34°24' N,	132°27' E
Hofu	34°03' N,	131°34' E
Iwaki	37°05' N,	140°50' E
Kagoshima	31°36' N,	130°33' E
Kanazawa	36°34' N,	136°39' E
Kawasaki	35°32' N,	139°43' E
Kita-Kyushu	33°50' N,	130°50' E
Kōbe	34°41' N,	135°10' E
Kōchi	33°33' N,	133°33' E
Kumamoto	32°48' N,	130°43' E
Kushiro	42°58' N,	144°23' E
Kutchan	42°54' N,	140°45' E
Kyōto	35°00' N,	135°45' E
Matsue	35°28' N,	133°04' E
Matsuyama	33°50' N,	132°45' E
Mito	36°22' N,	140°28' E
Miyazaki	31°52' N,	131°25' E
Morioka	39°42' N,	141°09' E
Muroran	42°18' N,	140°59' E
Nagano	36°39' N,	138°11' E
Nagasaki	32°48' N,	129°55' E

Nagoya. . . . . 35°10' N, 136°55' E
Naha . . . . 26°13' N, 127°40' E
Niigata. . . . . 37°55' N, 139°03' E
Obihiro . . . . 42°55' N, 143°12' E
Okayama . . . . 34°39' N, 133°55' E
Ōsaka. . . . . 34°40' N, 135°30' E
Otaru . . . . 43°13' N, 141°00' E
Sakai . . . . 34°35' N, 135°28' E
Sapporo. . . . . 43°03' N, 141°21' E
Sendai . . . . 31°49' N, 130°18' E
Shizuoka . . . . 34°58' N, 138°23' E
Tokyo . . . . 35°42' N, 139°46' E
Tomakomai . . . . 42°38' N, 141°36' E
Tottori . . . . 35°30' N, 134°14' E
Toyama . . . . 36°41' N, 137°13' E
Utsunomiya . . . . 36°33' N, 139°52' E
Wakayama. . . . . 34°13' N, 135°11' E
Wakkanai. . . . . 45°25' N, 141°40' E
Yaizu . . . . 34°52' N, 138°20' E
Yamagata. . . . . 38°15' N, 140°20' E
Yokohama . . . . 35°27' N, 139°39' E

JORDAN . . . . pg. 86

Adir . . . . 31°12' N, 035°46' E
Al-'Aqabah . . . . 29°31' N, 035°00' E
Al-Faydah . . . . 32°35' N, 038°13' E
Al-Ḥiṣn . . . . 32°29' N, 035°53' E
Al-Karak . . . . 31°11' N, 035°42' E
Al-Mafraq. . . . . 32°21' N, 036°12' E
Al-Mazra'ah . . . . 31°16' N, 035°31' E
Al-Mudawwarah . . . . 29°19' N, 035°59' E
Al-Qaṭrānah . . . . 31°15' N, 036°03' E
Amman ('Ammān). . . . . . . 31°57' N, 035°56' E
Ar-Ramthā . . . . 32°34' N, 036°00' E
Ash-Shawbak. . . . . 30°32' N, 035°34' E
Aṣ Ṣalt . . . . 32°03' N, 035°44' E
At-Ṭafilah. . . . . 30°50' N, 035°36' E
Az-Zarqā . . . . 32°05' N, 036°06' E
Bā'ir . . . . 30°46' N, 036°41' E
Dhāt Ra's. . . . . 31°00' N, 035°46' E
Irbid. . . . . 32°33' N, 035°51' E
Ma'ān . . . . 30°12' N, 035°44' E
Ma'dabā . . . . 31°43' N, 035°48' E
Maḥaṭṭat al-Ḥafif . . . . 32°12' N, 037°08' E
Maḥaṭṭat al-Jufūr. . . . . 32°30' N, 038°12' E
Ṣuwaylih . . . . 32°02' N, 035°50' E

KAZAKSTAN . . . . . pg. 87

Almaty (Alma-Ata) . . . . . . 43°15' N, 076°57' E
Aqtau (Aktau, or
  Shevchenko) . . . . 43°39' N, 051°12' E
Aqtöbe (Aktyubinsk) . . . . . 50°17' N, 057°10' E
Arqalyq . . . . 50°13' N, 066°50' E
Astana (Akmola,
  Akmolinsk, Aqmola,
  or Tselinograd) . . . . 51°10' N, 071°30' E
Atyraū (Atenau, Gurjev, or
  Guryev) . . . . 47°07' N, 051°53' E

Ayaguz. . . . . 47°56' N, 080°23' E
Balqash (Balkhash or
  Balchas) . . . . 46°49' N, 075°00' E
Dzhezkazgan . . . . 47°47' N, 067°46' E
Kokchetav . . . . 53°17' N, 069°30' E
Leningor (Leninogorsk
  or Ridder) . . . . 50°22' N, 083°32' E
Oral (Uralsk) . . . . 51°14' N, 051°22' E
Öskemen
  (Ust-Kamenogorsk) . . . . 49°58' N, 082°40' E
Panfilov (Zharkent) . . . . . . 44°10' N, 080°01' E
Pavlodar . . . . 52°18' N, 076°57' E
Petropavl
  (Petropavlovsk). . . . . . . 54°52' N, 069°06' E
Qaraghandy
  (Karaganda). . . . . 49°50' N, 073°10' E
Qostanay (Kustanay) . . . . . 53°10' N, 063°35' E
Qyzylorda (Kzyl-Orda) . . . 44°48' N, 065°28' E
Rūdnyy (Rudny) . . . . 52°57' N, 063°07' E
Semey (Semipalatinsk) . . . 50°28' N, 080°13' E
Shchūchinsk . . . . 52°56' N, 070°12' E
Shymkent (Chimkent or
  Cimkent) . . . . 42°18' N, 069°36' E
Taldyqorghan (Taldy
  -Kurgan) . . . . 45°00' N, 078°24' E
Talghar . . . . 43°19' N, 077°15' E
Termirtaū
  (Samarkand) . . . . 50°05' N, 072°56' E
Türkistan . . . . 43°20' N, 068°15' E
Tyuratam (Turaram or
  Leninsk) . . . . 45°40' N, 063°20' E
Zhambyl (Dzhambul) . . . . 42°54' N, 071°22' E
Zhangatas . . . . 43°34' N, 069°45' E
Zhetiqara . . . . 52°11' N, 061°12' E
Zhezqazghan . . . . 47°47' N, 067°46' E
Zyryan . . . . 49°43' N, 084°20' E

KENYA . . . . pg. 88

Bungoma . . . . 00°34' N, 034°34' E
Busia . . . . 00°28' N, 034°06' E
Eldoret . . . . 00°31' N, 035°17' E
Embu . . . . 00°32' S, 037°27' E
Garissa. . . . . 00°28' S, 039°38' E
Isiolo . . . . 00°21' N, 037°35' E
Kisii . . . . 00°41' S, 034°46' E
Kisumu . . . . 00°06' S, 034°45' E
Lamu . . . . 02°16' S, 040°54' E
Lodwar . . . . 03°07' N, 035°36' E
Machakos . . . . 01°31' S, 037°16' E
Malindi . . . . 03°13' S, 040°07' E
Mandera . . . . 03°56' N, 041°52' E
Maralal . . . . 01°06' N, 036°42' E
Marsabit . . . . 02°20' N, 037°59' E
Meru . . . . 00°03' N, 037°39' E
Mombasa. . . . . 04°03' N, 039°40' E
Murang'a . . . . 00°43' N, 037°09' E
Nairobi. . . . . 01°17' S, 036°49' E
Nakuru . . . . 00°17' S, 036°04' E
Nanyuki . . . . 00°01' N, 037°04' E

Wajir . . . . 01°45' N, 040°04' E

KIRIBATI . . . . pg. 89

Bairiki . . . . 01°20' N, 173°01' E

KUWAIT . . . . pg. 90

Al-Aḥmadī . . . . 29°05' N, 048°04' E
Al-Jahrah . . . . 29°20' N, 047°40' E
Ash-Shuʻaybah . . . . 29°03' N, 048°08' E
Ḥawallī . . . . 29°19' N, 048°02' E
Kuwait . . . . 29°20' N, 047°59' E
Umm Qasar . . . . 30°02' N, 047°55' E

KYRGYZSTAN . . . .pg. 91

Bishkek (Frunze) . . . . 42°54' N, 074°36' E
Dzhalal-Abad . . . . 40°56' N, 073°00' E
Irkeshtam . . . . 39°41' N, 073°55' E
Kara-Balta . . . . 42°50' N, 073°52' E
Karakol (Przhevalsk) . . . . 42°33' N, 078°18' E
Kök-Janggak . . . . 41°02' N, 073°12' E
Kyzyl-Kyya . . . . 40°16' N, 072°08' E
Mayly-Say . . . . 41°17' N, 072°24' E
Naryn . . . . 41°26' N, 075°58' E
Osh . . . . 40°32' N, 072°48' E
Sülüktü . . . . 39°56' N, 069°34' E
Talas . . . . 42°32' N, 072°14' E
Tash-Kömür . . . . 41°21' N, 072°14' E
Tokmok . . . . 42°52' N, 075°18' E
Ysyk-Kül (Rybachye) . . . . 42°26' N, 076°12' E

LAOS . . . . pg. 92

Attapu . . . . 14°48' N, 106°50' E
Ban Houayxay . . . . 20°18' N, 100°26' E
Champasak . . . . 14°53' N, 105°52' E
Louang Namtha . . . . 20°57' N, 101°25' E
Louangphrabang . . . . 19°52' N, 102°08' E
Muang Khammouan
 (Muang Thakhek) . . . . . 17°24' N, 104°48' E
Muang Pek . . . . 19°35' N, 103°19' E
Muang Xaignabouri
 (Sayaboury) . . . . 19°15' N, 101°45' E
Muang Xay . . . . 20°42' N, 101°59' E
Pakxé . . . . 15°07' N, 105°47' E
Phôngsali . . . . 21°41' N, 102°06' E
Saravan . . . . 15°43' N, 106°25' E
Savannakhét . . . . 16°33' N, 104°45' E
Vientiane
 (Viangchan) . . . . 17°58' N, 102°36' E
Xam Nua . . . . 20°25' N, 104°02' E

LATVIA . . . . pg. 93

Aizpute . . . . 56°43' N, 021°36' E

Alūksne . . . . 57°25' N, 027°03' E
Auce . . . . 56°28' N, 022°53' E
Balvi . . . . 57°08' N, 027°15' E
Bauska . . . . 56°24' N, 024°11' E
Cēsis . . . . 57°18' N, 025°15' E
Daugavpils . . . . 55°53' N, 026°32' E
Dobele . . . . 56°37' N, 023°16' E
Gulbene . . . . 57°11' N, 026°45' E
Ilūkste . . . . 55°58' N, 026°18' E
Jaunjelgava . . . . 56°37' N, 025°05' E
Jēkabpils . . . . 56°29' N, 025°51' E
Jelgava . . . . 56°39' N, 023°42' E
Jūrmala . . . . 56°58' N, 023°34' E
Kandava . . . . 57°02' N, 022°46' E
Kārsava . . . . 56°47' N, 027°40' E
Ķegums . . . . 56°44' N, 024°43' E
Krāslava . . . . 55°54' N, 027°10' E
Liepāja . . . . 56°31' N, 021°01' E
Limbaži . . . . 57°31' N, 024°42' E
Ludza . . . . 56°33' N, 027°43' E
Malta . . . . 56°23' N, 027°07' E
Mazsalace . . . . 57°52' N, 025°03' E
Ogre . . . . 56°49' N, 024°36' E
Piltene . . . . 57°13' N, 021°40' E
Preili . . . . 56°18' N, 026°43' E
Priekulē . . . . 55°33' N, 021°19' E
Rēzekne . . . . 56°30' N, 027°19' E
Riga (Rīga) . . . . 56°57' N, 024°06' E
Rujiena . . . . 57°54' N, 025°19' E
Sabile . . . . 57°03' N, 022°35' E
Salacgrīva . . . . 57°45' N, 024°21' E
Saldus . . . . 56°40' N, 022°30' E
Sigulda . . . . 57°09' N, 024°51' E
Stučka . . . . 56°35' N, 025°12' E
Talsi . . . . 57°15' N, 022°36' E
Valdemārpils . . . . 57°22' N, 022°35' E
Valmiera . . . . 57°33' N, 025°24' E
Ventspils . . . . 57°24' N, 021°31' E
Viesīte . . . . 56°21' N, 025°33' E
Viļaka . . . . 57°11' N, 027°41' E
Viļāni . . . . 56°33' N, 026°57' E
Zilupe . . . . 56°23' N, 028°07' E

LEBANON . . . . pg. 94

Ad-Dāmūr . . . . 33°44' N, 035°27' E
Al-ʻAbdah . . . . 34°31' N, 035°58' E
Al-Batrūn . . . . 34°15' N, 035°39' E
Al-Hirmīl . . . . 34°23' N, 036°23' E
Al-Labwah . . . . 34°12' N, 036°21' E
Al-Qubayyāt . . . . 34°34' N, 036°17' E
Amyūn . . . . 34°18' N, 035°49' E
An-Nabaṭīyah at-Taḥtā . . 33°23' N, 035°29' E
Aṣ-Ṣarafand . . . . 33°27' N, 035°18' E
Baalbek (Baʻlabakk) . . . . . 34°00' N, 036°12' E
Bʻaqlīn . . . . 33°41' N, 035°33' E
Beirut (Bayrut) . . . . 33°53' N, 035°30' E
Bḥamdūn . . . . 33°48' N, 035°39' E
Bint Jubayl . . . . 33°07' N, 035°26' E
Bsharri . . . . 34°15' N, 036°01' E

En-Nāqūrah . . . . 33°07' N, 035°08' E
Ghazir . . . . 34°01' N, 035°40' E
Ghazzah. . . . . 33°40' N, 035°49' E
Ghūmāh. . . . . 34°13' N, 035°42' E
Halbā . . . . 34°33' N, 036°05' E
Ḥaṣbayya. . . . . 33°24' N, 035°41' E
Ḥimlāyā . . . . 33°56' N, 035°42' E
Ihdin . . . . 34°17' N, 035°58' E
Jubayl (Byblos). . . . . 34°07' N, 035°39' E
Jubb Jannin. . . . . 33°37' N, 035°47' E
Jūniyah . . . . 33°59' N, 035°58' E
Jwayyā. . . . . 33°14' N, 035°19' E
Khaldah. . . . . 33°47' N, 035°29' E
Marj 'Uyūn . . . . 33°22' N, 035°35' E
Shḥim . . . . 33°37' N, 035°29' E
Shikkā . . . . 34°20' N, 035°44' E
Sidon (Sayda) . . . . 33°33' N, 035°22' E
Tripoli (Tarabulus). . . . . . 34°26' N, 035°51' E
Tyre (Ṣūr) . . . . 33°16' N, 035°11' E
Zaḥlah . . . . 33°51' N, 035°53' E
Zghartā . . . . 34°24' N, 035°54' E

LESOTHO . . . . . . .pg. 95

Butha-Butha . . . . 28°45' S, 028°15' E
Libono . . . . 28°38' S, 028°35' E
Mafeteng . . . . 29°49' S, 027°15' E
Maseru. . . . . 29°19' S, 027°29' E
Mohales Hoek . . . . 30°09' S, 027°28' E
Mokhotlong . . . . 29°22' S, 029°02' E
Qacha's Nek . . . . 30°08' S, 028°41' E
Quthing . . . . 30°24' S, 027°43' E
Roma. . . . . 29°27' S, 027°42' E
Teyateyaneng . . . . 29°09' S, 027°44' E

LIBERIA . . . . .pg. 96

Bentol . . . . 06°26' N, 010°36' W
Bopolu. . . . . 06°54' N, 010°46' W
Buchanan
  (Grand Bassa) . . . . 05°53' N, 010°03' W
Careysburg . . . . 06°24' N, 010°33' W
Gbarnga. . . . . 07°00' N, 009°29' W
Grand Cess
  (Grand Sesters) . . . . 04°34' N, 008°13' W
Greenville (Sino). . . . . 05°00' N, 009°02' W
Harbel . . . . 06°16' N, 010°21' W
Harper . . . . 04°22' N, 007°23' W
Kle . . . . 06°42' N, 010°53' W
Monrovia. . . . . 06°19' N, 010°48' W
Robertsport. . . . . 06°45' N, 011°22' W
Saniquellie
  (Sangbui) . . . . 07°22' N, 008°43' W
Tubmanburg
  (Vaitown) . . . . 06°52' N, 010°49' W
Voinjama . . . . 08°25' N, 009°45' W
Yekepa. . . . . 07°35' N, 008°32' W
Zorzor. . . . . 07°47' N, 009°26' W
Zwedru (Tchien). . . . . 06°04' N, 008°08' W

LIBYA . . . . .pg. 97

Al-Baydā (Baida or
  Zāwiyat al-Baydā) . . . . . 32°46' N, 021°43' E
Al-Kufrah . . . . 24°10' N, 023°15' E
Al-Marj (Barce) . . . . 32°30' N, 020°50' E
Al-'Uwaynāt
  (Sardalas). . . . . 25°48' N, 010°33' E
As-Sidrah (Es-Sidre) . . . . . 30°39' N, 018°22' E
Awbāri (Ubari) . . . . 26°35' N, 012°46' E
Az-Zuwaytinah . . . . 30°58' N, 020°07' E
Benghazi (Banghazi or
  Bengasi) . . . . 32°07' N, 020°04' E
Dahra. . . . . 29°30' N, 017°50' E
Darnah (Dērna). . . . . 32°46' N, 022°39' E
Ghadāmis (Ghadāmes) . . . 30°08' N, 009°30' E
Ghaddūwah (Goddua) . . . . 26°26' N, 014°18' E
Gharyān (Garian) . . . . 32°10' N, 013°01' E
Ghāt . . . . 24°58' N, 010°11' E
Marādah . . . . 29°14' N, 019°13' E
Miṣrātah (Misurata) . . . . . 32°23' N, 015°06' E
Murzuq . . . . 25°55' N, 013°55' E
Sabhā (Sebha). . . . . 27°02' N, 014°26' E
Sarīr . . . . 27°30' N, 022°30' E
Surt (Sirte) . . . . 31°13' N, 016°35' E
Tarabulus, see Tripoli
Tāzirbū . . . . 25°45' N, 021°00' E
Tobruk (Ṭubruq) . . . . 32°05' N, 023°59' E
Tripoli (Ṭarābulus). . . . . . . 32°54' N, 013°11' E
Waddān . . . . 29°10' N, 016°08' E
Wāw al-Kabīr . . . . 25°20' N, 016°43' E
Zalṭan (Zelten) . . . . 32°57' N, 011°52' E
Zlīṭan (Zliten) . . . . 32°28' N, 014°34' E
Zuwārah (Zuāra). . . . . 32°56' N, 012°06' E

LIECHTENSTEIN . pg. 98

Balzers. . . . . 47°04' N, 009°32' E
Eschen. . . . . 47°13' N, 009°32' E
Mauren . . . . 47°13' N, 009°33' E
Schaan . . . . 47°10' N, 009°31' E
Triesen . . . . 47°07' N, 009°32' E
Vaduz. . . . . 47°09' N, 009°31' E

LITHUANIA . . . . . .pg. 99

Alytus . . . . 54°24' N, 024°03' E
Anykščiai. . . . . 55°32' N, 025°06' E
Birštonas. . . . . 54°37' N, 024°02' E
Biržai . . . . 56°12' N, 024°45' E
Druskininkai . . . . 54°01' N, 023°58' E
Gargždai . . . . 55°43' N, 021°24' E
Ignalina . . . . 55°21' N, 026°10' E
Jonava . . . . 55°05' N, 024°17' E
Joniškis . . . . 56°14' N, 023°37' E
Jurbarkas. . . . . 55°04' N, 022°46' E
Kaunas. . . . . 54°54' N, 023°54' E
Kazly Rūda . . . . 54°46' N, 023°30' E
Kėdainiai . . . . 55°17' N, 023°58' E

Kelmé	55°38' N,	022°56' E
Klaipéda	55°43' N,	021°07' E
Kuršénai	56°00' N,	022°56' E
Lazdijai	54°14' N,	023°31' E
Marijampolé (Kapsukas)	54°34' N,	023°21' E
Mažeikiai	56°19' N,	022°20' E
Naujoji Akmené	56°19' N,	022°54' E
Neringa	55°22' N,	021°04' E
Pagégiai	55°09' N,	021°54' E
Pakruojis	58°58' N,	023°52' E
Palanga	55°55' N,	021°03' E
Pandélys	56°01' N,	025°13' E
Panevéžys	55°44' N,	024°21' E
Pasvalys	56°04' N,	024°24' E
Plungé	55°55' N,	021°51' E
Priekulé	55°33' N,	021°19' E
Radviliškis	55°49' N,	023°32' E
Ramygala	55°31' N,	024°18' E
Raseiniai	55°22' N,	023°07' E
Rokiškis	55°58' N,	025°35' E
Šalčininkai	54°18' N,	025°23' E
Šiauliai	55°56' N,	023°19' E
Šilalé	55°28' N,	022°12' E
Šiluté	55°21' N,	021°29' E
Širvintos	55°03' N,	024°57' E
Skuodas	56°16' N,	021°32' E
Tauragé	55°15' N,	022°17' E
Telšiai	55°59' N,	022°15' E
Trakai	54°38' N,	024°56' E
Utena	55°30' N,	025°36' E
Varéna	54°13' N,	024°34' E
Vilkaviškis	54°39' N,	023°02' E
Vilkija	55°03' N,	023°35' E
Vilnius	54°41' N,	025°19' E
Zarasai	55°44' N,	026°15' E

LUXEMBOURG . .pg. 100

Bains (Modorf-les-Bains)	49°30' N,	006°17' E
Bettembourg	49°31' N,	006°06' E
Capellen	49°39' N,	005°59' E
Clervaux	50°03' N,	006°02' E
Diekirch	49°52' N,	006°10' E
Differdange	49°31' N,	005°53' E
Dudelange	49°28' N,	006°06' E
Echternach	49°49' N,	006°25' E
Esch-sur-Alzette	49°30' N,	005°59' E
Ettlebruck	49°51' N,	006°07' E
Grevenmacher	49°41' N,	006°27' E
Hesperange	49°34' N,	006°09' E
Junglinster	49°43' N,	006°15' E
Lorentzweiler	49°42' N,	006°08' E
Luxembourg	49°36' N,	006°08' E
Mamer	49°38' N,	006°02' E
Mersch	49°45' N,	006°06' E
Niederanven	49°39' N,	006°16' E
Pétange	49°33' N,	005°53' E
Rambrouch	49°50' N,	005°51' E
Redange	49°46' N,	005°53' E

Remich	49°32' N,	006°22' E
Sanem	49°33' N,	005°56' E
Schifflange	49°30' N,	006°01' E
Vianden	49°56' N,	006°13' E
Walfedange	49°39' N,	006°08' E
Wiltz	49°58' N,	005°56' E
Wincrange	50°03' N,	005°55' E
Wormeldange	49°37' N,	006°25' E

MACEDONIA . . . .pg. 101

Bitola	41°02' N,	021°20' E
Gostivar	41°48' N,	020°54' E
Kavadarci	41°26' N,	022°00' E
Kičevo	41°31' N,	020°57' E
Kočani	41°55' N,	022°25' E
Kruševo	41°22' N,	021°15' E
Kumanovo	42°08' N,	021°43' E
Ohrid	41°07' N,	020°48' E
Prilep	41°21' N,	021°34' E
Skopje (Skoplje)	42°00' N,	021°29' E
Štip	41°44' N,	022°12' E
Strumica	41°26' N,	022°39' E
Tetovo	42°01' N,	020°59' E
Tito Veles	41°42' N,	021°48' E

MADAGASCAR . .pg. 102

Ambanja	13°41' S,	048°27' E
Ambatondrazaka	17°50' S,	048°25' E
Andapa	14°39' S,	049°39' E
Ankarana (Sosumav)	13°05' S,	048°55' E
Antalaha	14°53' S,	050°17' E
Antananarivo (Tananarive)	18°55' S,	047°31' E
Antsirabe	19°51' S,	047°02' E
Antsirañana (Diégo-Suarez)	12°16' S,	049°17' E
Antsohihy	14°52' S,	047°59' E
Fianarantsoa	21°26' S,	047°05' E
Ihosy	22°24' S,	046°07' E
Maevatanana	16°57' S,	046°50' E
Mahabo	20°23' S,	044°40' E
Mahajanga (Majunga)	15°43' S,	046°19' E
Mahanoro	19°54' S,	048°48' E
Mananjary	21°13' S,	048°20' E
Maroantsetra	15°26' S,	049°44' E
Marovoay	16°06' S,	046°38' E
Morombe	21°44' S,	043°21' E
Morondava	20°17' S,	044°17' E
Port-Bergé (Boriziny)	15°33' S,	047°40' E
Toamasina (Tamatave)	18°10' S,	049°23' E
Tôlañaro (Faradofay, Fort-Dauphin or Taolanaro)	25°02' S,	047°00' E
Toliara (Toliary or Tulear)	23°21' S,	043°40' E
Vangaindrano	23°21' S,	047°36' E
Vatomandry	19°20' S,	048°59' E

MALAWI . . . . pg. 103

Balaka . . . . 14°59' S, 034°57' E
Blantyre. . . . . 15°47' S, 035°00' E
Chikwawa . . . . 16°03' S, 034°48' E
Cholo (Thyolo) . . . . 16°04' S, 035°08' E
Dedza. . . . . 14°22' S, 034°20' E
Dowa . . . . 13°39' S, 033°56' E
Karonga. . . . . 09°56' S, 033°56' E
Kasungu. . . . . 13°02' S, 033°29' E
Lilongwe . . . . 13°59' S, 033°47' E
Mangoche
 (Fort Johnson). . . . . 14°28' S, 035°16' E
Mchinji (Fort Manning) . . . 13°48' S, 032°54' E
Monkey Bay . . . . 14°05' S, 034°55' E
Mzimba . . . . 11°54' S, 033°36' E
Mzuzu . . . . 11°27' S, 033°55' E
Nkhata Bay . . . . 11°36' S, 034°18' E
Nkhota Kota
 (Kota Kota) . . . . 12°55' S, 034°18' E
Nsanje (Port Herald) . . . . . 16°55' S, 035°16' E
Salima . . . . 13°47' S, 034°26' E
Zomba . . . . 15°23' S, 035°20' E

MALAYSIA . . . . . . pg. 104

Alor Setar . . . . 06°07' N, 100°22' E
Batu Pahat. . . . . 01°51' N, 102°56' E
Bau. . . . . 01°25' N, 110°09' E
Bentong. . . . . 03°32' N, 101°55' E
Bintulu. . . . . 03°10' N, 113°02' E
Butterworth . . . . 05°25' N, 100°24' E
George Town (Pinang) . . . . 05°25' N, 100°20' E
Ipoh . . . . 04°35' N, 101°05' E
Johor Baharu . . . . 01°28' N, 103°45' E
Kangar. . . . . 06°26' N, 100°12' E
Kelang (Klang) . . . . 03°02' N, 101°27' E
Keluang . . . . 02°02' N, 103°19' E
Kota Baharu . . . . 06°08' N, 102°15' E
Kota Kinabalu
 (Jesselton) . . . . 05°59' N, 116°04' E
Kota Tinggi . . . . 01°44' N, 103°54' E
Kuala Dungun (Dungun). . . 04°47' N, 103°26' E
Kuala Lumpur. . . . . 03°10' N, 101°42' E
Kuala Terengganu. . . . . 05°20' N, 103°08' E
Kuantan. . . . . 03°48' N, 103°20' E
Kuching . . . . 01°33' N, 110°20' E
Lundu . . . . 01°40' N, 109°51' E
Melaka (Malacca) . . . . 02°12' N, 102°15' E
Miri . . . . 04°23' N, 113°59' E
Muar
 (Bandar Maharani) . . . . . 02°02' N, 102°34' E
Petaling Jaya. . . . . 03°05' N, 101°39' E
Sandakan. . . . . 05°50' N, 118°07' E
Sarikei . . . . 02°07' N, 111°31' E
Seremban . . . . 02°43' N, 101°56' E
Sibu . . . . 02°18' N, 111°49' E
Song. . . . . 02°01' N, 112°33' E
Sri Aman (Simanggang) . . . 01°15' N, 111°26' E

Taiping . . . . 04°51' N, 100°44' E
Tawau . . . . 04°15' N, 117°54' E
Teluk Intan
 (Telok Anson) . . . . 04°02' N, 101°01' E
Victoria (Labuan) . . . . 05°17' N, 115°15' E

MALDIVES . . . . . . pg. 105

Male. . . . . 04°10' N, 073°30' E

MALI . . . . pg. 106

Ansongo . . . . 15°40' N, 000°30' E
Bafoulabé . . . . 13°48' N, 010°50' W
Bamako . . . . 12°39' N, 008°00' W
Diamou . . . . 14°05' N, 011°16' W
Diré . . . . 16°16' N, 003°24' W
Gao . . . . 16°16' N, 000°03' W
Goundam. . . . . 16°25' N, 003°40' W
Kalana . . . . 10°47' N, 008°12' W
Kangaba. . . . . 11°56' N, 008°25' W
Kayes . . . . 14°27' N, 011°26' W
Kolokani . . . . 13°35' N, 008°02' W
Koro. . . . . 14°04' N, 003°05' W
Labbezanga . . . . 14°57' N, 000°42' E
Ménaka . . . . 15°55' N, 002°24' E
Mopti . . . . 14°30' N, 004°12' W
Nara . . . . 15°10' N, 007°17' W
Niafounké . . . . 15°56' N, 004°00' W
Nioro Du Sahel . . . . 15°14' N, 009°35' W
San. . . . . 13°18' N, 004°54' W
Ségou . . . . 13°27' N, 006°16' W
Sikasso. . . . . 11°19' N, 005°40' W
Taoudenni. . . . . 22°40' N, 003°59' W
Timbuktu. . . . . 16°46' N, 003°01' W

MALTA . . . . pg. 107

Birkirkara . . . . 35°54' N, 014°28' E
Hamrun . . . . 35°53' N, 014°29' E
Mosta. . . . . 35°55' N, 014°26' E
Rabat . . . . 35°53' N, 014°24' E
Valletta (Valetta) . . . . 35°54' N, 014°31' E
Żabbar . . . . 35°52' N, 014°32' E
Żebbug . . . . 35°52' N, 014°26' E
Żejtun . . . . 35°51' N, 014°32' E

MARSHALL ISLANDS . . . . pg. 108

Majuro. . . . . 07°09' N, 171°12' E

MAURITANIA pg.109

Akjoujt . . . . 19°45' N, 014°23' W
Aleg . . . . 17°03' N, 013°55' W
Atar . . . . 20°31' N, 013°03' W

Ayoûn el 'Atroûs. . . . . 16°40' N, 009°37' W
Bir Mogrein. . . . . 25°14' N, 011°35' W
Bogué (Boghé) . . . . 16°35' N, 014°16' W
Boutilimit . . . . 17°33' N, 014°42' W
Chinguetti . . . . 20°27' N, 012°22' W
Fdérik . . . . 22°41' N, 012°43' W
Guérou. . . . . 16°48' N, 011°50' W
Kaédi. . . . . 16°09' N, 013°30' W
Kiffa. . . . . 16°37' N, 011°24' W
Maghama. . . . . 15°31' N, 012°51' W
M'Bout. . . . . 16°02' N, 012°35' W
Mederdra. . . . . 16°55' N, 015°39' W
Néma . . . . 16°37' N, 007°15' W
Nouadhibou . . . . 20°54' N, 017°04' W
Nouakchott . . . . 18°06' N, 015°57' W
Rosso. . . . . 16°30' N, 015°49' W
Sélibaby. . . . . 15°10' N, 012°11' W
Tichit . . . . 18°28' N, 009°30' W
Tidjikdja . . . . 18°33' N, 011°25' W
Timbédra. . . . . 16°15' N, 008°10' W
Zouirât. . . . . 22°42' N, 012°30' W

MEXICO . . . . .pg. 110

Acapulco . . . . 16°51' N, 099°55' W
Aguascalientes . . . . 21°53' N, 102°18' W
Caborca. . . . . 30°37' N, 112°06' W
Campeche . . . . 19°51' N, 090°32' W
Cananea. . . . . 30°57' N, 110°18' W
Cancún . . . . 21°05' N, 086°46' W
Carmen . . . . 18°38' N, 091°50' W
Casas Grandes . . . . 30°22' N, 107°57' W
Chetumal. . . . . 18°30' N, 088°18' W
Chihuahua. . . . . 28°38' N, 106°05' W
Ciudad Acuña (Las Vacas). 29°18' N, 100°55' W
Ciudad Juárez . . . . 31°44' N, 106°29' W
Ciudad Obregón . . . . 27°29' N, 109°56' W
Ciudad Victoria. . . . . 23°44' N, 099°08' W
Colima . . . . 19°14' N, 103°43' W
Culiacán. . . . . 24°48' N, 107°24' W
Durango. . . . . 24°02' N, 104°40' W
Guadalajara. . . . . 20°40' N, 103°20' W
Guadalupe. . . . . 25°41' N, 100°15' W
Guaymas . . . . 27°56' N, 110°54' W
Hermosillo. . . . . 29°04' N, 110°58' W
Jiménez . . . . 27°08' N, 104°55' W
Juchitán. . . . . 16°26' N, 095°01' W
La Paz . . . . 24°10' N, 110°18' W
León. . . . . 21°07' N, 101°40' W
Matamoros . . . . 25°53' N, 097°30' W
Matehuala . . . . 23°39' N, 100°39' W
Mazatlán . . . . 23°13' N, 106°25' W
Mérida. . . . . 20°58' N, 089°37' W
Mexicali. . . . . 32°40' N, 115°29' W
Mexico City
  (Ciudad de Mexico) . . . . 19°24' N, 099°09' W
Minatitlán . . . . 17°59' N, 094°31' W
Monterrey . . . . 25°40' N, 100°19' W
Morelia . . . . 19°42' N, 101°07' W
Nuevo Laredo . . . . 27°30' N, 099°31' W

Oaxaca. . . . . 17°03' N, 096°43' W
Poza Rica. . . . . 20°33' N, 097°27' W
Puebla . . . . 19°03' N, 098°12' W
Saltillo . . . . 25°25' N, 101°00' W
San Felipe . . . . 31°00' N, 114°52' W
San Ignacio . . . . 27°27' N, 112°51' W
Tampico . . . . 22°13' N, 097°51' W
Tijuana . . . . 32°32' N, 117°01' W
Torreón. . . . . 25°33' N, 103°26' W
Tuxtla . . . . 16°45' N, 093°07' W
Veracruz . . . . 19°12' N, 096°08' W
Villahermosa. . . . . 17°59' N, 092°55' W
Zapopan . . . . 20°43' N, 103°24' W

MICRONESIA, FEDERATED STATES OF . . . . .pg. 111

Colonia . . . . 09°31' N, 138°08' E
Kosrae . . . . 05°19' N, 162°59' E
Palikir . . . . 06°59' N, 158°08' E
Weno . . . . 07°26' N, 151°52' E

MOLDOVA . . . . . .pg. 112

Bălţi . . . . 47°46' N, 027°56' E
Calaras. . . . . 47°16' N, 028°19' E
Căuşeni . . . . 46°38' N, 029°25' E
Chişinău . . . . 47°00' N, 028°50' E
Ciadâr-Lunga . . . . 46°03' N, 028°50' E
Comrat (Komrat) . . . . 46°18' N, 028°39' E
Drochia . . . . 48°02' N, 027°48' E
Dubăsari . . . . 47°07' N, 029°10' E
Făleşti (Faleshty) . . . . 47°34' N, 027°42' E
Floreşti . . . . 47°53' N, 028°17' E
Hânceşti (Kotovsk). . . . . . 46°50' N, 028°36' E
Kagul . . . . 45°54' N, 028°11' E
Leova (Leovo). . . . . 46°28' N, 028°15' E
Orhei (Orgeyev) . . . . 47°22' N, 028°49' E
Râbnita . . . . 47°45' N, 029°00' E
Rezina . . . . 47°45' N, 028°58' E
Soroca (Soroki). . . . . 48°09' N, 028°18' E
Tighina . . . . 46°49' N, 029°29' E
Tiraspol . . . . 46°50' N, 029°37' E
Ungheni . . . . 47°12' N, 027°48' E

MONGOLIA . . . . . .pg. 113

Altay . . . . 46°20' N, 096°18' E
Arvayheer . . . . 46°15' N, 102°48' E
Baruun-Urt . . . . 46°42' N, 113°15' E
Bulgan . . . . 48°45' N, 103°34' E
Choybalsan (Bayan
  Tumen) . . . . 48°04' N, 114°30' E
Choyr. . . . . 46°20' N, 108°20' E
Dalandzadgad . . . . 43°34' N, 104°25' E
Darhan. . . . . 49°29' N, 105°55' E

Dariganga	45°18′ N,	113°52′ E
Dzüünharaa	48°52′ N,	106°28′ E
Erdenet	49°02′ N,	104°05′ E
Ereen	49°15′ N,	112°29′ E
Hanh	51°30′ N,	100°40′ E
Hatgal	50°26′ N,	100°09′ E
Hovd (Jirgalanta)	48°01′ N,	091°38′ E
Mörön	49°38′ N,	100°10′ E
Öndörhaan (Tsetsen Khan)	47°19′ N,	110°39′ E
Saynshand	44°52′ N,	110°09′ E
Sühbaatar	50°15′ N,	106°12′ E
Tes	49°41′ N,	095°48′ E
Tosontsengel	48°47′ N,	098°15′ E
Tsetserleg	47°30′ N,	101°27′ E
Tümentsogt	47°27′ N,	112°15′ E
Ulaanbaatar	47°55′ N,	106°53′ E
Uliastay	47°45′ N,	096°49′ E

MOROCCO ......pg. 114

Agadir	30°24′ N,	009°36′ W
Asilah (Arzila or Arcila)	35°28′ N,	006°02′ W
Beni Mellal	32°20′ N,	006°21′ W
Berkane	34°56′ N,	002°20′ W
Boudenib	31°57′ N,	003°36′ W
Boulemane	33°22′ N,	004°45′ W
Casablanca (Ad-Dār al-Bayḍā′ or Dar el-Beida)	33°37′ N,	007°35′ W
El Jadida (Mazagan)	33°15′ N,	008°30′ W
El-Kelaa des Srarhna	32°03′ N,	007°24′ W
Er-Rachidia (Ksar es-Souk)	31°56′ N,	004°26′ W
Fès (Fez)	34°02′ N,	004°59′ W
Figuig	32°06′ N,	001°14′ W
Guelmim (Goulimine)	28°56′ N,	010°04′ W
Kenitra (Mina Hassan Tani or Port-Lyautey)	34°16′ N,	006°36′ W
Khouribga	32°53′ N,	006°54′ W
Larache (El-Araish)	35°12′ N,	006°09′ W
Marrakech	31°38′ N,	008°00′ W
Meknès	33°54′ N,	005°33′ W
Mohammedia (Fedala)	33°42′ N,	007°24′ W
Nador	35°11′ N,	002°56′ W
Ouarzazate	30°55′ N,	006°55′ W
Oued Zem	32°52′ N,	006°34′ W
Oujda	34°40′ N,	001°54′ W
Rabat (Ribat)	34°02′ N,	006°50′ W
Safi (Asfi)	32°18′ N,	009°14′ W
Salé (Sla)	34°04′ N,	006°48′ W
Settat	33°00′ N,	007°37′ W
Tangier (Tanger)	35°48′ N,	005°48′ W
Tan-Tan	28°26′ N,	011°06′ W
Taounate	34°33′ N,	004°39′ W
Tarfaya	27°57′ N,	012°55′ W
Tata	29°45′ N,	007°59′ W
Taza	34°13′ N,	004°01′ W
Tétouan (Tetuan)	35°34′ N,	005°22′ W
Zagora	30°19′ N,	005°50′ W

MOZAMBIQUE ..pg. 115

Angoche	16°15′ S,	039°54′ E
Beira	19°50′ S,	034°52′ E
Chimoio (Vila Pery)	19°08′ S,	033°29′ E
Chokwe	24°32′ S,	032°59′ E
Inhambane	23°52′ S,	035°23′ E
Lichinga	13°18′ S,	035°14′ E
Maputo (Lourenço Marques)	25°58′ S,	032°34′ E
Massinga	23°20′ S,	035°22′ E
Memba	14°12′ S,	040°32′ E
Moçambique (Mozambique)	15°03′ S,	040°45′ E
Mocubúri	14°39′ S,	038°54′ E
Mopeia Velha	17°59′ S,	035°43′ E
Morrumbene	23°39′ S,	035°20′ E
Nacala	14°33′ S,	040°40′ E
Namapa	13°43′ S,	039°50′ E
Nampula	15°09′ S,	039°18′ E
Panda	24°03′ S,	034°43′ E
Pemba	12°57′ S,	040°30′ E
Quelimane	17°51′ S,	036°52′ E
Quissico	24°43′ S,	034°45′ E
Tete	16°10′ S,	033°36′ E
Vila da Manhiça	25°24′ S,	032°48′ E
Vila da Mocimboa da Praia	11°20′ S,	040°21′ E
Vila do Chinde (Chinde)	18°34′ S,	036°27′ E
Xai Xai (Joaõ Belo)	25°04′ S,	033°39′ E

MYANMAR ......pg. 116

Allanmyo	19°22′ N,	095°13′ E
Bassein (Pathein)	16°47′ N,	094°44′ E
Bhamo	24°16′ N,	097°14′ E
Chauk	20°53′ N,	094°49′ E
Henzada	17°38′ N,	095°28′ E
Homalin	24°52′ N,	094°55′ E
Kale	16°05′ N,	097°54′ E
Katha	24°11′ N,	096°21′ E
Kawthaung	09°59′ N,	098°33′ E
Kěng Tung	21°17′ N,	099°36′ E
Kyaikkami	16°04′ N,	097°34′ E
Kyaukpyu (Ramree)	19°05′ N,	093°52′ E
Labutta	16°09′ N,	094°46′ E
Loi-kaw	19°41′ N,	097°13′ E
Magwe (Magwa)	20°09′ N,	094°55′ E
Mandalay	22°00′ N,	096°05′ E
Mergui	12°26′ N,	098°36′ E
Minbu	20°11′ N,	094°53′ E
Monywa	22°07′ N,	095°08′ E
Moulmein (Mawlamyine)	16°30′ N,	097°38′ E
Myitkyina	25°23′ N,	097°24′ E
Palaw	12°58′ N,	098°39′ E
Pegu (Bago)	17°20′ N,	096°29′ E
Prome (Pye)	18°49′ N,	095°13′ E
Putao	27°21′ N,	097°24′ E

Sagaing	21°52' N,	095°59' E
Shwebo	22°34' N,	095°42' E
Sittwe (Akyab)	20°09' N,	092°54' E
Syriam	16°46' N,	096°15' E
Taunggyi	20°47' N,	097°02' E
Tavoy (Dawei)	14°05' N,	098°12' E
Tenasserim	12°05' N,	099°01' E
Thaton	16°55' N,	097°22' E
Tonzang	23°36' N,	093°42' E
Toungoo	18°56' N,	096°26' E
Yangon (Rangoon)	16°47' N,	096°10' E

NAMIBIA .... pg. 117

Aranos	24°08' S,	019°07' E
Bagani	18°07' S,	021°38' E
Gobabis	22°27' S,	018°58' E
Grootfontein	19°34' S,	018°07' E
Karasburg	28°01' S,	018°45' E
Karibib	21°56' S,	015°50' E
Keetmanshoop	26°35' S,	018°08' E
Khorixas	20°22' S,	014°58' E
Lüderitz	26°38' S,	015°09' E
Maltahöhe	24°50' S,	016°59' E
Mariental	24°38' S,	017°58' E
Okahandja	21°59' S,	016°55' E
Omaruru	21°26' S,	015°56' E
Ondangwa (Ondanga)	17°55' S,	015°57' E
Opuwo	18°04' S,	013°51' E
Oranjemund	28°33' S,	016°26' E
Oshakati	17°47' S,	015°41' E
Otjimbingwe	22°21' S,	016°08' E
Otjiwarongo	20°27' S,	016°39' E
Outjo	20°07' S,	016°09' E
Rehoboth	23°19' S,	017°05' E
Rundu	17°56' S,	019°46' E
Swakopmund	22°41' S,	014°32' E
Tsumeb	19°14' S,	017°43' E
Usakos	22°00' S,	015°36' E
Walvis Bay	22°57' S,	014°30' E
Warmbad	28°27' S,	018°44' E
Windhoek	22°35' S,	017°05' E

NEPAL .... pg. 118

Bāglūṅg	28°16' N,	083°36' E
Banepa	27°38' N,	085°31' E
Bhairahawā	27°30' N,	083°27' E
Bhaktapur (Bhadgaon)	27°41' N,	085°25' E
Bhojpūr	27°10' N,	087°03' E
Biratnagar	26°29' N,	087°17' E
Birendranagar	28°46' N,	081°38' E
Birganj	27°00' N,	084°52' E
Dailekh	28°50' N,	081°44' E
Dandeldhūrā	29°18' N,	080°35' E
Ilām	26°54' N,	087°56' E
Jājarkot	28°42' N,	082°12' E
Jalésvar	26°38' N,	085°48' E
Jomosom	28°47' N,	083°44' E
Jumlā	29°17' N,	082°10' E

Kathmandu	27°43' N,	085°19' E
Lahān	26°43' N,	086°29' E
Lalitpur (Patan)	27°40' N,	085°20' E
Lumbini (Rummin-dei)	27°29' N,	083°17' E
Mahendranagar	28°55' N,	080°20' E
Mustāng	29°11' N,	083°58' E
Nepālganj	28°03' N,	081°37' E
Pokharā	28°14' N,	083°59' E
Sallyān	28°22' N,	082°10' E
Simikot	29°58' N,	081°50' E
Taplejūṅg	27°21' N,	087°40' E

NETHERLANDS, THE .... pg. 119

Alkmaar	52°38' N,	004°45' E
Almelo	52°21' N,	006°40' E
Amersfoort	52°09' N,	005°23' E
Amstelveen	52°18' N,	004°52' E
Amsterdam	52°21' N,	004°55' E
Apeldoorn	52°13' N,	005°58' E
Arnhem	51°59' N,	005°55' E
Assen	53°00' N,	006°33' E
Bergen op Zoom	51°30' N,	004°18' E
Breda	51°34' N,	004°48' E
Delft	52°00' N,	004°22' E
Den Helder	52°58' N,	004°46' E
Deventer	52°15' N,	006°12' E
Dordrecht (Dort or Dordt)	51°48' N,	004°40' E
Drachten	53°06' N,	006°06' E
Ede	52°02' N,	005°40' E
Eindhoven	51°27' N,	005°28' E
Emmen	52°47' N,	006°54' E
Enschede	52°13' N,	006°54' E
Geleen	50°58' N,	005°50' E
Gendringen	51°52' N,	006°23' E
Groningen	53°13' N,	006°33' E
Haarlem	52°22' N,	004°39' E
Heerenveen	52°57' N,	005°56' E
Heerlen	50°54' N,	005°59' E
Helmond	51°29' N,	005°40' E
Hengelo	52°16' N,	006°48' E
Hilversum	52°14' N,	005°11' E
Hoofddorp (Haarlemmermeer)	52°18' N,	004°42' E
Hoorn	52°39' N,	005°04' E
IJmuiden	52°28' N,	004°36' E
Langedijk	52°42' N,	004°49' E
Leeuwarden (Ljouwert)	53°12' N,	005°47' E
Leiden (Leyden)	52°09' N,	004°30' E
Lelystad	52°31' N,	005°29' E
Maastricht	50°51' N,	005°41' E
Meppel	52°42' N,	006°12' E
Middelburg	51°30' N,	003°37' E
Nieuwegein	52°02' N,	005°06' E
Nijmegen (Nimwegen)	51°50' N,	005°52' E
Ommen	52°31' N,	006°26' E
Oostburg	51°20' N,	003°30' E
Oss	51°46' N,	005°32' E

Purmerend	52°31' N,	004°57' E
Ridderkerk	51°52' N,	004°36' E
Roermond	51°12' N,	006°00' E
Roosendaal	51°32' N,	004°28' E
Rosmalen	51°43' N,	005°22' E
Rotterdam	51°55' N,	004°30' E
Schiedam	51°55' N,	004°24' E
's-Hertogenbosch (Den		
Bosch or Bois-le-Duc)	51°42' N,	005°19' E
Sneek (Snits)	53°02' N,	005°40' E
Soest	52°11' N,	005°18' E
Steenwijk	52°47' N,	006°07' E
Stein	50°58' N,	005°46' E
Terneuzen	51°20' N,	003°50' E
The Hague ('s-Gravenhage,		
Den Haag, or La Haye)	52°05' N,	004°18' E
Tholen	51°32' N,	004°13' E
Tilburg	51°33' N,	005°07' E
Utrecht	52°05' N,	005°08' E
Veenendaal	52°02' N,	005°33' E
Venlo	51°22' N,	006°10' E
Vlaardingen	51°55' N,	004°21' E
Vlissingen (Flushing)	51°27' N,	003°35' E
Zaanstad	52°27' N,	004°50' E
Zoetermeer	52°03' N,	004°30' E
Zwolle	52°30' N,	006°05' E

NEW ZEALAND . .pg. 120

Auckland	36°52' S,	174°46' E
Blenheim	41°31' S,	173°57' E
Cheviot	42°49' S,	173°16' E
Christchurch	43°32' S,	172°39' E
Dunedin	45°53' S,	170°29' E
East Coast Bays	36°45' S,	174°45' E
Gisborne	38°39' S,	178°01' E
Greymouth	42°27' S,	171°12' E
Hamilton	37°47' S,	175°16' E
Hastings	39°39' S,	176°50' E
Invercargill	46°25' S,	168°22' E
Lower Hutt	41°13' S,	174°56' E
Manukau	36°57' S,	174°56' E
Milford Sound	44°41' S,	167°55' E
Napier	39°31' S,	176°54' E
Nelson	41°17' S,	173°17' E
New Plymouth	39°04' S,	174°04' E
Oamaru	45°06' S,	170°58' E
Paeroa	37°23' S,	175°40' E
Palmerston North	40°21' S,	175°37' E
Porirua	41°08' S,	174°51' E
Rotorua	38°10' S,	176°14' E
Takapuna	36°47' S,	174°45' E
Tauranga	37°42' S,	176°08' E
Timaru	44°24' S,	171°14' E
Upper Hutt	41°08' S,	175°03' E
Waihi	37°24' S,	175°56' E
Wanganui	39°56' S,	175°02' E
Wellington	41°18' S,	174°47' E
Westport	41°45' S,	171°36' E
Whangarei	35°43' S,	174°20' E

NICARAGUA . . . . .pg. 121

Bluefields	12°00' N,	083°45' W
Chinandega	12°37' N,	087°09' W
Esquipulas	12°40' N,	085°47' W
Estelí	13°05' N,	086°21' W
Granada	11°56' N,	085°57' W
Juigalpa	12°05' N,	085°24' W
León	12°26' N,	086°53' W
Managua	12°09' N,	086°17' W
Masaya	11°58' N,	086°06' W
Matagalpa	12°55' N,	085°55' W
Nandaime	11°45' N,	086°03' W
Ocotal	13°38' N,	086°29' W
Puerto Cabezas	14°02' N,	083°23' W
San Carlos	11°07' N,	084°47' W
San Juan del Norte		
(Greytown)	10°55' N,	083°42' W
San Juan del Sur	11°15' N,	085°52' W
Somoto	13°29' N,	086°35' W
Waspam	14°44' N,	083°58' W

NIGER . . . . .pg. 122

Agadez	16°58' N,	007°59' E
Ayorou	14°44' N,	000°55' E
Bilma	18°41' N,	012°56' E
Dakoro	14°31' N,	006°46' E
Diffa	13°19' N,	012°37' E
Dogondoutchi	13°38' N,	004°02' E
Dosso	13°03' N,	003°12' E
Filingué	14°21' N,	003°19' E
Gaya	11°53' N,	003°27' E
Gouré	13°58' N,	010°18' E
I-n-Gall	16°47' N,	006°56' E
Keïta	14°46' N,	005°46' E
Kolo	13°19' N,	002°20' E
Madaoua	14°06' N,	006°26' E
Magaria	13°00' N,	008°54' E
Maradi	13°29' N,	007°06' E
Mayahi	13°58' N,	007°40' E
Nguigmi	14°15' N,	013°07' E
Niamey	13°31' N,	002°07' E
Tahoua	14°54' N,	005°16' E
Tânout	14°58' N,	008°53' E
Zinder	13°48' N,	008°59' E

NIGERIA . . . . .pg. 123

Aba	05°07' N,	007°22' E
Abuja	09°15' N,	006°56' E
Ado-Ekiti	07°38' N,	005°13' E
Asari	10°31' N,	012°18' E
Awka	06°13' N,	007°05' E
Azare	11°41' N,	010°12' E
Bauchi	10°19' N,	009°50' E
Benin City	06°20' N,	005°38' E
Bida	09°05' N,	006°01' E
Birnin Kebbi	12°28' N,	004°12' E

Biu . . . . 10°37' N, 012°12' E
Calabar . . . . 04°57' N, 008°19' E
Deba Habe. . . . . 10°13' N, 011°23' E
Dikwa. . . . . 12°02' N, 013°55' E
Dukku . . . . 10°49' N, 010°46' E
Ede. . . . . 07°44' N, 004°26' E
Enugu. . . . . 06°26' N, 007°29' E
Funtua . . . . 11°32' N, 007°19' E
Garko. . . . . 11°39' N, 008°48' E
Gashua. . . . . 12°52' N, 011°03' E
Gboko . . . . 07°19' N, 009°00' E
Gombe. . . . . 10°17' N, 011°10' E
Gumel . . . . 12°38' N, 009°23' E
Gusau. . . . . 12°10' N, 006°40' E
Ibadan . . . . 07°23' N, 003°54' E
Ibi. 08°11' N, 009°45' E
Idah . . . . 07°06' N, 006°44' E
Ife. 07°28' N, 004°34' E
Ifon. . . . . 06°55' N, 005°46' E
Ikerre . . . . 07°30' N, 005°14' E
Ila . . . . 08°01' N, 004°54' E
Ilorin . . . . 08°30' N, 004°33' E
Iwo . . . . 07°38' N, 004°11' E
Jega . . . . 12°13' N, 004°23' E
Jimeta . . . . 09°17' N, 012°28' E
Jos . . . . 09°55' N, 008°54' E
Kaduna . . . . 10°31' N, 007°26' E
Kano . . . . 12°00' N, 008°31' E
Katsina . . . . 13°00' N, 007°36' E
Kaura Namoda . . . . 12°36' N, 006°35' E
Keffi . . . . 08°51' N, 007°52' E
Kishi. . . . . 09°05' N, 003°51' E
Kumo . . . . 10°03' N, 011°13' E
Lafia . . . . 08°29' N, 008°31' E
Lafiagi . . . . 08°52' N, 005°25' E
Lagos . . . . 06°27' N, 003°23' E
Lere . . . . 09°43' N, 009°21' E
Mada . . . . 12°09' N, 006°56' E
Maiduguri . . . . 11°51' N, 013°09' E
Makurdi . . . . 07°44' N, 008°32' E
Minna. . . . . 09°37' N, 006°33' E
Mubi . . . . 10°16' N, 013°16' E
Mushin. . . . . 06°32' N, 003°22' E
Ngurtuwa. . . . . 13°05' N, 013°34' E
Nguru . . . . 12°53' N, 010°28' E
Nsukka. . . . . 06°52' N, 007°23' E
Ogbomosho. . . . . 08°08' N, 004°16' E
Omoko. . . . . 05°21' N, 006°39' E
Onitsha . . . . 06°10' N, 006°47' E
Opobo Town . . . . 04°31' N, 007°32' E
Oron . . . . 04°50' N, 008°14' E
Oshogbo . . . . 07°46' N, 004°34' E
Oyo . . . . 07°51' N, 003°56' E
Pindiga. . . . . 09°59' N, 010°54' E
Port Harcourt . . . . 04°46' N, 007°01' E
Potiskum . . . . 11°43' N, 011°04' E
Sapele . . . . 05°55' N, 005°42' E
Shaki . . . . 08°40' N, 003°23' E
Sokoto . . . . 13°04' N, 005°15' E
Ugep . . . . 05°48' N, 008°05' E
Umuahia . . . . 05°32' N, 007°29' E

Uyo . . . . 05°03' N, 007°56' E
Warri . . . . 05°31' N, 005°45' E
Wukari . . . . 07°51' N, 009°47' E
Zaria . . . . 11°04' N, 007°42' E

NORTH KOREA. .pg. 124

Anju . . . . 39°36' N, 125°40' E
Ch'ŏngjin . . . . 41°46' N, 129°49' E
Cho'san . . . . 40°50' N, 125°48' E
Haeju . . . . 38°02' N, 125°42' E
Hamhŭng . . . . 39°54' N, 127°32' E
Hŭich'ŏn. . . . . 40°10' N, 126°17' E
Hyangsan . . . . 40°03' N, 126°10' E
Hyesan . . . . 41°24' N, 128°10' E
Ich'ŏn . . . . 38°29' N, 126°53' E
Kaesŏng . . . . 37°58' N, 126°33' E
Kanggye. . . . . 40°58' N, 126°36' E
Kimch'aek (Songjin) . . . . . 40°41' N, 129°12' E
Kŭmch'ŏn. . . . . 38°09' N, 126°29' E
Kusŏng. . . . . 39°59' N, 125°15' E
Kyŏngwŏn . . . . 42°49' N, 130°09' E
Manp'o. . . . . 41°09' N, 126°17' E
Myŏngch'ŏn . . . . 41°04' N, 129°26' E
Najin . . . . 42°15' N, 130°18' E
Namp'o . . . . 38°44' N, 125°24' E
P'anmunjŏm . . . . 37°57' N, 126°40' E
Puryŏng . . . . 42°04' N, 129°43' E
P'yŏngsŏng . . . . 39°15' N, 125°52' E
P'yŏngyang . . . . 39°01' N, 125°45' E
Sariwŏn . . . . 38°30' N, 125°45' E
Sinp'o . . . . 40°02' N, 128°12' E
Sinŭiju . . . . 40°06' N, 124°24' E
Songnim. . . . . 38°44' N, 125°38' E
Taegwan . . . . 40°13' N, 125°12' E
Tanch'ŏn . . . . 40°28' N, 128°55' E
Tŏkch'ŏn . . . . 39°45' N, 126°18' E
T'ongch'ŏn. . . . . 38°57' N, 127°52' E
Unggi . . . . 42°20' N, 130°24' E
Wŏnsan . . . . 39°10' N, 127°26' E

NORWAY . . . . .pg. 125

Ålesund . . . . 62°28' N, 006°09' E
Alta . . . . 69°58' N, 023°15' E
Båtsfjord . . . . 70°38' N, 029°44' E
Bergen . . . . 60°23' N, 005°20' E
Bodø . . . . 67°17' N, 014°23' E
Brønnøysund . . . . 65°28' N, 012°13' E
Drammen . . . . 59°44' N, 010°15' E
Elverum . . . . 60°53' N, 011°34' E
Evje . . . . 58°36' N, 007°51' E
Fauske . . . . 67°15' N, 015°24' E
Finnsnes . . . . 69°14' N, 017°59' E
Flekkefjord . . . . 58°17' N, 006°41' E
Hamar . . . . 60°48' N, 011°06' E
Hammerfest. . . . . 70°40' N, 023°42' E
Hareid . . . . 62°22' N, 006°02' E
Harstad . . . . 68°47' N, 016°33' E
Haugesund . . . . 59°25' N, 005°18' E

Hermansverk	61°11' N,	006°51' E
Karasjok	69°27' N,	025°30' E
Kautokeino	68°59' N,	023°08' E
Kolsås	59°55' N,	010°31' E
Kongsvinger	60°12' N,	012°00' E
Kristiansund	63°07' N,	007°45' E
Lillehammer	61°08' N,	010°30' E
Måløy	61°56' N,	005°07' E
Mandal	58°02' N,	007°27' E
Molde	62°44' N,	007°11' E
Mosjøen	65°50' N,	013°12' E
Narvik	68°26' N,	017°25' E
Nordfold	67°46' N,	015°12' E
Oslo (Christiania,		
Kristiania)	59°55' N,	010°45' E
Sandnessjøen	66°01' N,	012°38' E
Sarpsborg	59°17' N,	011°07' E
Skien	59°12' N,	009°36' E
Skjervøy	70°02' N,	020°59' E
Stavanger	58°58' N,	005°45' E
Steinkjer	64°01' N,	011°30' E
Svolvær	68°14' N,	014°34' E
Tønsberg	59°17' N,	010°25' E
Tromsø	69°40' N,	018°58' E
Trondheim	63°25' N,	010°25' E
Vadsø	70°05' N,	029°46' E
Vardø	70°22' N,	031°06' E

OMAN . . . . pg. 126

Al-Maṣna'ah	23°47' N,	057°38' E
Ar-Rustaq	23°24' N,	057°26' E
Bahlā' (Bahlah)	22°58' N,	057°18' E
Barkā'	23°43' N,	057°53' E
Ḍank	23°33' N,	056°16' E
Duqm	19°39' N,	057°42' E
Haymā'	19°56' N,	056°19' E
Ibrā'	22°43' N,	058°32' E
Khabura	23°59' N,	057°08' E
Khaṣab	26°12' N,	056°15' E
Khawr Rawrī (Khor Rori)	17°02' N,	054°27' E
Maṭraḥ	23°37' N,	058°34' E
Mirbāṭ	17°00' N,	054°41' E
Muscat (Masqat)	23°37' N,	058°35' E
Nizvā (Nazwah)	22°56' N,	057°32' E
Qurayyāt	23°15' N,	058°54' E
Rakhyūt	16°44' N,	053°20' E
Ṣalalah	17°00' N,	054°06' E
Shināṣ	24°46' N,	056°28' E
Ṣuḥār	24°22' N,	056°45' E
Ṣūr	22°34' N,	059°32' E
Tāqah	17°02' N,	054°24' E
Thamarīt	17°39' N,	054°02' E

PAKISTAN . . . . . . pg. 127

Badīn	24°39' N,	068°50' E
Bahāwalnagar	29°59' N,	073°16' E
Bannu	32°59' N,	070°36' E
Chitrāl	35°51' N,	071°47' E

Dādu	26°44' N,	067°47' E
Dera Ghazi Khan	30°03' N,	070°38' E
Dera Ismail Khan	31°50' N,	070°54' E
Faisalabad (Lyallpur)	31°25' N,	073°05' E
Gujranwala	32°09' N,	074°11' E
Gwadar	25°07' N,	062°19' E
Hyderabad	25°22' N,	068°22' E
Islamabad	33°42' N,	073°10' E
Karachi	24°52' N,	067°03' E
Khuzdār	27°48' N,	066°37' E
Kotri	25°22' N,	068°18' E
Larkana	27°33' N,	068°13' E
Las Bela	26°14' N,	066°19' E
Loralai	30°22' N,	068°36' E
Mardan	34°12' N,	072°02' E
Mianwali	32°35' N,	071°33' E
Mīrpur Khās	25°32' N,	069°00' E
Multan	30°11' N,	071°29' E
Nawabshah	26°15' N,	068°25' E
Panjgūr	26°58' N,	064°06' E
Peshawar	34°01' N,	071°33' E
Pishīn	30°35' N,	067°00' E
Quetta	30°12' N,	067°00' E
Rahīmyār Khān	28°25' N,	070°18' E
Rawalpindi	33°36' N,	073°04' E
Sahiwal (Montgomery)	30°40' N,	073°06' E
Sargodha	32°05' N,	072°40' E
Sūi	28°37' N,	069°19' E
Sukkur	27°42' N,	068°52' E
Thatta	24°45' N,	067°55' E
Turbat	25°59' N,	063°04' E
Wāh	33°48' N,	072°42' E
Zhob (Fort Sandeman)	31°20' N,	069°27' E

PALAU . . . . pg. 128

Airai	07°22' N,	134°33' E
Klouklubed	07°02' N,	134°15' E
Koror	07°20' N,	134°29' E
Melekeok	07°29' N,	134°38' E
Meyungs	07°20' N,	134°27' E
Ngardmau	07°37' N,	134°36' E

PANAMA . . . . . . pg. 129

Aguadulce	08°15' N,	080°33' W
Almirante	09°18' N,	082°24' W
Antón	08°24' N,	080°16' W
Boquete	08°47' N,	082°26' W
Cañazas	09°06' N,	078°10' W
Capira	08°45' N,	079°53' W
Changuinola	09°26' N,	082°31' W
Chepo	09°10' N,	079°06' W
Chitré	07°58' N,	080°26' W
Colón	09°22' N,	079°54' W
David	08°26' N,	082°26' W
Guararé	07°49' N,	080°17' W
La Chorrera	08°53' N,	079°47' W
La Concepción	08°31' N,	082°37' W
La Palma	08°25' N,	078°09' W

Las Cumbres	09°05' N, 079°32' W
Las Lajas	08°15' N, 081°52' W
Las Tablas	07°46' N, 080°17' W
Ocú	07°57' N, 080°47' W
Panama City (Panama)	08°58' N, 079°32' W
Pedregal	09°04' N, 079°26' W
Penonomé	08°31' N, 080°22' W
Portobelo (Puerto Bello)	09°33' N, 079°39' W
Puerto Armuelles	08°17' N, 082°52' W
San Miguelito	09°02' N, 079°30' W
Santiago	08°06' N, 080°59' W
Soná	08°01' N, 081°19' W
Yaviza (Yavisa)	08°11' N, 077°41' W

PAPUA NEW GUINEA . . . . pg. 130

Aitape	03°08' S, 142°21' E
Alotau	10°20' S, 150°25' E
Ambunti	04°14' S, 142°50' E
Arawa	06°13' S, 155°33' E
Baimuru	07°30' S, 144°49' E
Balimo	08°03' S, 142°57' E
Bogia	04°16' S, 144°54' E
Buin	06°50' S, 155°44' E
Bulolo	07°12' S, 146°39' E
Bwagaoia	10°42' S, 152°50' E
Daru	09°05' S, 143°12' E
Finschhafen	06°36' S, 147°51' E
Goroka	06°05' S, 145°23' E
Kandrian	06°13' S, 149°33' E
Kavieng	02°34' S, 150°48' E
Kerema	07°58' S, 145°46' E
Kikori	07°25' S, 144°15' E
Kimbe	05°33' S, 150°09' E
Kiunga	06°07' S, 141°18' E
Kupiano	10°05' S, 148°11' E
Lae	06°44' S, 147°00' E
Lorengau	02°01' S, 147°16' E
Losuia	08°32' S, 151°04' E
Madang	05°13' S, 145°48' E
Mt. Hagen	05°52' S, 144°13' E
Namatanai	03°40' S, 152°27' E
Popondetta	08°46' S, 148°14' E
Port Moresby	09°29' S, 147°11' E
Rabaul	04°12' S, 152°11' E
Saidor	05°38' S, 146°28' E
Samarai	10°37' S, 150°40' E
Tari	05°42' S, 142°57' E
Vanimo	02°41' S, 141°18' E
Wewak	03°33' S, 143°38' E

PARAGUAY . . . . . . pg. 131

Asunción	25°16' S, 057°40' W
Caacupé	25°23' S, 057°09' W
Caaguazú	25°26' S, 056°02' W
Caazapá	26°09' S, 056°24' W
Capitán Pablo Lagerenza	19°55' S, 060°47' W

Ciudad del Este (Puerto Presidente Stroessner)	25°31' S, 054°37' W
Concepción	23°25' S, 057°17' W
Encarnación	27°20' S, 055°54' W
Filadelfia	22°21' S, 060°02' W
Fuerto Olimpo	21°02' S, 057°54' W
General Eugenio A. Garay	20°31' S, 062°08' W
Luque	25°16' S, 057°34' W
Mariscal Estigarribia	22°02' S, 060°38' W
Paraguari	25°38' S, 057°09' W
Pedro Juan Caballero	22°34' S, 055°37' W
Pilar	26°52' S, 058°23' W
Pozo Colorado	23°26' S, 058°58' W
Salto del Guairá	24°05' S, 054°20' W
San Juan Bautista	26°38' S, 057°10' W
San Lázaro	22°10' S, 057°58' W
Villarica	25°45' S, 056°26' W

PERU . . . . pg. 132

Abancay	13°35' S, 072°55' W
Acomayo	13°55' S, 071°41' W
Arequipa	16°24' S, 071°33' W
Ayabaca	04°38' S, 079°43' W
Ayacucho	13°07' S, 074°13' W
Ayaviri	14°52' S, 070°35' W
Bagua	05°40' S, 078°31' W
Barranca	10°45' S, 077°46' W
Cajamarca	07°10' S, 078°31' W
Callao	12°04' S, 077°09' W
Castilla	05°12' S, 080°38' W
Cerro de Pasco	10°41' S, 076°16' W
Chiclayo	06°46' S, 079°51' W
Chimbote	09°05' S, 078°36' W
Contamana	07°15' S, 074°54' W
Cuzco	13°31' S, 071°59' W
Espinar	14°47' S, 071°29' W
Huacho	11°07' S, 077°37' W
Huancayo	12°04' S, 075°14' W
Huánuco	09°55' S, 076°14' W
Huaraz	09°32' S, 077°32' W
Huarmey	10°04' S, 078°10' W
Ica	14°04' S, 075°42' W
Iñapari	10°57' S, 069°35' W
Iquitos	03°46' S, 073°15' W
Juliaca	15°30' S, 070°08' W
Lagunas	05°14' S, 075°38' W
Lima	12°03' S, 077°03' W
Macusani	14°05' S, 070°26' W
Miraflores	12°07' S, 077°02' W
Moquegua	17°12' S, 070°56' W
Moyobamba	06°03' S, 076°58' W
Nauta	04°32' S, 073°33' W
Pampas	12°24' S, 074°54' W
Pisco	13°42' S, 076°13' W
Piura	05°12' S, 080°38' W
Pucallpa	08°23' S, 074°32' W
Puerto Maldonado	12°36' S, 069°11' W
Puno	15°50' S, 070°02' W
Requena	04°58' S, 073°50' W

San Juan . . . . 15°21′ S, 075°10′ W
Tacna. . . . . 18°01′ S, 070°15′ W
Tarapoto . . . . 06°30′ S, 076°25′ W
Trujillo. . . . . 08°07′ S, 079°02′ W
Tumbes . . . . 03°34′ S, 080°28′ W

PHILIPPINES . . . . .pg. 133

Angeles . . . . 15°09′ N, 120°35′ E
Aparri . . . . 18°22′ N, 121°39′ E
Bacolod . . . . 10°40′ N, 122°56′ E
Balabac . . . . 07°59′ N, 117°04′ E
Batangas . . . . 13°45′ N, 121°03′ E
Bayombong . . . . 16°29′ N, 121°09′ E
Borongan. . . . . 11°37′ N, 125°26′ E
Butuan. . . . . 08°54′ N, 125°35′ E
Cagayan de Oro . . . . 08°29′ N, 124°39′ E
Caloocan . . . . 14°39′ N, 120°58′ E
Cavite . . . . 14°29′ N, 120°55′ E
Cebu . . . . 10°18′ N, 123°54′ E
Daet . . . . 14°05′ N, 122°55′ E
Dagupan . . . . 16°03′ N, 120°20′ E
Dipolog . . . . 08°35′ N, 123°20′ E
Dumaguete . . . . 09°18′ N, 123°18′ E
General Santos . . . . 06°07′ N, 125°10′ E
Iligan . . . . 08°14′ N, 124°14′ E
Iloilo City. . . . . 10°42′ N, 122°33′ E
Isabela . . . . 06°42′ N, 121°58′ E
Jolo . . . . 06°03′ N, 121°00′ E
Laoag. . . . . 12°34′ N, 125°00′ E
Lucena. . . . . 13°56′ N, 121°37′ E
Manila . . . . 14°35′ N, 121°00′ E
Masbate. . . . . 12°22′ N, 123°36′ E
Mati . . . . 06°57′ N, 126°13′ E
Naga (Nueva Caceres) . . . . 13°37′ N, 123°11′ E
Ormoc . . . . 11°00′ N, 124°37′ E
Ozamiz. . . . . 08°08′ N, 123°50′ E
Pandan . . . . 14°03′ N, 124°10′ E
Puerto Princesa . . . . 09°44′ N, 118°44′ E
Quezon City . . . . 14°38′ N, 121°00′ E
Romblon . . . . 12°35′ N, 122°15′ E
Roxas (Capiz) . . . . 11°35′ N, 122°45′ E
Surigao . . . . 09°45′ N, 125°30′ E
Tagbilaran . . . . 09°39′ N, 123°51′ E
Tuguegarao . . . . 17°37′ N, 121°44′ E
Zamboanga . . . . 06°54′ N, 122°04′ E

POLAND . . . . .pg. 134

Biała Podlaska. . . . . 52°02′ N, 023°08′ E
Białystok . . . . 53°08′ N, 023°09′ E
Bielsko-Biała . . . . 49°49′ N, 019°02′ E
Bydgoszcz . . . . 53°09′ N, 018°00′ E
Ciechanów . . . . 52°53′ N, 020°37′ E
Częstochowa. . . . . 50°48′ N, 019°07′ E
Dąbrova Górnicza. . . . . . . 50°20′ N, 019°12′ E
Elbląg. . . . . 54°10′ N, 019°23′ E
Gdańsk (Danzig) . . . . 54°21′ N, 018°40′ E
Gdynia . . . . 54°30′ N, 018°33′ E
Gorzów Wielkopolski . . . . . 52°44′ N, 015°14′ E

Grudziądz . . . . 53°29′ N, 018°46′ E
Iława . . . . 53°36′ N, 019°34′ E
Inowrocław . . . . 52°48′ N, 018°16′ E
Kalisz. . . . . 51°45′ N, 018°05′ E
Katowice . . . . 50°16′ N, 019°01′ E
Kielce. . . . . 50°50′ N, 020°40′ E
Konin . . . . 52°13′ N, 018°16′ E
Koszalin. . . . . 54°12′ N, 016°11′ E
Kraków . . . . 50°05′ N, 019°55′ E
Krosno. . . . . 49°41′ N, 021°47′ E
Legnica . . . . 51°12′ N, 016°12′ E
Leszno . . . . 51°51′ N, 016°35′ E
Łódź. . . . . 51°45′ N, 019°28′ E
Łomża . . . . 53°11′ N, 022°05′ E
Lublin . . . . 51°15′ N, 022°34′ E.
Malbork. . . . . 54°02′ N, 019°03′ E
Mogilno. . . . . 52°40′ N, 017°58′ E
Nidzica. . . . . 53°22′ N, 020°26′ E
Nowy Sącz . . . . 49°38′ N, 020°43′ E
Olsztyn . . . . 53°47′ N, 020°29′ E
Opole. . . . . 50°40′ N, 017°57′ E
Ostrołęka . . . . 53°05′ N, 021°34′ E
Piła. . . . . 53°09′ N, 016°45′ E
Pińczów. . . . . 50°32′ N, 020°32′ E
Piotrków Trybunalski. . . . . 51°24′ N, 019°41′ E
Pisz . . . . 53°38′ N, 021°48′ E
Poznań. . . . . 52°25′ N, 016°58′ E
Radom . . . . 51°25′ N, 021°09′ E
Rybnik . . . . 50°07′ N, 018°32′ E
Rzeszów . . . . 50°03′ N, 022°00′ E
Siedlce . . . . 52°10′ N, 022°18′ E
Słupsk . . . . 54°27′ N, 017°02′ E
Suwałki . . . . 54°06′ N, 022°56′ E
Szczecin (Stettin) . . . . 53°25′ N, 014°35′ E
Tarnobrzeg . . . . 50°35′ N, 021°41′ E
Tarnów . . . . 50°01′ N, 020°59′ E
Tczew . . . . 54°06′ N, 018°48′ E
Tomaszów Mazowiecki . . . 51°32′ N, 020°01′ E
Toruń. . . . . 53°02′ N, 018°36′ E
Tuchola . . . . 53°35′ N, 017°51′ E
Tychy. . . . . 50°08′ N, 018°59′ E
Wałbrzych . . . . 50°46′ N, 016°17′ E
Warsaw (Warszawa). . . . . . 52°15′ N, 021°00′ E
Włocławek. . . . . 52°39′ N, 019°05′ E
Wrocław (Breslau) . . . . 51°06′ N, 017°02′ E
Zabrze . . . . 50°19′ N, 018°47′ E
Zamość . . . . 50°43′ N, 023°15′ E
Zielona Góra . . . . 51°56′ N, 015°30′ E

PORTUGAL . . . . . .pg. 135

Alcobaça . . . . 39°33′ N, 008°59′ W
Almada . . . . 38°41′ N, 009°09′ W
Amadora . . . . 38°45′ N, 009°14′ W
Aveiro . . . . 40°38′ N, 008°39′ W
Barreiro . . . . 38°40′ N, 009°04′ W
Batalha . . . . 39°39′ N, 008°50′ W
Beja . . . . 38°01′ N, 007°52′ W
Braga . . . . 41°33′ N, 008°26′ W
Bragança . . . . 41°49′ N, 006°45′ W
Castelo Branco . . . . 39°49′ N, 007°30′ W

Chaves	41°44' N,	007°28' W
Coimbra	40°12' N,	008°25' W
Elvas	38°53' N,	007°10' W
Évora	38°34' N,	007°54' W
Faro	37°01' N,	007°56' W
Fátima	39°37' N,	008°39' W
Figueira da Foz	40°09' N,	008°52' W
Guarda	40°32' N,	007°16' W
Guimarães	41°27' N,	008°18' W
Leiria	39°45' N,	008°48' W
Lisbon (Lisboa)	38°43' N,	009°08' W
Nazaré	39°36' N,	009°04' W
Odivelas	38°47' N,	009°11' W
Oeiras	38°41' N,	009°19' W
Portalegre	39°17' N,	007°26' W
Portimão (Vila Nova de Portimão)	37°08' N,	008°32' W
Porto (Oporto)	41°09' N,	008°37' W
Póvoa de Varzim	41°23' N,	008°46' W
Queluz	38°45' N,	009°15' W
Santarém	39°14' N,	008°41' W
Setúbal	38°32' N,	008°54' W
Sines	37°57' N,	008°52' W
Tomar	39°36' N,	008°25' W
Torres Vedras	39°06' N,	009°16' W
Urgeiriça	40°30' N,	007°53' W
Viana do Castelo	41°42' N,	008°50' W
Vila do Conde	41°21' N,	008°45' W
Vila Franca de Xira	38°57' N,	008°59' W
Vila Nova de Gaia	41°08' N,	008°37' W
Vila Real	41°18' N,	007°45' W
Viseu	40°39' N,	007°55' W

QATAR . . . . pg. 136

Al-Wakrah	25°10' N,	051°36' E
Ar Rayyān	25°18' N,	051°27' E
Ar-Ruways	26°08' N,	051°13' E
Doha (ad-Dawhah)	25°17' N,	051°32' E
Dukhān	25°25' N,	050°47' E
Musay'id	25°00' N,	051°33' E
Umm Bāb	25°09' N,	050°50' E

ROMANIA . . . . . . pg. 137

Alba Iulia (Gyulafehérvár)	46°04' N,	023°35' E
Alexandria	43°59' N,	025°20' E
Arad	46°11' N,	021°19' E
Bacău	46°34' N,	026°54' E
Baia Mare	47°40' N,	023°35' E
Bârlad	46°14' N,	027°40' E
Bistriţa	47°08' N,	024°29' E
Botoşani	47°45' N,	026°40' E
Brăila	45°16' N,	027°59' E
Braşov (Oraşul Stalin)	45°38' N,	025°35' E
Bucharest	44°26' N,	026°06' E
Buzău	45°09' N,	026°50' E
Calafat	43°59' N,	022°56' E
Călăraşi	44°12' N,	027°20' E

Cluj-Napoca	46°46' N,	023°36' E
Constanţa	44°11' N,	028°39' E
Craiova	44°19' N,	023°48' E
Dej	47°09' N,	023°52' E
Deva	45°53' N,	022°54' E
Drobeta-Turnu Severin	44°38' N,	022°40' E
Focşani	45°42' N,	027°11' E
Galaţi (Galatz)	45°27' N,	028°03' E
Giurgiu	43°53' N,	025°58' E
Hunedoara	45°45' N,	022°54' E
Iaşi (Jassy)	47°10' N,	027°36' E
Lugoj	45°41' N,	021°55' E
Mangalia	43°48' N,	028°35' E
Medgidia	44°15' N,	028°17' E
Mediaş	46°10' N,	024°21' E
Mizil	45°01' N,	026°27' E
Oneşti (Gheorghe Gheorghiu Dej)	46°15' N,	026°45' E
Oradea (Nagyvarad)	47°04' N,	021°56' E
Petroşani	45°25' N,	023°22' E
Piatra-Neamţ	46°55' N,	026°20' E
Piteşti	44°51' N,	024°52' E
Ploieşti (Ploesti)	44°57' N,	026°01' E
Reşiţa	45°18' N,	021°55' E
Roman	46°55' N,	026°55' E
Satu Mare	47°48' N,	022°53' E
Sebeş	45°58' N,	023°34' E
Slatina	44°26' N,	024°22' E
Suceava	47°38' N,	026°15' E
Ţăndărei	44°39' N,	027°40' E
Târgovişte	44°56' N,	025°27' E
Targu Jiu	45°03' N,	023°17' E
Târgu Mureş	46°33' N,	024°34' E
Tecuci	45°52' N,	027°25' E
Timişoara	45°45' N,	021°13' E
Tulcea	45°10' N,	028°48' E
Turda	46°34' N,	023°47' E
Vaslui	46°38' N,	027°44' E
Zalau	47°12' N,	023°03' E

RUSSIA . . . . pg. 138-9

Abakan	53°43' N,	091°26' E
Aginskoye	51°06' N,	114°32' E
Anadyr (Novo-Mariinsk)	64°45' N,	177°29' E
Angarsk	52°34' N,	103°54' E
Birobidzhan	48°48' N,	132°57' E
Biysk (Biisk)	52°34' N,	085°15' E
Cheboksary	56°09' N,	047°15' E
Chelyabinsk	55°10' N,	061°24' E
Cherepovets	59°08' N,	037°54' E
Chita	52°03' N,	113°30' E
Dudinka	69°25' N,	086°15' E
Gorno-Altaysk (Ulala, or Oyrot-Tura)	51°58' N,	085°58' E
Grozny	43°20' N,	045°42' E
Izhevsk (Ustinov)	56°51' N,	053°14' E
Kaluga	54°31' N,	036°16' E
Kazan	55°45' N,	049°08' E

Khanty-Mansiysk
(Ostyako-Vogulsk)...... 61°00' N, 069°06' E
Kirovsk .... 67°37' N, 033°40' E
Komsomol'sk-na-Amure .. 50°35' N, 137°02' E
Krasnoyarsk .... 56°01' N, 092°50' E
Kudymkar .... 59°01' N, 054°39' E
Kurgan.................. 55°26' N, 065°18' E
Kyzyl (Khem-Beldyr) .... 51°42' N, 094°27' E
Magadan .... 59°34' N, 150°48' E
Makhachkala............. 42°58' N, 047°30' E
Maykop (Maikop)........ 44°35' N, 040°10' E
Moscow (Moskva) .... 55°45' N, 037°35' E
Murmansk............... 68°58' N, 033°05' E
Nal'chik .... 43°29' N, 043°37' E
Nar'yan-Mar............. 67°39' N, 053°00' E
Nizhnekamsk............. 55°36' N, 051°47' E
Nizhny Novgorod
(Gorky).............. 56°20' N, 044°00' E
Novgorod .... 58°31' N, 031°17' E
Novokuznetsk
(Kuznetsk,
or Stalinsk) .... 53°45' N, 087°06' E
Novosibirsk.............. 55°02' N, 082°55' E
Omsk................... 55°00' N, 073°24' E
Orenburg (Chkalov) ..... 51°45' N, 055°06' E
Orsk................... 51°12' N, 058°34' E
Palana .... 59°07' N, 159°58' E
Penza.................. 53°13' N, 045°00' E
Perm' (Molotov) .... 58°00' N, 056°15' E
Petropavlovsk-
Kamchatsky.......... 53°01' N, 158°39' E
Petrozavodsk .... 61°49' N, 034°20' E
Rostov-na-Donu
(Rostov-on-Don) ..... 47°14' N, 039°42' E
St. Petersburg
(Leningrad,
or Sankt Peterburg)..... 59°55' N, 030°15' E
Salavat................. 53°21' N, 055°55' E
Salekhard .... 66°33' N, 066°40' E
Samara (Kuybyshev) ..... 53°12' N, 050°09' E
Saransk .... 54°11' N, 045°11' E
Saratov .... 51°34' N, 046°02' E
Smolensk............... 54°47' N, 032°03' E
Syktyvkar............... 61°40' N, 050°48' E
Tomsk .... 56°30' N, 084°58' E
Tver' (Kalinin)........... 56°52' N, 035°55' E
Tyumen'................ 57°09' N, 065°26' E
Ufa.................... 55°45' N, 055°56' E
Ulan-Ude .... 51°50' N, 107°37' E
Ussuriysk............... 43°48' N, 131°59' E
Ust'-Ordinsky .... 52°48' N, 104°45' E
Vladimir................ 56°10' N, 040°25' E
Vladivostok............. 43°08' N, 131°54' E
Volgograd (Stalingrad,
or Tsaritsyn)......... 48°45' N, 044°25' E
Vologda................ 59°13' N, 039°54' E
Voronezh............... 51°38' N, 039°12' E
Yakutsk................ 62°00' N, 129°40' E
Yaroslavl............... 57°37' N, 039°52' E
Yekaterinburg
(Sverdlovsk) .... 56°51' N, 060°36' E

Yuzhno-Sakhalinsk .... 46°57' N, 142°44' E

RWANDA ....pg. 140

Butare .... 02°36' S, 029°44' E
Gisenyi................. 01°42' S, 029°15' E
Kigali .... 01°57' S, 030°04' E
Ruhengeri .... 01°30' S, 029°38' E

SAINT KITTS AND NEVIS .....pg. 141

Basseterre.............. 17°18' N, 062°43' W
Brown Hill............. 17°08' N, 062°33' W
Cayon .... 17°22' N, 062°43' W
Challengers .... 17°18' N, 062°47' W
Charlestown .... 17°08' N, 062°37' W
Cotton Ground .... 17°11' N, 062°36' W
Half Way Tree .... 17°20' N, 062°49' W
Mansion............... 17°22' N, 062°46' W
Monkey Hill Village...... 17°19' N, 062°43' W
Newcastle .... 17°13' N, 062°34' W
New River .... 17°09' N, 062°32' W
Newton Ground .... 17°23' N, 062°51' W
Old Road Town .... 17°19' N, 062°48' W
Sadlers................ 17°24' N, 062°49' W
Saint Paul's .... 17°24' N, 062°49' W
Sandy Point Town....... 17°22' N, 062°50' W
Verchild's .... 17°20' N, 062°48' W
Zetlands............... 17°08' N, 062°34' W

SAINT LUCIA ....pg. 142

Anse La Raye........... 13°57' N, 061°03' W
Canaries .... 13°55' N, 061°04' W
Castries .... 14°01' N, 061°00' W
Dauphin............... 14°03' N, 060°55' W
Dennery .... 13°55' N, 060°54' W
Grande Anse .... 14°01' N, 061°45' W
Gros Islet .... 14°05' N, 060°58' W
Laborie .... 13°45' N, 061°00' W
Micoud .... 13°50' N, 060°54' W
Praslin................ 13°53' N, 060°54' W
Sans Soucis .... 13°59' N, 061°01' W
Soufrière .... 13°52' N, 061°04' W

SAINT VINCENT AND THE GRENADINES ....pg. 143

Ashton .... 12°36' N, 061°27' W
Barrouallie .... 13°14' N, 061°17' W
Calliaqua .... 13°08' N, 061°12' W
Chateaubelair .... 13°17' N, 061°15' W
Georgetown .... 13°16' N, 061°08' W
Kingstown .... 13°09' N, 061°14' W

SAMOA ....pg. 144

Apia	13°50' S,	171°44' W
Fa'aala	13°45' S,	172°16' W
Faleasi'u.	13°48' S,	171°54' W
Le'auva'a	13°48' S,	171°51' W
Lotofaga.	13°59' S,	171°50' W
Matavai (Asau)	13°28' S,	172°35' W
Safotu	13°27' S,	172°24' W
Sagone.	13°39' S,	172°35' W
Samatau	13°54' S,	172°02' W
Sili	13°43' S,	172°21' W
Si'umu	14°01' S,	171°47' W
Solosolo.	13°51' S,	171°36' W

SAN MARINO ....pg. 145

San Marino	43°56' N,	012°25' E

SÃO TOMÉ
AND PRÍNCIPE ..pg. 146

Infante Don Henrique	01°34' N,	007°25' E
Neves.	00°22' N,	006°33' E
Porto Alegre	00°02' N,	006°32' E
Santana	00°16' N,	006°45' E
Santo Amaro	00°22' N,	006°42' E
Santo António	01°39' N,	007°25' E
São Tomé	00°20' N,	006°44' E
Trindade	00°15' N,	006°40' E

SAUDI ARABIA ..pg. 147

Abhā	18°13' N,	042°30' E
Abqaiq (Buqayq)	25°56' N,	049°40' E
Ad-Dammām	26°26' N,	050°07' E
'Afif	23°55' N,	042°56' E
Al-Bāhah	20°01' N,	041°28' E
Al-Badī'	22°02' N,	046°34' E
Al-Bātin Hafar	28°27' N,	045°58' E
Al-Bi'ār	22°39' N,	039°40' E
Al-Hā'ir	24°23' N,	046°50' E
Al-Hufūf	25°22' N,	049°34' E
Al-Ju'aydah	19°40' N,	041°34' E
Al-Jubayl	27°01' N,	049°40' E
Al-Khubar	26°17' N,	050°12' E
Al-Mish'āb	28°12' N,	048°36' E
Al-Mubarraz	25°25' N,	049°35' E
Al-Qatīf	26°33' N,	050°00' E
Al-Qunfudhah	19°08' N,	041°05' E
Al-Ulā	26°38' N,	037°55' E
Ar'ar.	30°59' N,	041°02' E
As-Safrā'.	24°02' N,	038°56' E
As-Sulayyil.	20°27' N,	045°34' E
At-Ta'if.	21°16' N,	040°25' E
Az-Zilfi.	26°18' N,	044°48' E
Badanah	30°59' N,	040°58' E
Birkah	23°48' N,	038°50' E
Buraydah	26°20' N,	043°59' E
Buraykah	22°21' N,	039°20' E
Hā'il	27°33' N,	041°42' E
Halabān	23°29' N,	044°23' E
Harajah	17°56' N,	043°21' E
Jidda (Jiddah).	21°29' N,	039°12' E
Jizān (Qizān)	16°54' N,	042°32' E
Khamīs Mushayt	18°18' N,	042°44' E
Khawsh	18°59' N,	041°53' E
Laylā	22°17' N,	046°45' E
Madā'in Sālih.	26°48' N,	037°57' E
Mecca (Makkah).	21°27' N,	039°49' E
Medina (al-Madinah; Yathrib)	24°28' N,	039°36' E
Miskah	24°49' N,	042°56' E
Musābih.	18°42' N,	042°01' E
Na'jān.	24°05' N,	047°10' E
Najrān	17°26' N,	044°15' E
Qanā	27°47' N,	041°25' E
Rābigh	22°48' N,	039°02' E
Rafhā'.	29°38' N,	043°30' E
Ras Tanura	26°42' N,	050°06' E
Riyadh (ar-Riyad)	24°38' N,	046°43' E
Sahwah	19°19' N,	042°06' E
Sakākah	29°59' N,	040°12' E
Shidād	21°19' N,	040°03' E
Tabūk	28°23' N,	036°35' E
Taymā'.	27°38' N,	038°29' E
Turayf	31°41' N,	038°39' E
'Usfan	21°55' N,	039°22' E
Yanbu'	24°05' N,	038°03' E
Zahrān.	17°40' N,	043°30' E
Zalim	22°43' N,	042°10' E

SENEGAL ....pg. 148

Bakel	14°54' N,	012°27' W
Bignona	12°49' N,	016°14' W
Dagana.	16°31' N,	015°30' W
Dakar	14°40' N,	017°26' W
Diourbel	14°40' N,	016°15' W
Fatick	14°20' N,	016°25' W
Joal	14°10' N,	016°51' W
Kaffrine	14°06' N,	015°33' W
Kaolack	14°09' N,	016°04' W
Kédougou	12°33' N,	012°11' W
Kolda	12°53' N,	014°57' W
Koungheul	13°59' N,	014°48' W
Linguère	15°24' N,	015°07' W
Louga.	15°37' N,	016°13' W
Mbacké	14°48' N,	015°55' W
Mbour	14°24' N,	016°58' W
Mékhé	15°07' N,	016°38' W
Podor.	16°40' N,	014°57' W
Richard-Toll	16°28' N,	015°41' W
Saint Louis.	16°02' N,	016°30' W
Sédhiou	12°44' N,	015°33' W
Tambacounda	13°47' N,	013°40' W
Thiès	14°48' N,	016°56' W
Tivaouane	14°57' N,	016°49' W

Vélingara . . . . 13°09' N, 014°07' W
Ziguinchor . . . . 12°35' N, 016°16' W

SEYCHELLES . . . .pg. 149

Victoria . . . . 04°37' S, 055°27' E

SIERRA LEONE . .pg. 150

Bo . . . . 07°58' N, 011°45' W
Bonthe . . . . 07°32' N, 012°30' W
Freetown . . . . 08°30' N, 013°15' W
Kabala . . . . 09°35' N, 011°33' W
Kailahun . . . . 08°17' N, 010°34' W
Kambia . . . . 09°07' N, 012°55' W
Kenema . . . . 07°52' N, 011°12' W
Koidu-New Sembehun . . . . 08°38' N, 010°59' W
Lunsar . . . . 08°41' N, 012°32' W
Magburaka . . . . 08°43' N, 011°57' W
Makeni . . . . 08°53' N, 012°03' W
Mongeri . . . . 08°19' N, 011°44' W
Moyamba . . . . 08°10' N, 012°26' W
Pepel . . . . 08°35' N, 013°03' W
Port Loko . . . . 08°46' N, 012°47' W
Pujehun . . . . 07°21' N, 011°42' W
Sulima . . . . 06°58' N, 011°35' W

SINGAPORE . . . . .pg. 151

Singapore . . . . 01°16' N, 103°50' E

SLOVAKIA . . . . . .pg. 152

Banská Bystrica . . . . 48°44' N, 019°09' E
Bardejov . . . . 49°17' N, 021°17' E
Bratislava . . . . 48°09' N, 017°07' E
Čadca . . . . 49°26' N, 018°47' E
Fil'akovo . . . . 48°16' N, 019°50' E
Humenné . . . . 48°56' N, 021°55' E
Komárno . . . . 47°46' N, 018°08' E
Košice . . . . 48°42' N, 021°15' E
Levice . . . . 48°13' N, 018°36' E
Liptovský Mikuláš . . . . 49°05' N, 019°37' E
Lučenec . . . . 48°20' N, 019°40' E
Martin . . . . 49°04' N, 018°56' E
Michalovce . . . . 48°45' N, 021°56' E
Nitra . . . . 48°19' N, 018°05' E
Nové Zámky . . . . 47°59' N, 018°10' E
Partizánske . . . . 48°38' N, 018°23' E
Piešt'any . . . . 48°36' N, 017°50' E
Poprad . . . . 49°03' N, 020°18' E
Považská Bystrica . . . . 49°07' N, 018°27' E
Prešov . . . . 49°00' N, 021°15' E
Prievidza . . . . 48°46' N, 018°38' E
Rimavská Sobota . . . . 48°23' N, 020°02' E
Rožňava . . . . 48°40' N, 020°32' E
Skalica . . . . 48°51' N, 017°14' E
Spišská Nová Ves . . . . 48°57' N, 020°34' E

Topol'čany . . . . 48°34' N, 018°11' E
Trebišov . . . . 48°38' N, 021°43' E
Trenčín . . . . 48°54' N, 018°02' E
Trnava . . . . 48°22' N, 017°36' E
Žilina . . . . 49°13' N, 018°44' E
Zvolen . . . . 48°35' N, 019°08' E

SLOVENIA . . . . .pg. 153

Celje . . . . 46°14' N, 015°16' E
Hrastnik . . . . 46°09' N, 015°06' E
Idrija . . . . 46°00' N, 014°02' E
Javornik . . . . 46°14' N, 014°18' E
Jesenice . . . . 46°27' N, 014°04' E
Kočevje . . . . 45°39' N, 014°51' E
Koper . . . . 45°33' N, 013°44' E
Kranj . . . . 46°14' N, 014°22' E
Krško . . . . 45°58' N, 015°29' E
Ljubljana . . . . 46°02' N, 014°30' E
Maribor . . . . 46°33' N, 015°39' E
Murska Sobota . . . . 46°40' N, 016°10' E
Novo Mesto . . . . 45°48' N, 015°10' E
Postojna . . . . 45°47' N, 014°14' E
Ptuj . . . . 46°25' N, 015°52' E
Trbovlje . . . . 46°10' N, 015°03' E
Velenje . . . . 46°22' N, 015°07' E
Zagorje . . . . 46°08' N, 015°00' E

SOLOMON ISLANDS . . . . .pg. 154

Buala . . . . 08°08' S, 159°35' E
Honiara . . . . 09°26' S, 159°57' E
Kirakira . . . . 10°27' S, 161°55' E
Lata . . . . 10°44' S, 165°54' E
Maravovo . . . . 09°17' S, 159°38' E
Munda . . . . 08°19' S, 157°15' E
Sahalu . . . . 09°44' S, 160°31' E
Sasamungga . . . . 07°02' S, 156°47' E
Takwa . . . . 08°22' S, 160°48' E

SOMALIA . . . . . . .pg. 155

Baardheere (Bardera) . . . . 02°20' N, 042°17' E
Baraawe (Brava) . . . . 01°06' N, 044°03' E
Baydhabo (Baidoa) . . . . . . 03°07' N, 043°39' E
Beledweyne (Belet Uen) . . 04°45' N, 045°12' E
Berbera . . . . 10°25' N, 045°02' E
Boosaaso
   (Bender Cassim) . . . . . . 11°17' N, 049°11' E
Burao (Burco) . . . . 09°31' N, 045°32' E
Buulobarde (Bulo Burti) . . 03°51' N, 045°34' E
Eyl . . . . 07°59' N, 049°49' E
Hargeysa . . . . 09°35' N, 044°04' E
Hobyo (Obbia) . . . . 05°21' N, 048°32' E
Jamaame (Giamama or
   Jamame or Margherita) . 00°04' N, 042°45' E

Jawhar (Giohar)	02°46' N, 045°31' E
Kismaayo (Chisimayu)	00°22' S, 042°32' E
Marka (Merca)	01°43' N, 044°53' E
Mogadishu (Mogadiscio or Mogadisho)	02°04' N, 045°22' E
Seylac (Zeila)	11°21' N, 043°29' E
Xaafun	10°25' N, 051°16' E

SOUTH AFRICA . .pg. 156

Bellville	33°54' S, 018°38' E
Bisho	32°53' S, 027°24' E
Bloemfontein.	29°08' S, 026°10' E
Calvinia	31°28' S, 019°47' E
Cape Town (Kaapstad). . . .	33°55' S, 018°25' E
Durban (Port Natal)	29°51' S, 031°01' E
East London	33°02' S, 027°55' E
George.	33°58' S, 022°27' E
Germiston	26°13' S, 028°11' E
Hopefield	33°04' S, 018°21' E
Johannesburg	26°12' S, 028°05' E
Kimberley	28°45' S, 024°46' E
Klerksdorp	26°52' S, 026°40' E
Krugersdorp	26°06' S, 027°46' E
Kuruman	27°28' S, 023°26' E
Ladysmith	28°33' S, 029°47' E
Margate	30°51' S, 030°22' E
Newcastle	27°45' S, 029°56' E
Oudtshoorn.	33°35' S, 022°12' E
Pietermaritzburg.	29°37' S, 030°23' E
Port Elizabeth	33°58' S, 025°35' E
Port Nolloth	29°15' S, 016°52' E
Pretoria	25°45' S, 028°10' E
Queenstown	31°54' S, 026°53' E
Rustenburg	25°40' S, 027°15' E
Seshego	23°51' S, 029°23' E
Soweto	26°16' S, 027°52' E
Stellenbosch	33°56' S, 018°51' E
Uitenhage	33°46' S, 025°24' E
Upington	28°27' S, 021°15' E
Vanderbijlpark	26°42' S, 027°49' E
Welkom	27°59' S, 026°42' E
Worcester	33°39' S, 019°26' E

SOUTH KOREA . .pg. 157

Andong	36°34' N, 128°44' E
Anyang	37°23' N, 126°55' E
Ch'ang won	35°16' N, 128°37' E
Cheju	33°31' N, 126°32' E
Ch'ŏngju.	36°38' N, 127°30' E
Chŏnju	35°49' N, 127°09' E
Ch'unch'ŏn	37°52' N, 127°44' E
Inch'ŏn.	37°28' N, 126°38' E
Iri	35°56' N, 126°57' E
Kumi	36°08' N, 128°20' E
Kunsan	35°59' N, 126°43' E
Kwangju.	35°10' N, 126°55' E
Kyŏngju	35°50' N, 129°13' E
Masan	35°11' N, 128°34' E

Mokp'o.	34°47' N, 126°23' E
P'ohang	36°02' N, 129°22' E
Pusan.	35°06' N, 129°03' E
Samch'ŏnp'o	34°55' N, 128°04' E
Seoul (Soul).	37°34' N, 127°00' E
Sŏsan	36°47' N, 126°27' E
Sunch'ŏn	34°57' N, 127°29' E
Suwŏn	37°16' N, 127°01' E
T'aebaek	37°10' N, 128°59' E
Taech'ŏn	36°21' N, 126°36' E
Taegu (Daegu or Taiku)	35°52' N, 128°36' E
Taejon	36°20' N, 127°26' E
Uijŏngbu	37°44' N, 127°02' E
Ulsan	35°33' N, 129°19' E
Wŏnju	37°21' N, 127°58' E

SPAIN . . . . .pg. 158

Albacete	38°59' N, 001°51' W
Alcalá de Henares.	40°29' N, 003°22' W
Algeciras	36°08' N, 005°30' W
Alicante (Alacant).	38°21' N, 000°29' W
Avilés.	43°33' N, 005°55' W
Badajoz	38°53' N, 006°58' W
Barcelona	41°23' N, 002°11' E
Bilbao	43°15' N, 002°58' W
Burgos	42°21' N, 003°42' W
Cáceres	39°29' N, 006°22' W
Cádiz (Cadiz)	36°32' N, 006°18' W
Cartagena	37°36' N, 000°59' W
Castellón de la Plana	39°59' N, 000°02' W
Ciudad Real.	38°59' N, 003°56' W
Cordova (Córdoba)	37°53' N, 004°46' W
Cuenca	40°04' N, 002°08' W
Elche (Elx).	38°15' N, 000°42' W
Ferrol (El Ferrol del Caudillo)	43°29' N, 008°14' W
Gernika-Lumo (Guernica y Luno)	43°19' N, 002°41' W
Getafe	40°18' N, 003°43' W
Gijón	43°32' N, 005°40' W
Granada	37°11' N, 003°36' W
Huelva	37°16' N, 006°57' W
Jaén	37°46' N, 003°47' W
La Coruña (A Coruña) . . .	43°22' N, 008°23' W
León	42°36' N, 005°34' W
Lérida (Lleida)	41°37' N, 000°37' E
L'Hospitalet de Llobregat	41°22' N, 002°08' E
Logroño.	42°28' N, 002°27' W
Lugo.	43°00' N, 007°34' W
Madrid.	40°24' N, 003°41' W
Málaga	36°43' N, 004°25' W
Mérida	38°55' N, 006°20' W
Murcia	37°59' N, 001°07' W
Palencia.	42°01' N, 004°32' W
Pamplona (Iruña)	42°49' N, 001°38' W
Salamanca	40°58' N, 005°39' W
San Fernando	36°28' N, 006°12' W
Santander	43°28' N, 003°48' W

Santiago
de Compostela . . . . 42°53' N, 008°33' W
Saragossa (Zaragoza) . . . . 41°38' N, 000°53' W
Segovia . . . . 40°57' N, 004°07' W
Seville (Sevilla) . . . . 37°23' N, 005°59' W
Soria . . . . 41°46' N, 002°28' W
Tarragona . . . . 41°07' N, 001°15' E
Terrassa (Tarrasa) . . . . 41°34' N, 002°01' E
Teruel . . . . 40°21' N, 001°06' W
Toledo . . . . 39°52' N, 004°01' W
Valencia . . . . 39°28' N, 000°22' W
Valladolid . . . . 41°39' N, 004°43' W
Vigo . . . . 42°14' N, 008°43' W
Vitoria (Gasteiz) . . . . 42°51' N, 002°40' W

SRI LANKA . . . . . .pg. 159

Ambalangoda . . . . 06°14' N, 080°03' E
Anuradhapura . . . . 08°21' N, 080°23' E
Badulla . . . . 06°59' N, 081°03' E
Batticaloa . . . . 07°43' N, 081°42' E
Beruwala . . . . 06°29' N, 079°59' E
Chavakachcheri . . . . 09°39' N, 080°09' E
Colombo . . . . 06°56' N, 079°51' E
Dehiwala-
Mount Lavinia . . . . 06°51' N, 079°52' E
Eravur . . . . 07°46' N, 081°36' E
Galle . . . . 06°02' N, 080°13' E
Gampola . . . . 07°10' N, 080°34' E
Hambantota . . . . 06°07' N, 081°07' E
Jaffna . . . . 09°40' N, 080°00' E
Kalutara . . . . 06°35' N, 079°58' E
Kandy . . . . 07°18' N, 080°38' E
Kankesanturai . . . . 09°49' N, 080°02' E
Kegalla . . . . 07°15' N, 080°21' E
Kilinochchi . . . . 09°24' N, 080°24' E
Kotte . . . . 06°54' N, 079°54' E
Kurunegala . . . . 07°29' N, 080°22' E
Madampe . . . . 07°30' N, 079°50' E
Mannar . . . . 08°59' N, 079°54' E
Moratuwa . . . . 06°46' N, 079°53' E
Mullaittivu . . . . 09°16' N, 080°49' E
Mutur . . . . 08°27' N, 081°16' E
Negombo . . . . 07°13' N, 079°50' E
Nuwara Eliya . . . . 06°58' N, 080°46' E
Point Pedro . . . . 09°50' N, 080°14' E
Polonnaruwa . . . . 07°56' N, 081°00' E
Puttalam . . . . 08°02' N, 079°49' E
Ratnapura . . . . 06°41' N, 080°24' E
Tangalla . . . . 06°01' N, 080°48' E
Trincomalee . . . . 08°34' N, 081°14' E
Vavuniya . . . . 08°45' N, 080°30' E
Watugedara . . . . 06°15' N, 080°03' E
Weligama . . . . 05°58' N, 080°25' E
Yala . . . . 06°22' N, 081°31' E

SUDAN . . . . .pg. 160

Ad-Damazin
(Ed–Damazin) . . . . 11°46' N, 034°21' E

Ad-Dāmir . . . . 17°35' N, 033°58' E
Ad-Duwaym
(Ed-Dueim) . . . . 14°00' N, 032°19' E
Al-Fūlah . . . . 11°48' N, 028°24' E
Al-Fashir (El Fasher) . . . . . 13°38' N, 025°21' E
Al-Junaynah (Geneina) . . . 13°27' N, 022°27' E
Al-Mijlad . . . . 11°02' N, 027°44' E
Al-Qaḍārif (Gedaref) . . . . . 14°02' N, 035°24' E
Al-Ubbayid (El-Obeid) . . . . 13°11' N, 030°13' E
An-Nuhūd (An-Nahūd) . . . 12°42' N, 028°26' E
'Aṭbarah . . . . 17°42' N, 033°59' E
Bor . . . . 06°12' N, 031°33' E
Dunqulah (Dongola) . . . . . 19°10' N, 030°29' E
Juba . . . . 04°51' N, 031°37' E
Kāduqlī . . . . 11°01' N, 029°43' E
Kas . . . . 12°30' N, 024°17' E
Kassalā . . . . 15°28' N, 036°24' E
Khartoum . . . . 15°36' N, 032°32' E
Khartoum North . . . . 15°38' N, 032°33' E
Kūstī . . . . 13°10' N, 032°40' E
Malakāl . . . . 09°31' N, 031°39' E
Marawi . . . . 18°29' N, 031°49' E
Nagichot . . . . 04°16' N, 033°34' E
Nāṣir . . . . 08°36' N, 033°04' E
Nyala . . . . 12°03' N, 024°53' E
Omdurman . . . . 15°38' N, 032°30' E
Port Sudan . . . . 19°37' N, 037°14' E
Rumbek . . . . 06°48' N, 029°41' E
Sannār . . . . 13°33' N, 033°38' E
Sawākin . . . . 19°07' N, 037°20' E
Shandi . . . . 16°42' N, 033°26' E
Wadi Halfa' . . . . 21°48' N, 031°21' E
Wad Madanī . . . . 14°24' N, 033°32' E
Wāw (Wau) . . . . 07°42' N, 028°00' E

SURINAME . . . . . .pg. 161

Albina . . . . 05°30' N, 054°03' W
Benzdorp . . . . 03°41' N, 054°05' W
Bitagron . . . . 05°10' N, 056°06' W
Brokopondo . . . . 05°04' N, 054°58' W
Brownsweg . . . . 05°01' N, 055°10' W
Goddo . . . . 04°01' N, 055°28' W
Groningen . . . . 05°48' N, 055°28' W
Meerzorg . . . . 05°49' N, 055°09' W
Nieuw Amsterdam . . . . . . 05°53' N, 055°05' W
Nieuw Nickerie . . . . 05°57' N, 056°59' W
Onverwacht . . . . 05°36' N, 055°12' W
Paramaribo . . . . 05°50' N, 055°10' W
Totness . . . . 05°53' N, 056°19' W
Zanderij . . . . 05°27' N, 055°12' W

SWAZILAND . . . . .pg. 162

Hlatikulu . . . . 26°58' S, 031°19' E
Kadake . . . . 26°13' S, 031°02' E
Manzini (Bremersdorp) . . . 26°29' S, 031°22' E
Mbabane . . . . 26°19' S, 031°08' E
Nhlangono . . . . 27°07' S, 031°12' E
Piggs Peak . . . . 25°58' S, 031°15' E

Siteki (Stegi) . . . . 26°27' S, 031°57' E

SWEDEN . . . . .pg. 163

Älvsbyn	65°40' N,	021°00' E
Falun	60°36' N,	015°38' E
Gävle	60°40' N,	017°10' E
Göteborg	57°43' N,	011°58' E
Halmstad	56°39' N,	012°50' E
Haparanda	65°50' N,	024°10' E
Hudiksvall	61°44' N,	017°07' E
Jönköping	57°47' N,	014°11' E
Karlskrona	56°10' N,	015°35' E
Karlstad	59°22' N,	013°30' E
Kiruna	67°51' N,	020°13' E
Kristianstad	56°02' N,	014°08' E
Linköping	58°25' N,	015°37' E
Luleå	65°34' N,	022°10' E
Lycksele	64°36' N,	018°40' E
Malmberget	67°10' N,	020°40' E
Malmö	55°36' N,	013°00' E
Mariestad	58°43' N,	013°51' E
Mora	61°00' N,	014°33' E
Örebro	59°17' N,	015°13' E
Örnsköldsvik	63°18' N,	018°43' E
Östersund	63°11' N,	014°39' E
Piteå	65°20' N,	021°30' E
Skellefteå	64°46' N,	020°57' E
Söderhamn	61°18' N,	017°03' E
Stockholm	59°20' N,	018°03' E
Strömsund	63°51' N,	015°35' E
Sundsvall	62°23' N,	017°18' E
Umea	63°50' N,	020°15' E
Uppsala	59°52' N,	017°38' E
Vänersborg	58°22' N,	012°19' E
Västerås	59°37' N,	016°33' E
Växjö	56°53' N,	014°49' E
Vetalnda	57°26' N,	015°04' E
Visby	57°38' N,	018°18' E
Ystad	55°25' N,	013°49' E

SWITZERLAND . .pg. 164

Aarau	47°23' N,	008°03' E
Altdorf	46°53' N,	008°39' E
Arbon	47°31' N,	009°26' E
Appenzell	47°20' N,	009°24' E
Arosa	46°47' N,	009°40' E
Baden	47°28' N,	008°18' E
Basel	47°35' N,	007°32' E
Bellinzona	46°12' N,	009°01' E
Bern	46°55' N,	007°28' E
Biel (Bienne)	47°10' N,	007°15' E
Chur (Coire)	46°51' N,	009°30' E
Davos	46°49' N,	009°50' E
Delémont	47°22' N,	007°20' E
Frauenfeld	47°33' N,	008°54' E
Fribourg (Freiburg)	46°48' N,	007°09' E
Geneva	46°12' N,	006°10' E
Glarus	47°02' N,	009°04' E

Grindelwald	46°37' N,	008°03' E
Gstaad	46°28' N,	007°17' E
Herisau	47°24' N,	009°16' E
Interlaken	46°41' N,	007°51' E
La Chaux-de-Fonds	47°08' N,	006°51' E
Lausanne	46°32' N,	006°40' E
Liestal	47°28' N,	007°44' E
Locarno (Luggaras)	46°10' N,	008°48' E
Lucerne (Luzern)	47°05' N,	008°16' E
Lugano (Lauis)	46°00' N,	008°58' E
Montreux	46°26' N,	006°55' E
Neuchatel (Neuenburg)	47°00' N,	006°58' E
Saint Gall (Sankt Gallen)	47°28' N,	009°24' E
Saint Moritz (San Murezzan, Saint-Moritz, or Sankt Moritz)	46°30' N,	009°50' E
Sarnen	46°54' N,	008°14' E
Schaffhausen	47°42' N,	008°38' E
Sion (Sitten)	46°14' N,	007°21' E
Solothurn (Soleure)	47°14' N,	007°31' E
Stans	46°58' N,	008°21' E
Thun (Thoune)	46°45' N,	007°37' E
Vevey	46°27' N,	006°51' E
Winterthur	47°30' N,	008°45' E
Zermatt	46°01' N,	007°45' E
Zug	47°10' N,	008°31' E
Zürich	47°22' N,	008°33' E

SYRIA . . . . .pg. 165

Al-Bāb	36°22' N,	037°31' E
Al-Hasakah	36°29' N,	040°45' E
Al-Mayādin	35°01' N,	040°27' E
Al-Qāmishli (Al-Kamishly)	37°02' N,	041°14' E
Aleppo (Ḥalab)	36°12' N,	037°10' E
Ar-Raqqah (Rakka)	35°57' N,	039°01' E
As-Safirah	36°04' N,	037°22' E
As-Suwaydā'	32°42' N,	036°34' E
A'zāz (I'zaz)	36°35' N,	037°03' E
Damascus	33°30' N,	036°18' E
Dar'ā	32°37' N,	036°06' E
Dayr az-Zawr	35°20' N,	040°09' E
Dūmā (Douma)	33°35' N,	036°24' E
Hamāh (Hama)	35°08' N,	036°45' E
Ḥimṣ (Homs)	34°44' N,	036°43' E
Idlib	35°55' N,	036°38' E
Jablah (Jableh)	35°21' N,	035°55' E
Jarābulus	36°49' N,	038°01' E
Latakia (Al-Lādhiqīyah)	35°31' N,	035°47' E
Ma'arrat an-Nu'mān	35°38' N,	036°40' E
Ma'lūlā	33°50' N,	036°33' E
Manbij (Manbej)	36°31' N,	037°57' E
Mukharram al-Fawqāni	34°49' N,	037°05' E
Ra's al-'Ayn	36°51' N,	040°04' E
Salamīyah	35°01' N,	037°03' E
Tadmur	34°33' N,	038°17' E
Ṭarṭūs	34°53' N,	035°53' E

TAIWAN . . . . pg. 166

Chang-hua	24°05′ N,	120°32′ E
Ch'ao-chou	22°33′ N,	120°32′ E
Ch'e-ch'eng	22°05′ N,	120°42′ E
Chia-i	23°29′ N,	120°27′ E
Ch'ih-shang	23°07′ N,	121°12′ E
Chi-lung	25°08′ N,	121°44′ E
Chung-hsing Hsin-ts'un	23°57′ N,	120°41′ E
Chu-tung	24°44′ N,	121°05′ E
Erh-lin	23°54′ N,	120°22′ E
Feng-lin	23°45′ N,	121°26′ E
Feng-shan	22°38′ N,	120°21′ E
Feng-yüan	24°15′ N,	120°43′ E
Hsin-chu	24°48′ N,	120°58′ E
Hsin-ying	23°18′ N,	120°19′ E
Hua-lien	23°59′ N,	121°36′ E
I-lan	24°46′ N,	121°45′ E
Kang-shan	22°48′ N,	120°17′ E
Kao-hsiung	22°38′ N,	120°17′ E
Lan-yü	22°02′ N,	121°33′ E
Lo-tung	24°41′ N,	121°46′ E
Lu-kang	24°03′ N,	120°25′ E
Lü-tao	22°40′ N,	121°28′ E
Miao-li	24°34′ N,	120°49′ E
Nan-t'ou	23°55′ N,	120°41′ E
Pan-ch'iao	25°01′ N,	121°27′ E
P'ing-tung	22°40′ N,	120°29′ E
San-ch'ung	25°04′ N,	121°30′ E
Su-ao	24°36′ N,	121°51′ E
T'ai-chung	24°09′ N,	120°41′ E
T'ai-nan	23°00′ N,	120°12′ E
Taipei (T'ai-pei)	25°03′ N,	121°30′ E
T'ai-tung	22°45′ N,	121°09′ E
T'ao-yüan	25°00′ N,	121°18′ E
Tung-ho	22°58′ N,	121°18′ E
Yüan-lin	23°58′ N,	120°34′ E
Yung-k'ang	23°02′ N,	120°15′ E

TAJIKISTAN . . . . . pg. 167

Dushanbe	38°33′ N,	068°48′ E
Kalininobod	37°52′ N,	068°55′ E
Khorugh	37°30′ N,	071°36′ E
Khujand (Leninabad, or		
Khojand)	40°17′ N,	069°37′ E
Kofarniqon		
(Ordzhonikidzeäbad)	38°34′ N,	069°01′ E
Külob	37°55′ N,	069°46′ E
Norak	38°23′ N,	069°21′ E
Qayroqqum	40°16′ N,	069°49′ E
Qürghonteppa	37°50′ N,	068°47′ E
Uroteppa	39°55′ N,	069°01′ E

TANZANIA . . . . . pg. 168

Arusha	03°22′ S,	036°41′ E
Bagamoyo	06°26′ S,	038°54′ E
Bukoba	01°20′ S,	031°49′ E

Chake Chake	05°15′ S,	039°46′ E
Dar es Salaam	06°48′ S,	039°17′ E
Dodoma	06°11′ S,	035°45′ E
Ifakara	08°08′ S,	036°41′ E
Iringa	07°46′ S,	035°42′ E
Kigoma	04°52′ S,	029°38′ E
Korogwe	05°09′ S,	038°29′ E
Lindi	10°00′ S,	039°43′ E
Mbeya	08°54′ S,	033°27′ E
Mkoani	05°22′ S,	039°39′ E
Morogoro	06°49′ S,	037°40′ E
Moshi	03°21′ S,	037°20′ E
Mpwapwa	06°21′ S,	036°29′ E
Mtwara	10°16′ S,	040°11′ E
Musoma	01°30′ S,	033°48′ E
Mwanza	02°31′ S,	032°54′ E
Newala	10°56′ S,	039°18′ E
Pangani	09°32′ S,	035°31′ E
Shinyanga	03°40′ S,	033°26′ E
Singida	04°49′ S,	034°45′ E
Songea	10°41′ S,	035°39′ E
Sumbawanga	07°58′ S,	031°37′ E
Tabora	05°01′ S,	032°48′ E
Tanga	05°04′ S,	039°06′ E
Tunduru	11°07′ S,	037°21′ E
Wete	05°04′ S,	039°43′ E
Zanzibar	06°10′ S,	039°11′ E

THAILAND . . . . . . pg. 169

Bangkok (Krung Thep)	13°45′ N,	100°31′ E
Chanthaburi		
(Chantabun)	12°36′ N,	102°09′ E
Chiang Mai (Chiengmai)	18°47′ N,	098°59′ E
Chon Buri	13°22′ N,	100°59′ E
Hat Yai (Haad Yai)	07°01′ N,	100°28′ E
Khon Kaen	16°26′ N,	102°50′ E
Mae Sot	16°43′ N,	098°34′ E
Nakhon Phanom	17°24′ N,	104°47′ E
Nakhon Ratchasima		
(Khorat)	14°58′ N,	102°07′ E
Nakhon Sawan	15°41′ N,	100°07′ E
Nakhon Si Thammarat	08°26′ N,	099°58′ E
Nan	18°47′ N,	100°47′ E
Nong Khai	17°52′ N,	102°44′ E
Nonthaburi	13°50′ N,	100°29′ E
Pathum Thani	14°01′ N,	100°32′ E
Pattaya	12°54′ N,	100°51′ E
Phichit	16°26′ N,	100°22′ E
Phitsanulok	16°50′ N,	100°15′ E
Phra Nakhon Si Ayutthaya		
(Ayutthaya)	14°21′ N,	100°33′ E
Phuket	07°53′ N,	098°24′ E
Roi Et	16°03′ N,	103°40′ E
Sakon Nakhon	17°10′ N,	104°09′ E
Samut Prakan	13°36′ N,	100°36′ E
Samut Sakhon		
(Samut Sakorn)	13°32′ N,	100°17′ E
Sara Buri	14°32′ N,	100°55′ E
Trang	07°33′ N,	099°36′ E
Trat	12°14′ N,	102°30′ E

Ubon Ratchathani....... 15°14' N, 104°54' E
Udon Thani .... 17°26' N, 102°46' E
Uthai Thani .... 15°22' N, 100°03' E
Yala .... 06°33' N, 101°18' E

TOGO ....pg. 170

Aného .... 06°14' N, 001°36' E
Atakpamé .... 07°32' N, 001°08' E
Bassar .... 09°15' N, 000°47' E
Blitta .... 08°19' N, 000°59' E
Dapaong .... 10°52' N, 000°12' E
Kara (Lama Kara)...... 09°33' N, 001°12' E
Lomé .... 06°08' N, 001°13' E
Palimé .... 09°21' N, 002°37' E
Sokodé................ 08°59' N, 001°08' E
Tsévié .... 06°25' N, 001°13' E

TONGA ....pg. 171

Nuku'alofa............. 21°08' N, 175°12' E

TRINIDAD AND
TOBAGO ....pg. 172

Arima................. 10°38' N, 061°17' W
Arouca................ 10°38' N, 061°20' W
Chaguanas............ 10°31' N, 061°25' W
Charlotteville .... 11°19' N, 060°33' W
Couva .... 10°25' N, 061°27' W
Point Fortin........... 10°11' N, 061°41' W
Port of Spain.......... 10°39' N, 061°31' W
Princes Town .... 10°16' N, 061°23' W
Rio Claro .... 10°18' N, 061°11' W
Roxborough .... 11°15' N, 060°35' W
San Fernando .... 10°17' N, 061°28' W
Sangre Grande .... 11°11' N, 060°44' W
Scarborough .... 11°11' N, 060°44' W
Siparia............... 10°08' N, 061°30' W
Tunapuna .... 10°38' N, 061°23' W

TUNISIA ....pg. 173

Al-Ḥammāmāt
  (Hammamet) .... 36°24' N, 010°37' E
Al-Mahdīyah (Mahdia) .... 35°30' N, 011°04' E
Al-Metlaoui .... 34°20' N, 008°24' E
Al-Muknīn (Moknine) .. 35°38' N, 010°54' E
Al-Munastīr (Monastir or
  Ruspina)........... 35°47' N, 010°50' E
Al-Qaṣrayn (Kasserine) .. 35°11' N, 008°48' E
Al-Qayrawān (Kairouan
  or Qairouan) .... 35°41' N, 010°07' E
Bājah (Béja) .... 36°44' N, 009°11' E
Banzart (Bizerte) ...... 37°17' N, 009°52' E
Ḥammām al-Anf
  (Hammam-lif)........ 36°44' N, 010°20' E
Jarjīs (Zarzis) .... 33°30' N, 011°07' E

Madanīn (Medenine) ..... 33°21' N, 010°30' E
Makthar............... 35°51' N, 009°12' E
Manzil Bū Ruqaybah
  (Ferryville or Menzel-
  Bourguiba)........... 37°10' N, 009°48' E
Nābul (Nabeul or
  Neapolis) .... 36°27' N, 010°44' E
Nafṭah (Nefta)........... 33°52' N, 007°53' E
Qābis
  (Gabes or Tacape) ..... 33°53' N, 010°07' E
Qafṣah (Gafsa) .... 34°25' N, 008°48' E
Qibilī (Kebili) .... 33°42' N, 008°58' E
Safāqis (Sfax) .... 34°44' N, 010°46' E
Sūsah
  (Sousa or Sousse) ..... 35°49' N, 010°38' E
Tawzar (Tozeur)........ 33°55' N, 008°08' E
Tunis (Tunis) .... 36°48' N, 010°11' E
Zaghwān (Zaghouan) ..... 36°24' N, 010°09' E

TURKEY ....pg. 174

Adana .... 37°01' N, 035°18' E
Afyon .... 38°45' N, 030°33' E
Amasya .... 40°39' N, 035°51' E
Ankara (Angora)........ 39°56' N, 032°52' E
Antakya (Antioch) ...... 36°14' N, 036°07' E
Antalya
  (Attalia or Hatay) ..... 36°53' N, 030°42' E
Artvin................. 41°11' N, 041°49' E
Aydın .... 37°51' N, 027°51' E
Balıkesir.............. 39°39' N, 027°53' E
Bandırma (Panderma) ... 40°20' N, 027°58' E
Batman .... 37°52' N, 041°07' E
Bursa (Brusa) .... 40°11' N, 029°04' E
Çorum .... 40°33' N, 034°58' E
Denizli .... 37°46' N, 029°06' E
Diyarbakır (Amida)...... 37°55' N, 040°14' E
Elâzığ .... 38°41' N, 039°14' E
Erzincan .... 39°44' N, 039°29' E
Erzurum.............. 39°55' N, 041°17' E
Eskisehir .... 39°46' N, 030°32' E
Gaziantep .... 37°05' N, 037°22' E
Iğdır .... 39°56' N, 044°02' E
İskenderun
  (Alexandretta)........ 36°35' N, 036°10' E
Isparta (Hamid-Abad)..... 37°46' N, 030°33' E
Istanbul
  (Constantinople)...... 41°01' N, 028°58' E
İzmir (Smyrna) .... 38°25' N, 027°09' E
İzmit................. 40°46' N, 029°55' E
Kahramanmaraş
  (Maraş) .... 37°36' N, 036°55' E
Karabük.............. 41°12' N, 032°37' E
Karaman .... 37°11' N, 033°14' E
Kars .... 40°37' N, 043°05' E
Kayseri (Caesarea) ..... 38°43' N, 035°30' E
Kırıkkale .... 39°50' N, 033°31' E
Konya (Iconium) .... 37°52' N, 032°31' E
Kütahya.............. 39°25' N, 029°59' E
Manisa .... 38°36' N, 027°26' E
Mardin............... 37°18' N, 040°44' E

Mersin . . . . 36°48' N, 034°38' E
Muğla . . . . 37°12' N, 028°22' E
Nevşehir . . . . 38°38' N, 034°43' E
Niğde . . . . 37°59' N, 034°42' E
Ordu . . . . 41°00' N, 037°53' E
Samsun (Amisus) . . . . 41°17' N, 036°20' E
Sinop . . . . 42°01' N, 035°09' E
Sivas (Sebastia) . . . . 39°45' N, 037°02' E
Trabzon (Trapezus or
Trebizond) . . . . 41°00' N, 039°43' E
Urfa . . . . 37°08' N, 038°46' E
Uşak (Ushak) . . . . 38°41' N, 029°25' E
Van . . . . 38°30' N, 043°23' E
Yalova . . . . 40°39' N, 029°15' E
Yozgat . . . . 39°50' N, 034°48' E
Zonguldak . . . . 41°27' N, 031°49' E

TURKMENISTAN pg. 175

Ashgabat (Ashkhabad) . . . . 37°57' N, 058°23' E
Bayramaly . . . . 37°37' N, 062°10' E
Büzmeyin . . . . 38°05' N, 058°12' E
Chärjew . . . . 39°06' N, 063°34' E
Cheleken . . . . 39°26' N, 053°07' E
Chirchiq . . . . 41°29' N, 069°35' E
Dashhowuz . . . . 41°50' N, 059°58' E
Gowurdak . . . . 37°50' N, 066°04' E
Kerki . . . . 37°50' N, 065°12' E
Mary (Merv) . . . . 37°36' N, 061°50' E
Nebitdag . . . . 39°30' N, 054°22' E
Türkmenbashy
(Krasnovodsk) . . . . 40°00' N, 053°00' E
Yolöten . . . . 37°18' N, 062°21' E

TUVALU . . . . pg. 176

Fongafale . . . . 08°31' S, 179°13' E

UGANDA . . . . pg. 177

Entebbe . . . . 00°04' N, 032°28' E
Gulu . . . . 02°47' N, 032°18' E
Jinja . . . . 00°26' N, 033°12' E
Kabarole . . . . 00°39' N, 030°16' E
Kampala . . . . 00°19' N, 032°35' E
Masaka . . . . 00°20' S, 031°44' E
Mbale . . . . 01°05' N, 034°10' E
Soroti . . . . 01°43' N, 033°37' E
Tororo . . . . 00°42' N, 034°11' E

UKRAINE . . . . pg. 178

Alchevsk . . . . 48°30' N, 038°47' E
Berdyansk . . . . 46°45' N, 036°47' E
Berdychiv . . . . 49°54' N, 028°35' E
Bila Tserkva . . . . 49°47' N, 030°07' E
Cherkasy . . . . 49°26' N, 032°04' E

Chernihiv . . . . 51°30' N, 031°18' E
Chernivtsi . . . . 48°18' N, 025°56' E
Chornobyl (Chernobyl) . . 51°16' N, 030°14' E
Dnipropetrovs'k . . . . 48°27' N, 034°59' E
Donetsk . . . . 48°00' N, 037°48' E
Kerch . . . . 45°21' N, 036°28' E
Kharkiv . . . . 50°00' N, 036°15' E
Khmelnytskyy . . . . 49°25' N, 027°00' E
Kiev (Kyyiv) . . . . 50°26' N, 030°31' E
Korosten . . . . 50°57' N, 028°39' E
Kovel . . . . 51°13' N, 024°43' E
Krasny Luch . . . . 48°08' N, 038°56' E
Kryvyy Rih . . . . 47°55' N, 033°21' E
Luhansk . . . . 48°34' N, 039°20' E
Lutsk . . . . 50°45' N, 025°20' E
Lviv . . . . 49°50' N, 024°00' E
Makiyivka . . . . 48°02' N, 037°58' E
Marhanets . . . . 47°38' N, 034°38' E
Mariupol . . . . 47°06' N, 037°33' E
Melitopol . . . . 46°50' N, 035°22' E
Mykolayiv . . . . 46°58' N, 032°00' E
Myrhorod . . . . 49°58' N, 033°36' E
Novhorod-Siverskyy . . . . . 52°00' N, 033°16' E
Odessa . . . . 46°28' N, 030°44' E
Pavlograd . . . . 48°31' N, 035°52' E
Poltava . . . . 49°35' N, 034°34' E
Pryluky . . . . 50°36' N, 032°24' E
Rivne . . . . 50°37' N, 026°15' E
Rubizhne . . . . 49°01' N, 038°23' E
Sevastopol . . . . 44°36' N, 033°32' E
Shostka . . . . 51°52' N, 033°29' E
Simferopol . . . . 44°57' N, 034°06' E
Sumy . . . . 50°54' N, 034°48' E
Syeverodonets'k . . . . 48°58' N, 038°26' E
Uzhhorod . . . . 48°37' N, 022°18' E
Vinnytsya . . . . 49°14' N, 028°29' E
Voznesensk . . . . 47°33' N, 031°20' E
Yevpatoriya . . . . 45°12' N, 033°22' E
Zaporizhzhya . . . . 47°49' N, 035°11' E
Zhytomyr . . . . 50°15' N, 028°40' E

UNITED ARAB EMIRATES . . . . pg. 179

Abu Dhabi . . . . 24°28' N, 054°22' E
'Ajmān . . . . 25°25' N, 055°27' E
Al-'Ayn . . . . 24°13' N, 055°46' E
Al-Fujayrah . . . . 25°08' N, 056°21' E
Al-Khīs . . . . 23°00' N, 054°12' E
Al-Māriyah . . . . 23°08' N, 053°44' E
'Arādah . . . . 22°59' N, 053°26' E
Ash-Shāriqah . . . . 25°22' N, 055°23' E
Diqdāqah . . . . 25°40' N, 055°58' E
Dubayy . . . . 25°16' N, 055°18' E
Kalbā . . . . 025°05' N, 056°22' E
Khawr Fakkān . . . . 25°21' N, 056°22' E
Ra's Al-Khaymah . . . . 25°47' N, 055°57' E
Tarīf . . . . 24°03' N, 053°46' E
Umm Al-Qaywayn . . . . . . 25°35' N, 055°34' E
Wadhīl . . . . 23°03' N, 054°08' E

UNITED KINGDOM . . . . . .pg. 180-1

Aberdeen. . . . . 57°09' N, 002°08' W
Barrow-in-Furness. . . . . . . 54°07' N, 003°14' W
Bath. . . . . 51°23' N, 002°22' W
Belfast . . . . 54°35' N, 005°56' W
Birmingham. . . . . 52°29' N, 001°51' W
Bradford . . . . 53°47' N, 001°45' W
Bristol . . . . 51°26' N, 002°35' W
Cambridge. . . . . 52°12' N, 000°09' E
Cardiff . . . . 51°29' N, 003°11' W
Carlisle . . . . 54°53' N, 002°57' W
Cheltenham. . . . . 51°54' N, 002°05' W
Colchester. . . . . 51°54' N, 000°54' E
Coventry . . . . 52°24' N, 001°31' W
Darlington. . . . . 54°32' N, 001°34' W
Dartford. . . . . 51°26' N, 000°12' W
Derby. . . . . 52°55' N, 001°28' W
Derry (Londonderry) . . . . 55°00' N, 007°20' W
Dundee . . . . 56°29' N, 003°02' W
Dunfermline . . . . 56°04' N, 003°26' W
Eastbourne . . . . 50°47' N, 000°16' E
Edinburgh . . . . 55°57' N, 003°10' W
Exeter . . . . 50°43' N, 003°31' W
Glasgow. . . . . 55°52' N, 004°15' W
Great Yarmouth . . . . 52°36' N, 001°44' E
Grimsby. . . . . 53°34' N, 000°05' W
Hamilton . . . . 55°47' N, 004°02' W
Harrogate . . . . 54°00' N, 001°32' W
Hartlepool . . . . 54°41' N, 001°13' W
Hastings. . . . . 50°52' N, 000°35' E
High Wycombe . . . . 51°38' N, 000°45' W
Hove . . . . 50°50' N, 000°11' W
Ipswich . . . . 52°03' N, 001°09' E
Kilmarnock . . . . 55°36' N, 004°30' W
King's Lynn . . . . 52°45' N, 000°24' E
Kingston upon Hull. . . . . . 53°45' N, 000°20' W
Leeds . . . . 53°48' N, 001°32' W
Leicester . . . . 52°38' N, 001°08' W
Lincoln. . . . . 53°14' N, 000°32' W
Liverpool. . . . . 53°25' N, 002°57' W
London . . . . 51°30' N, 000°07' W
Lowestoft . . . . 52°28' N, 001°45' E
Maidstone . . . . 51°16' N, 000°32' E
Manchester . . . . 53°29' N, 002°15' W
Margate . . . . 51°23' N, 001°23' E
Newcastle upon Tyne. . . . . 54°58' N, 001°36' W
Newtownabbey. . . . . 54°40' N, 005°57' W
Norwich. . . . . 52°38' N, 001°18' E
Nottingham. . . . . 52°58' N, 001°10' W
Paisley. . . . . 55°50' N, 004°25' W
Peterborough . . . . 52°35' N, 000°14' W
Plymouth. . . . . 50°23' N, 004°09' W
Poole . . . . 50°43' N, 001°59' W
Portsmouth. . . . . 50°49' N, 001°04' W
Rhondda . . . . 51°39' N, 003°29' W
Royal Tunbridge Wells. . . . 51°08' N, 000°16' E
Sheffield. . . . . 53°23' N, 001°28' W
South Shields . . . . 54°59' N, 001°26' W

Southampton . . . . 50°55' N, 001°24' W
Staines. . . . . 51°26' N, 000°30' W
Stevenage . . . . 51°54' N, 000°12' W
Stoke-on-Trent . . . . 53°01' N, 002°11' W
Swansea . . . . 51°38' N, 003°58' W
Torquay. . . . . 50°29' N, 003°32' W
Walsall. . . . . 52°35' N, 001°59' W
Warrington . . . . 53°24' N, 002°36' W
York. . . . . 53°57' N, 001°06' W

UNITED STATES . . . . .pg. 182-3

Aberdeen, S.D. . . . . 45°28' N, 098°29' W
Aberdeen, Wash.. . . . . 46°59' N, 123°50' W
Abilene, Kan. . . . . 38°55' N, 097°13' W
Abilene, Tex. . . . . 32°28' N, 099°43' W
Ada, Okla. . . . . 34°46' N, 096°41' W
Akron, Ohio. . . . . 41°05' N, 081°31' W
Alamogordo, N.M. . . . . . . 32°54' N, 105°57' W
Alamosa, Colo. . . . . 37°28' N, 105°52' W
Albany, Ga. . . . . 31°35' N, 084°10' W
Albany, N.Y. . . . . 42°39' N, 073°45' W
Albuquerque, N.M. . . . . . . 35°05' N, 106°39' W
Alexandria, La. . . . . 31°18' N, 092°27' W
Alexandria, Va. . . . . 38°48' N, 077°03' W
Alliance, Neb. . . . . 42°06' N, 102°52' W
Alpena, Mich. . . . . 45°04' N, 083°27' W
Alton, Ill. . . . . 38°53' N, 090°11' W
Alturas, Calif. . . . . 41°29' N, 120°32' W
Altus, Okla. . . . . 34°38' N, 099°20' W
Amarillo, Tex. . . . . 35°13' N, 101°50' W
Americus, Ga. . . . . 32°04' N, 084°14' W
Anaconda, Mont.. . . . . 46°08' N, 112°57' W
Anchorage, Alaska . . . . 61°13' N, 149°54' W
Andalusia, Ala. . . . . 31°18' N, 086°29' W
Ann Arbor, Mich. . . . . 42°17' N, 083°45' W
Annapolis, Md. . . . . 38°59' N, 076°30' W
Appleton, Wis. . . . . 44°16' N, 088°25' W
Arcata, Calif. . . . . 40°52' N, 124°05' W
Arlington, Tex. . . . . 32°44' N, 097°07' W
Arlington, Va. . . . . 38°53' N, 077°07' W
Asheville, N.C. . . . . 35°36' N, 082°33' W
Ashland, Ky. . . . . 38°28' N, 082°38' W
Ashland, Wis. . . . . 46°35' N, 090°53' W
Aspen, Colo. . . . . 39°11' N, 106°49' W
Astoria, Ore. . . . . 46°11' N, 123°50' W
Athens, Ga. . . . . 33°57' N, 083°23' W
Atlanta, Ga. . . . . 33°45' N, 084°23' W
Atlantic City, N.J. . . . . 39°21' N, 074°27' W
Augusta, Ga. . . . . 33°28' N, 081°58' W
Augusta, Me. . . . . 44°19' N, 069°47' W
Aurora, Colo. . . . . 39°43' N, 104°49' W
Austin, Minn. . . . . 43°40' N, 092°58' W
Austin, Tex. . . . . 30°17' N, 097°45' W
Baker, Mont. . . . . 46°22' N, 104°17' W
Baker, Ore. . . . . 44°47' N, 117°50' W
Bakersfield, Calif. . . . . 35°23' N, 119°01' W
Baltimore, Md. . . . . 39°17' N, 076°37' W
Bangor, Me. . . . . 44°48' N, 068°46' W

Bar Harbor, Me.	44°23' N, 068°13' W
Barrow, Alaska	71°18' N, 156°47' W
Bartlesville, Okla.	36°45' N, 095°59' W
Baton Rouge, La.	30°27' N, 091°11' W
Bay City, Mich.	43°36' N, 083°54' W
Beaumont, Tex.	30°05' N, 094°06' W
Bellingham, Wash.	48°46' N, 122°29' W
Beloit, Wis.	42°31' N, 089°01' W
Bemidji, Minn.	47°28' N, 094°52' W
Bend, Ore.	44°04' N, 121°19' W
Berlin, N.H.	44°28' N, 071°11' W
Bethel, Alaska	60°48' N, 161°45' W
Beulah, N.D.	47°15' N, 101°46' W
Billings, Mont.	45°47' N, 108°30' W
Biloxi, Miss.	30°24' N, 088°53' W
Birmingham, Ala.	33°31' N, 086°48' W
Bismarck, N.D.	46°48' N, 100°47' W
Bloomington, Ind.	39°10' N, 086°32' W
Blythe, Calif.	33°37' N, 114°36' W
Boca Raton, Fla.	26°21' N, 080°05' W
Bogalusa, La.	30°47' N, 089°52' W
Boise, Idaho	43°37' N, 116°13' W
Boston, Mass.	42°22' N, 071°04' W
Boulder, Colo.	40°01' N, 105°17' W
Bowling Green, Ky.	36°59' N, 086°27' W
Bozeman, Mont.	45°41' N, 111°02' W
Bradenton, Fla.	27°30' N, 082°34' W
Brady, Tex.	31°09' N, 099°20' W
Brainerd, Minn.	46°22' N, 094°12' W
Bremerton, Wash.	47°34' N, 122°38' W
Brigham City, Utah	41°31' N, 112°01' W
Brookings, S.D.	44°19' N, 096°48' W
Brownsville, Tex.	25°54' N, 097°30' W
Brunswick, Ga.	31°10' N, 081°30' W
Bryan, Tex.	30°40' N, 096°22' W
Buffalo, N.Y.	42°53' N, 078°53' W
Buffalo, Tex.	31°28' N, 096°04' W
Burlington, Ia.	40°48' N, 091°06' W
Burlington, Vt.	44°29' N, 073°12' W
Burns, Ore.	43°35' N, 119°03' W
Butte, Mont.	46°00' N, 112°32' W
Cairo, Ill.	37°00' N, 089°11' W
Caldwell, Idaho	43°40' N, 116°41' W
Canton, Ohio	40°48' N, 081°23' W
Cape Girardeau, Mo.	37°19' N, 089°32' W
Carbondale, Ill.	37°44' N, 089°13' W
Carlsbad, N.M.	32°25' N, 104°14' W
Carson City, Nev.	39°10' N, 119°46' W
Casa Grande, Ariz.	32°53' N, 111°45' W
Casper, Wyo.	42°51' N, 106°19' W
Cedar City, Utah	37°41' N, 113°04' W
Cedar Rapids, Ia.	41°59' N, 091°40' W
Chadron, Neb.	42°50' N, 103°00' W
Champaign, Ill.	40°07' N, 088°15' W
Charleston, S.C.	32°46' N, 079°56' W
Charleston, W.Va.	38°21' N, 081°39' W
Charlotte, N.C.	35°13' N, 080°51' W
Chattanooga, Tenn.	35°03' N, 085°19' W
Chesapeake, Va.	36°50' N, 076°17' W
Cheyenne, Wyo.	41°08' N, 104°49' W
Chicago, Ill.	41°53' N, 087°38' W

Chico, Calif.	39°44' N, 121°50' W
Chula Vista, Calif.	32°38' N, 117°05' W
Cincinnati, Ohio	39°06' N, 084°31' W
Clarksdale, Miss.	34°12' N, 090°35' W
Clayton, N.M.	36°27' N, 103°11' W
Clearwater, Fla.	27°58' N, 082°48' W
Cleveland, Ohio	41°30' N, 081°42' W
Clinton, Okla.	35°31' N, 098°58' W
Clovis, N.M.	34°24' N, 103°12' W
Cody, Wyo.	44°32' N, 109°03' W
Coeur d'Alene, Idaho	47°41' N, 116°46' W
College Station, Tex.	30°37' N, 096°21' W
Colorado Springs, Colo.	38°50' N, 104°49' W
Columbia, S.C.	34°00' N, 081°03' W
Columbus, Ga.	32°29' N, 084°59' W
Columbus, Miss.	33°30' N, 088°25' W
Columbus, Ohio	39°58' N, 083°00' W
Concord, N.H.	43°12' N, 071°32' W
Coos Bay, Ore.	43°22' N, 124°12' W
Coral Gables, Fla.	25°45' N, 080°16' W
Cordele, Ga.	31°58' N, 083°47' W
Cordova, Alaska	60°33' N, 145°45' W
Corinth, Miss.	34°56' N, 088°31' W
Corpus Christi, Tex.	27°47' N, 097°24' W
Corsicana, Tex.	32°06' N, 096°28' W
Corvallis, Ore.	44°34' N, 123°16' W
Council Bluffs, Ia.	41°16' N, 095°52' W
Covington, Ky.	39°05' N, 084°31' W
Crescent City, Calif.	41°45' N, 124°12' W
Crystal City, Tex.	28°41' N, 099°50' W
Dalhart, Tex.	36°04' N, 102°31' W
Dallas, Tex.	32°47' N, 096°49' W
Dalton, Ga.	34°46' N, 084°58' W
Danville, Va.	36°36' N, 079°23' W
Davenport, Ia.	41°32' N, 090°35' W
Davis, Calif.	38°33' N, 121°44' W
Dayton, Ohio	39°45' N, 084°12' W
Daytona Beach, Fla.	29°13' N, 081°01' W
Decorah, Ia.	43°18' N, 091°48' W
Denver, Colo.	39°44' N, 104°59' W
Des Moines, Ia.	41°35' N, 093°37' W
Detroit, Mich.	42°20' N, 083°03' W
Dickinson, N.D.	46°53' N, 102°47' W
Dillingham, Alaska	59°03' N, 158°28' W
Dillon, Mont.	45°13' N, 112°38' W
Dodge City, Kan.	37°45' N, 100°00' W
Dothan, Ala.	31°13' N, 085°24' W
Dover, Del.	39°10' N, 075°32' W
Dover, N.H.	43°12' N, 070°53' W
Dubuque, Ia.	42°30' N, 090°41' W
Duluth, Minn.	46°47' N, 092°07' W
Duncan, Okla.	34°30' N, 097°57' W
Durango, Colo.	37°17' N, 107°53' W
Durham, N.C.	36°00' N, 078°54' W
Dutch Harbor, Alaska	53°53' N, 166°32' W
East St. Louis, Ill.	38°37' N, 090°09' W
Eau Claire, Wis.	44°49' N, 091°30' W
El Cajon, Calif.	32°48' N, 116°58' W
El Dorado, Ark.	33°12' N, 092°40' W
El Paso, Tex.	31°45' N, 106°29' W
Elko, Nev.	40°50' N, 115°46' W

Ely, Minn.	47°55' N, 091°51' W		Greeley, Colo.	40°25' N, 104°42' W
Ely, Nev.	39°15' N, 114°54' W		Green Bay, Wis.	44°31' N, 088°00' W
Emporia, Kan.	38°25' N, 096°11' W		Greensboro, N.C.	36°04' N, 079°48' W
Enid, Okla.	36°24' N, 097°53' W		Greenville, Ala.	31°50' N, 086°38' W
Erie, Pa.	42°08' N, 080°05' W		Greenville, Miss.	33°24' N, 091°04' W
Escanaba, Mich.	45°45' N, 087°04' W		Greenwood, S.C.	34°12' N, 082°10' W
Escondido, Calif.	33°07' N, 117°05' W		Griffin, Ga.	33°15' N, 084°16' W
Eugene, Ore.	44°05' N, 123°04' W		Gulfport, Miss.	30°22' N, 089°06' W
Eunice, La.	30°30' N, 092°25' W		Guymon, Okla.	36°41' N, 101°29' W
Eureka, Calif.	40°47' N, 124°09' W		Hampton, Va.	37°02' N, 076°21' W
Eustis, Fla.	28°51' N, 081°41' W		Hannibal, Mo.	39°42' N, 091°22' W
Evanston, Wyo.	41°16' N, 110°58' W		Harlingen, Tex.	26°12' N, 097°42' W
Everett, Wash.	47°59' N, 122°12' W		Harrisburg, Pa.	40°16' N, 076°53' W
Fairbanks, Alaska.	64°51' N, 147°45' W		Hartford, Conn.	41°46' N, 072°41' W
Falls City, Neb.	40°03' N, 095°36' W		Hattiesburg, Miss.	31°20' N, 089°17' W
Fargo, N.D.	46°53' N, 096°48' W		Helena, Mont.	46°36' N, 112°02' W
Farmington, N.M.	36°44' N, 108°12' W		Henderson, Nev.	36°02' N, 114°59' W
Fayetteville, Ark.	36°03' N, 094°09' W		Hialeah, Fla.	25°51' N, 080°16' W
Fayetteville, N.C.	35°03' N, 078°53' W		Hilo, Hawaii	19°44' N, 155°05' W
Fergus Falls, Minn.	46°17' N, 096°04' W		Hobbs, N.M.	32°42' N, 103°08' W
Flagstaff, Ariz.	35°12' N, 111°39' W		Hollywood, Fla.	26°01' N, 080°09' W
Flint, Mich.	43°01' N, 083°41' W		Honokaa, Hawaii	20°05' N, 155°28' W
Florence, S.C.	34°12' N, 079°46' W		Honolulu, Hawaii	21°19' N, 157°52' W
Fort Bragg, Calif.	39°26' N, 123°48' W		Hope, Ark.	33°40' N, 093°36' W
Fort Collins, Colo.	40°35' N, 105°05' W		Hot Springs, Ark.	34°31' N, 093°03' W
Fort Dodge, Ia.	42°30' N, 094°11' W		Houghton, Mich.	47°07' N, 088°34' W
Fort Lauderdale, Fla.	26°07' N, 080°08' W		Houston, Tex.	29°46' N, 095°22' W
Fort Madison, Ia.	40°38' N, 091°27' W		Hugo, Okla.	34°01' N, 095°31' W
Fort Myers, Fla.	26°39' N, 081°53' W		Huntsville, Ala.	34°44' N, 086°35' W
Fort Pierce, Fla.	27°26' N, 080°19' W		Hutchinson, Kan.	38°05' N, 097°56' W
Fort Smith, Ark.	35°23' N, 094°25' W		Idaho Falls, Idaho	43°30' N, 112°02' W
Fort Wayne, Ind.	41°04' N, 085°09' W		Independence, Mo.	39°05' N, 094°24' W
Fort Worth, Tex.	32°45' N, 097°18' W		Indianapolis, Ind.	39°46' N, 086°09' W
Frankfort, Ky.	38°12' N, 084°52' W		International Falls, Minn.	48°36' N, 093°25' W
Freeport, Ill.	42°17' N, 089°36' W		Iron Mountain, Mich.	45°49' N, 088°04' W
Freeport, Tex.	28°57' N, 095°21' W		Ironwood, Mich.	46°27' N, 090°09' W
Fremont, Neb.	41°26' N, 096°30' W		Ithaca, N.Y.	42°26' N, 076°30' W
Fresno, Calif.	36°44' N, 119°47' W		Jackson, Miss.	32°18' N, 090°12' W
Gadsden, Ala.	34°01' N, 086°01' W		Jackson, Tenn.	35°37' N, 088°49' W
Gainesville, Fla.	29°40' N, 082°20' W		Jacksonville, Fla.	30°20' N, 081°39' W
Gainesville, Ga.	34°17' N, 083°49' W		Jacksonville, N.C.	34°45' N, 077°26' W
Galena, Alaska.	64°44' N, 156°56' W		Jamestown, N.Y.	42°06' N, 079°14' W
Gallup, N.M.	35°31' N, 108°45' W		Jefferson City, Mo.	38°34' N, 092°10' W
Galveston, Tex.	29°18' N, 094°48' W		Jersey City, N.J.	40°44' N, 074°04' W
Garden City, Kan.	37°58' N, 100°52' W		Joliet, Ill.	41°32' N, 088°05' W
Garland, Tex.	32°54' N, 096°38' W		Jonesboro, Ark.	35°50' N, 090°42' W
Gary, Ind.	41°36' N, 087°20' W		Jonesboro, Ga.	33°31' N, 084°22' W
Georgetown, S.C.	33°23' N, 079°17' W		Juneau, Alaska	58°20' N, 134°27' W
Gillette, Wyo.	44°18' N, 105°30' W		Kaktovik, Alaska	70°08' N, 143°38' W
Glasgow, Ky.	37°00' N, 085°55' W		Kalamazoo, Mich.	42°17' N, 085°35' W
Glasgow, Mont.	48°12' N, 106°38' W		Kalispell, Mont.	48°12' N, 114°19' W
Glendive, Mont.	47°07' N, 104°43' W		Kansas City, Kan.	39°07' N, 094°38' W
Glenwood Springs, Colo.	39°33' N, 107°19' W		Kansas City, Mo.	39°06' N, 094°35' W
Goliad, Tex.	28°40' N, 097°23' W		Kapaa, Hawaii	22°05' N, 159°19' W
Goodland, Kan.	39°21' N, 101°43' W		Kearney, Neb.	40°42' N, 099°05' W
Grand Forks, N.D.	47°55' N, 097°03' W		Kenai, Alaska.	60°33' N, 151°16' W
Grand Island, Neb.	40°55' N, 098°21' W		Ketchikan, Alaska	55°21' N, 131°39' W
Grand Junction, Colo.	39°04' N, 108°33' W		Key Largo, Fla.	25°06' N, 080°27' W
Grand Rapids, Mich.	42°58' N, 085°40' W		Key West, Fla.	24°33' N, 081°49' W
Granite Falls, Minn.	44°49' N, 095°33' W		King City, Calif.	36°13' N, 121°08' W
Great Falls, Mont.	47°30' N, 111°17' W		Kingman, Ariz.	35°12' N, 114°04' W

Kingsville, Tex.	27°31' N, 097°52' W
Kirksville, Mo.	40°12' N, 092°35' W
Klamath Falls, Ore.	42°12' N, 121°46' W
Knoxville, Tenn.	35°58' N, 083°55' W
Kodiak, Alaska	57°47' N, 152°24' W
Kokomo, Ind.	40°30' N, 086°08' W
La Crosse, Wis.	43°48' N, 091°15' W
Lafayette, La.	30°14' N, 092°01' W
La Junta, Colo.	37°59' N, 103°33' W
Lake Charles, La.	30°14' N, 093°13' W
Lake Havasu City, Ariz.	34°29' N, 114°19' W
Lakeland, Fla.	28°03' N, 081°57' W
Lansing, Mich.	42°44' N, 084°33' W
Laramie, Wyo.	41°19' N, 105°35' W
Laredo, Tex.	27°30' N, 099°30' W
Las Cruces, N.M.	32°19' N, 106°47' W
Las Vegas, Nev.	36°01' N, 115°09' W
Las Vegas, N.M.	35°36' N, 105°13' W
Laurel, Miss.	31°41' N, 089°08' W
Lawton, Okla.	34°37' N, 098°25' W
Lebanon, N.H.	43°39' N, 072°15' W
Lewiston, Idaho	46°25' N, 117°01' W
Lewiston, Me.	44°06' N, 070°13' W
Lewiston, Mont.	47°03' N, 109°25' W
Lexington, Ky.	38°01' N, 084°30' W
Liberal, Kan.	37°02' N, 100°55' W
Lihue, Hawaii	21°59' N, 159°23' W
Lima, Ohio.	40°44' N, 084°06' W
Lincoln, Me.	45°22' N, 068°30' W
Lincoln, Neb.	40°50' N, 096°41' W
Little Rock, Ark.	34°45' N, 092°17' W
Logan, Utah.	41°44' N, 111°50' W
Long Beach, Calif.	33°47' N, 118°11' W
Los Alamos, N.M.	35°53' N, 106°19' W
Los Angeles, Calif.	34°04' N, 118°15' W
Louisville, Ky.	38°15' N, 085°46' W
Lowell, Mass.	42°38' N, 071°19' W
Lubbock, Tex.	33°35' N, 101°51' W
Lynchburg, Va.	37°25' N, 079°09' W
Macomb, Ill.	40°27' N, 090°40' W
Macon, Ga.	32°51' N, 083°38' W
Madison, Wis.	43°04' N, 089°24' W
Manchester, N.H.	43°00' N, 071°28' W
Mandan, N.D.	46°50' N, 100°54' W
Mankato, Minn.	44°10' N, 094°00' W
Marietta, Ohio.	39°25' N, 081°27' W
Marinette, Wis.	45°06' N, 087°38' W
Marion, Ind.	40°32' N, 085°40' W
Marquette, Mich.	46°33' N, 087°24' W
Massillon, Ohio.	40°48' N, 081°32' W
McAllen, Tex.	26°12' N, 098°14' W
McCall, Idaho	44°55' N, 116°06' W
McCook, Neb.	40°12' N, 100°38' W
Medford, Ore.	42°19' N, 122°52' W
Meeker, Colo.	40°02' N, 107°55' W
Melbourne, Fla.	28°05' N, 080°37' W
Memphis, Tenn.	35°08' N, 090°03' W
Meridian, Miss.	32°22' N, 088°42' W
Mesa, Ariz.	33°25' N, 111°49' W
Miami, Fla.	25°47' N, 080°11' W
Midland, Mich.	43°36' N, 084°14' W

Midland, Tex.	32°00' N, 102°05' W
Miles City, Mont.	46°25' N, 105°51' W
Milledgeville, Ga.	33°05' N, 083°14' W
Milwaukee, Wis.	43°02' N, 087°55' W
Minneapolis, Minn.	44°59' N, 093°16' W
Minot, N.D.	48°14' N, 101°18' W
Missoula, Mont.	46°52' N, 114°01' W
Mitchell, S.D.	43°43' N, 098°02' W
Moab, Utah	38°35' N, 109°33' W
Mobile, Ala.	30°41' N, 088°03' W
Moline, Ill.	41°30' N, 090°31' W
Monterey, Calif.	36°37' N, 121°55' W
Montgomery, Ala.	32°23' N, 086°19' W
Montpelier, Vt.	44°16' N, 072°35' W
Montrose, Colo.	38°29' N, 107°53' W
Morehead City, N.C.	34°43' N, 076°43' W
Morgan City, La.	29°42' N, 091°12' W
Morgantown, W.Va.	39°38' N, 079°57' W
Moscow, Idaho	46°44' N, 117°00' W
Mount Vernon, Ill.	38°19' N, 088°55' W
Murfreesboro, Ark.	34°04' N, 093°41' W
Murfreesboro, Tenn.	35°50' N, 086°23' W
Muskogee, Okla.	35°45' N, 095°22' W
Myrtle Beach, S.C.	33°42' N, 078°53' W
Naples, Fla.	26°08' N, 081°48' W
Nashville, Tenn.	36°10' N, 086°47' W
Natchez, Miss.	31°34' N, 091°24' W
Needles, Calif.	34°51' N, 114°37' W
Nevada, Mo.	37°51' N, 094°22' W
New Albany, Ind.	38°18' N, 085°49' W
Newark, N.J.	40°44' N, 074°10' W
New Bedford, Mass.	41°38' N, 070°56' W
New Bern, N.C.	35°07' N, 077°03' W
Newcastle, Wyo.	43°50' N, 104°11' W
New Haven, Conn.	41°18' N, 072°55' W
New Madrid, Mo.	36°36' N, 089°32' W
New Orleans, La.	29°58' N, 090°04' W
Newport, Ore.	44°39' N, 124°03' W
Newport, R.I.	41°29' N, 071°18' W
Newport News, Va.	36°59' N, 076°25' W
New York City, N.Y.	40°43' N, 074°00' W
Niagara Falls, N.Y.	43°06' N, 079°03' W
Nogales, Ariz.	31°20' N, 110°56' W
Nome, Alaska	64°30' N, 165°25' W
Norfolk, Va.	36°51' N, 076°17' W
Norman, Okla.	35°13' N, 097°26' W
North Augusta, S.C.	33°30' N, 081°59' W
North Platte, Neb.	41°08' N, 100°46' W
Oakland, Calif.	37°49' N, 122°16' W
Ocala, Fla.	29°11' N, 082°08' W
Oceanside, Calif.	33°12' N, 117°23' W
Odessa, Tex.	31°52' N, 102°23' W
Ogallala, Neb.	41°08' N, 101°43' W
Ogden, Utah	41°13' N, 111°58' W
Oklahoma City, Okla.	35°30' N, 097°30' W
Olympia, Wash.	47°03' N, 122°53' W
Omaha, Neb.	41°17' N, 096°01' W
O'Neill, Neb.	42°27' N, 098°39' W
Orem, Utah	40°18' N, 111°42' W
Orlando, Fla.	28°33' N, 081°23' W
Oshkosh, Wis.	44°01' N, 088°33' W

Ottawa, Ill.	41°20' N, 088°50' W
Ottumwa, Ia.	41°01' N, 092°25' W
Overton, Nev.	36°33' N, 114°27' W
Owensboro, Ky.	37°46' N, 087°07' W
Paducah, Ky.	37°05' N, 088°37' W
Pahala, Hawaii.	19°12' N, 155°29' W
Palm Springs, Calif.	33°50' N, 116°33' W
Palo Alto, Calif.	37°27' N, 122°10' W
Panama City, Fla.	30°10' N, 085°40' W
Paris, Tex.	33°40' N, 095°33' W
Parsons, Kan.	37°20' N, 095°16' W
Pasadena, Calif.	34°09' N, 118°09' W
Pasadena, Tex.	29°43' N, 095°13' W
Pascagoula, Miss.	30°21' N, 088°33' W
Paterson, N.J.	40°55' N, 074°11' W
Pecos, Tex.	31°26' N, 103°30' W
Pendleton, Ore.	45°40' N, 118°47' W
Pensacola, Fla.	30°25' N, 087°13' W
Peoria, Ill.	40°42' N, 089°36' W
Petoskey, Mich.	45°22' N, 084°57' W
Philadelphia, Pa.	39°57' N, 075°10' W
Phoenix, Ariz.	33°27' N, 112°04' W
Pierre, S.D.	44°22' N, 100°21' W
Pine Bluff, Ark.	34°13' N, 092°01' W
Pittsburgh, Pa.	40°26' N, 080°01' W
Plano, Tex.	33°01' N, 096°41' W
Plattsburgh, N.Y.	44°42' N, 073°27' W
Pocatello, Idaho	42°52' N, 112°27' W
Point Hope, Alaska	68°21' N, 166°41' W
Port Gibson, Miss.	31°58' N, 090°59' W
Port Lavaca, Tex.	28°37' N, 096°38' W
Port Royal, S.C.	32°23' N, 080°42' W
Portland, Me.	43°39' N, 070°16' W
Portland, Ore.	45°32' N, 122°37' W
Prescott, Ariz.	34°33' N, 112°28' W
Presque Isle, Me.	46°41' N, 068°01' W
Providence, R.I.	41°49' N, 071°24' W
Provo, Utah	40°14' N, 111°39' W
Pueblo, Colo.	38°15' N, 104°36' W
Pullman, Wash.	46°44' N, 117°10' W
Racine, Wis.	42°44' N, 087°48' W
Raleigh, N.C.	35°46' N, 078°38' W
Rapid City, S.D.	44°05' N, 103°14' W
Red Bluff, Calif.	40°11' N, 122°15' W
Redding, Calif.	40°35' N, 122°24' W
Redfield, S.D.	44°53' N, 098°31' W
Reno, Nev.	39°31' N, 119°48' W
Rice Lake, Wis.	45°30' N, 091°44' W
Richfield, Utah	38°46' N, 112°05' W
Richmond, Ind.	39°50' N, 084°54' W
Richmond, Va.	37°33' N, 077°27' W
Riverside, Calif.	33°59' N, 117°22' W
Riverton, Wyo.	43°02' N, 108°23' W
Roanoke, Va.	37°16' N, 079°56' W
Rochester, Minn.	44°01' N, 092°28' W
Rochester, N.Y.	43°10' N, 077°37' W
Rock Hill, S.C.	34°56' N, 081°01' W
Rock Island, Ill.	41°30' N, 090°34' W
Rock Springs, Wyo.	41°35' N, 109°12' W
Rockford, Ill.	42°16' N, 089°06' W
Rolla, Mo.	37°57' N, 091°46' W
Rome, Ga.	34°15' N, 085°09' W
Roseburg, Ore.	43°13' N, 123°20' W
Roswell, N.M.	33°24' N, 104°32' W
Sacramento, Calif.	38°35' N, 121°29' W
Saginaw, Mich.	43°26' N, 083°56' W
Salem, Ore.	44°56' N, 123°02' W
Salina, Kan.	38°50' N, 097°37' W
Salinas, Calif.	36°40' N, 121°39' W
Salmon, Idaho	45°11' N, 113°54' W
Salt Lake City, Utah	40°45' N, 111°53' W
San Angelo, Tex.	31°28' N, 100°26' W
San Antonio, Tex.	29°25' N, 098°30' W
San Bernardino, Calif.	34°07' N, 117°19' W
San Diego, Calif.	32°43' N, 117°09' W
San Francisco, Calif.	37°47' N, 122°25' W
San Jose, Calif.	37°20' N, 121°53' W
San Luis Obispo, Calif.	35°17' N, 120°40' W
Sanderson, Tex.	30°09' N, 102°24' W
Santa Ana, Calif.	33°46' N, 117°52' W
Santa Barbara, Calif.	34°25' N, 119°42' W
Santa Fe, N.M.	35°41' N, 105°57' W
Santa Maria, Calif.	34°57' N, 120°26' W
Sarasota, Fla.	27°20' N, 082°32' W
Sault Ste. Marie, Mich.	46°30' N, 084°21' W
Savannah, Ga.	32°05' N, 081°06' W
Scott City, Kan.	38°29' N, 100°54' W
Scottsbluff, Neb.	41°52' N, 103°40' W
Scottsdale, Ariz.	33°29' N, 111°56' W
Searcy, Ark.	35°15' N, 091°44' W
Seattle, Wash.	47°36' N, 122°20' W
Sebring, Fla.	27°30' N, 081°27' W
Seguin, Tex.	29°34' N, 097°58' W
Selawik, Alaska	66°36' N, 160°00' W
Seldovia, Alaska	59°26' N, 151°43' W
Selma, Ala.	32°25' N, 087°01' W
Sharpsburg, Md.	39°28' N, 077°45' W
Sheboygan, Wis.	43°45' N, 087°42' W
Sheridan, Wyo.	44°48' N, 106°58' W
Show Low, Ariz.	34°15' N, 110°02' W
Shreveport, La.	32°31' N, 093°45' W
Sierra Vista, Ariz.	31°33' N, 110°18' W
Silver City, N.M.	32°46' N, 108°17' W
Sioux City, Ia.	42°30' N, 096°24' W
Sioux Falls, S.D.	43°33' N, 096°44' W
Skagway, Alaska	59°28' N, 135°19' W
Snyder, Tex.	32°44' N, 100°55' W
Socorro, N.M.	34°04' N, 106°54' W
Somerset, Ky.	37°05' N, 084°36' W
South Bend, Ind.	41°41' N, 086°15' W
Sparks, Nev.	39°32' N, 119°45' W
Spencer, Ia.	43°09' N, 095°10' W
Spokane, Wash.	47°40' N, 117°24' W
Springfield, Ill.	39°48' N, 089°38' W
Springfield, Mo.	37°13' N, 093°17' W
St. Augustine, Fla.	29°54' N, 081°19' W
St. Cloud, Minn.	45°34' N, 094°10' W
St. George, Utah	37°06' N, 113°35' W
St. Joseph, Mo.	39°46' N, 094°50' W
St. Louis, Mo.	38°37' N, 090°11' W
St. Maries, Idaho	47°19' N, 116°35' W
St. Paul, Minn.	44°57' N, 093°06' W

St. Petersburg, Fla. . . . . . . 27°46' N, 082°39' W
State College, Pa. . . . . 40°48' N, 077°52' W
Ste. Genevieve, Mo. . . . . . 37°59' N, 090°03' W
Steamboat Springs, Colo. . . 40°29' N, 106°50' W
Stillwater, Minn. . . . . 45°03' N, 092°49' W
Sumter, S.C. . . . . 33°55' N, 080°21' W
Sun Valley, Idaho . . . . 43°42' N, 114°21' W
Superior, Wis. . . . . 46°44' N, 092°06' W
Syracuse, N.Y. . . . . 43°03' N, 076°09' W
Tacoma, Wash. . . . . 47°14' N, 122°26' W
Tallahassee, Fla. . . . . 30°27' N, 084°17' W
Tampa, Fla. . . . . 27°57' N, 082°27' W
Tempe, Ariz. . . . . 33°25' N, 111°56' W
Temple, Tex. . . . . 31°06' N, 097°21' W
Terre Haute, Ind. . . . . 39°28' N, 087°25' W
Texarkana, Ark. . . . . 33°26' N, 094°03' W
Thief River Falls, Minn. . . . 48°07' N, 096°10' W
Tifton, Ga. . . . . 31°27' N, 083°31' W
Titusville, Fla. . . . . 28°37' N, 080°49' W
Toledo, Ohio . . . . 41°39' N, 083°33' W
Tonopah, Nev. . . . . 38°04' N, 117°14' W
Topeka, Kan. . . . . 39°03' N, 095°40' W
Traverse City, Mich. . . . . . 44°46' N, 085°38' W
Trenton, N.J. . . . . 40°14' N, 074°46' W
Trinidad, Colo. . . . . 37°10' N, 104°31' W
Troy, Ala. . . . . 31°48' N, 085°58' W
Troy, N.Y. . . . . 42°44' N, 073°41' W
Tucson, Ariz. . . . . 32°13' N, 110°58' W
Tulsa, Okla. . . . . 36°10' N, 095°55' W
Tupelo, Miss. . . . . 34°16' N, 088°43' W
Tuscaloosa, Ala. . . . . 33°12' N, 087°34' W
Twin Falls, Idaho. . . . . 42°34' N, 114°28' W
Tyler, Tex. . . . . 32°21' N, 095°18' W
Ukiah, Calif. . . . . 39°09' N, 123°12' W
Utica, N.Y. . . . . 43°06' N, 075°14' W
Uvalde, Tex. . . . . 29°13' N, 099°47' W
Valdez, Alaska. . . . . 61°07' N, 146°16' W
Valdosta, Ga. . . . . 30°50' N, 083°17' W
Valentine, Neb. . . . . 42°52' N, 100°33' W
Vero Beach, Fla. . . . . 27°38' N, 080°24' W
Vicksburg, Miss. . . . . 32°21' N, 090°53' W
Victoria, Tex. . . . . 28°48' N, 097°00' W
Vincennes, Ind. . . . . 38°41' N, 087°32' W
Virginia Beach, Va. . . . . . . 36°51' N, 075°59' W
Waco, Tex. . . . . 31°33' N, 097°09' W
Wahpeton, N.D. . . . . 46°15' N, 096°36' W
Wailuku, Hawaii . . . . 20°53' N, 156°30' W
Walla Walla, Wash. . . . . . . 46°04' N, 118°20' W
Warren, Pa. . . . . 41°51' N, 079°08' W
Washington, D.C. . . . . 38°54' N, 077°02' W
Waterloo, Ia. . . . . 42°30' N, 092°21' W
Watertown, N.Y. . . . . 43°59' N, 075°55' W
Waycross, Ga. . . . . 31°13' N, 082°21' W
Wayne, Neb. . . . . 42°14' N, 097°01' W
Weiser, Idaho . . . . 44°45' N, 116°58' W
West Palm Beach, Fla. . . . . 26°43' N, 080°03' W
Wheeling, W.Va. . . . . 40°04' N, 080°43' W
Wichita, Kan. . . . . 37°42' N, 097°20' W
Wichita Falls, Tex. . . . . . . 33°54' N, 098°30' W
Williamsport, Pa. . . . . 41°15' N, 077°00' W
Wilmington, N.C. . . . . 34°14' N, 077°55' W

Winfield, Kan. . . . . 37°15' N, 096°59' W
Winnemucca, Nev. . . . . . . 40°58' N, 117°44' W
Winslow, Ariz. . . . . 35°02' N, 110°42' W
Winston-Salem, N.C. . . . . . 36°06' N, 080°14' W
Worcester, Mass. . . . . 42°16' N, 071°48' W
Worthington, Minn. . . . . . . 43°37' N, 095°36' W
Wrangell, Alaska. . . . . 56°28' N, 132°23' W
Yakima, Wash. . . . . 46°36' N, 120°31' W
Yankton, S.D. . . . . 42°53' N, 097°23' W
Yazoo City, Miss. . . . . 32°51' N, 090°25' W
Youngstown, Ohio . . . . . . 41°06' N, 080°39' W
Yuba City, Calif. . . . . 39°08' N, 121°37' W
Yuma, Ariz. . . . . 32°43' N, 114°37' W
Zanesville, Ohio . . . . 39°56' N, 082°01' W

URUGUAY . . . . . . .pg. 184

Aiguá . . . . 34°12' S, 054°45' W
Artigas . . . . 30°24' S, 056°28' W
Belén . . . . 30°47' S, 057°47' W
Bella Unión . . . . 30°15' S, 057°35' W
Carmelo . . . . 34°00' S, 058°17' W
Castillos. . . . . 34°12' S, 053°50' W
Casupá . . . . 34°07' S, 055°39' W
Chuy . . . . 33°41' S, 053°27' W
Colonia . . . . 34°28' S, 057°51' W
Constitución . . . . 31°05' S, 057°50' W
Dolores . . . . 33°33' S, 058°13' W
Durazno . . . . 33°22' S, 056°31' W
Florida . . . . 34°06' S, 056°13' W
Lascano . . . . 33°40' S, 054°12'W
Las Piedras . . . . 34°44' S, 056°13' W
Maldonado . . . . 34°54' S, 054°57' W
Melo . . . . 32°22' S, 054°11' W
Mercedes . . . . 33°16' S, 058°01' W
Minas . . . . 34°23' S, 055°14' W
Montevideo . . . . 34°53' S, 056°11' W
Nuevo Berlín . . . . 32°59' S, 058°03' W
Pando . . . . 34°43' S, 055°57' W
Paysandú . . . . 32°19' S, 058°05' W
Rio Branco . . . . 32°34' S, 053°25' W
Rivera . . . . 30°54' S, 055°31' W
Rocha . . . . 34°29' S, 054°20' W
Salto. . . . . 31°23' S, 057°58' W
San Carlos . . . . 34°48' S, 054°55' W
San Gregorio . . . . 32°37' S, 055°40' W
San José. . . . . 34°20' S, 056°42' W
Santa Clara . . . . 32°55' S, 054°58' W
Suárez (Tarariras) . . . . 34°17' S, 057°37' W
Tacuarembó
   (San Fructuoso). . . . . . . 31°44' S, 055°59' W
Tranqueras . . . . 31°12' S, 055°45' W
Treinta y Tres . . . . 33°14' S, 054°23' W
Trinidad . . . . 33°32' S, 056°54' W
Vergara . . . . 32°56' S, 053°57' W
Young . . . . 32°41' S, 057°38' W

UZBEKISTAN . . . .pg. 185

Andijon . . . . 40°45' N, 072°22' E

Angren	41°01' N,	070°12' E
Bekobod	40°13' N,	069°14' E
Beruniy (Biruni)	41°42' N,	060°44' E
Bukhara (Bokhoro)	39°48' N,	064°25' E
Chirchiq	41°29' N,	069°35' E
Denow	38°16' N,	067°54' E
Fergana (Farghona)	40°23' N,	071°46' E
Guliston	40°29' N,	068°46' E
Jizzakh	40°06' N,	067°50' E
Kattaqŭrghon	39°55' N,	066°15' E
Khiva (Khiwa)	41°24' N,	060°22' E
Khonqa	41°28' N,	060°47' E
Kogon	39°43' N,	064°33' E
Marghilon	40°27' N,	071°42' E
Namangan	41°00' N,	071°40' E
Nawoiy	40°09' N,	065°22' E
Nukus	42°29' N,	059°38' E
Olmaliq	40°50' N,	069°35' E
Qarshi	38°53' N,	065°48' E
Qŭqon	40°30' N,	070°57' E
Samarkand	39°40' N,	066°58' E
Tashkent (Toshkent)	41°20' N,	069°18' E
Termiz	37°14' N,	067°16' E
Urganch	41°33' N,	060°38' E
Zarafshon	41°31' N,	064°15' E

VANUATU . . . . pg. 186

Ipayato	15°38' S,	166°52' E
Isangel	19°33' S,	169°16' E
Lakatoro	16°07' S,	167°25' E
Lalinda	16°21' S,	168°03' E
Laol	16°41' S,	168°16' E
Loltong	15°33' S,	168°09' E
Luganville	15°32' S,	167°10' E
Lumbukuti	16°55' S,	168°32' E
Natapao	17°37' S,	168°13' E
Norsup	16°04' S,	167°23' E
Port Olry	15°03' S,	167°04' E
Unpongkor	18°49' S,	169°01' E
Veutumboso	13°54' S,	167°27' E
Vila (Port-Vila)	17°44' S,	168°18' E

VENEZUELA . . . . . pg. 187

Barcelona	10°08' N,	064°42' W
Barinas	08°38' N,	070°12' W
Barquisimeto	10°04' N,	069°19' W
Cabimas	10°23' N,	071°28' W
Caicara (Caicara de		
Orinoco)	07°37' N,	066°10' W
Caicara	09°49' N,	063°36' W
Caracas	10°30' N,	066°55' W
Ciudad Bolívar	08°08' N,	063°33' W
Ciudad Guayana		
(San Felix)	08°23' N,	062°40' W
Coro	11°25' N,	069°41' W
Cumaná	10°28' N,	064°10' W
Guasdualito	07°15' N,	070°44' W
La Asunción	11°02' N,	063°53' W

Maracaibo	10°40' N,	071°37' W
Maracay	10°15' N,	067°36' W
Maturín	09°45' N,	063°11' W
Mérida	08°36' N,	071°08' W
Pariaguán	08°51' N,	064°43' W
Petare	10°29' N,	066°49' W
Puerto Ayacucho	05°40' N,	067°35' W
Punto Fijo	11°42' N,	070°13' W
San Carlos de		
Río Negro	01°55' N,	067°04' W
San Cristóbal	07°46' N,	072°14' W
San Fernando de Apure	07°54' N,	067°28' W
San Fernando		
de Atabapo	04°03' N,	067°42' W
Santa Elena	04°37' N,	061°08' W
Tucupita	09°04' N,	062°03' W
Upata	08°01' N,	062°24' W
Valencia	10°11' N,	068°00' W
Valera	09°19' N,	070°37' W

VIETNAM . . . . pg. 188

Bac Can	22°08' N,	105°50' E
Bac Giang	21°16' N,	106°12' E
Bac Lieu	09°17' N,	105°43' E
Bien Hoa	10°57' N,	106°49' E
Buon Me Thuot		
(Lac Giao)	12°40' N,	108°03' E
Ca Mau	09°11' N,	105°08' E
Cam Pha	21°01' N,	107°19' E
Cam Ranh	11°54' N,	109°13' E
Can Tho	10°02' N,	105°47' E
Chau Doc	10°42' N,	105°07' E
Da Lat	11°56' N,	108°25' E
Da Nang (Tourane)	16°04' N,	108°13' E
Dong Ha	16°49' N,	107°08' E
Dong Hoi	17°29' N,	106°36' E
Go Cong	10°22' N,	106°40' E
Ha Giang	22°50' N,	104°59' E
Hai Duong	20°56' N,	106°19' E
Haiphong (Hai Phong)	20°52' N,	106°41' E
Hanoi (Ha Noi)	21°02' N,	105°51' E
Ha Tinh	18°20' N,	105°54' E
Hoa Binh	20°50' N,	105°20' E
Ho Chi Minh City		
(Saigon)	10°45' N,	106°40' E
Hoi An	15°52' N,	108°19' E
Hong Gai (Hon Gai)	20°57' N,	107°05' E
Hue	16°28' N,	107°36' E
Kon Tum (Cong Tum or		
Kontun)	14°21' N,	108°00' E
Lai Chau	22°04' N,	103°10' E
Lao Caí	22°30' N,	103°58' E
Long Xuyen	10°23' N,	105°25' E
Minh Hoa	17°47' N,	106°01' E
My Tho	10°21' N,	106°21' E
Nam Dinh	20°25' N,	106°10' E
Nha Trang	12°15' N,	109°11' E
Phan Rang	11°34' N,	108°59' E
Phan Thiet	10°56' N,	108°06' E
Pleiku (Play Cu)	13°59' N,	108°00' E

Quan Long	09°11' N,	105°08' E
Quang Ngai	15°07' N,	108°48' E
Qui Nhon	13°46' N,	109°14' E
Rach Gia	10°01' N,	105°05' E
Sa Dec	10°18' N,	105°46' E
Soc Trang	09°36' N,	105°58' E
Son La	21°19' N,	103°54' E
Tam Ky	15°34' N,	108°29' E
Tan An	10°32' N,	106°25' E
Thai Binh	20°27' N,	106°20' E
Thai Nguyen	21°36' N,	105°50' E
Thanh Hoa	19°48' N,	105°46' E
Tuy Hoa	13°05' N,	109°18' E
Viet Tri	21°18' N,	105°26' E
Vinh	18°40' N,	105°40' E
Vung Tau	10°21' N,	107°04' E
Yen Bai	21°42' N,	104°52' E

YEMEN . . . . pg. 189

Aden ('Adan)	12°46' N,	045°02' E
Aḥwar	13°31' N,	046°42' E
Al-Bayḍā'	13°58' N,	045°35' E
Al-Ghaydah	16°13' N,	052°11' E
Al-Ḥudaydah	14°48' N,	042°57' E
Al-Luḥayyah	15°43' N,	042°42' E
Al-Mukallā	14°32' N,	049°08' E
Balḥāf	13°58' N,	048°11' E
Dhamār	14°33' N,	044°24' E
Ibb	13°58' N,	044°11' E
Laḥij	13°04' N,	044°53' E
Madīnat ash-Sha'b	12°50' N,	044°56' E
Ma'rib	15°25' N,	045°21' E
Min'ar	16°43' N,	051°18' E
Mocha (al-Mukha)	13°19' N,	043°15' E
Niṣāb	14°31' N,	046°30' E
Raydah	15°50' N,	044°03' E
Sa'dah	16°57' N,	043°46' E
Ṣalīf	15°18' N,	042°41' E
Ṣan'ā'	15°21' N,	044°12' E
Sayḥūt	15°12' N,	051°14' E
Saywūn (Say'un)	15°56' N,	048°47' E
Shabwah	15°22' N,	047°01' E
Shahārah	16°11' N,	043°42' E
Ta'izz	13°34' N,	044°02' E
Tarīm	16°03' N,	049°00' E
Zabīd	14°12' N,	043°19' E
Zinjibār	13°08' N,	045°23' E

YUGOSLAVIA . . . . pg. 190

Bar	42°05' N,	019°06' E
Belgrade	44°50' N,	020°30' E
Bor	44°06' N,	022°06' E
Cacak	43°54' N,	020°21' E
Gornji Milanovac	44°02' N,	020°27' E
Kikinda	45°50' N,	020°29' E
Knjaževac	43°34' N,	022°15' E
Kosovska Mitrovica (Titova Mitrovica)	42°53' N,	020°52' E

Kragujevac	44°01' N,	020°55' E
Kraljevo	43°44' N,	020°43' E
Kruševac	43°35' N,	021°20' E
Leskovac	42°59' N,	021°57' E
Majdanpek	44°25' N,	021°56' E
Nikšić	42°46' N,	018°58' E
Nis	43°19' N,	021°54' E
Novi Beograd	44°49' N,	020°27' E
Novi Pazar	43°08' N,	020°31' E
Novi Sad	45°15' N,	019°50' E
Pancevo	44°52' N,	020°39' E
Pirot	43°09' N,	022°36' E
Podgorica (Titograd)	42°26' N,	019°16' E
Priboj	43°35' N,	019°32' E
Priština	42°40' N,	021°10' E
Prizren	42°13' N,	020°45' E
Sabac	44°45' N,	019°43' E
Smederevo	44°39' N,	020°56' E
Sombor	45°46' N,	019°07' E
Sremski Karlovci	45°12' N,	019°56' E
Subotica	46°06' N,	019°40' E
Titovo Užice (Užice)	43°52' N,	019°51' E
Valjevo	44°16' N,	019°53' E
Vranje	42°33' N,	021°54' E
Zrenjanin	45°23' N,	020°23' E

ZAMBIA . . . . pg. 191

Chililabombwe (Bancroft)	12°22' S,	027°50' E
Chingola	12°32' S,	027°52' E
Chipata (Fort Jameson)	13°39' S,	032°40' E
Isoka	10°08' S,	032°38' E
Kabwe (Broken Hill)	14°27' S,	028°27' E
Kalabo	14°58' S,	022°41' E
Kalulushi	12°50' S,	028°05' E
Kasama	10°13' S,	031°12' E
Kawambwa	09°47' S,	029°05' E
Kitwe	12°49' S,	028°13' E
Livingstone (Maramba)	17°51' S,	025°52' E
Luanshya	13°08' S,	028°25' E
Lusaka	15°25' S,	028°17' E
Mansa (Fort Rosebery)	11°12' S,	028°53' E
Mazabuka	15°51' S,	027°46' E
Mongu	15°17' S,	023°08' E
Monze	16°16' S,	027°29' E
Mpika	11°50' S,	031°27' E
Mumbwa	14°59' S,	027°04' E
Mwamfuli (Samfya)	11°21' S,	029°33' E
Nchelenge	09°21' S,	029°44' E
Ndola	12°58' S,	028°38' E
Senanga	16°07' S,	023°16' E
Serenje	13°14' S,	030°14' E
Zambezi	13°33' S,	023°07' E

ZIMBABWE . . . . . . pg. 192

Beitbridge	22°13' S,	030°00' E
Bulawayo	20°09' S,	028°35' E

Chimanimani (Mandidzudzure, or Melsetter)	19°48' S,	032°52' E
Chinhoyi (Sinoia)	17°22' S,	030°12' E
Chipinge	20°12' S,	032°37' E
Chiredzi	21°03' S,	031°40' E
Chitungwiza	18°47' S,	032°37' E
Empress Mine Township	18°27' S,	029°27' E
Gweru (Gwelo)	19°27' S,	029°49' E
Harare (Salisbury)	17°50' S,	031°03' E
Hwange (Wankie)	18°22' S,	026°29' E
Inyanga	18°13' S,	032°45' E
Kadoma (Gatooma)	18°21' S,	029°55' E
Kariba	16°31' S,	028°48' E
Karoi	16°49' S,	029°41' E
Kwekwe (Que Que)	18°55' S,	029°49' E

Marondera (Marandellas)	18°11' S,	031°33' E
Mashava	20°03' S,	030°29' E
Masvingo (Fort Victoria, or Nyanda)	20°05' S,	030°50' E
Mhangura	16°54' S,	030°09' E
Mount Darwin	16°47' S,	031°35' E
Mvuma	19°17' S,	030°32' E
Mutare (Umtali)	18°58' S,	032°40' E
Norton	17°53' S,	030°42' E
Redcliff	19°02' S,	029°47' E
Shamva	17°19' S,	031°34' E
Shurugwi (Selukwe)	19°40' S,	030°00' E
Triangle	21°02' S,	031°27' E
Tuli	21°55' S,	029°12' E
Victoria Falls	17°56' S,	025°50' E

Acronyms for International Organizations

ACP	African, Caribbean, and Pacific Convention
ADB	Asian Development Bank
APEC	Asia-Pacific Economic Cooperation Council
CARICOM	Caribbean Community and Common Market
EEC	European Economic Community
EU	The European Union
FAO	Food and Agriculture Organization
GCC	Gulf Cooperation Council
I-ADB	Inter-American Development Bank
IDB	Islamic Development Bank
ILO	International Labour Organization
IMF	International Monetary Fund
ITU	International Telecommunications Union
OAS	Organization of American States
OAU	Organization of African Unity
OPEC	Organization of Petroleum Exporting Countries
SPC	South Pacific Commission
UNICEF	United Nations Children's Fund
UNESCO	United Nations Educational, Scientific, and Cultural Organization
WHO	World Health Organization
WTO	World Trade Organization (formerly General Agreement on Tariffs and Trade, GATT)

Country	National Capital	Population of National Capital	United Nations (date of admission)	UNICEF	FAO	ILO
Afghanistan	Kābul	700,000	1946	•	•	•
Albania	Tiranë	300,000	1955	•	•	•
Algeria	Algiers	1,507,241	1962	•	•	•
Andorra	Andorra la Vella	22,821	1993			
Angola	Luanda	2,000,000	1976	•	•	•
Antigua and Barbuda	Saint John's	21,514	1981	•	•	•
Argentina	Buenos Aires	2,988,006	1945	•	•	•
Armenia	Yerevan	1,226,000	1992	•	•	•
Australia	Canberra	303,700	1945	•	•	•
Austria	Vienna	1,539,848	1955	•	•	•
Azerbaijan	Baku	1,087,000	1992	•	•	•
Bahamas, The	Nassau	172,196	1973	•	•	•
Bahrain	Manama	140,401	1971	•	•	•
Bangladesh	Dhākā (Dacca)	3,839,000	1974	•	•	•
Barbados	Bridgetown	6,070	1966	•	•	•
Belarus	Minsk	1,700,000	1945	•		•
Belgium	Brussels	136,424	1945	•	•	•
Belize	Belmopan	3,927	1981	•	•	•
Benin	Cotonou (official)	533,212	1960	•	•	•
	Porto-Novo (de facto)	177,660				
Bhutan	Thimphu	30,340	1971	•	•	
Bolivia	La Paz (administrative)	784,976	1945	•	•	•
	Sucre (judicial)	144,994				
Bosnia and Herzegovina	Sarajevo	250,000	1992	•	•	•
Botswana	Gaborone	156,803	1966	•	•	•
Brazil	Brasília	1,492,542	1945	•	•	•
Brunei	Bandar Seri Begawan	21,484	1984			
Bulgaria	Sofia	1,116,823	1955	•	•	•
Burkina Faso	Ouagadougou	690,000	1960	•	•	•
Burundi	Bujumbura	300,000	1962	•	•	•
Cambodia	Phnom Penh	920,000	1955	•	•	•
Cameroon	Yaoundé	800,000	1960	•	•	•
Canada	Ottawa	313,987	1945	•	•	•
Cape Verde	Praia	61,644	1975	•	•	•
Central African Republic	Bangui	524,000	1960	•	•	•
Chad	N'Djamena	530,965	1960	•	•	•
Chile	Santiago	5,076,808	1945	•	•	•
China	Beijing (Peking)	7,000,000	1945	•	•	•
Colombia	Bogotá	5,237,635	1945	•	•	•
Comoros	Moroni	30,000	1975	•	•	•
Congo, Democratic Republic of the	Kinshasa	4,655,313	1960	•	•	•
Congo, Republic of the	Brazzaville	937,579	1960	•	•	•
Costa Rica	San José	321,193	1945	•	•	•
Croatia	Zagreb	867,717	1992	•	•	•
Cuba	Havana	2,241,000	1945	•	•	•
Cyprus	Nicosia (Lefkosia)	186,400	1960	•	•	•
Czech Republic	Prague	1,213,299	1993	•		•
Denmark	Copenhagen	1,353,333	1945	•	•	•
Djibouti	Djibouti	317,000	1977	•	•	•
Dominica	Roseau	15,853	1978	•	•	•

IMF	ITU	UNESCO	WHO	WTO	Commonwealth of Nations	EU	GCC	OAS	OAU	SPC	ACP	ADB	APEC	CARICOM	EEC	I-ADB	IDB	OPEC	Country
•	•	•	•									•					•		Afghanistan
•	•	•	•	•													•		Albania
•	•	•	•	•					•								•	•	Algeria
	•	•	•					•											Andorra
•	•	•	•	•					•		•								Angola
•	•	•	•	•	•			•			•			•					Antigua and Barbuda
•	•	•	•	•				•								•			Argentina
•	•	•	•																Armenia
•	•	•	•	•	•					•		•	•						Australia
•	•	•	•	•		•						•			•	•			Austria
•	•	•	•														•		Azerbaijan
•	•	•	•		•			•			•			•		•			Bahamas, The
•	•	•	•	•			•										•		Bahrain
•	•	•	•	•	•							•					•		Bangladesh
•	•	•	•	•	•			•			•			•		•			Barbados
•	•	•	•	•															Belarus
•	•	•	•	•		•						•			•	•			Belgium
•	•	•	•	•	•			•			•			•		•			Belize
•	•	•	•	•					•		•						•		Benin
•	•	•	•									•							Bhutan
•	•	•	•	•				•								•			Bolivia
•	•	•	•																Bosnia and Herzegovina
•	•	•	•	•	•				•		•								Botswana
•	•	•	•	•				•								•			Brazil
	•	•	•	•	•								•				•		Brunei
•	•	•	•	•															Bulgaria
•	•	•	•	•					•		•						•		Burkina Faso
•	•	•	•	•					•		•								Burundi
•	•	•	•									•							Cambodia
•	•	•	•	•	•				•		•						•		Cameroon
•	•	•	•	•	•			•				•	•			•			Canada
•	•	•	•						•		•								Cape Verde
•	•	•	•	•					•		•								Central African Republic
•	•	•	•	•					•		•						•		Chad
•	•	•	•	•				•					•			•			Chile
•	•	•	•	•								•	•						China
•	•	•	•	•				•								•			Colombia
•	•	•	•						•		•						•		Comoros
•	•	•	•	•					•		•								Congo, Democratic Republic of the
•	•	•	•	•					•		•								Congo, Republic of the
•	•	•	•	•				•								•			Costa Rica
•	•	•	•	•															Croatia
	•	•	•	•				•											Cuba
•	•	•	•	•	•											•			Cyprus
•	•	•	•	•															Czech Republic
•	•	•	•	•		•						•			•	•			Denmark
•	•	•	•	•					•		•						•		Djibouti
•	•	•	•	•	•			•			•			•		•			Dominica

Country	National Capital	Population of National Capital	United Nations (date of admission)	UNICEF	FAO	ILO
Dominican Republic	Santo Domingo	2,138,262	1945	•	•	•
Ecuador	Quito	1,444,363	1945	•	•	•
Egypt	Cairo	6,849,000	1945	•	•	•
El Salvador	San Salvador	422,570	1945	•	•	•
Equatorial Guinea	Malabo	58,040	1968	•	•	•
Eritrea	Asmara	367,300	1993	•	•	•
Estonia	Tallinn	434,763	1991	•	•	•
Ethiopia	Addis Ababa	2,316,400	1945	•	•	•
Fiji	Suva	200,000	1970	•	•	•
Finland	Helsinki	525,031	1955	•	•	•
France	Paris	2,175,200	1945	•	•	•
Gabon	Libreville	362,386	1960	•	•	•
Gambia, The	Banjul	42,407	1965	•	•	•
Georgia	Tbilisi	1,279,000	1992	•	•	•
Germany	Berlin	293,072	1973	•	•	•
Ghana	Accra	1,781,100	1957	•	•	•
Greece	Athens	748,110	1945	•	•	•
Grenada	Saint George's	4,621	1974	•	•	•
Guatemala	Guatemala City	823,301	1945	•	•	•
Guinea	Conakry	1,508,000	1958	•	•	•
Guinea-Bissau	Bissau	197,610	1974	•	•	•
Guyana	Georgetown	248,500	1966	•	•	•
Haiti	Port-au-Prince	846,247	1945	•	•	•
Honduras	Tegucigalpa	775,300	1945	•	•	•
Hungary	Budapest	1,909,000	1955	•	•	•
Iceland	Reykjavik	104,276	1946	•	•	•
India	New Delhi	301,297	1945	•	•	•
Indonesia	Jakarta	8,259,266	1950	•	•	•
Iran	Tehrān	11,000,000	1945	•	•	•
Iraq	Baghdad	4,478,000	1945	•	•	•
Ireland	Dublin	478,389	1955	•	•	•
Israel	Jerusalem (Yerushalayim, Al-Quds)	591,400	1949	•	•	•
Italy	Rome (Roma)	2,687,881	1955	•	•	•
Ivory Coast	Yamoussoukro (de jure; administrative)	106,786	1960	•	•	•
Jamaica	Kingston	103,771	1962	•	•	•
Japan	Tokyo	7,966,195	1956	•	•	•
Jordan	Amman	963,490	1955	•	•	•
Kazakstan	Astana	1,150,500	1992	•	•	•
Kenya	Nairobi	2,000,000	1963	•	•	•
Kiribati	Bairki	2,226	1999	•		
Kuwait	Kuwait (Al-Kuwayt)	31,241	1963	•	•	•
Kyrgyzstan	Bishkek (Frunze)	597,000	1992	•	•	•
Laos	Vientiane (Viangchan)	442,000	1955	•	•	•
Latvia	Rīga	839,670	1991	•	•	•
Lebanon	Beirut (Bayrūt)	1,100,000	1945	•	•	•
Lesotho	Maseru	170,000	1966	•	•	•
Liberia	Monrovia	668,000	1945	•	•	•
Libya	Tripoli (Ṭarābulus)	591,062	1955	•	•	•
Liechtenstein	Vaduz	5,067	1990			

IMF	ITU	UNESCO	WHO	WTO	Commonwealth of Nations	EU	GCC	OAS	OAU	SPC	ACP	ADB	APEC	CARICOM	EEC	I-ADB	IDB	OPEC	Country
•	•	•	•	•				•			•			•		•			Dominican Republic
•	•	•	•	•				•								•			Ecuador
•	•	•	•	•					•		•						•	•	Egypt
•	•	•	•	•				•								•			El Salvador
•	•	•	•						•		•								Equatorial Guinea
•	•	•	•						•										Eritrea
•	•	•	•	•															Estonia
•	•	•	•						•		•								Ethiopia
•	•	•	•	•	•					•	•	•							Fiji
•	•	•	•	•		•						•			•	•			Finland
•	•	•	•	•		•				•		•			•	•			France
•	•	•	•	•					•		•						•	•	Gabon
•	•	•	•	•	•				•		•						•		Gambia, The
•	•	•	•																Georgia
•	•	•	•	•		•						•			•	•			Germany
•	•	•	•	•	•				•		•								Ghana
•	•	•	•	•		•									•				Greece
•	•	•	•	•	•			•			•			•		•			Grenada
•	•	•	•	•				•								•			Guatemala
•	•	•	•	•					•		•						•		Guinea
•	•	•	•						•		•						•		Guinea-Bissau
•	•	•	•	•	•			•			•			•		•			Guyana
•	•	•	•	•				•			•			•		•			Haiti
•	•	•	•	•				•								•			Honduras
•	•	•	•	•															Hungary
•	•	•	•	•															Iceland
•	•	•	•	•	•							•							India
•	•	•	•	•								•	•				•	•	Indonesia
•	•	•	•														•	•	Iran
•	•	•	•														•	•	Iraq
•	•	•	•	•		•									•				Ireland
•	•	•	•	•												•			Israel
•	•	•	•	•		•						•			•	•			Italy
•	•	•	•						•		•								Ivory Coast
•	•	•	•	•	•			•			•			•		•			Jamaica
•	•	•	•	•								•	•			•			Japan
•	•	•	•	•													•		Jordan
•	•	•	•									•							Kazakhstan
•	•	•	•	•	•				•		•								Kenya
•	•	•	•		•					•	•	•							Kiribati
•	•	•	•	•			•										•	•	Kuwait
•	•	•	•									•							Kyrgyzstan
•	•	•	•									•							Laos
•	•	•	•	•															Latvia
•	•	•	•														•		Lebanon
•	•	•	•	•	•				•		•								Lesotho
•	•	•	•						•		•								Liberia
•	•	•	•						•								•	•	Libya
	•		•	•															Liechtenstein

Country	National Capital	Population of National Capital	United Nations (date of admission)	UNICEF	FAO	ILO
Lithuania	Vilnius	590,100	1991	•	•	•
Luxembourg	Luxembourg	76,446	1945	•	•	•
Macedonia	Skopje (Skopije)	541,280	1993	•	•	•
Madagascar	Antananarivo	1,052,835	1960	•	•	•
Malawi	Lilongwe	395,500	1964	•	•	•
Malaysia	Kuala Lumpur	1,145,075	1957	•	•	•
Maldives	Male'	62,973	1965	•	•	•
Mali	Bamako	800,000	1960	•	•	•
Malta	Valletta	9,129	1964	•	•	•
Marshall Islands	Majuro	20,000	1991	•		
Mauritania	Nouakchott	735,000	1961	•	•	•
Mexico	Mexico City	9,815,795	1945	•	•	•
Federated States of Micronesia	Palikir		1991	•		
Moldova	Chişinău	662,000	1992	•	•	•
Mongolia	Ulaanbaatar (Ulan Bator)	619,000	1961	•	•	•
Morocco	Rabat	1,220,000	1956	•	•	•
Mozambique	Maputo (Lourenço Marques)	931,591	1975	•	•	•
Myanmar	Yangōn (Rangoon)	3,851,000	1948	•	•	•
Namibia	Windhoek	161,000	1990	•	•	•
Nepal	Kāthmāndu	535,000	1955	•	•	•
Netherlands, The	Amsterdam (de jure)	722,245	1945	•	•	•
New Zealand	Wellington	158,275	1945	•	•	•
Nicaragua	Managua	1,195,000	1945	•	•	•
Niger	Niamey	391,876	1960	•	•	•
Nigeria	Abuja	339,100	1960	•	•	•
North Korea	P'yŏngyang	2,355,000	1991	•	•	•
Norway	Oslo	487,908	1945	•	•	•
Oman	Muscat	51,869	1971	•	•	•
Pakistan	Islāmābād	204,364	1947	•	•	•
Palau	Koror	10,500	1994	•		
Panama	Panama City	445,902	1945	•	•	•
Papua New Guinea	Port Moresby	193,242	1975	•	•	•
Paraguay	Asunción	502,426	1945	•	•	•
Peru	Lima	421,570	1945	•	•	•
Philippines	Manila	1,894,667	1945	•	•	•
Poland	Warsaw (Warszawa)	1,640,700	1945	•	•	•
Portugal	Lisbon	677,790	1955	•	•	•
Qatar	Doha	313,639	1971	•	•	•
Romania	Bucharest	2,343,824	1958	•	•	•
Russia	Moscow	8,717,000	1991	•	•	•
Rwanda	Kigali	232,733	1962	•	•	•
St. Kitts and Nevis	Basseterre	15,000	1983	•	•	
St. Lucia	Castries	13,615	1979	•	•	•
St. Vincent and The Grenadines	Kingstown	15,466	1980	•	•	•
Samoa	Apia	32,859	1976	•	•	•
San Marino	San Marino	2,316	1992			
São Tomé and Príncipe	São Tomé	43,420	1975	•	•	•
Saudi Arabia	Riyadh (Ar-Riyadh)	1,800,000	1945	•	•	•

IMF	ITU	UNESCO	WHO	WTO	Commonwealth of Nations	EU	GCC	OAS	OAU	SPC	ACP	ADB	APEC	CARICOM	EEC	I-ADB	IDB	OPEC	Country
•	•	•	•	•		•													Lithuania
•	•	•	•	•		•									•				Luxembourg
•	•	•	•	•															Macedonia
•	•	•	•	•					•			•							Madagascar
•	•	•	•	•	•				•			•							Malawi
•	•	•	•	•	•							•	•				•		Malaysia
•	•	•	•	•	•							•					•		Maldives
•	•	•	•	•					•		•						•		Mali
•	•	•	•	•	•										•				Malta
•			•							•		•							Marshall Islands
•	•	•	•						•		•						•		Mauritania
•	•	•	•	•				•					•			•			Mexico
•	•									•		•							Federated States of Micronesia
•	•	•	•																Moldova
•	•	•	•									•							Mongolia
•	•	•	•														•		Morocco
•	•	•	•		•				•		•								Mozambique
•	•	•	•	•								•							Myanmar
•	•	•	•	•					•		•								Namibia
•	•	•	•	•								•							Nepal
•	•	•	•	•		•							•		•				Netherlands, The
•	•	•	•	•	•					•		•	•						New Zealand
•	•	•	•	•				•								•			Nicaragua
•	•	•	•	•					•		•						•		Niger
•	•	•	•	•	•				•		•						•		Nigeria
	•	•	•																North Korea
•	•	•	•	•								•					•		Norway
•	•	•	•	•			•										•		Oman
•	•	•	•	•	•							•					•		Pakistan
												•							Palau
•	•	•	•	•				•								•			Panama
•	•	•	•	•	•					•	•	•	•						Papua New Guinea
•	•	•	•	•				•								•			Paraguay
•	•	•	•	•				•					•			•			Peru
•	•	•	•	•								•	•						Phillippines
•	•	•	•	•															Poland
•	•	•	•	•		•									•	•			Portugal
•	•	•	•	•			•										•	•	Qatar
•	•	•	•	•															Romania
•	•	•	•										•						Russia
•	•	•	•						•		•								Rwanda
•	•	•	•	•	•			•			•			•		•			St. Kitts and Nevis
•	•	•	•	•	•			•			•			•		•			St. Lucia
•	•	•	•	•	•			•			•			•					St. Vincent and the Grenadines
•	•	•	•	•	•					•	•	•							Samoa
•	•	•	•																San Marino
•	•	•	•	•					•		•						•	•	São Tomé and Príncipe
•	•	•	•	•			•										•	•	Saudi Arabia

Country	National Capital	Population of National Capital	United Nations (date of admission)	UNICEF	FAO	ILO
Senegal	Dakar	785,071	1960	•	•	•
Seychelles	Victoria	25,000	1976	•	•	•
Sierra Leone	Freetown	669,000	1961	•	•	•
Singapore	Singapore	3,045,000	1965	•		•
Slovakia	Bratislava	450,776	1993	•	•	•
Slovenia	Ljubljana	276,119	1992	•	•	•
Solomon Islands	Honiara	43,643	1978	•	•	•
Somalia	Mogadishu	900,000	1960	•	•	•
South Africa	Bloemfontein (judicial)	126,867	1945	•	•	•
	Cape Town (legislative)	854,616				
	Pretoria (executive)	525,583				
South Korea	Seoul (Sŏul)	10,229,262	1991	•	•	•
Spain	Madrid	3,041,101	1955	•	•	•
Sri Lanka	Colombo	615,000	1955	•	•	•
Sudan	Khartoum	924,505	1956	•	•	•
Suriname	Paramaribo	200,970	1975	•	•	•
Swaziland	Mbabane	47,000	1968	•	•	•
Sweden	Stockholm	711,119	1946	•	•	•
Switzerland	Bern (Berne)	128,422	-	•	•	•
Syria	Damascus (Dimashq)	1,549,932	1956	•	•	•
Taiwan	Taipei (T'ai-pei)	2,626,138	-			
Tajikistan	Dushanbe	524,000	1992	•	•	•
Tanzania	Dar es Salaam	1,360,850	1961	•	•	•
Thailand	Bangkok	5,584,288	1946	•	•	•
Togo	Lomé	513,000	1960	•	•	•
Tonga	Nuku'alofa	34,000	1999	•	•	•
Trinidad and Tobago	Port-of-Spain	52,451	1962	•	•	•
Tunisia	Tunis	674,100	1956	•	•	•
Turkey	Ankara	2,782,200	1945	•	•	•
Turkmenistan	Ashkhabad (Ashgabat)	518,000	1992	•	•	•
Tuvalu	Funafuti	3,839	-	•		
Uganda	Kampala	773,463	1962	•	•	•
Ukraine	Kiev (Kyyiv)	2,630,000	1945	•		•
United Arab Emirates	Abu Dhabi (Abū Ẓaby)	363,432	1971	•	•	•
United Kingdom	London	6,967,500	1945	•	•	•
United States	Washington, D.C.	567,094	1945	•	•	•
Uruguay	Montevideo	1,378,707	1945	•	•	•
Uzbekistan	Tashkent	2,106,000	1992	•		
Vanuatu	Vila	26,100	1981	•	•	
Venezuela	Caracas	1,822,465	1945	•	•	•
Vietnam	Hanoi	2,154,900	1977	•	•	•
Yemen	Şan'ā'	503,600	1947	•	•	•
Yugoslavia	Belgrade (Beograd)	1,168,454	1945	•	•	•
Zambia	Lusaka	982,362	1964	•	•	•
Zimbabwe	Harare	1,184,169	1980	•	•	•

IMF	ITU	UNESCO	WHO	WTO	Commonwealth of Nations	EU	GCC	OAS	OAU	SPC	ACP	ADB	APEC	CARICOM	EEC	I-ADB	IDB	OPEC	Country
•	•	•	•	•					•								•		Senegal
•	•	•	•	•	•				•		•								Seychelles
•	•	•	•	•	•				•		•					•			Sierra Leone
•	•	•	•	•	•							•	•						Singapore
•	•	•	•	•															Slovakia
•	•	•	•	•												•			Slovenia
•	•	•	•	•	•					•	•	•							Solomon Islands
•	•	•	•	•					•		•						•		Somalia
•	•	•	•	•	•				•										South Africa
•	•	•	•	•								•	•						South Korea
•	•	•	•	•		•						•				•	•		Spain
•	•	•	•	•	•							•							Sri Lanka
•	•	•	•	•					•		•						•		Sudan
•	•	•	•	•				•			•			•			•		Suriname
•	•	•	•	•	•				•		•								Swaziland
•	•	•	•	•		•						•				•	•		Sweden
•	•	•	•	•								•				•			Switzerland
•	•	•	•	•													•		Syria
				•															Taiwan
•		•	•																Tajikistan
•	•	•	•	•	•				•		•								Tanzania
•	•	•	•	•								•	•						Thailand
•	•	•	•	•					•		•						•		Togo
•	•	•	•	•	•					•	•	•							Tonga
•	•	•	•	•	•			•			•			•			•		Trinidad and Tobago
•	•	•	•	•					•							•			Tunisia
•	•	•	•	•								•			•		•		Turkey
•	•	•	•	•													•		Turkmenistan
	•	•	•	•	•					•	•								Tuvalu
•	•	•	•	•	•				•		•								Uganda
•	•	•	•	•															Ukraine
•	•	•	•	•			•										•	•	United Arab Emirates
•	•	•	•	•	•	•					•	•			•	•			United Kingdom
•	•	•	•	•				•				•	•			•			United States
•	•	•	•	•				•								•			Uruguay
•	•	•	•	•															Uzbekistan
•	•	•	•	•	•					•	•	•							Vanuatu
•	•	•	•	•				•						•		•		•	Venezuela
•	•	•	•	•								•							Vietnam
•	•	•	•	•													•		Yemen
•	•	•	•																Yugoslavia
•	•	•	•	•	•				•		•								Zambia
•	•	•	•	•	•				•		•								Zimbabwe

Country	Airports with scheduled flights (1996)	Persons per Television (1995)	Persons per Telephone (1993)	Mobile Phones per 1000 people (1995)	Computers per 1000 people (1995)
Afghanistan	3	181	770	...	...
Albania	1	11	70	0	...
Algeria	28	14	25	0.2	3
Andorra	0	2.8	2.4	...	...
Angola	17	220	190	0.2	...
Antigua and Barbuda	2	2.3	3.5	...	...
Argentina	43	4.8	8.1	9.9	24.6
Armenia	1	4.7	6.4	0	...
Australia	400	2.3	2.1	127.7	275.8
Austria	6	3	2.2	47.6	124.2
Azerbaijan	1	4.7	11	0.1	...
Bahamas, The	23	5.5	3.3	...	...
Bahrain	1	2.1	4.3	...	...
Bangladesh	8	200	440	0	...
Barbados	1	4.1	3.2	...	...
Belarus	2	3.7	5.7	0.6	...
Belgium	2	2.4	2.3	23.2	138.3
Belize	11	9.4	7.1	...	...
Benin	1	270	260	0.2	...
Bhutan	1	...	400	...	...
Bolivia	14	8.8	33	1	...
Bosnia and Herzegovina	1	3.4	7.3	0	...
Botswana	4	111	32	0	...
Brazil	139	5.2	13	8	13
Brunei	1	3.2	5.1	...	...
Bulgaria	3	2.7	3.8	...	21.4
Burkina Faso	2	244	460	0	0
Burundi	1	1320	390	0.1	...
Cambodia	7	137	1670	1.5	...
Cameroon	5	882	220	0.2	...
Canada	301	1.5	1.7	86.5	192.5
Cape Verde	9	371	26	...	...
Central African Republic	1	419	480	0	...
Chad	4	127	1430	0	0
Chile	18	7.1	9.1	13.8	37.8
China	113	5.3	68	3	2.2
Colombia	63	6.4	8.9	7.1	16.2
Comoros	4	2550	130	...	...
Congo, Democratic Republic of the	12	2000	1110	0.2	...
Congo, Republic of the	5	305	130	0	...
Costa Rica	14	9.8	11	5.5	...
Croatia	5	6	4.5	7.1	20.9
Cuba	14	4.4	31	0.1	...
Cyprus	2	6.3	2	...	...
Czech Republic	2	2.1	5.3	4.7	53.2
Denmark	13	10.2	1.7	157.3	270.5
Djibouti	1	34	78	...	...

Country	Airports with scheduled flights (1996)	Persons per Television (1995)	Persons per Telephone (1993)	Mobile Phones per 1000 people (1995)	Computers per 1000 people (1995)
Dominica	2	14	5.3	...	...
Dominican Republic	4	11	13	...	...
Ecuador	14	13	19	4.6	3.9
Egypt	14	12	24	0.1	3.4
El Salvador	1	12	26	2.5	...
Equatorial Guinea	2	158	290	...	...
Eritrea	2	...	170	0	...
Estonia	3	2.5	4.3	20.5	6.7
Ethiopia	31	367	400	0	...
Fiji	13	59	11	...	...
Finland	24	2.7	1.8	199.2	182.1
France	66	2	1.9	23.8	134.3
Gabon	23	29	41	2.5	4.5
Gambia, The	1	186	63	1.3	...
Georgia	1	...	9.6	0	...
Germany	40	2.7	2.2	42.8	164.9
Ghana	1	66	330	0.4	1.2
Greece	36	4.6	2.2	26.1	33.4
Grenada	2	6.1	4.5	...	...
Guatemala	2	22	43	2.8	2.8
Guinea	2	103	560	0.1	0.2
Guinea-Bissau	2	...	120	0	...
Guyana	1	51	20	...	...
Haiti	2	264	150	0	...
Honduras	8	34	48	0	...
Hungary	1	2.4	6.9	25.9	39.2
Iceland	24	3.5	1.8	...	...
India	66	47	110	0.1	1.3
Indonesia	81	18	110	1.1	3.7
Iran	19	8.8	17	0.1	...
Iraq	...	20	29	0	...
Ireland	9	3.6	3.1	44.1	145
Israel	7	3.6	2.7	153.5	99.8
Italy	31	3.4	2.4	67.4	83.7
Ivory Coast	11	18	140	0	...
Jamaica	5	5.2	9.5	17.9	...
Japan	73	1.3	2.1	81.5	152.5
Jordan	2	17	14	2.6	8
Kazakstan	6	3.5	11	0.3	...
Kenya	13	57	120	0.1	0.7
Kiribati	17	115	43	...	...
Kuwait	1	2.1	4.1	70.7	57.1
Kyrgyzstan	2	5.1	12	0	...
Laos	11	61	530	0.1	...
Latvia	1	2.2	3.7	6	7.9
Lebanon	1	2.7	11	30	12.5
Lesotho	1	8.2	179	0	...

Country	Airports with scheduled flights (1996)	Persons per Television (1995)	Persons per Telephone (1993)	Mobile Phones per 1000 people (1995)	Computers per 1000 people (1995)
Liberia	1	53	590	...	...
Libya	12	9.8	21	0	...
Liechtenstein	0	3	1.6	...	...
Lithuania	3	2.4	4.4	4	6.5
Luxembourg	1	4.1	1.9	...	...
Macedonia	1	5.9	6.8	0	...
Madagascar	19	114	370	0	...
Malawi	4	...	290	0	...
Malaysia	36	6.5	7.9	43.4	39.7
Maldives	5	53	24	...	...
Mali	1	901	670	0	...
Malta	1	2.6	2.3	...	...
Marshall Islands	23	...	23	...	...
Mauritania	10	2070	290	0	...
Mexico	83	6.5	11	7	26.1
Micronesia, Federated States of	4	15	18	...	...
Moldova	1	3.5	8.3	0	2.1
Mongolia	1	17	36	0	0.2
Morocco	12	22	32	1.1	1.7
Mozambique	7	511	270	0	...
Myanmar (Burma)	19	47	560	0	...
Namibia	13	42	22	2.3	...
Nepal	24	80	290	0	...
Netherlands, The	6	2.4	2	33.2	200.5
New Zealand	36	3.2	2.2	108	222.7
Nicaragua	10	21	60	1.1	...
Niger	6	366	830	0	...
Nigeria	12	16	300	0.1	4.1
North Korea	1	12	21	0	...
Norway	50	2.2	1.8	224.4	273
Oman	6	1.4	8.6	3.7	...
Pakistan	34	68	76	0.3	1.2
Palau	1	11	...	...	...
Panama	10	13	9.8	0	...
Papua New Guinea	129	43	100	0	...
Paraguay	5	14	33	3.2	...
Peru	27	12	34	3.1	5.9
Philippines	21	10	76	7.3	11.4
Poland	12	3.9	8.7	1.9	28.5
Portugal	14	5.6	3.2	34.3	60.4
Qatar	1	2.3	4.7	...	...
Romania	12	5.7	8.7	0.4	5.3
Russia	58	2.7	6.3	0.6	17.7
Rwanda	3	...	630	0	...
St. Kitts and Nevis	2	4.2	3.4	...	...
St. Lucia	2	5.7	6.5	...	...
St. Vincent and the Grenadines	4	6.2	6.7	...	...

Country	Airports with scheduled flights (1996)	Persons per Television (1995)	Persons per Telephone (1993)	Mobile Phones per 1000 people (1995)	Computers per 1000 people (1995)
Samoa	2	33	25	...	...
San Marino	0	3	1.6	...	...
São Tomé and Príncipe	2	6.2	52	...	...
Saudi Arabia	25	3.8	11	0.9	25.1
Senegal	7	136	130	0	7.2
Seychelles	2	5.8	6.2	...	...
Sierra Leone	1	180	310	0	...
Singapore	1	4.6	2.3	97.7	172.4
Slovakia	2	4.2	6	2.3	41
Slovenia	1	3.5	3.9	13.6	47.7
Solomon Islands	30	...	65	...	...
Somalia	1	55	560	...	...
South Africa	24	12	11	12.9	26.5
South Korea	14	4.3	2.7	36.6	120.8
Spain	25	2.3	2.7	24.1	81.6
Sri Lanka	1	26	111	2.8	1.1
Sudan	10	112	440	0	...
Suriname	2	10	8.6	...	...
Swaziland	1	73	56	...	...
Sweden	48	2.4	1.5	229.4	192.5
Switzerland	5	2.7	1.6	63.5	348
Syria	5	20	24	0	0.1
Taiwan	13	3	2.6	...	...
Tajikistan	1	6.3	22	0	...
Tanzania	11	351	313	0.1	...
Thailand	25	18	27	18.5	15.3
Togo	1	28	230	0	0
Tonga	6	40	16	...	...
Trinidad and Tobago	2	5.1	6.5	4.3	19.2
Tunisia	5	14	20	0.4	6.7
Turkey	26	5.9	5.4	7	12.5
Turkmenistan	1	5.3	15	0.2	...
Tuvalu	1	...	77	...	...
Uganda	1	162	830	0.1	0.5
Ukraine	20	3	6.7	0.3	5.6
United Arab Emirates	6	13	2.6	54.2	48.4
United Kingdom	50	2.9	2	98	186.2
United States	834	1.2	1.7	128.4	328
Uruguay	1	5.3	5.9	12.6	22
Uzbekistan	9	6.3	15	...	...
Vanuatu	29	80	39	...	...
Venezuela	24	5.9	10	18	16.7
Vietnam	12	30	270	0.2	...
Yemen	11	131	83	0.5	...
Yugoslavia	5	6.4	5.6	0	11.8
Zambia	4	47	110	0.2	...
Zimbabwe	7	82	84	0	3

Name and location	Area (sq mi)
WORLD	
Caspian Sea, *Turkmenistan–Kazakstan–Russia–Azerbaijan-Iran*	149,200
Superior, *Canada–United States*	31,700
Victoria, *Kenya–Tanzania–Uganda*	26,828
Huron, *Canada–United States*	23,000
Michigan, *United States*	22,300
Aral Sea, *Kazakstan–Uzbekistan*	13,000
Tanganyika, *Burundi–Tanzania–Dem. Rep. Congo–Zambia*	12,700
Baikal, *Russia*	12,200
AFRICA	
Victoria, *Kenya-Tanzania–Uganda*	26,828
Tanganyika, *Burundi–Tanzania-Dem. Rep. Congo–Zambia*	12,700
Nyasa (Malawi), *Malawi–Mozambique–Tanzania*	11,430
Chad, *Cameroon–Chad–Niger–Nigeria*	6,875
Bangweulu, *Zambia*	3,800
AMERICA, NORTH	
Superior, *Canada–United States*	31,700
Huron, *Canada–United States*	23,000
Michigan, *United States*	22,300
Great Bear, *Northwest Territories, Canada*	12,028
Great Slave, *Northwest Territories, Canada*	11,031
AMERICA, SOUTH	
Maracaibo, *Venezuela*	5,150
Titicaca, *Peru–Bolivia*	3,200
Poopó, *Bolivia*	1,000
Buenos Aires (General Carrera), *Chile–Argentina*	865
Chiquita, *Argentina*	714
ASIA	
Caspian Sea, *Turkmenistan–Kazakstan–Russia–Azerbaijan-Iran*	149,200
Aral Sea, *Kazakstan–Uzbekistan*	13,000
Baikal, *Russia*	12,200
Balkhash, *Kazakstan*	6,650
Tonle Sap, *Cambodia*	2,525
EUROPE	
Ladoga, *Russia*	6,826
Onega, *Russia*	3,753
Vänern, *Sweden*	2,156
Iso Saimaa, *Finland*	1,690
Peipsi, *Estonia–Russia*	1,373
OCEANIA	
Eyre, *South Australia*	3,600
Torrens, *South Australia*	2,230
Gairdner, *South Australia*	1,845
Frome, *South Australia*	900

Name	Outflow	Length (miles)
WORLD		
Nile	Mediterranean Sea	4,132
Amazon–Ucayali–Apurimac	South Alantic Ocean	4,000
Chang (Yangtze)	East China Sea	3,915
Mississippi–Missouri–Red Rock	Gulf of Mexico	3,710
Yenisey–Baikal–Selenga	Kara Sea	3,442
Huang (Yellow)	Bo Hai (Gulf of Chihli)	3,395
Ob–Irtysh	Gulf of Ob	3,362
Paraná	Río de la Plata	3,032
AFRICA		
Nile	Mediterranean Sea	4,132
Congo	South Alantic Ocean	2,900
Niger	Bight of Biafra	2,600
Zambezi	Mozambique Channel	2,200
Kasai	Congo River	1,338
AMERICA, NORTH		
Mississippi–Missouri–Red Rock	Gulf of Mexico	3,710
Mackenzie–Slave–Peace	Beaufort Sea	2,635
Missouri–Red Rock	Mississippi River	2,540
St. Lawrence–Great Lakes	Gulf of St. Lawrence	2,500
Mississippi	Gulf of Mexico	2,340
AMERICA, SOUTH		
Amazon–Ucayali–Apurimac	South Alantic Ocean	4,000
Paraná	Río de la Plata	3,032
Madeira–Mamoré–Guaporé	Amazon River	2.082
Jurua	Amazon River	2,040
Purus	Amazon River	1,995
ASIA		
Chang (Yangtze)	East China Sea	3,915
Yenisey–Baikal–Selenga	Kara Sea	3,442
Huang (Yellow)	Bo Hai (Gulf of Chihli)	3,395
Ob–Irtysh	Gulf of Ob	3,362
Amur–Argun	Sea of Okhotsk	2,761
EUROPE		
Volga	Caspian Sea	2,193
Danube	Black Sea	1,770
Ural	Caspian Sea	1,509
Dnieper	Black Sea	1,367
Don	Sea of Azov	1,162
OCEANIA		
Darling	Murray River	1,702
Murray	Great Australian Bight	1,609
Murrumbidgee	Murray River	981
Lachlan	Murrumbidgee River	992

Name and location	Height (feet)
AFRICA	
Kilimanjaro (Kibo Peak), *Tanzania*	19,340
Mt. Kenya (Batian Peak), *Kenya*	17,058
Margherita, Ruwenzori Range, *Dem. Rep. Congo–Uganda*	16,795
Ras Dashen, Simyen Mts., *Ethiopia*	15,157
AMERICA, NORTH	
McKinley, Alaska Range, *Alaska, U.S.*	20,320
Logan, St. Elias Mts., *Yukon, Canada*	19,524
Citlaltépetl (Orizaba), Cordillera Neo-Volcánica, *Mexico*	18,406
St. Elias, St Elias Mts., *Alaska, U.S.–Canada*	18,009
AMERICA, SOUTH	
Aconcagua, Andes, *Argentina–Chile*	22,831
Ojos del Salado, Andes, *Argentina–Chile*	22,615
Bonete, Andes, *Argentina*	22,546
Tupungato, Andes, *Argentina–Chile*	22,310
Pissis, Andes, *Argentina*	22,241
ANTARCTICA	
Vinson Massif, Sentinel Range, Ellsworth Mts.	16,066
Tyree, Sentinel Range, Ellsworth Mts.	15,919
Shinn, Sentinel Range, Ellsworth Mts.	15,751
Kirkpatrick, Queen Alexandra Range	14,856
ASIA	
Everest (Chomolungma), Himalayas, *Nepal–Tibet, China*	29,028
K2 (Godwin Austen), Karakoram Range, *Pakistan–Xinjiang, China*	28,251
Kānchenjunga I, Himalayas, *Nepal–India*	28,169
Lhotse I, Himalayas, *Nepal–Tibet, China*	27,940
EUROPE	
Mont Blanc, Alps, *France–Italy*	15,771
Dufourspitze (Monte Rosa), Alps, *Switzerland–Italy*	15,203
Dom (Mischabel), Alps, *Switzerland*	14,911
Weisshorn, Alps, *Switzerland*	14,780
OCEANIA	
Jaya (Sukarno, Carstensz), Sudirman Range, *Indonesia*	16,500
Pilimsit (Idenburg), Sudirman Range, *Indonesia*	15,750
Trikora (Wilhelmina), Jayawijaya Mts., *Indonesia*	15,580
Mandala (Juliana), Jayawijaya Mts., *Indonesia*	15,420
CAUCASUS	
Elbrus, Caucasus, *Russia*	18,510
Dyhk-Tau, Caucasus, *Russia*	17,073
Koshtan-Tau, Caucasus, *Russia*	16,900
Shkhara, Caucasus, *Russia–Georgia*	16,627